MW01068981

Tropical Riffs

Tropical

Jason Borge

Riffs Latin America and the Politics of Jazz

Duke University Press : Durham and London : 2018

© **2018 Duke University Press.** All rights reserved
Printed in the United States of America on acid-free paper ∞
Cover designed by Heather Hensley
Interior designed by Courtney Leigh Baker
Typeset in Garamond Premier Pro and Clarendon by
Westchester Publishing Services

Library of Congress Cataloging-in-Publication Data
Names: Borge, Jason, [date] author.
Title: Tropical riffs : Latin America and the politics of jazz / Jason Borge.
Description: Durham : Duke University Press, 2018. | Includes bibliographical references
and index.
Identifiers: LCCN 2017035987 (print)
LCCN 2017044574 (ebook)
ISBN 9780822372332 (ebook)
ISBN 9780822369875 (hardcover : alk. paper)
ISBN 9780822369905 (pbk. : alk. paper)
Subjects: LCSH: Jazz—Social aspects—Latin America. | Jazz—Latin America—History and
criticism. | Jazz—Latin America—History—20th century.
Classification: LCC ML3918.J39 (ebook) | LCC ML3918.J39 B674 2018 (print) | DDC
306.4/8425098—dc23
LC record available at https://lccn.loc.gov/2017035987

COVER ART: Chano Pozo. Photograph by Allan Grant/The LIFE Picture Collection/
Getty Images.

Contents

Acknowledgments

The beginnings of the project that eventually became *Tropical Riffs* date back to my last years as a graduate student at the University of California, Berkeley, when, like so many Latin Americanists and jazz enthusiasts, I watched Ken Burns's PBS series *Jazz* and was both enraptured and horrified by what I saw. Newly attuned to the dissonances of North-South cultural politics, I was deeply unsettled by what I considered the series' criminal indifference to the central contributions of Latin American and US Latino/a musicians, bandleaders, and composers.

My indignation never fully subsided. In the years that followed, though, I gradually realized that the story that mattered most to me was not what Latin America meant to the US jazz establishment so much as what jazz meant to Latin America, particularly during the music's heyday between the 1920s and the 1960s. I knew that it was a book that still had not been written, and I felt that it needed to be. In thinking about how I could approach the sheer enormity of the topic, one of the first challenges I faced as a specialist in literature and film was how to tackle what was ostensibly a music studies project. The answer came at a panel on Latin America and new jazz studies at the 2013 meeting of the Latin American Studies Association in Washington, DC, when I was fortunate to be able to exchange ideas with a small group of first-rate scholars—Matthew Karush, Robin Moore, Jairo Moreno, and Chris Washburne. Although from different fields and regional specialties, the five of us shared a common interest in Latin America and jazz and a common desire to address theoretical and historical questions yet to be fully explored.

The success of the panel, which eventually led to a special dossier on the subject in the *Journal of Latin American Cultural Studies* (including an essay by Lara Putnam), convinced me that the book project I had long envisioned could and should be interdisciplinary in scope. The main challenge that remained was how to speak with depth, rigor, and specificity about the cultural politics of jazz without losing myself in the fascinating minutiae of the myriad jazz scenes across the hemisphere. In the end I decided to focus on the cities that had given the jazz world many, if not most, of its most luminous talents. Perhaps not surprisingly, these places turned out to be the twentieth-century cultural capitals of the region: Mexico City, Havana, Rio de Janeiro, Buenos Aires, and New York City.

For research on early Argentine jazz journals, a summer grant from Vanderbilt University's Center for the Americas allowed me to conduct important research in the Biblioteca Nacional Mariano Moreno, not to mention in the wonderful jazz clubs, used bookstores, and book fairs of Buenos Aires, a largely informal network that helped me track down jazz treasures large and small. Archival research on Cuba and Brazil was made possible in part by a College of Liberal Arts Research Fellowship from the University of Texas at Austin. Especially fruitful were the many hours spent reviewing periodicals at the University of Miami's Cuban Heritage Collection, the Biblioteca Nacional do Brasil in Rio de Janeiro, the Museu Lasar Segall in São Paulo, and the indispensable Institute of Jazz Studies at Rutgers University–Newark. Finally, I should mention the excellent libraries and librarians of my home institution, the University of Texas at Austin, in particular the Benson Latin American Collection and the Harry Ransom Center, both of which proved essential for research on Mexico.

Some of the chapters of the book expand upon and rearticulate previously published works of mine. I would like to thank a few scholarly journals and presses for allowing me to use portions of previously published essays. My discussion of Josephine Baker expands on work first appearing in the edited volume *Urban Latin America: Images, Words, and the Built Environment* (Routledge, 2018). Portions of chapter 2 dealing with early Argentine jazz journals draw from an article in the *Afro-Hispanic Review* (2011). In chapter 3, my discussion of the jazz-samba debates originally appeared in different form as an article in the *Journal of Latin American Cultural Studies* (2016). Finally, portions of my analysis of mambo films in chapter 4 were first published in the volume *Cosmopolitan Visions: Transnational Horizons of Latin American Film Culture, 1896–1960* (Indiana University Press, 2017).

My research on a project covering such a wide range of times, places, and materials has relied not just on institutions but also on people. For crucial encouragement, research tips, and feedback at various points over the last five years, I would like to thank Carlos Jáuregui, Micol Seigel, Charles Perrone, Chris Washburne, and Jairo Moreno, not to mention my present and former colleagues and students in the Department of Spanish and Portuguese at

UT–Austin. For the time and care they took to sift through the finer points of structure and argumentation, I owe a debt of gratitude to the two anonymous readers of my manuscript. I would also like to thank my editor, Gisela Fosado, for her trust in the project and her clear-eyed guidance throughout the process. For their generosity and extremely useful comments on early drafts of several chapters, extra special thanks go to Matthew Karush (for the chapter concerning Argentina), Robin Moore (Cuba), Sônia Roncador (Brazil), and finally Randolph Lewis, whose extensive feedback on the book's introduction and conclusion was absolutely crucial. In different ways, all of these friends and colleagues managed to shine light on aspects of the book that I hadn't fully grasped initially.

In any book about music, an uncommon love of music and aural culture inevitably plays a central role. With this in mind, I want to voice my deepest love and appreciation to my artist mother, Martha Borge, who never ceases to amaze me with her keen insights into the creative process; and to my late father, Ralph Borge, and my sister, Michele McCulloch, for instilling in me a lifelong reverence not just for music and musicianship, but also for the intimately linked arts of listening and record collecting—eclectically, adventurously, and insatiably.

As usual, my final thanks go to Sônia: inevitably my first reader and my last, my partner in crime, my sounding board, my unfailing companion, *meu amor*.

INTRODUCTION. **Kindred Sounds and Latin Cats**

Ken Burns's sprawling, ten-part documentary *Jazz* (PBS, 2001) was a watershed cultural event that helped to rekindle long-standing debates about the cultural politics of music, race, and nationality. Backed by major contributions from corporate behemoths such as Starbucks and Amazon, the series brought jazz back into the national spotlight and, however temporarily, helped to make the music commercially viable again after a nearly four-decade decline. The opening episode alone reached an estimated thirteen million viewers; books, CDs, DVDs, and related merchandise eventually generated hundreds of millions of dollars in revenue.[1] As with the case of Burns's previous projects *The Civil War* (1990) and *Baseball* (1994), the series allowed US public television to reassert itself as an essentially patriotic enterprise.[2] Beautifully produced and epic in scope, *Jazz* painted a moving portrait of African Americans' triumph over adversity, consecrating the music as a symbol of the uniquely democratic ethos of the United States.

But something was clearly amiss with Burns's brand of storytelling. With its technically sophisticated yet politically simplistic approach to the topic, *Jazz* was more a coronation of "America's classical music" and "America's art form" than a true celebration of democratic diversity, let alone a balanced account of the persistent racial struggles, economic exploitation, and transnational complexities of jazz history.[3] In spite of a general consensus about the contributions of jazz icons like Armstrong, Ellington, and Parker, whom Burns extolled, many critics bluntly denounced the omission or reduction of key secondary figures, especially Latin American musicians. Ben Ratliff complained in his *New York Times* review that the documentary was "stubbornly Americanist" in overlooking Africa, Cuba, and the Caribbean. He added, "That there's little more than a peep of Latin jazz since the 1940's is weird indeed."[4] In a damning article published in *Jazz Times*, Bobby Sanabria stressed the importance of recognizing influential musicians not often mentioned by mainstream jazz critics. Citing Burns's omission of Tito Puente, the Cuban percussionist Mongo Santamaría, and the legendary Nuyoricans Eddie Palmieri and Willie Bobo, Sanabria lamented that "in terms of jazz history, we basically didn't exist."[5] Clearly, for jazz to be sold to US audiences on a massive scale, the music needed first to be branded as quintessentially American. In a maneuver that cloaked overarching nationalist imperatives, in other words, Burns had sold a nostalgic, reductive vision of jazz to a US public eager for redeeming, black-and-white narratives about the nation's recent past. The undeniably protectionist slant of Burns's *Jazz* therefore should not be seen as simple negligence. On the contrary, the exclusion of Latin America from the grand narrative of jazz was the main price to be paid in order to claim the music as a national heirloom.

By severing Latin America from the jazz corpus, Burns reinforced what scores of US and European historians, critics, and musicians had done for decades: he rendered jazz something less capacious, muddled, and global than it actually was. During much of the twentieth century, jazz played a vitally important but too often overlooked role in the elaboration of far-flung musical practices. But it was never just about the music. Jazz, in fact, was a central conduit for the negotiation of cultural identity, race, and gender politics, for transnational flows of bodies and technologies, ideas and feelings. The music's impact was felt well beyond Latin America. As a number of recent scholarly accounts have documented, the acoustic, visual, and symbolic reach of jazz extended from Nazi Germany to the Soviet Union, China to Africa.[6] What is striking about these pioneering studies is their nearly unanimous insistence that locally generated jazz or jazz-inflected performances, even when xenophobic state apparatuses intervened, never managed to remain "authentically" national any more than jazz could be considered a purely American import. Far from simply reproducing capitalist or colonial ideologies, local performances and nodes of reception often served as sites of ambivalence and contention. This was true of unapologetic US jazz imitators as well as stalwart nationalists.

As Everett Taylor Atkins points out, for example, the "strategies of authentication" that informed attempts in interwar and wartime Japan to reproduce the sounds of North American swing bands involved not only stylistic replication but also ritualistic sojourns to the United States and even claims of racial solidarity, as some Japanese performers sought to ally themselves with black jazz musicians by proclaiming themselves "yellow Negroes." At the same time, a nativist imperative to produce inimitable national music compelled many local jazz musicians to instill into their work "indigenous" and/or traditional "textures, instruments, or aesthetic principles."[7]

As I will discuss in subsequent chapters, early to mid-twentieth-century Latin American jazz interpreters (in the sense of both intellectual mediators and also musical practitioners), storm-tossed by the frequently countervailing winds of global capital and cultural nationalism, faced similar pressures. Yet close cultural and economic ties combined with frequent geopolitical rifts between the United States and Latin American nations placed the region in a unique category with respect to jazz. The many parallels and frequent interactions and overlaps between jazz and loosely analogous Latin American forms—from choro, maxixe, tango, and samba to son, rumba, mambo, and even salsa—strongly suggest that the word "jazz" was better suited as an umbrella term for a whole range of musical practices in the hemisphere than as a stable signifier for a discretely national form. To a greater extent than any other region outside the United States, I would argue, Latin America did not just embrace and repudiate, consume and purge, imitate and appropriate jazz. The region and its musicians actively participated in the global jazz enterprise to such a degree that its imprint eventually had to be acknowledged, even if ultimately disavowed, marginalized, or bracketed off as "Latin jazz."[8] The fundamental problem that Latin America presents to US jazz historiography, therefore, can be seen in part as one of cultural blowback: how to reconcile "banal" or "quiet" nationalist claims to cultural ownership and imperial conquest with the inherent porousness of musical borders and instability of musical practices?[9]

The problem is not just a unilateral one. One of the more striking phenomena is the extent to which twentieth-century Latin American intellectuals, politicians, fans, and musicians, echoing their US counterparts, tended to celebrate local jazz musicians and enthusiasts while also excluding them from the category of authentic jazz. Such cultural policing signaled at once an admiration for jazz's tantalizingly kindred pedigree—a shimmering (and shimmying) product tied to New World modernity—and also an apprehension of the music's penetration of local and national landscapes. Indeed, in the early to mid-twentieth century, I would like to propose, popular and elite Latin

American audiences alike understood jazz as the product, however strange, of conditions fundamentally analogous to their own disjunctive social environments, a range of cultural expressions seemingly both modern and primal, timely and syncopated.[10] Even conservative Latin American intellectuals were hard pressed to dismiss the music as entirely foreign to local and national sensibilities. One minute emblematic of savage Northern modernity, the next evoking retooled national narratives of racial difference and New World ingenuity, jazz oscillated between the familiar and the remote, signifying different things at different times to distinct nations, communities, and ideological factions within the region. Jazz thus emerged as particularly illustrative of overlapping yet divergent—syncopated—experiences of modernity within the Americas.[11] What joined Latin Americans of myriad stripes—writers and intellectuals, musicians and composers, filmmakers and fans—was how they offered up original and compelling narratives about the central role jazz has played in questions of race and gender, power and nation.

For the most part, as I discuss in chapter 1, jazz arrived in Latin American cities as an exotic oddity and quickly mutated into a contentious emblem of cosmopolitanism. The music's cachet lay in the fact that it was an aggressively modern export nonetheless imbued with seductive yet potentially discomforting moral laxity and racial alterity. For many Latin American intellectuals of the 1920s, news of jazz washed ashore muddled and secondhand by way of written accounts, drawings, and photographs as often as through hard-to-find recordings and sporadic live performances. Early icons of the Jazz Age, such as the singer-actor Al Jolson (star of *The Jazz Singer*), the white bandleader Paul Whiteman, and the Paris-based African American singer and dancer Josephine Baker, left an impression of the music constantly in flux and sometimes at odds with the more stable but still variegated jazz imaginary that would emerge in the 1930s. With her aggressively erotic, explicitly racialized revue spectacle, Baker proved an especially alluring and divisive entertainer, one who introduced many Latin American audiences to the emancipatory potential of jazz while still clinging to the demeaning lexicon of minstrelsy.

The idea of jazz as an avatar of vernacular modernism generally prevailed in the 1920s, thanks in part to the growing prominence of young lions associated with avant-garde movements at home and abroad—Latin American intellectuals such as Alejo Carpentier, Mário de Andrade, Miguel Covarrubias, and Ulises Petit de Murat and Europeans such as Blaise Cendrars, Darius Milhaud, Robert Goffin, and António Ferro. By the late 1930s, however, many critics, composers, public officials, and other denizens of the Latin American lettered city began to treat jazz warily if not with open hostility—attempting, in effect, to sanitize the music just as its popularity spread. Fearful of the US culture industry's moral corruption of the lower classes, many intellectuals turned against jazz, typecasting the sounds of Goodman and Gillespie as the antinational music par excellence. In chapters 2, 3, and 4, I examine how Argentine, Brazilian, and Cuban intellectuals, composers, and musicians came to terms with jazz's meteoric popularity during the mid-twentieth century. As we shall see, the music frequently clashed with the pedagogical narratives of Latin American cultural nationalism. These discourses stressed not only the primacy of favored styles like samba, tango, and son, but also the erection of rigid barriers between national practices and the "American," "capitalist," "foreignizing," or "antipeople" qualities with which jazz was variously associated.[12]

Among the most powerful institutions were national film industries in Argentina, Mexico, and Brazil, all of which capitalized on popular dances and associated musical performances to bring local spectators to the box office in droves during the 1930s, 1940s, and 1950s. Musical melodramas in various guises had an undeniably decisive impact on what constituted the national in the popular imagination. At a time of considerable musical heterogeneity and generic fluidity, however, most productions felt compelled to strip down myriad expressions to a single form, to the exclusion of others: in Argentina, tango; in Brazil, samba.[13] Such disjunctures between unitary narratives and the actual diversity of musical practices lent cinematic discourse an ambivalent and inherently unstable quality, or "double time."[14] The disciplinary forces of nationalist populism did not simply keep marginal musical idioms from the soundstage. In the name of the nation, such films also promoted views of race that excluded in the name of inclusion by, as the cultural theorist John Beverly puts it, "rhetorically sutur[ing] over the gaps and discontinuities internal to 'the people.'"[15]

As might be expected, the racial politics of musical nationalism in the region varied from country to country, according to a whole host of factors including divergent colonial legacies, migrational and other demographic trends, and particular strategies embraced by individual governments and their various intellectual and institutional supports. In spite of these differences, though, in official and unofficial narratives from the 1930s through the 1960s jazz consistently played what I am calling the "kindred foil": an object of strange familiarity at odds with ideological goals yet also deeply resonant with local populations at social and affective levels.[16] Indeed, in an ironic twist, the very Latin American nations that had their own flourishing culture industries during the middle decades of the twentieth century—industries at various moments placed in the service of racialized nationalist objectives— would also prove to be hotbeds of jazz consumption and production. It is precisely these nations (Argentina, Brazil, Mexico, and Cuba) that I focus on in *Tropical Riffs*.

In Argentina, as I discuss in chapter 2, even intellectuals favorably disposed toward jazz held up the music as a modern, exogenous expression fit for selective consumption if not quite wholesale appropriation. Although Argentine fans and critics of the 1930s and 1940s were among the first in the region to celebrate local exponents of jazz, ultimately they viewed North American and especially African American musicians as the music's only authentic practitioners. Their paradoxically distant embrace of jazz—both celebratory and self-preserving, negrophile and negrophobic—makes more sense when we consider that the Afro-Argentine provenance of tango had been all but expunged from mainstream discourse by the end of the 1930s, only to be picked up again several decades later.[17] Jazz—as *arte negro* par excellence—therefore assumed a uniquely contradictory and prosthetic role in national debates over several decades, a role ultimately challenged by the fictional writing of Julio Cortázar and the international fame of musicians such as Oscar Alemán, Lalo Schifrin, and Leandro "Gato" Barbieri.

In Brazil, by contrast, such an odd typecasting of jazz in the national narrative was not an option. As I examine in chapter 3, the political-symbolic paradigm that came to haunt the Brazilian cultural arena in the late 1930s and through the 1940s and 1950s explicitly promoted the incorporation of racial admixture into the national imaginary. As critics such as Hermano Vianna have written, however, the ideology of *mestiçagem* was so internally flawed and fictitious that it demanded the scaffolding of xenophobia to hold it erect. In cultural debates of the period, jazz served as an emblem of Americanization as well as a suitable countermodel to samba since it seemed to epitomize at once the decadence of foreign capitalism, the moral excesses of liberal democracy, and the racial hypocrisy of US society and institutions. A peculiar legacy of the Estado Novo's antijazz ideology was that it helped brand North American popular music as a fundamentally middle-class and even "white" pursuit—a critical legacy that would carry over into raucous debates over bossa nova in the 1960s. With its cool jazz cadences, I maintain, the music of João Gilberto, Tom Jobim, and others made an easy target for Brazilian musical nationalists and samba purists. Yet the international success of bossa nova undermined US exceptionalist claims to jazz at the same time that it weakened Brazilian antijazz rhetoric, while also further infusing vernacular idioms from both countries with new rhythms, modalities, and compositional range.

Unlike Brazil and Argentina, prerevolutionary Cuba "enjoyed" considerable geographical, political, and economic proximity to the United States, which in turn encouraged intensive musical exchange, seasonal employment, and, in many cases, emigration. Yet, as I discuss in chapter 4, in the first half of the twentieth century Cuba lacked the sort of consolidated, freestanding culture industry that characterized Mexico, Argentina, and, to a lesser extent, Brazil. This was especially true in the realm of film musicals. Whereas Cuba's prodigious talent was well represented abroad, prerevolutionary governments in Cuba failed to develop stable institutional supports with which to foster cultural production and pedagogical narratives typical of larger populist regimes in the rest of the region. As a result, compared to Argentina and Brazil, Cuban performers were highly susceptible to economic and symbolic poaching on the part of more powerful film and music industries—namely, in Mexico and the United States. It was out of this triangulation of cultural production in the 1940s and 1950s that both Afro-Cuban jazz and mambo—although usually segregated in critical discourse, they were in many ways two sides of the same coin—emerged to challenge the United States' monopolization of jazz and big band. As I will argue, innovative figures like Chano Pozo and Dámaso Pérez Prado plied their trade in hybridized transnational settings that challenged generic orthodoxies. After the triumph of the revolution, Cuban musicians remained in the forefront of what was now becoming known as Latin jazz. The nationalist orthodoxy and anti-yanqui stance of the Castro regime, however, disavowed the very idea of Cuban jazz even as cultural institutions fostered the music's development.

In the 1960s, 1970s, and 1980s, as jazz gradually lost its commercial clout, the music's artistic and countercultural cachet grew, lending it symbolic currency among new generations of writers, intellectuals, and listeners. In chapter 5, therefore, I return to fiction and poetry as key archival repositories through which to trace the afterlives of jazz in the region during the Cold War. While these literary and cultural interventions constituted in a narrow sense a return to the cosmopolitan stance of the historical vanguard, in the last few decades of the twentieth century jazz was just as likely to play the part of outsider or anachronism as savior or scapegoat. If Latin American writers such as Julio Cortázar and Alain Derbez frequently spun jazz into nostalgic metaphors of personal and creative freedom against the oppression of nationalist autocracy and populist vulgarity, others, such as Hermenegildo Sábat, César Aira, and Silviano Santiago, probed the contradictions, limits, and post-Utopian hauntings of the music's liberatory potential.

One of the more ambitious goals of *Tropical Riffs* is to introduce a decentered, expansive notion of what constitutes jazz discourse and criticism. In his study *Blowin' Hot and Cool*, John Gennari has made a compelling case for the unique mediating power of US intellectual jazz discourse compared to that of other musical genres.[18] To an unusual degree, critics like Marshall Stearns, Leonard Feather, Gary Giddins, and Stanley Crouch have helped to shape "the terms and conditions on which the music and the musicians reach the public." What is more, they have done so not just as writers, but also as promoters, educators, radio and television hosts, and even spoken-word participants in concerts and recordings.[19] As Gennari concedes, though, the transnational dimensions of the jazz "superstructure" point to the urgent need for a more comprehensive survey of jazz criticism, one that goes beyond the signature racial tensions and other particularities of North American discourse and specifically takes into account the rest of the hemisphere. The long-standing prestige enjoyed by Latin American *letrados* gave many such intellectuals a peculiar stranglehold over the "order of signs" of modernizing cities and cultures.[20] This in turn made erudite advocacy of jazz (particularly among music scholars) a risky endeavor in the region until the emergence of a "jazz art world" in North America and Europe during the postwar period.[21]

Even so, scores of other jazz interpreters, from marginal musicians and small-time editors to poets and *cronistas*, had begun to engage critically with the new music almost as soon as the word "jazz" entered into circulation. At a basic level, what most separated Latin American jazz literature from analogous practices in North America and Europe was the former region's relative lack of strategic agency vis-à-vis the invention of jazz orthodoxy and coproduction of hegemonic jazz scenes. In short, Argentina and Brazil did not produce any equivalent of Feather or Crouch, nor should they have been expected to. Like critics from Asia, Africa, and much of Europe, Latin American writers simply lacked the personal access and linguistic and cultural authority to mediate jazz at a global level for a global audience.[22] To be sure, the absence of a professional class of jazz gatekeepers in Latin America intimately involved in the international music industry at the level of production came with certain advantages. For one thing, it left those writers and intellectuals who wrote about jazz less susceptible to accusations of parasitism—one of the hallmarks of the often contentious relationship between African American jazz musicians and white critics from North America and Europe.[23] Yet, more important, the very autonomy of informal jazz discourse created ample opportunities for poetic license—Cortázar's novella *El perseguidor* (The Pursuer, 1959) perhaps being the foremost example—in which literary and film fiction absorbed and subverted the mediating function of the metropolitan Jazz Critic. Such activities were not limited to imaginative pursuits. As will become apparent at various moments of this book, intellectual interventions of different stripes, found in a wide range of media—jazz as liberator, jazz as modern vulgarity, jazz as the mask of cultural invasion—can be seen as arbitrary and therefore essentially fictive devices.

The full political complexity of jazz in Latin America was negotiated not just through narrative fiction, music criticism, radio broadcasts, live performances, or the circulation of records and liner notes, but also, and at times quite centrally, through film and television. To those seeking an exclusive focus on musical practices, recordings, and music criticism per se, my attention to the latter in *Tropical Riffs* may at first glance seem disproportionate, and no doubt reflects my own scholarly background and interests. But an analysis of relevant audio-visual culture is also crucial to understanding how the idea of jazz morphed and spread in Latin America, especially in regard to race. In shedding light on the cultural politics of jazz in Latin America, particularly during the middle decades of the twentieth century, popular cinema and television lend us key methodological tools with which to uncover the strategic positions of south-of-the-border intellectuals, politicians, and culture industries.

That jazz had a jarring impact on twentieth-century debates about race, nation, and cultural production is not just a testament to the singularity of the music's formal innovations or its peculiar sway over political debates in the region. Jazz also reveals the geopolitical dimensions of what Ana María Ochoa Gautier calls the "aural public sphere" of Latin American intellectual and cultural channels, a discursive space that channeled a common interest in "identifying and visibilizing local musics as part of a project of valorizing sonic localism." Rooted in folklore studies, yet ultimately the by-product of diverse interests and institutional investments, this frequently contentious forum of debate articulated and mediated a whole range of local, national, and international expressions.[24] Vernacular music's pervasiveness in political, social, and cultural discussions during the first half of the twentieth century ensured that jazz would also find a distinct place in the public sphere. Ever mindful of facilitating the "aural differential modernity" of national expressions, critical discourses in Latin America sought to advocate and shape—and conversely, to police and discourage—the consumption of competing transnational idioms, particularly jazz.[25] Rarely achieving the status of industry players beyond the relatively insular music scenes in Buenos Aires and São Paulo, Havana and Mexico City, critics in various guises nonetheless played central roles in interpreting the meaning of jazz for local readers, listeners, and fans.

Throughout *Tropical Riffs*, I argue that jazz has operated in various Latin American settings as a vital touchstone, bearing the risks and benefits of urban modernization, hemispheric geopolitics, and transnational cultural production.

Initially, the music provided intellectuals a shiny new instrument with which to navigate rapidly evolving attitudes toward race and sexuality, national identity, and mass consumption. As I will show in the chapters that follow, however, the acquisition of this useful tool of metropolitan citizenship required a crucial trade-off. Like popular cinema, jazz in early twentieth-century Latin America was widely associated with the very nation-state that posed the most palpable economic and military threat to regional stability and integrity. Above all, though, the United States loomed as a *cultural* force of the first order whose bag of tricks prominently featured popular dance music assisted by a formidable trio of technological-industrial supports: radio, the phonograph, and the film industry itself. For many Latin Americans, jazz gave vivid—even cruel—aural and visual form to North America's cultural, political, and economic dominance.

In the remainder of this book I will examine how and why jazz—whether embraced or denounced, exploited or obstructed, diverted or repatriated— echoed in peculiar ways with Latin American audiences, artists, and intellectuals of the twentieth century. To a greater extent than Hollywood, whose systemic racism excluded African Americans from all but token roles in the vast majority of films throughout the first half of the century, jazz forced proponents and critics alike to grapple with the cultural matrix of modern capitalism in all shades of its political complexity. The sheer power with which jazz penetrated Latin America was not just proof of the unyielding might of the US imperial machine, what Ronald Radano and Tejumola Olaniyan have referred to as "the pernicious vibrations of rapacious capitalists, the sound of bad men."[26] It also served as clear evidence of how mightily critics, intellectuals, and fans in the region struggled with questions of race, technology, sexuality, and nation during a period marked by disorientating social and demographic change. Sensitive to such issues yet also seduced by jazz's musical vitality and symbolic cachet, *jazzistas* and other performers from Buenos Aires and Rio de Janeiro to Mexico City and Havana—Oscar Alemán and Chano Pozo, João Gilberto and Gato Barbieri, Arturo Santoval and Danilo Pérez—ultimately transformed the music they played in ways few critics could have predicted.

Jazz music's ambiguous but abiding relationship with Latin America demonstrates the sheer volume, mutability, and mobility of musical currents within and across national borders. Yet that is not all it does. Any book about cultural politics should, of course, make every attempt to steer clear of facile premises about a form or genre's supposed country of origin. This is especially true for jazz, which perhaps more than any musical expression of the twentieth century enjoyed an unusually prominent and enduring global profile, but also was (and still is) subjected to an inordinate number of nationalist claims. What I propose to do in the chapters that follow is not to define jazz as Argentine or Cuban or Brazilian, or to deny that most of its innovators or practitioners were US-born. Rather, I hope to reveal the uniquely multipurpose, shape-shifting, mobile character of jazz, qualities that owed their strength not just to the intrinsic dynamism of the music, but also to its perceived Americanness. Jazz thus contained an unavoidable paradox. While consistently seen in Latin America as yanqui in provenance, "America's art form" was and remains a transnational project and a collective idea.

1

La Civilizada Selva Latin America and the Jazz Age

En la civilizada selva luchan felinos ojos de automóviles
— BERNANDO ORTIZ DE MONTELLANO, "Motivos negros" (1928)

Latin Americans of the 1920s were first exposed to what they understood to be jazz through a highly variable array of records, sheet music, traveling orchestras, revues, newspapers, magazines, radio, and cinema. South of the border, the Jazz Age initially was something of an upscale affair. Despite the increasing availability of print media and new technologies over the course of the decade, routes of access generally favored literate, male urban dwellers of some economic means. Although working classes in larger cities such as Havana, Rio de Janeiro, São Paulo, Buenos Aires, Lima, and Mexico City generally enjoyed easy enough access to cinemas, cheap live music venues, and cabarets, the barriers to obtaining and listening to recorded music in the region were considerable until at least the latter part of the decade. In smaller markets this problem was compounded by the fact that radio was slow to develop, while recording industries were dominated by foreign labels like RCA Victor, Columbia, and Odeon.[1] Finally, even in the late 1920s, the cost of record players and radio sets privileged the buying power and musical tastes of middle- and upper-class consumers.

What first characterized jazz listenership and performance in cities such as Buenos Aires was confusion about what exactly the music was supposed to sound like. One of the first successful Argentine jazz musicians and bandleaders, René Cóspito, later recalled: "Contacts with jazz in those years were very sporadic. Practically no [jazz] musicians made it to the country and imported records were scarce. . . . In reality, no one knew very well what the new music was about."[2] Another Latin American jazz pioneer, the Chilean bandleader Pablo Garrido, held a similar view. The few jazz records that made it to Santiago and Valparaiso in the first half of the decade, Garrido later wrote, were those of Paul Whiteman and similar "sweet" (as opposed to "hot") ensembles. Since there were relatively few capable instrumentalists in Chile, not to mention a scarcity of standard jazz instruments, attempts to reproduce Whiteman's ornate arrangements quickly led to a "pastiche or parody of jazz" in which overmatched smaller bands endeavored to assign three and four parts to each instrument.[3]

In a number of Latin American cities, what compensated for the initial scarcity of jazz records and limited access to radio broadcasts was that homegrown musicians and bandleaders began to incorporate jazz compositions and dance styles into their *típico* (national/traditional) repertoires. Hollywood silent films such as those featuring the "jazz baby" Clara Bow popularized dances like the fox-trot and the shimmy, which in turn encouraged local orchestras to diversify their offerings. Social elites in Caracas, partying under cover during the dictatorship of Juan Vicente Gómez, hired small ensembles to play fox-trots along with waltzes, joropos, and pasodobles.[4] In the salons, cafés, and carnival societies of Porto Alegre in southern Brazil, local bands like Jazz Espia Só interspersed Charlestons with choros, polcas, and marchas.[5] In Argentina, well-known tango bandleaders of the early 1920s such as Francisco Canaro, Osvaldo Fresedo, Roberto Firpo, and Adolfo Carabelli frequently made jazz records as well. In the year 1924 alone, Canaro's orchestra cut 202 records. Of these, 124 were labeled as típico, of which 108 were tangos. Of the 78 records categorized as "jazz-band," 44 were said to be shimmies, 26 fox-trots, 6 pasodobles, 1 camel trot, and 1 blues.[6] And while Canaro, like Firpo and Fresedo, remained mostly a performer of tangos, Carabelli increasingly gravitated toward jazz.[7]

While jazz was quickly finding its way into record stores and seeping into urban dance halls, other forces shaped the critical sensibilities of Latin American consumers and audiences. The ascendance of Hollywood in the region coincided with the rise of jazz. Even during the silent era, the hegemony of the US film industry at once benefited from jazz and consecrated the music as its unofficial soundtrack. Upscale movie theaters in Latin American cities served as emblems of cosmopolitan progress, and as such, economically and symbolically important venues for the music most associated with yanqui films. In Mexico City, for example, jazz "was perceived to be a key element of the cinema-going experience," a fact borne out by the box office success of films such as Tiffany Productions' 1924 hit *Jazzmania*.[8] Even when silent pictures were not jazz-themed, the music proved a major draw for Mexican movie-goers. Purpose-built theaters such as the Cine Royal, the Cine-Odeon, and the Cine Progreso Mundial regularly hired jazz bands to accompany screenings and to provide entertainment, some going so far as to hold fox-trot, shimmy, and Charleston lessons during intermissions.[9]

Of course, not all of the information Latin Americans received about jazz was acoustic in nature. This was especially true of the literate classes. In addition to chronicling the latest trends in Paris, New York, and Los Angeles, newspapers and magazines from Mexico City and Havana to Buenos Aires and Santiago gave readers previews of jazz, often before they had a chance to hear the music for themselves. As early as December 1917, for example, Havana's *El Mundo* surmised that jazz was a "nervous," "spicy," and yet innocent music that would soon provide a wholesome diversion for high-spirited dancers in the "distinguished cabarets" of Cuba's capital.[10] By 1918, newspapers in Chile and Argentina were advertising jazz dance lessons alongside tango and maxixe. Caracas's *El Universal* published a step-by-step description of how to do the fox-trot to the "strange rhythm" of jazz.[11] In 1919 the same newspaper reported that the jazz "had spread like a plague throughout the United Kingdom," a fact proven by the "250,000 dancers" that were supposedly flooding London's dance halls on a nightly basis.[12]

These initial accounts read jazz mostly as a harmlessly frenetic, fashionably risqué soundtrack to the fox-trot and related salon dances, many of them fleeting in their popularity. By the early 1920s, as jazz consolidated its position as a full-blown musical genre and not just a passing fad, descriptions of innocent hysteria yielded to more racialized, often moralizing denouncements of the new music. Argentina's *Crítica* bemoaned the "veritable furor" and "insanity" provoked by the jazz band's "exotic discord."[13] Mexico's *El Universal* used even more emphatic language when it reported on a petition to the Mexican government on the part of a Catholic women's organization. Citing the scores of "dance addicts" who would be disappointed by the petition, the newspaper soundly condemned jazz as an antiaesthetic, immoral, inane "Black dance" that threatened to "drive young people of both sexes crazy."[14] Such judgments were common in the US Hispanophone press as well. San Antonio's *La Prensa* reported in May 1924, for instance, that jazz had invaded all of Spanish America due to "our imitative spirit," and bemoaned the encroachment on the superior musicality and "Romanticism of our race."[15]

Latin American journalists of the period consistently confused early jazz with associated popular dances such as the fox-trot and the shimmy, and sometimes wrote about the music as if it were a product of Paris, London, or Honolulu rather than New York, Chicago, and New Orleans. That many articles offered secondhand news—or worse, imperfect reprintings and mistranslations of secondhand accounts—compounded misinformation about jazz's formal characteristics and cultural origins. The correctness of details often took a back seat to the perceived moral consequences of the music's "savage" provenance. In an essay translated from English and published in Mexico's *El Universal* in 1922, for example, an unnamed author bitterly denounced jazz as a product of the "heat-atrophied brains" and "well-known lasciviousness" of "the poor Indians of the Hawaiian Islands."[16] Latin American newspapers frequently used reports of antijazz declarations in the United States and Europe as evidence that the music was divisive, aesthetically suspect, and morally dangerous. In an article published in May 1922, *O Estado de São Paulo* reported that New York pastor Percy Grant had condemned jazz in a sermon titled "Is Jazz our National Anthem?" as "music of bestial noise that obliges [one] to yell and tap furiously." As opposed to "progressive" vanguard schools such as cubism, Grant intoned, jazz "makes us regress, returning [us] to the forests of primitive times." Although the Brazilian article glossed at least one other report in its account, and therefore could hardly be considered veridical, the spin that the newspaper gave Grant's sermon was that of a widespread frenzy seizing the entire nation rather than the incendiary remarks of a single clergyman.[17]

By branding jazz as a modern-primitive practice, denunciatory newspaper accounts inadvertently paved the way for the music's acceptance in Latin America by pairing depictions of sexual degeneration with liberation, racial otherness with urban fashion. Kwame Anthony Appiah has argued that cosmopolitan societies, both modern and ancient, have invariably depended on the "impurities" of strangers through the productive influx and assimilation of exogenous subjects, texts, and practices. Central to Appiah's view is the notion that cosmopolitanism was "invented by contaminators."[18] This turn of phrase underscores the fact that cultural impurities do not merely flavor cosmopolitan settings but also constitute them. Jazz's appeal to progress-minded Latin Americans of the 1920s illustrates the inseparability of "clean" and "dirty" conceptions of the modern at a moment of rapid urbanization, political upheaval, and social turmoil in the region. The primitive spirit and moral dubiousness commonly attributed to jazz in early newspaper accounts highlighted the music's "contaminating" influence, at the same time that these writers underscored its quintessentially modern sounds and seductive appeal, often in the same breath.

In Latin America, as elsewhere, acute social fears were frequently tied to claims about the pathogenic qualities of vernacular and certain forms of erudite music—claims that could be found in medical and moral discourse dating back to the early nineteenth century. By the mid-1920s, jazz music's frequent association with lower-class bars, brothels, theatrical venues, women's liberation, and black bodies raised fears of frenetic gyrations and unhygienic contact on the dance floor. It also directly or indirectly raised the specter of miscegenation.[19] The perceived threat posed by jazz was heightened in Latin America by the peculiar resilience of eugenics in intellectual circles, even in Brazil, where alternative models of social and cultural nationalism championed "racially mixed people of increasing ethnic and eugenic soundness."[20]

In a certain sense, early Latin American writing about jazz was not entirely unique. According to Ronald Radano, North American and European critics and intellectuals of the late nineteenth and early twentieth centuries tended to associate the "hotness" of black urban music with one of two extremes: primordial salvation ("descent") or jarring social and demographic change ("displacement").[21] Such racialized binaries were also present in Latin America. Yet rose-tinted primitivism and racial hysteria were not the only reactions that greeted jazz in the region. Emerging at a time when a new generation of urban intellectuals and lower- and middle-class consumers had begun to embrace mass culture, jazz stood as a symbol of increasing access to modernity, social and sexual liberation, and metropolitan citizenship. For the cultural avant-garde, jazz kept time to modern urban culture, its trademark speed and syncopation the flip side of the contagious freneticism so feared by the music's anxious critics. For urban denizens generally, the strange appeal of jazz signaled a vaguely defined notion of a deeply problematic "good life." Even before the widespread penetration of Hollywood talkies beginning in 1927, the international stardom afforded to many North American performers (whether actors, musicians, or dancers) intensified jazz music's affective claims on Latin American consumers.[22] The virtues of jazz were sometimes expressed in the same technological or pathological language used by its detractors. Enthusiasts frequently championed the music as a beacon of modernity and modern expression, a therapeutic salve and even an energizing cure-all, one promising not just social or epistemological salvation but physical regeneration as well.

The basis for such an attraction was not just geopolitical. It was also rooted in unique experiences and conceptions of time. Néstor García Canclini has argued that the marked "multitemporal heterogeneity" of Latin American societies is largely the result of "ruptures provoked by industrial development and urbanization that, although they occurred after those of Europe, were more accelerated."[23] Jazz, like ragtime before it, emanated from a highly stratified ecosystem in which subaltern subjects and antiquated systems of knowledge awkwardly rubbed shoulders with modern ones. The speed and strangeness of jazz played out in peculiar ways in Latin American settings. The music's sonic audacity and racial profile posed unique challenges to conventional notions of erudite culture and social hierarchies. In short, they positioned jazz as an emblem of international mass culture reminiscent of national expressions yet conveniently external to them: a transcontinental sign (North American, European, African) that enabled new strategies of self-identification while invoking the cachet of a particularly risky—and risqué—brand of the modern. Jazz thus allowed a new generation of critics and intellectuals to grapple with the contradictions of Latin America's long promised but troubled membership in the club of modern nations, a relationship marked by difference as much as by affiliation, by gaping rifts as much as common ties.

These negotiations, as early newspaper accounts illustrate, were often plagued by confusion as to what exactly jazz *was* and ambivalence toward its association with the United States, a country that loomed ominously not just as a very real geopolitical threat to many Latin American nations, but also as an emblem of boorish capitalism. In the second decade of the twentieth century, jazz surfaced amid a larger wave of vernacular musical idioms washing over many parts of the world, part of what Michael Denning has termed the revolutionary "polyphony of colonial ports."[24] In what remains of this chapter, I am interested in mapping the music's first encroachment into Latin American urban imaginaries once the word, and with it the idea of, jazz had taken hold, even if the music's precise characteristics were still largely in flux. In this sense, an especially useful realm of analysis of the Latin American Jazz Age is the widespread, contentious reception given to touring singer and dancer Josephine Baker in the late 1920s. In some ways the ideal courier of African-American vernacular music to middle-brow and elite audiences, Baker's Parisian residence and affectations mitigated her North American origins, consecrating her Latin American performances as "civilized" in spite of the fact that they often exhibited the most debasing qualities of minstrelsy, all under the rubric of jazz and *le nègre*. As I will discuss later in this chapter, if Baker's rhetoric of tropical shock and excess brought to Latin American audiences a caricature of cosmopolitan impurities, her performances also distilled the analogousness and adaptability of jazz to local idioms and social conditions that would supply the backbeat of musical nationalism in the decades to come.

Call of the Urban Wild

If Josephine Baker came to the attention of many Latin Americans by European proxy, so too did jazz itself. In the late 1910s and early 1920s, it was not New York or Los Angeles but rather Paris that was to play an especially salient role for modern-minded artists, writers, composers, and musicians in the region. While this was due in part to the long-standing prestige of French high culture among Latin American intellectuals, France also served to mediate, depurate, and consecrate far-flung popular dances and musical idioms during the interwar period. It is hardly surprising, therefore, that the City of Light should have played a central role in the unfolding of jazz history in the waning days of the First World War.

The seminal event leading to the music's international popularity was a six-week tour of France by James Reese Europe's Harlem Hellfighters (the 369th Infantry Band) in early 1918, a smashing success that led to more performances once the war had definitively ended.[25] Even before the "Europe" fever hit Europe, however, major artists and intellectuals such as Jean Cocteau and Igor Stravinsky were avidly integrating rag and early jazz elements into their modernist compositions. Together with Erik Satie, Pablo Picasso, and the Ballets Russes, and inspired by the music of Scott Joplin, Cocteau turned the ballet *Parade* (1917) into an avant-garde celebration of modern life in the United States and France.[26] Although other composers, including Debussy (*Golliwog's Cakewalk*, 1908) and Stravinsky (*Histoire du soldat* and *Ragtime pour onze instruments*, 1918), also experimented with ragtime, it was the Swiss-born Darius Milhaud who first systematically based a classical composition on jazz. The culmination of Paris's obsession with jazz was Milhaud's jazz-inspired ballet *La création du monde*, composed in collaboration with poet Blaise Cendrars and first staged in 1923.

The rising fervor for things nègre was never focused exclusively on jazz. For European intellectuals of the 1910s, ragtime, and later jazz, often overlapped with other Afro-diasporic styles such as tango, maxixe, rumba, danzón, and son.[27] The maxixe was a highly malleable musical and dance form that briefly benefited from intensive transnational negotiations across cultural circuits. Reaching its international zenith in 1914, maxixe quickly suffered a "conflationary flattening" alongside tango and jazz.[28] Such generic confusion eventually led to the maxixe's curious erasure, which scholar Micol Seigel has attributed to the music's inability to brand itself as Brazilian without also placing its blackness in the foreground. By contrast, tango's promoters managed to "erase its blackness without deleting its *Argentinidad*."[29] Jazz emerged later on the international scene than either tango or maxixe. Yet considering a number of advantages held by the United States over Brazil and Argentina—North American companies' stranglehold on the recording industry, Hollywood's unparalleled promotional machinery, not to mention the hundreds of US musicians who remained in Europe after World War I—it is easy to see why jazz quickly eclipsed tango and maxixe in the postwar, transnational marketplace.[30]

Interestingly, Milhaud's brief but intense love affair with jazz was immediately preceded by an equally fervent obsession with maxixe during the composer's two-year stay in Brazil at the end of the war as secretary to the French ambassador. "Haunted" by the fervor surrounding the seminal samba recording "Pelo telefone" (1917), Milhaud praised the compositional abilities of Ernesto Nazareth and Marcelo Tupinambá owing to what he calls their "rhythmic richness . . . , verve, vivacity, and melodic invention of prodigious imagination."[31] Sometimes dubbed the Brazilian Scott Joplin for similarities between his syncopated songs and North American rags, Nazareth was widely considered the period's foremost composer of maxixes and *tangos brasileiros*.[32] Milhaud later recalled having witnessed Nazareth play "mournful" piano at the entrance of a cinema on Rio de Janeiro's Avenida Rio Branco.[33]

The Swiss composer's short-lived fixation on Brazilian culture culminated after his return to France with the staging of the maxixe- and samba-based ballet *Le boeuf sur le toit* (1919). Originally conceived by Milhaud as a silent film soundtrack (an association perhaps inspired by the spectacle of Nazareth playing at a Rio movie house), the piece featured the lyrics of poet and budding Brazil enthusiast Blaise Cendrars.[34] *Le boeuf sur le toit* was built on a pastiche of popular songs, although not all Brazilians appreciated the tribute. According to a 1967 study by Baptista Siqueira, Milhaud had borrowed substantially and without attribution from Nazareth's "Escovado," a wholesale appropriation Siqueira characterized as a "cold, revolting, unspeakable usurpation."[35] *Le boeuf sur le toit* got its name from a tune ("O boi no telhado") written by José Monteiro of the Oito Batutas, a celebrated Brazilian ensemble with which Milhaud was quite familiar.[36] Led by the brilliant flautist and later saxophonist Pixinguinha (Alfredo da Rocha Viana Jr.), the Oito Batutas performed and recorded extensively in Brazil, Argentina, and Europe during the late 1910s and 1920s. In fact, as a number of scholars have pointed out, the group covered much the same ground musically and geographically as the touring US jazz bands and impressed some of the same intellectuals, including Milhaud and Cendrars.

Europeans were not the only ones to take notice of the Oito Batutas. In a column published in the *Gazeta de Notícias* in January 1922, when the Oito Batutas were about to embark on a trip to Europe as part of Rio's centennial exhibition, the novelist and journalist Benjamim Costallat argued that "we

[Brazilians] should look to be recognized in Europe as we are. *With our Negroes and all the rest.*[37] Costallat's defense of the group on racial grounds signaled a shift from just a few years earlier, when Brazilian elites had often worried that the Afro-Brazilian strains of the fashionable maxixe would give a false, vulgar impression of the country abroad.[38] Yet Costallat's impassioned intervention was couched in bias against what he saw as the Oito Batutas' main competition in Europe: jazz bands. The Parisian public, he wrote, "should know how to distinguish between our musicians and those American clowns, men of tin cans, horns and whistles." Based on his own travels to France months earlier, Costallat contended that "prosaic" US jazz bands were winning over audiences by injecting noisy gimmickry into their performances, the horns and whistles products of their "morbid imagination." That was about to change. "Hearing our *modinhas*," he writes, "listening to [the Oito Batutas] sing about our moonlit nights, our *sertão*, our dark-skinned women, our love and our *saudade*, many French people will be moved."[39]

Viewed in hindsight, the main problem with such a defense of the Oito Batutas is that, like most music and cultural critics of the period, Costallat presumed a strict division between national idioms. Actual musical practices were not so segregated. The cavaquinho player Nelson Alves reported having played alongside US jazz musicians on numerous occasions during the Oito Batutas' first stint in Paris.[40] In the aftermath of the visit, jazz strains began to embellish and even to eclipse Brazilian rhythms in performance venues in São Paulo and Rio de Janeiro. Tellingly, the Oito Batutas returned to Brazil having added a banjo and a saxophone to their arsenal. At the same time, new orchestras, such as the Oito Cotubas (a split-off group of the Batutas, featuring Donga), the Jazz-Band Sul-Americano, and the Jazz-Band Brasil-América, responding to a demand for North American dances, increasingly favored fox-trots, shimmies, and later, Charlestons over sambas, maxixes, and tangos.[41] In a 1923 interview, Romeu Silva, the founder and leader of the Jazz Band Sul-Americano, boasted of having won over audiences not just in Rio, São Paulo, and Santos, but also in Montevideo and New York. Yet even as Silva unabashedly embraced non-Brazilian music, he echoed Costallat's remark about the vulgar "clownishness" of many of his competitors. "Always uniformed and decent," he writes, "our fine band is fit to perform in any high society Rio ballroom. No monkeying around or mockery, like certain French and American bands around here. We are artists and not clowns."[42]

French avant-garde intellectuals tended to conceive of jazz as an accepted, stable sign rather than as a socially constructed emblem in flux, one that in the early 1920s, as we have already seen, referred rather clumsily to a wide-ranging and shifting set of musical practices. Intellectuals like Milhaud and Cocteau, while frequenting Parisian venues such as Le Boeuf sur le Toit (named after Milhaud's hit ballet), engaged in spirited slumming through which they promoted jazz as "secondary aesthetic production" that stimulated and underpinned their modernist works. This strongly connotative function of jazz would prove crucial to Paris-based intellectuals of the period.[43] Erudite treatments of jazz seduced emerging Latin American intellectuals of the period like the Cuban writer Alejo Carpentier, who praised the jazz-inspired pieces of Ravel and Stravinsky as much as he did jazz itself.[44] Carpentier spoke particularly often and well of Milhaud, whom he described as "one of the strongest and most original creators of contemporary music."[45] The young Cuban's "secondary" enthusiasm for jazz reveals the extent to which Latin American vanguard intellectuals often took their cues from European high-culture mediators, whose authority had the dual effect of disinfecting Afro-descendant music and dance and also bypassing the generic untidiness that characterized vernacular idioms.

As the decade progressed, what might be called the techno-primitivism of nègre discourses and compositional practices of the late teens and early 1920s yielded to more exuberant negrophilia, a shift that eventually facilitated jazz's seduction of Latin American vanguardists.[46] Among the leaders of the charge were Robert Goffin, André Coeuroy, André Schaeffner, and Hugues Panassié, who championed hot jazz of the 1920s and early 1930s as a vital crossroads of rigidly segregated white cultivation and black inspiration.[47] The Belgian-born Goffin would prove especially pivotal in transforming jazz criticism from an extension of vanguard poetics into something that increasingly resembled a vocation. Cofounder and editor of *Le Disque Vert*, a journal of literature and culture to which he contributed numerous jazz-oriented articles and poems during the 1920s, Goffin trumpeted jazz music's revolutionary preeminence among the arts of the early twentieth century.[48] Proclaiming jazz "the first form of Surrealism," Goffin (a surrealist poet himself) emphasized the need for emotive, naive folk-art forms to rescue interwar Europe from a cold, cerebral decadence, likening the continent to a patient in need of non-Western medicine for whom jazz was the cure-all.[49]

The Francophone critics were not the only European writers of the period to praise jazz as a restorative expression. The Jazz Age arrived in Spain at roughly the same time as the nation's first important vanguard school, *ultraísmo*. In January 1921, Madrid's first jazz venue, the Club Parisiana, hosted an important *ultraísta* happening attended by such intellectuals as Guillermo de Torre, Gerardo Diego, and Jorge Luis Borges during the Argentine writer's first stay in Spain.[50] Yet it was the Portuguese writer António Ferro (later closely associated with António Salazar's Estado Novo) who would play a crucial early role in Latin America by putting the jazz-band stamp on emerging Brazilian vanguard projects. During a long stint in Brazil in 1922 and 1923, he gave a number of public lectures in several cities, often embellishing his verbal pyrotechnics with musical performances.[51] Ferro's "A idade do jazz-band" quickly became his signature performance. First giving the talk-performance on June 30 in Rio de Janeiro's Teatro Lírico, Ferro went on to present it in a number of different venues, including São Paulo's Teatro Municipal (September 12), Santos's Teatro Guarany (October 9), São Paulo's Automóvel Club (November 10), and Belo Horizonte's Teatro Municipal (February 6, 1923).[52]

The talk itself, first released in book form in 1923, presented a curious mix of sober reflection and giddy sensationalism. Ferro was particularly eager to link jazz's paradigmatic significance to the emergence of cinema. Yet he did so in a way that explicitly gendered jazz. If the jazz band, "like the *écran*, contains all the images of modern life," it was women, drawn away from the artificial confines of the boudoir, who were most completely liberated by the music's "insane" spectacle and "triumph of dissonance."[53] What was more, Ferro suggested that jazz created or "improvised" women by setting their bodies in motion on the dance floor.[54] As if to prove his point, Ferro's signature talk was apparently interrupted several times by the performance of a jazz band accompanied by a female dancer—presumably performing a fox-trot, since this was the dance form of which Ferro spoke most frequently in his lecture.[55]

Modernist writers from the late nineteenth century onward frequently associated the devalued and devaluating "menace" of mass culture with women.[56] For Ferro, however, such dangers assumed positively transformative qualities. Jazz was not just any agent of change, but an "alchemist of bodies" and "the great furnace of humanity."[57] Ferro explicitly linked the music to both race and *novomundismo*. While a somber Europe lived in the darkness of the Great War, jazz was the "siren of peace" and restorer of light. Echoing the contemporaneous criticism of Robert Goffin and others, Ferro flattered his audience by declaring Europe Americanized—a turn of phrase Brazilians of the time would have understood in national as well as hemispheric terms.[58] Further, the Old Continent had been "blackened" by jazz, and the Portuguese showman ostensibly served as the evidence. Before another interruption by the jazz band, Ferro announced that the "Hour of the Negro" was upon them, and explicitly alluded to the ostensibly mixed-race makeup of the Brazilian audience. "The jazz-band is the chessboard of the moment," he wrote. "*Jazz*-white; *band*-black.

Alabaster bodies—dancing; ebony bodies—touching. The jazz-band is the *ex-libris* of the century. May your souls dance to the rhythm of this jazz-band of white men masked by the blackface of my words."[59]

Many Brazilian modernists of the early 1920s were already predisposed to accept Ferro's jazz gospel. During the second night of the watershed avant-garde event Semana de Arte Moderna, held in São Paulo's Teatro Municipal just three months before Ferro's arrival, Paulo Menotti del Picchia gave a provocative lecture proposing jazz as a metaphor for the liberation of Brazilian cultural production from the shackles of tradition—and from classical poetics in particular. "Enough with describing the rushing around of scruffy satyrs in pursuit of soft-footed nymphs," he challenged his audience. "The Babylon of São Paulo is full of urban fauns and modern nymphs dancing *maxixes* to the sound of jazz."[60] Meanwhile, in the first issue of the short-lived but influential avant-garde journal *Klaxon* (which coincided almost to the day with Ferro's arrival in the country), Mário de Andrade's manifesto declared the "Jazz-Band" one of the pillars of Brazilian modernism: "[Ours] is the age of the Oito Batutas, of the Jazz Band, of Chicharrão, Charlie Chaplin, Mutt and Jeff. The Age of Construction. The Age of KLAXON." Picking up where Menotti del Picchia left off, Mário de Andrade invoked jazz to rail against the "artistic tears" of the previous generation of Brazilian intellectuals, and to advocate instead for revolutionary levity and "surgical" farce.[61]

Anti-moralistic and aesthetically rebellious, the young lions of Brazilian modernism saw a kindred spirit in António Ferro. In its third issue (July 1922), *Klaxon* published Ferro's delirious manifesto "Nós." That September, the *klaxistas* feted the Portuguese visitor at a dinner during which the guest of honor and his hosts flattered one another with clever wordplay: "São Paulo precisa importar ferro" (São Paulo needs to import iron [ferro]), one Brazilian quipped, to which the Portuguese writer responded, "because Ferro is valued by São Paulo."[62] In a 1923 interview appearing in *Diário de Lisboa*, an acerbic Oswald de Andrade acknowledged that the "backward" Brazilian modernists had benefited considerably from the visit of the agitator Ferro.[63] That the Portuguese jazz messenger had been greeted as an antidote to cultural anachronism became apparent in an article published in *Diário de Minas* in which Carlos Drummond de Andrade wrote that Ferro "lived in 1923 as though it were the year 2000." If Ferro could be "irritatingly modern, noisy" and even "perverse and immoral," it was because—Drummond speculated—he had "poisoned himself with all the marvelous toxins of the century." It was as if, in other words, Ferro had "a jazz-band in his soul."[64]

The frenzy surrounding Ferro's lecture and visit ebbed and flowed in the ensuing years. In the mid-1920s many Brazilian critics began to reject jazz with increasing stridency, just as the hot sound was beginning to permeate the urban music of Brazil, thus endangering the "authenticity" of national idioms.[65] In a series of newspaper articles written in the early 1920s, a young Gilberto Freyre lamented the popularization of jazz in Brazil even as he praised analogous urban music such as the choro and samba for exhibiting what many other critics considered jazz-like characteristics: namely, formal hybridity and transatlantic provenance. Lauding the "voluptuousness" of certain Old World forms like the waltz, the future author of the landmark work *The Masters and the Slaves* (Casa Grande e Senzala; 1933) declared jazz, by contrast, "barbarous" and full of "sensuality without a single note of grace or spirit."[66] Freyre carefully avoided racializing jazz so as not to have to acknowledge parallels between African American and Afro-Brazilian vernacular idioms at the level of production. Instead, he focused primarily on jazz's putative national traits and secondarily on its potential impact on local audiences, a maneuver the anthropologist Hermano Vianna has identified as the result of political, rather than intellectual, conviction.[67] Like the United States itself, Freyre suggested, "the 'whoof-whoof' of jazz-bands" expressed a puerile, commercialized, and spiritually lacking quality to which Brazilian listeners and spectators were particularly vulnerable.[68]

Freyre's disgust with jazz reflected not just his distrust of cosmopolitanism—which he saw as the bearer of exotic imports and as such a menace to authentic regional expression—but also Brazil's relative isolation from Spanish American avant-garde circuits in the 1920s and 1930s. In short, Freyre could ill afford to invoke analogous Brazilian musical idioms like samba as worthy vessels of *mestiçagem* without seeming to disqualify non-Brazilian musical expressions such as tango or rumba as invalid in other national contexts.[69] As historian Dain Borges has suggested, moreover, Brazilian modernists (including Freyre) preferred to legitimize Afro-Creole cultures without mobilizing them in any specific ways that might jeopardize the purity of the *mestiço* ideal.[70] Seen in this way, Freyre's rejection of jazz was symptomatic of a general refusal to mobilize or legitimize cultural practices that lay outside the narrow parameters of his nationalist yearnings. It may also have been a question of timing. Freyre's denigration of jazz contrasted sharply with his favorable assessment of the jazz-inflected work of Donga and Pixinguinha from the late 1920s. As Vianna has noted, it was surely no small coincidence that the celebrated author's earlier jazz writings had emerged at a moment when the commercialized, sweet sounds of Paul Whiteman and others were first exploding onto international cultural markets.[71]

In any case, Freyre's antijazz stance of the 1920s evoked the specter of eugenic discourse that would continue to haunt his major works. The backdrop of racial "hygiene" and "progress" both confounded and enabled the provocative thesis developed in *The Masters and the Slaves*.[72] Taking stock of the climate of eugenics in which Freyre emerged makes it possible to understand the ambivalence with which he and many other intellectuals of the period regarded urban dance music. Nineteenth- and early twentieth-century medical eugenicists and educators frequently pathologized musical expression, particularly when vernacular music was associated with racial otherness and the culture industry. As a result, new idioms like ragtime and jazz were widely seen as contaminants of the body politic. Many elites feared that jazz's "primitive" rhythms, delivered by emerging technologies, might not only fray the nerves of young listeners, but also lead to debauchery, sexual licentiousness, and even miscegenation. And their fears did not stop there. In the 1920s, scores of writers, intellectuals, and educators in Europe and North America warned that the syncopated rhythms of jazz might well "change human physiology, damaging the medulla in the brain and leading to insomnia, dizziness, nervous spasms, impotence in men, and to depression and infertility in women."[73]

Clearly, though, not all Brazilian intellectuals of the 1920s shared such misgivings about the social and hygienic consequences of North American urban dance music. The jazz-band euphoria proclaimed by *Klaxon*'s team of cosmopolitans was still palpable, for example, in António Alcântara Machado's unique vanguard travel narrative *Pathé-Baby* (1926). Named after the popular home-movie system, Alcântara's percussive literary montage of the European cities he visited—from Lisbon to Paris, Milan to Seville—seemed to respond to Ferro's entreaty to write tumultuously about modern life in all its speed and vulgarity. The Brazilian's camera eye, juxtaposing cabaret dancers and bullfights, automobiles and fox-trots, was clearly trained to the Jazz Age now in full swing on the Continent. To underscore the musical subtext of Alcântara's narrative, the book's first edition featured a series of illustrations by António Paim Vieira showing a small, animated jazz ensemble (including a black-haired, bare-shouldered flapper on piano) performing in the bottom frame, with representative images of each city projected onto to a screen above them. The overall effect was that of a Latin American traveler visibly up to the task of translating the dizzying spectacles he encountered, employing an innovative language with which to celebrate and match the sights and sounds of modernity.

It could be said that *Pathé-Baby* was ultimately a derivative, eccentric product in the sense that it depended on European cityscapes to provide the inspiration for Brazilian vanguard aesthetics. Such dependence masks a deep irony, since, as we have already seen, Europe so frequently relied on the New World's stock of otherness for its own inspiration. As cultural historian Nicolau Sevcenko later remarked about 1920s intellectuals in São Paulo, "Brazilian travelers and tourists, desirous of taking the traditional *banho de civilização* (bath of civilization) in Paris, discovered how 'important' and 'ingenious' [the French] considered the culture of the population that shamed [Brazilian travelers] with its misery, ignorance and skin color."[74] Brazilian elites, though, were not the only ones in the region to encounter revealing racial contradictions abroad. The basic incongruity between the ways Latin American and European intellectuals thought about New World others, and jazz itself, would be further challenged in the second half of the decade.

El Chamaco and La Baker

The visibility and influence of the Mexican illustrator, caricaturist, and designer Miguel Covarrubias stands as vivid proof of two underappreciated realities of the Jazz Age as it related to Latin America: first, regional jazz discourse in the 1920s was not limited to written expression; and second, Latin American intellectuals did not merely take their cultural cues from third-party European sources such as Milhaud, Cendrars, and Ferro. Covarrubias's profile as a key eyewitness to the Jazz Age and an honorary member of the Harlem Renaissance has a curious backstory: he was something of an outcast in Mexico.[75] Following a pivotal conversation with José Juan Tablada, the renowned poet, journalist, and sometime diplomat who found himself banished from Mexico due to a political dispute, Covarrubias moved to New York in 1923. With the help of Tablada, who secured the young artist a job at the Mexican consulate, and shortly later Carl van Vechten, a well-connected US journalist with a keen nose for talent, Covarrubias quickly established himself as a caricaturist of uncommon style and satirical deftness. If revolutionary orthodoxy proved daunting for Covarrubias, the US publishing industry embraced his fresh approach to illustration with open arms. By 1924, the artist had his first one-man show. His work, moreover, was appearing routinely in such newspapers as the *New York Tribune* and magazines like *Vanity Fair*.[76] One of his favorite subjects became black urban culture. Here, van Vechten's influence would prove crucial. As a chronicler and patron of the Harlem Renaissance, van Vechten introduced

Covarrubias not just to the intellectuals associated with the movement—writers like Langston Hughes, Zora Neale Hurston, and James Weldon Johnson—but also the neighborhood itself, which by this time had displaced New Orleans and Chicago as ground zero of the Jazz Age.

Covarrubias's illustrations for *Vanity Fair* set the stage for a number of subsequent works, including the cover of Langston Hughes's *The Weary Blues* (1925), a set of illustrations for composer W. C. Handy's *Blues: An Anthology* (1926), and Covarrubias's stand-alone collection *Negro Drawings* (1927). Seen as a whole, the renderings show the extent to which jazz and blues spectacles had quickly captured Covarrubias's visual imagination. While exaggerating the features and movements of their subjects, the illustrations could hardly be called satirical, much less grotesque. If anything, Covarrubias's work from the period reveals a subtlety of observation and clear-eyed, if stylized, appreciation for black musicians, singers, and dancers, as well as the uptown venues where they performed. *Blues* presents images of individuals and couples striking poses that vacillate between smoky languor and religious ecstasy, including a compelling study of celebrated singer Bessie Smith. *Negro Drawings*, despite its somber title, captures the jaunty, playful spirit of the Harlem clubs. Without sacrificing entirely the lyric quality characteristic of the *Blues* illustrations, Covarrubias renders jazz patrons, performers, and even instruments into lithe, modern, elegant figures.

Covarrubias's singular portraits of the 1920s seduced not only New York publishers but also a number of prominent writers associated with jazz and blues. Langston Hughes and James Weldon Johnson praised the Mexican's work in book reviews published respectively in *Opportunity* and the *Saturday Review of Literature*. In a letter to the artist written after seeing the jacket for *Weary Blues*, Hughes proclaimed Covarrubias "the only artist I know whose Negro things have a 'Blues' touch about them."[77] Such a combination of private praise and generally glowing press coverage, along with the wide distribution enjoyed by the Mexican artist's illustrations, soon made Covarrubias a crucial interloper between artistic and literary circles in the United States, the Caribbean, Europe, and South America.[78]

Initially it would be Tablada who would prove Covarrubias's most dogged promoter in Mexico. In late November 1924 (in the wake of *Vanity Fair*'s publication of Covarrubias's work) Tablada made the extraordinary claim in the Mexican newspaper *El Universal* that Covarrubias had "discovered" blacks in the United States. Presenting both the artist and his Afro-descendant subjects as virtual unknowns, Tablada argued that "just as America existed before Columbus, and African art existed before it was discovered by Picasso and

Apollinaire," the culture of the "North American Negro" also existed before Covarrubias brought it to the world's attention in the *Vanity Fair* illustrations. By "revealing beauty where no one had seen it," Covarrubias had rescued black Americans from a long history of debasing stereotypes and exploitation. "Our artist," Tablada wrote emphatically, "has revealed that the Negro is not the laughingstock, not the black and bowlegged clown of the white man."[79] Tablada thus invoked both European colonial conquest and vanguard negrophilia to suggest that Covarrubias was performing a similar function in the United States. In one fell swoop, the poet placed his countryman in the dual role of refined observer and Lincolnesque liberator.

Several months before Tablada's provocative article, in February of 1924, "Caballero Puck" (Manuel Horta) had published an introductory sketch of the artist in *El Universal Ilustrado*. The profile did not include caricatures of jazz or blues musicians. Yet its appearance signaled Covarrubias's rising fame in the United States and Mexico, and also the key role he had played years earlier in the foundation of the magazine, one of the first in Mexico to embrace modernity and mass culture.[80] In a special issue several months later (July 1924), a number of Mexican writers and intellectuals approached the jazz phenomenon from various angles. In a feature that would be repeated in Argentine and Brazilian journals in the coming decades, *El Universal Ilustrado* asked modern classical composers, conductors, and musicians to express their candid opinions about jazz. The response of composer Manuel Ponce typified the ambivalence expressed by all those interviewed. While lightly praising the "melodious" sound of the jazz saxophone, Ponce took exception to jazz bands generally, dismissing typical rhythm sections as "musical gibberish, cacophony without precedent, an amalgam of inharmonious noises and sounds." Moreover, it was precisely these "vile," "vulgar," and "animalistic" qualities of jazz, according to Ponce, that expressed the essence of the "North American soul."[81]

Ponce's remarks gave stark, racialized expression to fears of yanqui cultural invasion commonly heard among Mexican intellectuals with respect to US cinema during the same period.[82] Like Hollywood films, jazz music (as we have already seen in early newspaper accounts) was frequently associated with shifting sartorial fashion and sexual provocation, and sometimes ironically praised by older male writers as a vehicle of youthful indiscretion and women's sexual liberation. In *El Universal Ilustrado*'s survey of composers and musicians, the violinist José Rocabruna echoed Ponce's comments when he lamented that jazz rhythms "awaken muscular movements of our youth" and therefore cannot help but be "disastrous for the spiritual education of [our] race." Even jazz proponents hinted at the music's putative dangers. "Sánchez Filmador"

Fig. 1.1. Miguel Covarrubias, "Orchestra," from *Negro Drawings* (1927).

Fig. 1.2. Miguel Covarrubias, "Double Charleston," from *Negro Drawings* (1927).

(Gustavo F. Aguilar) wrote in a satirical poem that the music's secret appeal was the tendency of female dance partners, caught up in jazz's "vertigo of pleasure," to display their bodies more brazenly. "The corset is now used under no circumstances," he marveled, since "women wear a blouse and nothing else."[83]

As the comments by Ponce and Rocabruna suggest, nationalist fears and moral trepidation were overlaid with a heightened sense of racial anxiety not generally seen in Mexican intellectuals' criticism of silent-era Hollywood. For example, the *cronista* "Jacobo Dalevuelta" (Fernando Ramírez de Aguilar) bemoaned the music's arrival in working-class Mexican neighborhoods. "The dangerous germ invaded the organism of our interesting commoners," he wrote. "The North American clowns left behind the brilliant tuxedos with which they had disguised their histrionics [while they played] in elegant cabarets smelling of champagne and Black Narcissus, and now play with the blue denim outfits of our lowly brothers." Dalevuelta's sardonic tone betrayed an elitist disdain for the vulgarity of jazz. While acknowledging the music's penetration of all rungs of Mexican society, the cronista suggested that "our lowly brothers" were more susceptible to yanqui contagion and lowbrow pedigree.[84]

Of all the pieces included in the special volume of *El Universal Ilustrado*, the most daring was Manuel Maples Arce's delirious poetic essay "Jazz=XY." Painstakingly framing jazz in futurist language, Maples Arce proclaimed his own endeavor a theoretical one constituting "a constructive proposition" and "the expository equivalent of . . . neo-musical poetics."[85] The Mexican writer characterized the music as a "new state of the spirit" emblematic of a return to primitive chaos, and traced the music's origins to "a few cannibalistic tribes from South Africa [*sic*], where North American jazz took its primordial technical elements and dynamic, polyrhythmic structure."[86] In spite of his shaky grasp of cultural geography, Maples Arce localized jazz in ways that subverted prevailing primitivist dichotomies, concluding his article in typically eccentric fashion: "Black music, a vital and *estridentista* success, holds the secret of an animalistic, violent and subversive ideology. The bourgeoisie may rise up in protest, but despite it all they live the rhythm of its mechanized animalism."[87]

By describing jazz with the same adjective used to define his own aesthetic-political platform—estridentista—Maples Arce staked a claim to a common primeval source shared by jazz music and Mexican avant-garde literary production, or so he hoped. His audacious pronouncements somewhat resembled those the Brazilian monthly *Klaxon* published two years earlier. The imagined alliance between jazz and Latin American literary modernism is not surprising when we consider that both were cultural practices "out of place" in the 1920s, albeit in distinct ways.[88] At the same time, Maples Arce's use of language echoed the ways jazz music of the period fashioned itself after the technological flows of mass culture, through an embrace of syncopation and sometimes extramusical sounds. This was precisely the side of the music most strenuously repudiated by the likes of Manuel Ponce, with his stalwart modernism and revolutionary orthodoxy. Maples Arce's essay thus turned a common criticism of jazz—that it was mechanical "noise"—into an affirmative assessment of jazz's potential as a model for newfangled literature. The many antijazz opinions included in the special issue of *El Universal Ilustrado* may have revealed the cultural conservatism that was widespread among his countrymen but they also threw into relief Maples Arce's unique claim to avant-gardism. Not content simply to echo European intellectuals by proclaiming jazz avant-garde, as it were, avant la lettre ("the first form of Surrealism"), the Mexican poet conceived of the music as a cultural practice uniquely relevant to the Americas. Emblematic of the vernacular and the modern in equal measure, jazz was New World capitalism's reconversion of the primitive.

Covarrubias's caricatures were nowhere to be found in *El Universal Ilustrado*'s special volume, even though the Mexican artist had not yet abandoned jazz illustrations entirely. In 1925, Covarrubias was asked to design the sets for the landmark musical *Le Revue Nègre*. The show would make a star of the dancer and singer Josephine Baker and inaugurate the second wave of negrophilia in Paris through its lurid exhibition of novel dances and black bodies, particularly Baker's. More than merely exoticizing jazz, as the ballets of the early 1920s had done, *Le Revue Nègre* fully eroticized the music. As Baker biographer Phyllis Rose aptly puts it, "With Baker's triumph, the erotic gaze of a nation moved downward: she had uncovered a new region for desire."[89] The various sketches presented to the audience at the Théâtre des Champs-Élysées ranged from bucolic plantation scenes to urban tableaus. In one of the latter sketches, a peanut vendor played a plaintive tune on the clarinet before a backdrop of a Manhattan skyscraper. The name of the clarinetist was Sidney Bechet; the skyscraper was by Covarrubias.[90]

The Mexican artist's sets greatly influenced other illustrators and designers. Yet it was an earlier caricature of his—"Jazz Baby" from the December 1924 *Vanity Fair* series—that directly influenced French illustrator Paul Colin's posters and other renderings of Baker. When we compare Covarrubias's work with Colin's posters, we indeed find some common themes. Perhaps inspired by the over-the-top performances, costumes, and design motifs of *Le Revue Nègre*, though, Colin augmented the nuances of Covarrubias's illustrations. While the Mexican artist represented Baker as earthy, if coquettish, for Colin she was so sexually provocative as to seem predatory. In an early poster for *La*

Fig. 1.3. Miguel Covarrubias, "Jazz Baby," from *Negro Drawings* (1927).

Revue Nègre, the French artist positioned Baker between two dark-skinned, wide-eyed, big-lipped black men—a choice that both lightened Baker's skin color and, more to the point, represented a nod to minstrelsy largely absent from Covarrubias's image.[91] Colin thus participated simultaneously in the minstrelization of Baker and Covarrubias's depictions of the Jazz Age. His makeover of Baker's already heavily mediated image, one that accompanied her rising celebrity, would impress a number of Latin American spectators and intellectuals in years to come.

Primitives and Prudes

In 1927, the renowned Brazilian poet, fiction writer, and ethnomusicologist Mário de Andrade brought a poem about Josephine Baker to the attention of the Minas Gerais–based avant-garde journal *Verde*.[92] Written by the young Argentine poet Marcos Fingerit, the poem updated the jazz-as-panacea language typical of nègre enthusiasts since the early interwar period:

> You turned
> the tables
> on Western fatigue
> with the dynamism
> of your mercurial body

The verses echoed the frequent celebration of jazz's ascent as a quasi-messianic event and a salve for modernity's perceived ailments. Yet there was something different this time. The dreaded dark side of primitivist optimism had long been the panic over racial contamination and displacement that surrounded urban vernacular music. Here, though, the Argentine poet was proclaiming that the disruptive capacity of jazz was precisely its greatest gift. Fingerit exalted Baker not just as an exotic cure-all, but also as an incendiary, erotic rabble-rouser. He thus tailored the Black Venus for vanguard revolution while endorsing her as an all-purpose, combustible trope of the Jazz Age, "a hot metaphor / of magical Charlestons."[93]

The poem previewed how and why Josephine Baker would take Latin American avant-gardism by storm in the final years of the decade. It also showed that *letrados*' attitudes toward jazz were becoming more complex. As we have seen, early Latin American critics of jazz tended to see the music rather simplistically as a modern-savage sign of the times. They were willing to do so in part because modernists on both sides of the Atlantic, anxious for renovation and innovation, now questioned the blind celebration of erudite expressions and found themselves willing to risk the potential pitfalls of mass culture.[94] In embracing jazz, Latin American intellectuals had even more to gain than Europeans. As media scholar Jesús Martín-Barbero has observed, Latin American societies depended greatly on "the 'dirty' culture industry and the dangerous aesthetic avant-garde . . . to incorporate black rhythms into the urban culture and legitimize the urban-popular as culture."[95] Such affinities had socioeconomic and racial dimensions as well as geopolitical ones: by embracing the North's others, including jazz musicians, south-of-the-border vanguard intellectuals were able to engage mass culture "identified with an elsewhere" by postcolonial proxy, without fully abandoning local and national nuances and cultural-political projects.[96]

Vanguardistas' euphoric celebration of jazz was not without its critics. Urban, complex, and dynamic, jazz was neither primitive materia prima ready-made for elite consumption nor an innocently venal product of mass culture. Nevertheless, many Latin American intellectuals were tempted to reduce the music to a bare essence in order to strike a fashionable pose. In a frequently cited 1926 essay, Peruvian poet César Vallejo denounced what he saw as the superficial invocation of modern artifacts such as jazz in avant-garde literary production: "It doesn't matter whether or not the lexicon corresponds to an authentically new sensibility," he wrote scoldingly. "What matters are the words."[97] It is certainly true, as Vallejo suggested, that too many vanguardists did not interrogate the terms of modern capitalism in substantive ways. Even so, a number of literary works and journals from the period used the connotative potency of jazz and blues to deliver oblique commentaries on the racial and sexual politics of the interwar culture industry.

Josephine Baker, meanwhile, remained at the heart of the avant-garde's struggles to come to terms with the complexities of the Jazz Age. One reason for her disproportionate presence as a metonym of jazz was the strikingly racialized visuality of her celebrity, which flooded late 1920s mediascapes in the form of newspaper photos, illustrations, and eventually film appearances. Her association with the recording industry also played a role. In his poem "Motivos negros" (1928), the Mexican writer Bernardo Ortiz de Montellano linked Baker's magnetism to the materiality and functionality of the phonograph:

> On the island of your belly—a black disc
> the cry of the bird impaled
> by the movement of the palm tree

The sex-charged political economy of "Motivos negros" extends to Baker's band as well:

Revenge of the serpent, the saxophone lulls the flutes
in the black market of the orchestra.[98]

Ortiz de Montellano's condemnation of the exploitative music industry—a black market in more than one sense—belied what many Francophone writers of the early 1920s saw as the artistic integrity of jazz; that is, vernacular music evincing spontaneity unsullied by modern capital and matched by the purity of its expression. Jazz performance, the Mexican poet suggested, should not be seen as a felicitous expression of pure art but rather as a powerful if naive commodity.

A furious debate in the radical Peruvian magazine *Amauta* in March 1928 perhaps best exemplifies the deep ambivalence of the Latin American vanguards toward Baker and jazz. In spite of its generally spirited defense of vernacular idioms and subaltern subjects, *Amauta*, led by its founder and guiding light José Carlos Mariátegui, frequently showed disdain for the commercialism of jazz and its supposedly corrosive effect on impressionable national audiences. The Baker debate was set off by one particularly provocative poem published by the magazine that stretched the boundaries of moral permissibility. Enrique Peña Barrenechea's "In Praise of Miss Baker" celebrated Baker as a kind of pagan harlot meant for the enjoyment of the poet-sailor, for whom her "brightly feathered buttocks" served as a "magic guide to new ports." Yet Peña Barrenechea did not see Baker as wholly primitive, nor even entirely female. At times, the poet wrote, "she is a naive civilized African boy and pogo-stick," while at others "her tongue plays lustful shimmies on the keyboard of her smile."[99] Peña Barrenechea also hinted at a third role for Baker, that of cultural interlocutor. "Negress," the poet intoned,

> ambassador of the jungle to the Paris of Paul Morand
> Baudelaire from his grave takes in your scent of dynamic flesh
> fantastic volcano spilling out of French ermines the lava of your guttural
> moans unlevels the terrain of the Americas[100]

With a remarkable lack of irony and hints of Pan-Americanism, the Peruvian mimicked the way European intellectuals had for years mined the materia prima of non-European cultures and metropolitan marginalia.

Peña Barrenechea's unbridled celebration of Baker's jazz spectacle predictably drew the ire of *Amauta*'s editors. Indeed, it is likely that Mariátegui had staged the controversy by allowing the offending poem to be published in the first place. In any case, the poet Martín Adán began his withering rebuttal by citing a disclaimer (in English) no doubt familiar to transatlantic travelers of the time: "Neither the captain nor agents of the steamer X will be responsible for debts contracted by the crew while in this port unless duly authorized by the captain." By invoking the authority and prestige of its "captain" Mariátegui, *Amauta* ostensibly meted out discipline to an errant "sailor," cleverly using Peña Barrenechea's own metaphor against him.[101] Adán's main tactic was to demystify Baker, berating her spectacle as little edifying, her style as "the failure of virtue," and her Charlestons as "instinctive, perfect and unconvincing epileptic seizures." Whereas Peña Barrenechea found in Baker a realization of Baudelaire's "barbarous and elemental *Malabaraise*," Adán saw instead "a Virginia [*sic*] mulatto woman, standardized and conformist, with something of *yanqui* manufacturing."[102] Although Adán wrote categorically that the errant poet "should know that the acoustics of the Teatro *Amauta* are not suitable for a jazz band," his censure did not rise above the level of mild, condescending reproach. The "chaste and sober" Peña Barrenechea, normally "one of our purest and truest lyricists," had been led astray, reduced to a childish trance by "a noisy, monstrous, shiny toy."[103]

The lustrous monstrosity attributed to the performer undercuts Adán's condescending dismissal of Baker and the music she embodied. Indeed, it is a testament to the disruptive power of jazz in Latin America that both its admirers and its critics often resorted to similar language: when it came to jazz, and especially when it came to Josephine Baker, moral panic, sexual desire, and anti-capitalist paranoia often lived side by side, and sometimes overlapped. *Amauta's* strange disavowal of Peña Barrenechea's poem showed how some voices of the Latin American avant-garde refused on political grounds to accept jazz as the happy marriage of the primitive and the modern. But the internecine debate also provided evidence of just how completely the Jazz Siren disturbed and bewitched lettered audiences of various ideological stripes.

Josephine Baker's smashing success in Paris and the ambivalent buzz generated in Latin American avant-garde circles led later in the decade to a major tour of a number of South American cities, including Buenos Aires, Santiago, Montevideo, São Paulo, and Rio de Janeiro. Baker took with her much of the visual and aural vocabulary developed in her successful Parisian shows. By virtually all accounts, her tour was an elaborate, hybrid, and changeable affair, featuring top-notch musicians of different racial and national backgrounds. Baker culled songs and performative styles from a range of sources and sang not only in French and English but also in Spanish and possibly Portuguese.[104] The ornate sets and costumes that surrounded her reflected urban and rural themes and borrowed omnivorously from art deco design and graphic arts, vaudeville, high burlesque, and of course minstrelsy. Indeed, it was not just Baker's ambiguously metropolitan patina that attracted South American audiences, but also the distinct colonial flavor of her touring spectacle. As she spun fantasies about North Africa, the Caribbean, and Southeast Asia, she reminded spectators of "the gifts of civilization with which the French bequeathed their colonies."[105] But above all, Baker brought the Charleston. With its brazen exhibition of the female body and jaunty back-and-forth movements, the dance posed a menace to the conventionally gendered space of South American dance floors. It indexed race and colonial displacement by exhibiting, as Jayna Brown writes, "the multijoints of the fragmented modern body corresponding with a multisited sense of being in the world."[106]

Baker's appearances were highly polarizing, to say the least. In Argentina, the performer's scanty costumes and provocative dance numbers met with harsh criticism from Catholic nationalists and moralists, among the latter the nation's president, Hipólito Yrigoyen. By the time of Baker's inaugural performance at the Teatro Astral on May 29, 1929, the municipal government of Buenos Aires had already passed a decree establishing standards of moral decency in public performances. President Yrigoyen had made a point of supporting such measures, pleasing conservative publications such as *Calle* and incurring the wrath of left-wing newspapers such as *Crítica* and *La Nación*.[107] All sides understood that the arrival of the controversial "Ebony Venus" would test a city and a nation in turmoil. Prior to Baker's arrival, the local press was already debating the performer's artistic merits, how Argentines would receive her and, of course, whether or not she would appear in the nude.[108] Once her ship landed, the furor only intensified. Popular plays made open reference to her. An illustrator, Alberto Iraberren, published a detailed study of her body and dance movements in the magazine *Caras y Caretas*.[109] Baker herself clearly perceived the political significance of her performances, later describing that she was "being used in Buenos Aires as a banner waved by some in the name of free expression and by others in defense of public morality."[110]

Matters came to a head during a subsequent performance at the Astral on June 6. As Baker took the stage, pro- and anti-Yrigoyen demonstrators traded heated insults. When a number of spectators set off firecrackers and clashed violently, the police were forced to intervene.[111] In the next few days several newspapers criticized the near riot that preceded the show. *Crítica* accused a combination of clerics and *irigoyenistas* of bringing shame to the city; *La Prensa*, meanwhile, took aim at the president directly, accusing him of zealously overstepping his jurisdiction, using the Jazz Empress as a pretext to press for censorship at the city level.[112] Baker's tour of Córdoba and Mendoza over the summer did little to quiet passions. Though her performances remained wildly popular, there were protests wherever she went. After her return to Buenos Aires in September 1929, one newspaper reprinted a negative review of Baker's starring role on film in *La Sirène des Tropiques*, which happened to open in the United States during Baker's stay in Argentina. The review accused Baker not just of indecency, but also of "imitating the French" and thus selling out her American Negro identity.[113]

The Argentine reaction to Baker went beyond mere moral objection or petty domestic politics. The Buenos Aires theater journal *Comoedia* condemned the dancer in explicitly racist terms. "All the emotive art of this epileptic negress is done with a monkey's rhythm," the reviewer declared, "[for] she is a monkey on whom the modern hunter has placed a bunch of feathers in the same place where until yesterday she had a hairy, prehensile tail." Calling the dancer "a sexual organ that moves . . . and nothing more," the author accused her of "shaking her body crudely and wantonly to the *candombero* sound of brass instruments that other blacks blow with a simian air."[114] The piece represents a nadir of Bakerphobia, and is particularly striking when we consider the serious theater criticism to which the magazine presumably aspired. Yet it is interesting to note that the reviewer compares the sound of Baker's "simian" musicians to that of candombe. Lodged in the fissures of reactionary criticism, the analogy acknowledges jazz music's ties to local cultural practices while simultaneously disavowing them.

By most accounts, the rest of Baker's 1929 South American tour was somewhat less contentious. In Chile, the Jazz Empress was already a star. Prior to her arrival, shimmy, Charleston, and black bottom lessons were all the rage in Santiago; noisy, raucous "dancings" captivated young audiences and rankled local authorities.[115] Santiago's Nascimento Press published a translation of Baker's memoirs, and music publisher Casa Amarilla printed two fox-trots dedicated to the Ebony Venus, one of which provocatively proclaimed,

> Santiago will applaud you
> with a vibrant frenzy,
> bataclana,
> you will spark her nocturnal orgies.[116]

The popular magazine *Zig Zag* predicted that fans from all corners of the nation would flock to the capital. Such curiosity, moreover, "[could] not be written off as mere ignorance or 'Indian rabble' [*indiada*]," since the "fantastic Negress . . . had already captured ancient civilizations, had roused the enthusiasm of the youth of America, and continues to be the entire world's main female attraction."[117] Though enthusiastic, *Zig Zag*'s tone was defensive: the recent scandals in Europe and Argentina had cast a pall over Baker's celebrity. Her promoters obviously had to overcome commercial as well as moral barriers in order to bring the star to Chile. The magazine took particular aim at the hypocrisy of unnamed critics who accused Baker of immorality while themselves attending "theatrical spectacles that [went] against the most basic principles of good taste."[118]

Zig Zag's insinuation that Baker's Chilean critics were elitist prigs was somewhat justified. In a 1927 *crónica* eulogizing Isadora Duncan, for example, future Nobel laureate Gabriela Mistral had exhibited Baker as a vulgar counterpoint to Duncan's style and elegance. For Mistral, Duncan epitomized corporeal modesty, classical refinement, and artistic integrity that went unappreciated by the masses. By contrast, Baker won over modern audiences, and particularly the bourgeoisie, with her venal display of "simian gesticulation" and a "preponderance of the belly and the buttocks over the shoulder, the neck and the feet." If Duncan's graceful, fluid movements belonged to the ethereal realm of the spirits and the air—spaces Mistral associated alternately with contemporary northern Europe and ancient Greece—Baker's "bestial" powers derived from the "foul-smelling depths of the slave trade."[119]

Mistral's harsh rebuke of Baker's "slavish" prurience reveals the writer's preference for high art over vernacular culture, a sensibility frequently plaguing conservative intellectuals of the period, and sometimes professed Marxists as well—as the *Amauta* debate showed. At the same time, the explicitly racial terms with which the Chilean writer dismissed Baker's performances implicitly condemned virtually all black American cultural agency. As scholar Licia Fiol-Matta has noted, blackness for Mistral was generally incompatible with the ideals of Latin American (read: indigenous-European) *mestizaje*, as the "discursive operations of Latin Americanism obliterated the black subject from aesthetic and also political representation."[120] For Mistral, mass cultural production of African slave descendants, jazz included, necessarily carried with it the "foul-smelling" and "simian" debasement of colonial bondage. What was worse, the "strong and fetid tobacco of black dance" had polluted the world, turning it into one big "Charleston dance hall."[121]

In an article in *El Mercurio* written in response to Baker's visit, journalist Daniel de la Vega echoed Mistral's lament over a jazz-saturated world. He bemoaned Baker's bewitchment of Chilean audiences, even if he saw little use in fighting against something that had already taken hold of urban society. "Josephine Baker is nothing less than the banner of our aesthetic decadence," de la Vega wrote. "How to protest against her if practically all of today's public carries her inside them?" The journalist did not stop there. He railed against the always suspect taste of the lower classes, but in a dig at the literary avant-garde, also condemned unnamed "young poets" who had valorized such tastes, assuring readers that "millions of black dancers . . . dance in our conversations, drag us to the theatre, choose our reading and impose themselves on our decisions."[122] Such fears of jazz performance in some ways paralleled the anxiety over a "Yankee invasion" that accompanied the arrival of sound cinema. This was an abrupt transition that for many Latin American critics constituted a violation of the supposed aesthetic purity of silent film while laying bare the widening hegemony of Hollywood, made more audible through English dialogue.[123] Yet Mistral and de la Vega were not only talking about an invasion in the sense of a proliferation of mass-market objects such as records, fan magazines, and movies. They were also alluding to a kind of bodily possession of local audiences, one that presumably would alter the very patterns of consumption.

Such fears were sexual insofar as they revealed Baker's reputation as an erotic dancer. But they also echoed the tendency among modernist intellectuals to associate women (particularly fans and readers, but performers as well) with the dangers of mass culture. Compounding Baker's gender problem was a propensity among admirers and detractors to imagine her sexuality itself as ambiguous, as anxious accusations of androgyny coexisted with fears of racial indeterminacy.[124] Further, in spite of the prestige of the large venues where she sang and danced during her tour, Baker's nominal status as a female jazz performer thwarted attempts by her advocates to defend her artistry. As a nonmale, noninstrumentalist, Baker was hardly in an advantageous position to promote jazz as art. The journalist and scholar Lara Pelligrinelli has noted that jazz singers, who have historically made up the overwhelming majority of female performers, have consistently received short shrift in jazz historiography. In the 1920s, female jazz and blues singers were often written off as comediennes and entertainers rather than being viewed as artists or musicians. In spite of the important antecedents of spiritual hymns and blues, and the abiding centrality of vocal performance in early jazz, Pelligrinelli argues, "the divorce between jazz and its entertainment contexts, the removal of its associations with vernacular culture . . . all contribute to the erasure of women" from the "serious" domain of music history.[125]

Based on gender and genre alone, then, Baker was not well positioned to win accolades for her artistry. But both Mistral's "bestial" epithets and de la Vega's "millions of black dancers" comment carried strong overtones of negrophobia, and not just xenophobia or misogyny. Afro-descendant observers and critics of Josephine Baker frequently inverted these paranoid fears of racial possession.

Even before Baker and her band embarked for Brazil later in the year, the Brazilian press was abuzz with the contentious reception she had received in Argentina. Afro-Brazilian publications such as *Progresso* and *O Clarim da Alvorada* tended to defend Baker preemptively. If her shows in Buenos Aires caused pandemonium, one contributor to *Progresso* speculated, it was no doubt due to the hypocrisy of the audience members, who protested the salacious aspects of her performance only to imitate her "crazy expressions" once they were safely back at home.[126]

The Brazilian writer thus began with some of the same premises as the Chilean Daniel de la Vega, namely that Baker exercised great influence on young audiences and dancers intent on learning the black bottom and mastering Baker's clowning and acrobatic moves. Instead of seeing her as a threat, though, the *Progresso* writer viewed Baker as a useful teacher, capable of undoing the severe education many Brazilian students had received in schools. Moreover, he wrote, the dancer synthesized the "extraordinary and picturesque" aspects of her ancestors in order to "reveal to the world . . . the most characteristic art form of the current period."[127] The *Progresso* piece dismissed the vulgarity rap invoked by writers such as Mistral by asserting the opposite. Baker's nudity was that of a "dark statue," her clownish gimmickry the "stunning feats" and "prodigious" acts of a virtuoso. To prove his point, the anonymous writer used Paris as an unimpeachable benchmark of aesthetic judgment. If France's "demanding multitudes" had proclaimed Baker a queen, then how dare "mediocre minds" in Buenos Aires think any differently?[128]

Brazilian antipathy toward Baker's rude reception in Argentina was fomented by Baker herself once she arrived. The film journal *Cinearte* reported that she had found her experience in Buenos Aires frankly disappointing, and the city "without personality," whereas Brazil was a "great, unforgettable country."[129] During her stint in Rio de Janeiro, Baker stayed with renowned avant-gardists Tarsila do Amaral and Oswald de Andrade at their house in Santa Teresa do Alto. Her hosts threw a lavish party for Baker and the renowned French architect Le Corbusier, with whom the dancer became fast friends and reputedly had a passionate affair.[130] In *Progresso*, Baker declared Rio the most beautiful capital she had ever seen, and professed an ardent wish to learn about the coffee plantations of São Paulo.[131] The feeling, it seems, was mostly mutual. One reporter observed the contrast between the ebullient applause Baker received from *paulista* audiences and the hypocrisy supposedly demonstrated by their *porteño* counterparts.[132]

Not everyone in Brazil approved of the Jazz Siren's presence, much less the influence they feared she had on local audiences. Months after Baker's series of concerts in Rio de Janeiro and São Paulo, a new theatrical revue emerged called the Companhia de Mulatas Rosadas, apparently inspired by Baker's visit. In the *crônica* "Pré, Pró e Post-Josephine," short-story writer and journalist Orígenes Lessa suggested that the new company provided fresh evidence that Baker's performances had despoiled the purity of Brazilian culture.[133] The Companhia de Mulatas Rosadas was not the first revue of its kind. The Companhia Negra de Revista had arrived on the national scene in 1926, piggybacking on the success of the French revue Bataclan's celebrated appearances in Rio during the same year—spectacles that featured several Afro-descendant performers. Founded by the Afro-Brazilian composer De Chocolat and the Portuguese choreographer Jaime Silva, the Companhia Negra de Revista explicitly identified itself as a black ensemble and openly took on previously taboo issues of race and mestiçagem in Brazilian society.[134] The Companhia also coalesced into a laboratory for young Afro-Brazilian performers such as the actor Grande Otelo and the ubiquitous Pixinguinha. When the latter, tongue in cheek, called a split-off group of the Companhia Negra the "black Bataclan," the name stuck.[135] Featuring members of the already well-traveled Oito Batutas, the groups toured Brazil and several cities in Europe in the late 1920s.

The Companhia Negra's *Tudo Negro* (All Black) and subsequent Brazilian revues were not quite the risky ventures they might seem, given the relatively race-favorable climate of the Jazz Age, including the precedent set by Baker herself well before her South American tour. But the politically fraught local references and the Batutas' peculiar mélange of vernacular musical styles certainly contrasted in daringly original ways with the French stage productions. As scholar Tiago de Melo Gomes has noted, the immediate precedence and stylistic vocabulary of the international revue styles permitted the Companhia Negra and Bataclan Preta a certain visual and thematic latitude they would not otherwise have enjoyed. Still, the homegrown nègre performances were not merely exotic shows featuring safely foreign subjects, but rather national spectacles performed by *conterrâneos* (countrymen) all too often feared, disdained, and even reviled by elite audiences.[136] This was true even though Afro-Brazilians were increasingly associated with a larger category of celebrated, if essentialized, Afro-descendant performers, namely US jazz and blues singers, dancers, and musicians.

Josephine Baker's arrival at the end of the decade seemed to reactivate race ambivalence among many Brazilian intellectuals. If her performances shifted blackness to an international setting, mercifully turning the spotlight away from Afro-Brazilian conterrâneos, writers such as Orígenes Lessa nevertheless saw heightened dangers of emulation in Baker's rekindled celebrity. His fears were not unfounded. Besides spectacles like the Companhia de Mulatas Rosa-das, Baker's tour spawned highly popular musical tributes, from Eduardo Sou-to's "Eu quero uma mulher bem preta" to De Chocolat's own "Mulata." Both songs were fox-trots soon made famous by crooner Francisco Alves, an enor-mously popular singer of European descent whose work spanned the worlds of samba, Whiteman-style "straight" jazz, and swing.[137]

Such popular theatrical spin-offs and sound recordings were a sure sign that Baker's travels to Brazil had won her significant crossover success with audiences of different races and social classes.[138] And Brazil was not alone in this regard. Baker's shows in Montevideo, for example, inspired numerous songs and per-formances of carnival troupes known as *murgas*. One Afro-Uruguayan murga called La Jazz Band affected provocative attitudes and struck poses reminiscent of Baker's controversial shows. While carnival blackface experienced a resur-gence in Uruguay in the years that followed—in part inspired by Al Jolson's performance in *The Jazz Singer* (1927)—the sheer popularity of Afro-diasporic representations among mixed-race murga troupes following Baker's visit com-pelled white women-only comparsas to integrate their ranks.[139] Clearly, if the Jazz Siren had arrived in South America as an avant-garde fetish and dance trendsetter, she returned to Europe having brought the racial and sexual politics of the Jazz Age to a large cross section of audiences, dancers, and performers.

Jazz after the Jazz Age

In two related essays first published in the early 1930s, the Cuban writer Alejo Carpentier announced the decline of jazz and the rise of Cuban dance forms as the standard-bearers of modern hemispheric "roots" music. Appearing in the vanguard-leaning magazine *Social* in December 1931, the first piece chronicles the Paris performance of Josephine Baker accompanied by the pianist and composer Moisés Simons. For the previous ten years, Carpentier writes, jazz had reigned supreme in Europe, to the point that even the snootiest of classical performers had been forced to familiarize themselves with popular jazz tunes and syncopation. Yet audiences were now tiring of the monotony of jazz bands' "constant freneticism"; they needed "new rhythms" and a "different melodic spirit" such as those of the son and the rumba. Carpentier held up Simons, author of the massive hit "El manisero" (The Peanut Vendor) as a symbol of the revitalization of jazz and the emergence of Cuba on the international stage. For the young Cuban, "El manisero" signaled a shift in the balance of power. "Our native rhythms," he wrote, "having already dominated the market, [now] occupy all the areas left free by the retreat of jazz."[140] To soften his argument,

Carpentier described Baker as the perfect accompanist to Simons—something of a stretch, since Baker was still at the peak of her popularity. Still, given her "primitive instinct" and elegant "spontaneity," only "an artist of color [like Baker], from the New World, could have brought us the primal violence that our nerves demanded."[141] Carpentier thus likened the passing of the dance-music baton from jazz to rumba to a harmonious pan-Afro treaty signed, oddly enough, on the supposedly neutral site of a medieval concert hall.

In an essay published in *Carteles* nearly one year later, Carpentier further developed his Cuban succession thesis. This time he focused on the Paris arrival of Don Azpiazu's Orchestra, a later version of the same ensemble that had made Simons's "El manisero" famous. Like the work of Duke Ellington's orchestra, and unlike the straight jazz of Paul Whiteman's band, don Azpiazu had brought uncommon sophistication to the European stages without polishing the edges of the music into something that sounded like "well-groomed folklore."[142] Carpentier's praise of Ellington and dig at Whiteman suggest that the Cuban writer was listening to wider swaths of jazz than many of his contemporaries.[143] Carpentier maintained that the Cuban orchestra had "come to definitively dislodge [Whiteman-style jazz] from Parisian dancehalls," due, presumably, to its combination of technical vigor and ungroomed vitality. As proof, he pointed to the fact that audiences at the Champs-Élysées had supposedly yawned their way through opening sets of straight jazz and tango while eagerly waiting for don Azpiazu to take the stage.[144]

In both of these remarkable essays, Carpentier invoked the language of military conquest and royal succession to celebrate Cuban music's putative dethronement of jazz. With the "masterpiece" of Don Azpiazu's Orchestra, he wrote, "we march on the world in the vanguard of Latin American music, and plenty of time will pass before another music forces our retreat."[145] While he used Baker conveniently as a primitive foil to Simons's regal sophistication (the Cuban composer apparently performed "El manisero" on a Louis XV grand piano), Carpentier also implicitly cubanized the Ebony Venus. Rather than write her off as a has-been, Carpentier portrayed the singer and dancer as a useful, kindred subordinate to Afro-Cuban music's surging fortune and prestige. The Cuban's invocation of the term vanguard to describe Don Azpiazu's Orchestra is particularly arresting, since it reveals an anxious desire, long manifested in Latin American intellectuals' praise of jazz, to place the avant-garde moniker on local musical practices as well. Ever in awe of the erudite, Carpentier attempted to soften the daring of his maneuver by placing Simons and Baker in a noble setting. Yet his final verdict was clear enough: the emblem of national advancement and social ascension would be vernacular music—like jazz, only Afro-Cuban.

Provocative, if occasionally hyperbolic, Carpentier's essays were prescient in two important ways. As music historian Leonardo Acosta has pointed out, the success of Don Azpiazu's Orchestra in the early 1930s indeed signaled new international possibilities for Afro-Cuban music and musicians, and suggested that jazz had serious competition in international salons and concert halls. For years the orchestras of Azpiazu, Simons, and Julio Cueva, along with Rita Montaner and countless other Cuban musicians, would be fixtures not only in Havana but also in Paris and New York, presenting a variety of concerts, cabarets, and operettas to leagues of new listeners.[146] Their success was not limited to live performances. Azpiazu's recording of "El manisero" was a huge crossover hit. In addition to radio airplay, the song would resurface in numerous Hollywood feature films and shorts of the period. Azpiazu and his orchestra would perform the rumba "Por tus ojos negros" in one of Carlos Gardel's successful Paramount productions, *Espérame* (dir. Louis Gasnier, 1933).[147]

The 1930s and 1940s did little to diminish Josephine Baker's celebrity in Europe and Latin America. As Carpentier suggested, though, the Ebony Venus no longer stood purely as a symbol of jazz. Increasingly singing in Spanish and Portuguese in addition to English and French, Baker returned to Latin American stages several times over the rest of her career. On many occasions, Baker performed with local musical celebrities and hobnobbed with political figures. As the Afro-Cuban poet Nicolás Guillén later noted, the celebrated *vedette* became close friends with the Cuban composer Eliseo Grenet, who cowrote the score for her 1935 film *Princesse Tam-Tam*.[148] In addition to recording two of Agustín Lara's songs ("María Bonita" and "Madrid"), Baker "fell passionately" for the Mexican composer, who happened to be married at the time to María Félix.[149] Film director and tango legend Hugo del Carril, meanwhile, facilitated Baker's comeback performances in Argentina after World War II, in a three-month stint that would lead to subsequent shows in Chile, Peru, and Mexico.[150] In Argentina and Chile, the diva met personally with presidents Juan Perón and Carlos Ibáñez del Campo and praised their commitment to racial equality.[151] On tour in Brazil, Baker echoed Gilberto Freyre's vision of a racial democracy: "I have always believed that different races can live together in harmony and I am full of admiration for the way the Brazilians have made this idea a reality."[152]

It was in Cuba, though, where Baker would create the biggest stir in years to come. When she encountered racial discrimination in several Havana establishments in the 1950s, Baker encouraged Afro-Cubans to rally around her. Leveraging her considerable charm and compelling personal narrative—besides contributing greatly to the resistance in World War II, she and her French husband Jo Bouillon had already begun to adopt children of different races, in part to raise awareness of barriers to interracial families *and* musical ensembles—Baker parleyed rising anti-American sentiment on the island into renewed popular support for her career.[153] She also began to give more public lectures. When her frequent criticism of US racial politics incurred a backlash from the Truman and Eisenhower administrations and their allies, including a resurgent Fulgencio Batista, Baker became more intransigent than ever. If somewhat susceptible to local demagoguery, her transformation in two decades from feather-clad queen of the Charleston to war hero, civil rights activist, and stateswoman was nothing short of remarkable.

In her first Latin American tour in 1929, Josephine Baker had exemplified what scholar Fiona I. B. Ngô has called the "imperial logic" of Jazz Age performance. The mutable and unstable signs of imperialism made visible in such exotic spectacles, Ngô writes, formed "concepts of distance and intimacy" that enabled complex understandings of race, sexuality, pleasure, and consumption.[154] Baker's immersion in things Latin American upon her return to Europe anticipated the ways jazz itself would increasingly absorb south-of-the-border styles and musicians, especially after World War II. Yet perhaps it would be more accurate to say that Baker's own *latinización* mirrored the ways many Latin American admirers (from intellectuals like Carpentier to Uruguayan *murgistas*) wished to see her: at first, as a pliable and borrowable black body, a kindred other willing to forgo her national fealty and succumb to the charms of the tropics; later, as an elegant spokesperson for racial equality frequently at odds with the United States—a position with which Latin Americans of different stripes could readily identify. In short, Baker's iconic performance style, frequent tours to the region, public mingling with local celebrities, and open criticism of social discrimination made her appear to be as receptive to the influences of her encounters with Latin Americans as they were to her.

And so it turns out that Alejo Carpentier was not incorrect to suggest Baker's growing *cubanía*. Significantly, though, the second of his predictions—that rumba's gain would be jazz's loss—proved dead wrong. Even if it did not divide and conquer intellectuals in the manner hot jazz had in the 1920s, swing music, catapulted by radio and film, in the end would enjoy even broader international appeal. By the late 1930s, Latin American music critics could no longer write off jazz so easily as the music of vulgar flappers, trendy aficionados, and vanguardistas. But big band would be only one of jazz's many manifestations. The arrival of figures like Dizzy Gillespie and Charlie Parker confirmed jazz's stature in some Latin American intellectual circles as a unique cultural practice of profound social significance marked by technical virtuosity and conceptual complexity. The impact of bebop and other iterations of modern jazz in Latin America was staggered and uneven, and would not take hold in even the most progressive circles until well into the 1950s. Already by the mid-1930s, though, a new generation of fans and critics was emerging in Argentina and Uruguay, one that would extensively examine the social history, racial politics, and formal characteristics of jazz, and in so doing challenge the way many Latin Americans thought about popular music.

2

Dark Pursuits Argentina, Race, and Jazz

Lo malo es que si sigo así voy a acabar escribiendo más sobre mí mismo
que sobre Johnny.
— JULIO CORTÁZAR, *El perseguidor* (The Pursuer, 1959)

Vicente Rossi's landmark study *Cosas de negros* (1926) brought race into the
foreground of debates surrounding popular music and national identity in Argentina and Uruguay. Writing at the height of tango's international popularity,
Rossi brazenly argued for "rectifications and revelations" of the region's cultural
history by underscoring the African antecedents of *rioplatense* popular music.[1]
His main objective was to document the African origins of the candombe and
milonga, and by extension the Afro-Uruguayan pedigree of the tango. Of those
who took issue with Rossi's controversial thesis, perhaps the most outspoken
was a patriotic young Argentine poet named Jorge Luis Borges, who insisted
that "the tango is not rural but *porteño* [from Buenos Aires]. Its fatherland
is the little pink street corners of the suburbs, not the countryside; its atmosphere, the slums; its symbol, the weeping willow of the riverbanks, never the
ombú [of the pampas]." Borges did not deny the African influence on the development of the tango, even going so far as to acknowledge that batuque was
practiced in Buenos Aires' Plaza del Once in the nineteenth century.[2] Writing
for the magazine *Síntesis* in 1928, he went out of his way to praise Rossi's largely
unheralded contributions to regional cultural history. Yet Borges implicitly reduced the Uruguayan's racial argument to one of place and nation. However

much *Cosas de negros* may have sought to "color" the history of River Plate popular music, for the Argentine writer the tango was finally and essentially a product of Buenos Aires.[3]

Rossi, though, was not solely concerned with challenging the conventional wisdom about the origins of the tango or even criollo identity generally. In fact, he dedicated parts of the last chapter of *Cosas negras* to jazz, which he saw as exhibiting some of the same cultural underpinnings as local musical styles. Although white musicians and audiences might well take issue with Afro-descendants' musical unorthodoxy, Rossi writes, "the Negro is the sorcerer of disciplined disharmony; no discordant or grating note can befuddle him; he receives it with his perpetual smile and submits it to his ingenuity." Rossi praises the ability of black US jazz musicians to make innovative use of "inarticulate noises," syncopation and improvisation, without resorting to the "pose and artificiality" of Western erudite music.[4] While strains of primitivism are audible in the Uruguayan's assessment of jazz, Rossi's thoughtful appreciation of the new form goes beyond the realm of race essentialisms that generally characterized avant-garde jazz discourse of the period. In effect, *Cosas de negros* does not merely place tango and milonga in a larger, hemispheric and transatlantic context. The book also previews a shift in the conversation in Argentina about jazz and African American idioms generally, from one of aesthetics and morality to a more nuanced discussion of cultural politics, social value, and racial identity.

As suggested by the "rectifications" of the book's early title, *Cosas de negros* was clearly written against the grain of cultural criticism in the River Plate region.[5] In the century since achieving their independence, studies of race and popular music in Uruguay and especially Argentina had frequently written off black identity as either an exotic import or a historical anomaly remote from current criollo subjectivity.[6] Despite the frequent disavowal of *negritud* in Argentine intellectual discourse, nowhere in Latin America has jazz criticism been so prolific and intense. This was particularly true in the pivotal period of the 1930s, when African American musicians like Louis Armstrong and Duke Ellington first came to the attention of local intellectuals and musicians. Indeed, Argentine writers were the first in Latin America to rigorously examine jazz not only as a technically sophisticated musical idiom but also as a cultural practice inseparable from the African diaspora and postcolonial legacies of slavery. In the 1930s and 1940s, a number of Argentine jazz journals—beginning with *Síncopa y Ritmo*, *Swing*, and *Jazz Magazine*, on which I will focus in the first part of this chapter—sought to promote and at the same time normalize "black" jazz as a legitimate art form. In this sense, their efforts constitute a significant departure from common cultural paradigms of the period, not just in Argentina but also throughout Latin America.

In his study of Afro-Caribbean *negrista* poetry of the 1920s and 1930s, Jerome Branche notes that "racial ventriloquism in negrismo was achieved on the basis of the removal of the referent from the realm of agency."[7] While at first glance it would seem tempting to liken porteños' praise of hot jazz to negrismo's "ventriloquism," a closer look reveals that early Argentine jazz criticism engages not in ethnic stagecraft but rather in a kind of ambivalent hermeneutics based on a perceived affinity with, and also insulation from, the otherness of jazz. These discourses combined race-based authentication, exhaustive musical appraisal (including countless comparisons to tango), and the lionization of black US jazz performers. Such critical production—culminating in Julio Cortázar's early jazz writing—enabled River Plate fans, promoters, and intellectuals to engage openly with questions of race, social class, and the recording industry. In most cases they did so, however, without subjecting themselves to a sufficiently rigorous self-examination on these very issues.

The unusual abundance of Argentine jazz criticism in the middle decades of the twentieth century therefore masked a central ambivalence toward the music. The recognition and promotion of national and Latin American jazz musicians in a spirit of solidarity and civic pride served to underscore the marginality, redundancy, and even artificiality of such local practices compared to North American (and particularly African American) jazz performers. Such a maneuver was hardly coincidental. Argentine intellectuals of the mid-twentieth century, I would like to propose, depended on an *autre* jazz subject to lend themselves legitimacy as modern critics, musical tastemakers, advocates of local cultural consumption, and finally self-designated gatekeepers of the national patrimony. *El perseguidor*, Cortázar's brilliant fictional treatment of Charlie Parker, ultimately complicated this critical stance. So too did the rise to international prominence of Lalo Schifrin, Astor Piazzolla, and Gato Barbieri in the 1960s and 1970s. While their success illustrated how musicians could excel on the world stage beyond the parochial limits of *argentinidad*, it also revealed the persistent challenges to inscribing Argentine musicians generically within the increasingly transnational jazz canon.

Syncopation and Swing

As I suggested in the previous chapter, Josephine Baker's dazzling performances in the twilight of the 1920s gave South American audiences not only a jolt of metropolitan citizenship, but also, for some, sanctioned reprieves from racial, social, and moral taboos: one-night stands of pleasurable turmoil and cosmopolitan vulgarity. Even the much-discussed "primitive" components of Baker's traveling show can be construed as productive mechanisms within the "heterogeneous-homogeneous" dialectic of cultural nationalism.[8] As Florencia Garramuño has pointed out, musical primitivism was central to the elaboration of Latin American identity projects of the early twentieth century. Garramuño argues that Modernist intellectuals in Brazil and Argentina gradually transformed the "primitive-savage" elements of samba and tango into "primitive-modern" subjects that would serve as the ideological basis of the nationalist-populist campaigns of the 1930s and 1940s.[9] Baker's landmark 1929 tour, then, performed two quite important though contradictory functions. On one hand, the very hybridity of her spectacle served as a model for the discursive elaboration of national-vernacular musical idioms that incorporated elements of the modern. At the same time, the mostly negative reaction to Baker's spectacle by journalists and *letrados* anticipated the revolt against jazz in nationalist-populist discourse of the 1930s, 1940s, and 1950s. Posing a constant threat to the commercial and symbolic hegemony of national forms, jazz in all its permutations would help Latin American intellectuals to define the parameters of the normative practices and consumption of vernacular music and performance years after the decline of the Jazz Age.

The increasing maturity of jazz music and its growth beyond the peculiarities of the 1920s were of course not specific to Argentina. The 1930s and early 1940s witnessed the surging popularity of swing music, first represented by the pioneering ensembles of Chick Webb, Duke Ellington, Benny Goodman, Count Basie, and others, then increasingly by commercially inclined big bands such as those led by the Dorsey brothers, Glenn Miller, and Harry James. Yet a new kind of jazz fandom also emerged in Europe, North America, and Argentina in the 1930s, one closer to the idiosyncratic and affective realm of "cult" fandom.[10] These jazz enthusiasts often looked back to the hot era for inspiration, and regularly spurned the market-oriented tastes of mainstream swing fans, focusing their energies instead on hard-to-find recordings, small-circulation publications, and (somewhat later) jazz fan clubs, rather than on dance concerts and the latest radio hits. Jazz collectors in the 1930s tended to be white male elites, often in search of rare 1920s "race" records previously owned by black consumers. That record collecting assumed special importance as a defining practice of elite jazz aficionados was obvious to critics as early as 1939, when journalist Steve Smith remarked that collectors engaged "in competitive displays of symbolic capital both privately and publicly through the medium of specialist magazines."[11]

Initially, the cult of jazz fandom in Argentina and Uruguay was an even more select group than in Europe and North America. The main reason, as Sergio Pujol points out, was twofold. First, the burgeoning rioplatense jazz market had to compete against a local style still in its apogee—tango—relegating jazz to minority status during a difficult time for the record business. Second, interwar jazz collectors confronted a perennial problem in gaining access to the kinds of recordings they desired. Consequently, the most successful collectors were those who could afford to pay exorbitant sums for imports from specialized European sellers such as Hot Record Exchange and Alfred Imhof.[12] In spite of such obstacles, by the mid-1930s the community of collectors and cult fans in Argentina had grown to such an extent that demand emerged for specialized publications and radio programs that could serve as forums for debate and sources of information about recordings and live performances (supported partly through paid advertising).

The seminal magazine *Síncopa y Ritmo* was first published in August 1934, the same year that two better-known jazz publications also appeared for the first time: Chicago's *Down Beat* and the Parisian *Jazz Hot*.[13] The Argentine magazine's publisher was Fernando Iriberri, a foundational figure in the Buenos Aires jazz scene who, in addition to his work for the magazine, produced records, promoted shows, and hosted an influential hot jazz program on Radio Splendid.[14] From the inaugural issue of *Síncopa y Ritmo*, it became clear that race would play a central, though carefully circumscribed, role in the magazine's platform. For his first editorial, Iriberri borrowed a page from avant-garde jazz discourse, praising "black" records as indispensable agents of diplomacy. While conflating the aesthetic novelty and commercial success of jazz, Iriberri was careful to assign each a different race, and to avoid the anti–mass culture tone that haunted so much 1920s writing about jazz. What black slaves brought to the United States through toil and suffering, he wrote, "Americans in turn spread throughout the world through records, black pieces of a whole world of black feelings."[15] Iriberri thus consigned African Americans to creative and inspirational roles, whereas he praised whites—tellingly identified simply as *americanos*—for spreading the music throughout the world through their mastery of marketing and technological means.

That Iriberri would write so favorably about the conquests of global capital is hardly surprising. He clearly wished *Síncopa y Ritmo* to serve as a means to facilitate an increase in the supply and diversity of international jazz offerings for local audiences. Specifically, Iriberri praised the efforts of Buenos Aires importers and record stores, and eagerly awaited the moment when "an entrepreneur with a good idea" would invite the biggest stars to perform live in local venues.[16] Yet *Síncopa y Ritmo* contributors did not promote just any jazz performers or recordings. Ulises Petit de Murat (who had written vividly about jazz in the 1920s for the journal *Martín Fierro*) argued that African descent was the sine qua non of authentic musical expression. "The White man is afforded the luxury of not being authentic," he declared flatly, "not the Negro."[17] As such, only black musicians were deemed capable of summoning the primitive inspiration necessary to perform jazz. Conversely, that whites had the luxury of "not being authentic" implied that if jazz was the natural domain of black musicians, Petit de Murat and other Argentine critics like him possessed the unique capacity to interpret such special intelligence.[18]

The tendency to proclaim certain jazz performances or performers authentic or inauthentic was not limited to either rioplatense writers or even the early twentieth century generally. Scholar Eric Porter has observed that the early jazz criticism of *Down Beat* and *Metronome*, "by and large created by whites for a white readership," frequently echoed the primitivist language of the 1920s.[19] As one might well expect, *Síncopa y Ritmo* likewise championed African American figures such as Louis Armstrong and Duke Ellington above all others, dedicating a number of covers and extensive profiles to their lives and work. The magazine's slant provoked some reactions from its own correspondents. Pablo Álvarez Nájera denounced the tendency to equate authenticity solely with black musicians. Jazz, he wrote, should be seen less as a folkloric expression or even a category of musical production than a new way of playing music, "an interpretive modality to which different types of pieces can be adapted."[20] He mentioned cornetist Bix Beiderbecke—also widely celebrated by *Síncopa y Ritmo*—as an example of how white musicians too could master such an interpretative approach.

Yet Álvarez Nájera's warning against race essentialism caved in under the weight of the temptation that he himself decried. If jazz should be reserved as an exclusively black domain, he wrote, blues was another matter entirely, "impregnated with an intense racial spirit" that lay beyond the "interpretative powers" of white musicians. To bring his point home, the critic claimed that it would be futile for a singer from Buenos Aires, who would have little difficulty interpreting various national idioms, to attempt to master traditional African American songs. "A Buenos Aires resident may well learn how to play perfectly a *vidala*, and a *puntano*, a tango; but a white man will never be able to sing a 'work song' well."[21] Álvarez Nájera thus equated the porteño with "the white man" under cover of making general claims about race—and in an article that was ostensibly about something other than race.

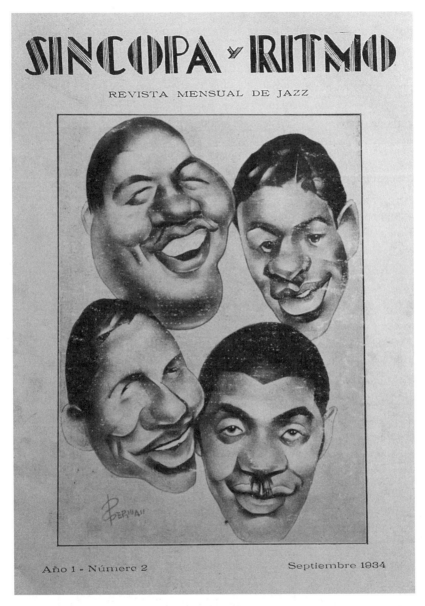

Fig. 2.1. The pioneering Argentine jazz journal *Síncopa y Ritmo* consistently promoted African American performers as the key purveyors of jazz authenticity.

Such a maneuver reveals the distance, benevolent or otherwise, with which blackness was customarily treated in Argentine intellectual discourse of the 1930s and '40s in spite of the key role played by Afro-Argentines in postindependence daily life and in the foundational cultural myths and practices of the nation.[22] It was in Juan José Hernández Arregui's essay "Sentido social del jazz," however, where *Síncopa y Ritmo* published perhaps its most provocative social claims about jazz. Later to become an important Peronist essayist and historian, Hernández Arregui was in his early years a jazz aficionado and one of *Síncopa y Ritmo*'s most frequent contributors, penning a number of analytical essays and even a short story, "La tragedia del crooner," one of the magazine's few forays into fiction. In "Sentido social del jazz," Hernández Arregui denounced racialist theories and also Oswald Spengler's claim that jazz constituted a disturbing sign of modern decadence. Yet he also made the argument (long expressed by Francophone critics such as *Jazz Hot* cofounder Hugues Panassié) that jazz synthesized the best of white intellectualism and black spontaneity.[23] The end result, the Argentine maintained, was "an indiscernible mixture" in which, however, white and black performances continued to set themselves apart from each other, albeit with subtlety. Indeed, the originality of black jazz musicians consisted of the "slight difference in which their intellect [captured] the civilization surrounding them."[24]

What distinguished Hernández Arregui's praise of jazz from others' was not so much his contradictory stance—after all, his fellow *Síncopa y Ritmo* contributors disavowed the racist underpinnings of their claims in much the same way. But Hernández Arregui placed his dubious biopolitical claims in social context in a slightly more nuanced way. A number of influential writers of the time, starting with Spengler and José Ortega y Gasset, had foregrounded the supposed social dangers posed by jazz, namely that the vulgarity and hysteria generated by the "irrational" sounds of the music would infect modern (white) audiences.[25] Hernández Arregui, by contrast, welcomed the ways in which the popular masses had expressed their desires and "evolution" through their embrace of black urban music. If such an embrace included the emulation of certain "superfluous" qualities of African American visual style— what he somewhat anxiously called their *engalanamiento personal* (personal embellishment)—then it was a small price to pay for gleaning the benefits of their "ardent instinct" through fan participation.[26]

Síncopa y Ritmo was not the last word in interwar Argentine jazz criticism. Founded in 1936 by Evar Méndez, and featuring early articles by such important figures as Néstor R. Ortiz Oderigo, the magazine *Swing* shared with *Síncopa y Ritmo* a slightly defensive sense of jazz advocacy in the face of conservative social criticism. In an essay comparing jazz with classical music, for example, Albert H. Roth conceded that jazz could not compete with erudite music in the realm of composition and theoretical sophistication. Even so, he maintained, musicians like Armstrong and Ellington combined a mastery of theory and technique with unparalleled creative looseness and intuitive virtuosity. Though Roth relied on some of the same key words as his *Síncopa y Ritmo* colleagues—"that overflowing, passionate, spontaneous feeling"—he asserted that jazz musicians' execution of "simple ideas" could nevertheless be "transcendental and of as much artistic importance as any classical work, and perhaps of even greater interest considering their innovation."[27]

To a greater extent than *Síncopa y Ritmo*, *Swing* underscored the strengths and limitations of national jazz production. The publication frequently criticized Argentine jazz for being too commercial, and on numerous occasions identified authentic jazz as being not just black, but more broadly North American in origin. In its sixth issue, however, declaring itself "an eminently Argentine publication," the magazine proclaimed its solidarity with local jazz musicians against what it called "the constant invasion of foreign elements." *Swing*'s newfound anxiety about musical influence was directed mainly at the United States. Even in the midst of xenophobic fervor, however, the magazine's editorial page declared the need for European jazz models: "Here in Argentina we need to produce jazz as interesting as that found in Paris or London. And we need to follow the rhythm of European scholars of North American creative work—its origins, development and achievements."[28]

While *Swing*'s prescription for homegrown jazz strongly implied that Argentine critical production should emulate European models, the topic of the proper role of jazz criticism was given a different focus by Carlos Sandoval in a short essay dedicated to the subject. The author warned, in particular, against anecdotal or superficial assessments of jazz. Large record collections and knowledge of bibliographical minutiae, Sandoval argued, should not be deemed qualifications per se, hence "knowing the name of Duke Ellington's sister's nanny or the street where Gene Krupa's uncle was born is not enough to judge Ellington and Krupa themselves." The article was generally consistent with *Swing*'s tendency to strike an unsteady balance between a defense of jazz's supposedly spontaneous, passionate authenticity and highbrow assessments that insisted on its equal footing with European art music. Since jazz was "complicated" and "enigmatic," jazz criticism should be practiced only by "extremely cultured critics."[29] The very mystery of jazz—its inscrutability, its obscurity—thus became a pretext for the publication of illuminating, learned commentary of the sort *Swing* ostensibly provided.

The music lost its patina of exoticism when critics turned their gaze on local jazz artists, as Sandoval did in a series of profiles written for *Síncopa y Ritmo*. One of the early homegrown stars of the Buenos Aires jazz scene was the singer Paloma Efron, widely known during her career by her stage name, Blackie. Efron had received her moniker by popular vote in 1934 after winning a singing competition held by Radio Stentor.[30] Born in Buenos Aires to Jewish parents, Blackie capitalized on the minstrel imaginary evoked by her nickname to lend herself an aura of alterity. Strategic nomenclature was a common practice among porteño jazz artists of the period. Two popular Argentine jazz orchestras of the time were the Dixy Pals (featuring the pianist Adolfo Ortiz) and the Santa Paula Serenaders.[31] Besides Efron, and some time later the even bigger star Lois Blue, another popular Argentine jazz singer of the day went by the name of Mabel Wayne, getting her start with Don Dean's orchestra.[32] Sandoval praised Wayne as "the beauty of the microphone, a sports lover, a beautiful little blonde Argentine who speaks English as perfectly as she does her own language."[33] Whether or not this was actually the case, Wayne's jazz credentials would seem to have been bolstered by her manufactured profile as a virtual yanqui.

By her own account, Blackie owed her ascent in large part to the agency of jazz aficionado and journalist León Klimovsky, himself a contributor to *Síncopa y Ritmo*.[34] Sandoval underscored the crucial role played by Klimovsky. Without the constant direction and financial support of her "discoverer," Sandoval suggested, Blackie would have been incapable of realizing her star potential. Under Klimovsky's tutelage, on the other hand, the singer was "capable of taking on difficult jazz genres, including the hardest of all to interpret: spirituals." The language Sandoval used to describe the difficulty of interpreting African American blues and folk exposed Blackie not just as non-African in origin but also non–North American.[35] Her true nationality and ethnicity were never really in question, since Sandoval ironically declared the "dear 'black' girl" to be one of Argentina's most distinguished cultivators of jazz.[36] Still, it is interesting to note how Sandoval evoked Klimovsky as the enabler of Blackie's performance of authenticity. Clearly, he suggested, if an Argentine jazz artist were to achieve international celebrity, it would have to be through the prosthesis of a pseudonym, mimetic capacity, a physical resemblance to North American prototypes, and the patronage of a learned expert.

Even in a case where an Argentine jazz musician hardly needed the aid of sponsorship or nomenclature to achieve international renown—that of the guitarist Oscar Alemán—local writers tended to compensate for the performer's argentinidad by stressing his exile and personal acquaintance with foreign

SWING

REVISTA DE JAZZ PARA TODO EL MUNDO

Lea en este número:

LA ORIGINAL DIXIELAND JAZZ-BAND
por NESTOR ORTIZ ODERIGO

LA MISION DEL CRITICO
por CARLOS SANDOVAL

ANNIE WHILSON
por ZILENIUS

¡ESTO ES JAZZ!
por "EL GUARDA Nº 13"

DECLARACIONES DE DON MAURICIO GODARD
de las Industrias Eléctricas y Musicales "ODEON"

SANDOVALERIAS

JAZZ DE NOVIEMBRE

LOS DISCOS NUEVOS

CLUBS DE JAZZ

NOTAS DE RADIO

JAZZ EN LOS FILMS

BLACKIE, la popular y admirada cancionista.

EN EL MUNDO DEL JAZZ: Orquestas, músicos y vocalistas. • Fiesta de jazz de SWING en Radio Stentor. • Veladas de jazz de Klimovsky. • Sophie Tucker en Londres, sus opiniones. • ¿El jazz no nació en Dixie? • Irving Mills funda una empresa de discos. • El "Cotton Club" se fué de Harlem a Broadway, con Calloway y Robinson.

20 cts.   BUENOS AIRES, NOVIEMBRE DE 1936   **Nº 2**

ESTA ES UNA PUBLICACION DE JAMES PINKERTON, INC., PUBLICITY - Florida 478

Fig. 2.2. To achieve jazz credibility, white Argentine singer Blackie (Paloma Efron) capitalized not just on her nickname but also on a carefully engineered media image, with the help of Buenos Aires publications such as *Síncopa y Ritmo* and *Swing*.

OSCAR ALEMAN

EL MUSICO ARGENTINO
MAS FAMOSO EN EL
MUNDO DEL JAZZ

●

UN argentino es, en su instrumento, uno de los mejores ejecutantes en el mundo. Nos referimos al guitarrista Oscar Alemán, nacido en el Chaco y consagrado en Europa, que ha regresado recientemente al país.

En 1928, a los dos años de haber regresado del Brasil, país al que marchó siendo un niño, se embarcó rumbo a Eu-

ropa iniciando en España la que se constituiría en carrera triunfal. En la madre patria formó una orquesta y con ella tocó sus primeros coros de guitarra. Estando en España fué llamado por Josefina Baker para actuar en el Casino de París como solista, sin orquesta y con ella. En otros países, además de España y Francia tuvieron el placer de escu-

Fig. 2.3. Oscar Alemán, Argentina's foremost jazz export of the swing era, in a *Síncopa y Ritmo* profile (1941).

stars. By any definition, Alemán was a singular figure in the annals of Argentine popular music. Born in the remote Chaco region in 1909, orphaned and homeless at age ten, he spent a large part of his later childhood in Brazil, where he earned his keep playing Argentine and Brazilian songs on the streets and in popular theaters. Alemán returned to Argentina in 1927 with the slide guitarist Gastão Bueno Lobo as a part of the "exotic" duo Les Loups. Ostensibly specializing in the Hawaiian music in vogue at the time, he and Lobo (later joined by the violinist Elvino Vardaro) played in a variety of other styles as well, including tango, choro, and jazz. Attracting the attention of the touring tap dancer and revue director Harry Flemming in 1929, Les Loups traveled to France, where Alemán eventually established himself as Josephine Baker's indispensable sideman and occasional music director. His career blossomed. By the end of the 1930s, Alemán was, after Django Reinhardt, the most accomplished guitarist of the European jazz scene.[37]

The Nazi occupation of Paris compelled Alemán to return to Argentina. By then he had made a deep impression on jazz critics back home. In a 1941 profile that declared Alemán "the most famous Argentine musician in the jazz world," *Síncopa y Ritmo* underscored the native son's childhood experience in Brazil and long career in Europe. The musician's important collaborations with Josephine Baker, however, were reduced to a short paragraph in which Alemán's stellar musicianship was said to have earned no more admiration from Baker than his role as the famous singer's assistant and confidante.[38] Although the article did not mention Alemán's ethnicity, his racially mixed features (clearly evident in an accompanying photo) could hardly have escaped readers' notice. It might even be argued that Alemán's phenotypic *mulatez* precluded the necessity of an anglicized moniker such as Lois Blue's. If his racial makeup implicitly lent him "Afro" credibility, his lengthy tenure abroad and extensive interaction with many giants of jazz added to his exotic profile upon his celebrated return to Buenos Aires. In an important sense Alemán had become, as Pujol remarks, "the 'blackest' of all the jazzmen this country has given to the world."[39]

Tango and Bebop

By the 1920s, tango had been consecrated as the Argentine music par excellence, though not—as the Borges-Rossi debate shows—without some disagreement over which bank of the Rio de la Plata could claim the music as its own.[40] Tango was not without its rivals on the national music scene. As we have seen, jazz in the 1920s emerged as a contentious emblem of modernity and a formidable draw for urban listeners and leisure dancers. The North American idiom also encroached on the tango-dominated repertoires of such *típica* bandleaders as Francisco Canaro and Roberto Firpo, and especially on the work of Adolfo Carabelli and Osvaldo Fresedo, all of whom regularly performed and recorded fox-trots, shimmies, and other jazz-flavored numbers. Nevertheless, tango held its ground once hot and "sweet" jazz gave way to big-band swing in the 1930s.

The productive, dynamic tension between jazz and tango can be explained by several factors. While jazz epitomized the seductions of the urban metropolis through its association with the United States and to a lesser extent Europe, tango held special appeal for a wider swath of the Argentine population. Like jazz, tango could position itself as a modern expression, thanks in part to the absorption of jazz and the adoption of other international modalities and instrumentation by the likes of Canaro and Carabelli. But to a greater extent than jazz, tango struck a balance between cosmopolitan modernity and "authenticity" (represented by traditional folk forms) under the banner of the national.[41]

Even so, jazz appealed to a sizable minority of Argentine listeners, and this was partly a by-product of the peculiar growth pattern of the music industry in the 1920s. As the historian Matthew Karush points out, the four dominant record labels of the time were foreign (US companies Victor, Columbia, and Brunswick, and the German Odeon), an asymmetrical commercial arrangement that gave a wide berth to jazz recordings.[42] Despite such availability in Argentina and elsewhere in Latin America, the prohibitive cost of phonographs and even records themselves (especially imports) made jazz records something of a luxury item for much of the interwar period, particularly during the Great Depression. In contrast, by the 1930s radio was reaching a wide audience; unlike the record industry, radio was not dominated by foreign companies, nor did it require repeated expenditures by music consumers. The result was greater airtime for national styles such as the tango, even as swing began to inundate international record markets.[43]

Another important medium in the development of critical discourse about tango (and popular music generally) was cinema. In the earliest Argentine ventures of the sound era such as *¡Tango!* (dir. Luis Moglia Barth, 1933), *Los tres berretines* (dir. Enrique Telémaco Susini, 1933), and *El alma del bandoneón* (dir. Mario Soffici, 1935), tango performance, lyrics, and themes formed the backbone of plot development. The appeal of tango also boosted attendance. The films were bolstered at the box office by the singing and acting talents of established theatrical stars such as Libertad Lamarque, Tita Merello, and Luis Sandrini. While Argentine stations like Radio Belgrade controlled the airwaves, however, it was Hollywood that ruled the movie houses. In the late 1920s and early 1930s, the US film industry attempted to secure its dominance over Latin American markets through Spanish-language productions. Today considered among the few failures in Hollywood's century-long attempt to maintain a stranglehold on foreign markets, simultaneous and foreign-language productions were Hollywood's first attempt to adjust to the daunting technical demands of talking pictures. One exception to this rule was a series of films produced by Paramount in Joinville (France) and New York City during the early 1930s and starring the established recording star Carlos Gardel.

The impact of Gardel's cinematic performances on how Argentines imagined themselves is difficult to quantify, but it should not be underestimated. Films such as *Las luces de Buenos Aires* (dir. Adelqui Migliar, 1931), *Espérame* (dir. Louis Gasnier, 1933), *Melodía de arrabal* (dir. Louis Gasnier, 1933), *El tango en Broadway* (dir. Louis Gasnier, 1934), and *El día que me quieras* (dir. John Reinhardt, 1935) situated the tango idol in Argentina as well as international settings alongside Spanish- and English-speaking characters of different nationalities. In spite of the frequent clumsiness of the productions from a technical standpoint, the films firmly established Gardel as a Latin American star and helped to popularize tango films in Argentina.[44] Importantly, the Paramount pictures also codified tango as a kind of super-Argentine musical genre capable of selectively embracing other idioms. Indeed, in this sense the Joinville and Astoria Studios (New York) pictures made tango look and sound more jazz-like. Perhaps the most famous song from *El tango en Broadway*, for example, was the fox-trot "Rubias de New York." *Espérame* featured the rumba "Por tus ojos negros," backed by none other than the Cuban bandleader don Azpiazu. Still, Gardel's dabbling in foreign flavors and rhythms on the big screen did not sacrifice the national appeal of the music. Rumbas and fox-trots were simply subsumed under the sign of tango, and Gardel's argentinidad only grew stronger amid Hollywood's short-lived transnational experiment.

Nonetheless, Gardel certainly felt pressure to demonstrate his loyalty to River Plate audiences and musical styles. As the historian Simon Collier would later point out, the fact that Gardel returned to touring extensively in the Argentine and Uruguayan provinces even after his Joinville successes of 1932 and early 1933 suggests that "he was trying hard to convince the public—maybe himself?—that . . . his Argentine roots were still firmly entrenched."[45] Although the increasingly international character and adaptability of tango were undoubtedly keys to its survival in the face of the onslaught of swing, one of the inevitable controversies that arose in the mid-1930s revolved around the supposed corruption of tango music by jazz. With the rather ominous headline "American Music has begun to displace the Tango," the magazine *La Canción Moderna* voiced its concern that Argentine musicians were being "conquered by syncopation" and that local singers had become "completely dedicated to interpreting American songs in such poor English that, in some cases, their linguistic knowledge is reduced to the study of phonetics." Perhaps not surprisingly, *La Canción Moderna* laid most of the blame on Hollywood for orchestrating the swing jazz invasion. "The vacuous, frivolous, and untranscendent qualities made known to us by the syrupy manners of Yankee films have taken hold on our own customs, to the point of seizing control of the radio waves."[46] Never mind that the Joinville and Astoria productions, guided by the same "syrupy" bottom-line principles, gave birth to some of Gardel's most popular recordings and augmented tango's prestige not only abroad but also in Argentina and Uruguay. Hollywood hegemony was only perceived as a threat if it served as a vehicle for yanqui idioms and narratives.

The reactionary tone of some of tango's defenders was not lost on Buenos Aires-based jazz writers. *Síncopa y Ritmo* wasted no time in directly contesting the trumped-up war waged on nationalist grounds by such publications as *La Canción Moderna*. In a pointed editorial piece, the magazine asserted that jazz was "not limited, as many believe, to a blues number or some catchy fox-trot from a talking picture" and in fact "encompasse[d] a much broader field than the merely danceable." Yet in his efforts to elevate jazz, the same editorial writer resorted to equally objectionable essentialisms. While jazz had constantly reinvented itself and attracted large numbers of highly skilled composers and musicians, tango, since its heyday in the 1920s—or so the magazine claimed— had increasingly suffered from "an almost total lack of renovation among the orchestras and in the spirit of the bandleaders."[47]

La Canción Moderna subsequently asked for the opinions of a number of leading Argentine composers and bandleaders on the subject. Their responses, reprinted in *Síncopa y Ritmo,* generally showed a more nuanced and favorable view of jazz than *La Canción Moderna*'s initial editorial slant. Musician, bandleader, and composer Osvaldo Fresedo remarked that musically "[jazz bands] are much more advanced than us," particularly in terms of harmonic sophistication and variety of instrumentation, though he pointed out that like tango, "jazz also began with rudimentary 'typical' orchestras."[48] Composer Francisco Lomuto avoided formal comparisons by focusing on questions of nationality. While the "undeniable beauty" of tango melodies constituted the "faithful expression of the sentiment of this Argentina," jazz was "undoubtedly the music of another people, agreeable, rhythmic, but we should receive it like a visitor one treats with all due courtesy because it pleases us."[49]

Perhaps the most poignant insights of the survey came from composer Adolfo Ortiz who, like Lomuto and others, downplayed the putative competition between tango and jazz. While praising jazz as a culturally complex, sophisticated, and ever-changing musical form as well as the consummate expression of modern life, Ortiz insisted that tango offered "infinite possibilities, as many as jazz itself." Moreover, he rightly pointed out that since tango had also enjoyed great success abroad, particularly in other Latin American countries—here he would have been thinking mostly about Gardel—then it was as absurd to talk about the "invasion" of jazz as it was to decry the "danger of the tango."[50]

While the question of race only appeared in passing in these offhand comparative assessments, the tango-jazz debate forced several leading figures to acknowledge that jazz was harmonically more sophisticated than tango, even if the latter's emphasis on melody was said to have more visceral appeal. The polled composers and intellectuals often measured the value of tango from the point of view of criollo identity and emotional connection. Declaring that tango was simply more moving to him than the fox-trot, for example, Lomuto admitted that North Americans would likely have felt the opposite way, "but I speak based on my own standards and temperament and not theirs."[51] Lomuto and others thus sought to safeguard tango from foreign defilement, not as a logical demonstration of the Argentine form's sophistication or complexity, but rather by asserting value through a nativist appeal to the senses. If avant-garde primitivists had championed jazz as a privileged space of otherness unfettered by reason and historical time—what the Spanish writer Ramón Gómez de la Serna a few years earlier had called a domain of *sinhistoria* and *sinrazónes*[52]—here Argentine composers and musicians couched their preference for tango in similar language, retreating rhetorically into the realm of affect so as to discredit jazz as an overly cerebral, modern form. In short, jazz was a kind of music "much more advanced than us."[53]

It is not my intention to expose composers like Lomuto as hypocrites, but rather to show that even critical censure of jazz was, by the mid-1930s, increasingly drifting away from the premises held by many Latin American intellectuals just a few years earlier. The arrival of bebop in the 1940s further challenged the conventional assessment of jazz as a nonrational expression. On the whole, Argentine intellectuals and jazz aficionados were rather slow to embrace Charlie Parker and Dizzy Gillespie as the legitimate successors to hot jazz. A key shaper of critical orthodoxy in the region, Néstor Ortiz Oderigo, in a number of articles and three major monographs—*Panorama de la música afroamericana* (1944), *Estética del jazz* (1951), and *Historia del jazz* (1952)—laid down the fundamentals of jazz history through the midcentury. Ortiz Oderigo's work was instrumental in bringing Latin American readers up to speed on international and critical trends and helping to elucidate the importance of blues and Negro spirituals to the development of early jazz. Above all, he forcefully distinguished the seminal work of Jelly Roll Morton, Louis Armstrong, and Duke Ellington from the commercialized appropriations of such bandleaders as Paul Whiteman and Harry James.[54]

As musically literate as his writing was, however, Ortiz Oderigo used race as an essential marker separating what he considered canonical from apocryphal jazz practices. "As is well known," he wrote in *Jazz Magazine*, "the Afro-American songbook has exerted a singular influence on the aesthetic formation, structure and even the spirit of legitimate expressions of jazz of pure black roots." For the Argentine music historian, the qualifier "of pure black roots" (de castiza raigambre negra) clearly indicated that the most authentic type of jazz music was that which preserved the "purity" of popular African American anteced-ents. Jazz, he wrote, drew thematically not just from the blues tradition, but also from typical "blue" modes of expression and harmonic traits and from in-tonations "derived from the hoarse voices of uneducated singers," making such qualities "freer and less exact than those of whites."[55]

Ortiz Oderigo made his pronouncement in October 1945, a pivotal time in Argentine and jazz history. If the last years of the Second World War turned out to be the twilight of big band's reign elsewhere, they marked the peak of the music's popularity in the River Plate region. By the middle of the decade, jazz records and broadcasts of various stripes were widely available in urban markets. A whole assortment of jazz venues (especially so-called *confiterías*) now dotted the urban landscape of cities such as Buenos Aires, Córdoba, and Rosario, as Juan Perón's ascendance to the presidency briefly lent buying power to a larger-than-ever cross section of music enthusiasts.[56] Most of these new fans were casual listeners and devoted dancers enamored mostly of white bandleaders such as Goodman, Artie Shaw, and Tommy Dorsey.[57] By the early 1940s, though, it could hardly be said that jazz fandom was a predominantly cult pursuit.

Meanwhile, though at first almost imperceptibly, a sea change was taking place. In the United States, commercial swing bands lost bandleaders, musi-cians, and dance audiences to the war effort, and postwar public tastes shifted away from unwieldy, expensive dance orchestras. It was in this vacuum that more challenging, listener-oriented jazz groups emerged in North American, European, and (shortly afterward) Latin American cities. In Argentina the de-mise of big bands roughly coincided with a decline in tango as well. This was due not only to the changing political economy of the popular music industry, but also to the fact that US and Argentine *música bailable* had long shared the same dance floors, sound stages, and even bandleaders and musicians. Since the

1920s, as I have already suggested, countless Argentine performers had regularly alternated between two or more styles of music, donning different hats for genre-hopping audiences. The conclusion of the Second World War soon ended such a complementary arrangement. By the end of the 1940s, as Perón's economic reforms stagnated, larger *orquestas típicas* began to fail in much the same manner as North American big bands. The downsizing of larger orchestras revealed after the fact the long-standing interconnectedness of jazz and tango performances. As Karush points out, "with the decline of big band jazz, tango lost its dance partner."[58]

The emergence of bebop in the 1940s suggested a vindication of "serious" music after the commercial excesses and concomitant whitening of jazz during the reign of big-band swing. Even so, most River Plate jazz critics did not immediately greet the new style with open arms. It is important to remember that the rise of the young bop lions Gillespie and Parker also coincided with the revival of Dixieland and hot jazz. A clear sign of the times occurred in 1947, when Louis Armstrong abandoned the big-band format and returned triumphantly to the New Orleans and Chicago styles that had made him famous; Earl Hines, Jack Teagarden, Sidney Bechet, and others soon followed suit.[59] And in Argentina, too, traditional jazz underwent a sharp resurgence in the postwar era. The Hot Club de Buenos Aires was founded in 1948 and quickly led to the formation of local hot and New Orleans ensembles—the Guardia Vieja Jazz Band, the Dixielanders, the Porteña Jazz Band—several of which would flourish over the next two decades.[60]

Perhaps out of reverence for the sanctity of African American jazz idioms and their "uneducated" pedigree, Ortiz Oderigo was very reluctant to acknowledge bebop as a viable path for the music's future. *Historia del jazz*, despite being published in 1952, recognized the work of Gillespie and Parker only to characterize it—in language that verged on Adornian—as a cold and mechanical affront to the accessible phrasing and polyphony that made "authentic" jazz swing. Ortiz Oderigo saw bebop not as evidence of mass culture's victory over high art, though, but rather the opposite: a misguided rejection of the music's popular heritage by "serious" and "educated" musicians. The Argentine critic's account of bebop's supposed erudite desecration of jazz's vernacular roots even assumed racial overtones. Although bebop's most important pioneers were black musicians, he acknowledged, "the results . . . could not be more nefarious, as with all attempts made to turn one's back on the vigorous Afro-American roots of 'hot' art."[61]

Ortiz Oderigo was not the only Argentine critic of the early 1950s to reject or downplay bebop's contribution to jazz, even though Buenos Aires institutions such as the Bop Club Argentino (founded in 1950) and musicians like Enrique "Mono" Villegas and a young Lalo Schifrin were openly embracing the work of Gillespie and Thelonious Monk.[62] The general reluctance to praise bebop reflected the persistent influence of Francophone critics Robert Goffin, Charles Delaney, and Hugues Panassié, whose critical oeuvre was frequently cited and reviewed and occasionally published in translation in Argentine jazz journals of the period.[63] The backlash, though, was not unanimous. In a 1946 *Jazz Magazine* piece, Edgardo Fiore praised Gillespie as a highly innovative musician, as influential for younger musicians as Louis Armstrong had been fifteen years earlier. Fiore also answered his more conservative colleagues (whom he pointedly called "pseudocritics") by defending Gillespie against the common accusation that the accelerated tempo and dissonance common to bebop frequently grated on the ears. On the contrary, Fiore maintained, Gillespie's virtuosic flourishes were signs of jazz's progress, not its decadence.[64]

By the early 1950s, *Jazz Magazine* could afford to be less defensive in its embrace of bebop. In one essay, A. César Di Baja completely refuted any notion that bebop was an effete dead end. "Of all the offspring of traditional 'jazz' nurtured by improvisation," he wrote, "the strongest and most indispensable originality has been that of Gillespie and Parker." Arguing that the "furiously antiromantic" bebop liberated jazz from European influences and "brought back the almost barbaric impetus and vigor of primitive jazz," Di Baja maintained that bebop only fully realized its revolutionary potential when it steered clear of extraneous influences, notably the Afro-Cuban rhythms that marked Gillespie's 1940s collaborations with Mario Bauzá and Chano Pozo.[65] This was exactly the opposite of the remarks made by Ortiz Oderigo, who had begrudgingly praised the rhythmic independence and "Afro-Cuban blood" leeched by Gillespie during his forays into Caribbean music.[66] Though ultimately drawing opposite conclusions about the value of bebop's contributions to jazz tradition, both Di Baja and Ortiz Oderigo proposed just such an "authentic," "primitive" tradition as the music's hallmark.

Charlie Parker the Porteño

Julio Cortázar's early jazz criticism stands as a fascinating if paradoxical counterpoint to Argentine jazz criticism of the period. In two early essays, Cortázar, to an even greater extent than Ortiz Oderigo, held up hot jazz as the height of pure poetic creativity, synonymous with the enviable "irrationality" of black American cultural traditions. In "Soledad de la música" (written in 1941), a young Cortázar framed jazz music as the ideal channel for what he considered unmediated musical expression. According to Cortázar, the notation of erudite music required an extra step of interpretation that diluted the intentions of the composer. By contrast, jazz, "that created by Blacks, and the only kind deserving of the name," had avoided such a fate. "Black jazzmen," Cortázar wrote, "did not come to ask the question that I have wanted to examine: with ignorant wisdom they had answered it beforehand."[67]

Cortázar developed his argument even further a decade later in a long and frequently acerbic letter written to the musicologist-critic Daniel Devoto. Not only did Cortázar reaffirm that African American culture was single-handedly responsible for the development of hot jazz (although he failed at this point to include bebop, to which he was a late convert). He also claimed that jazz had had a transformative influence on Western culture generally, leading to a "parallel liberation" in which the improvisational genius of jazz echoed the extemporaneous creativity of surrealism.[68] Iconoclastic as always, Cortázar was dismissive of the tendency among conservative music critics and musicologists to praise jazz only insofar as it bore a resemblance to erudite music. To clamor over technical analogues between the two, he wrote, only revealed a failure to realize that jazz was essentially a poetic practice, not an aesthetic one. The emphasis placed on notation and interpretation in classical music, moreover, simply intensified the search for the composer's original intent. If "cultured music is always a type of hypostasis of its author," then *jazz is its own author.*[69]

These last aspects of Cortázar's thesis foreshadowed the critical insights of African American intellectual Amiri Baraka in the following decade.[70] In other ways, though, the Argentine's argument reverted to commonplaces of 1920s primitivism.[71] By declaring jazz "irreducible to any mediation," Cortázar channeled the avant-garde's celebration of jazz as an admirably direct, intuitive vessel of creative expression.[72] More to the point, his privileging of blackness as an enabler of creative instinct distilled the residue of race essentialism running through much Argentine jazz criticism of the previous two decades. Like Hernández Arregui, Ortiz Oderigo, and others, the young Cortázar explained the conundrum of jazz—its brazen departures from musical convention yet massive and often unseemly popularity, its primitive modernity, its "ignorant wisdom"—by attributing it primarily to blackness: the catch-all for ineffable difference.

This would all change with *El perseguidor*, in which Cortázar ambitiously attempted to deconstruct the very modern-primitive binaries on which jazz criticism (including his own) had too often relied. Indeed, what is most remarkable about the 1959 novella, particularly when read alongside Cortázar's earlier musings on jazz, is the extent to which it resists simple analysis. On its surface, the story recounts African American jazz musician Johnny Carter's tailspin into drug-addled extremes of creative sublimity and pathetic collapse, anger and tenderness, insight and incoherence. His key interlocutor—the narrator of the story—is the Parisian jazz critic and historian Bruno, an alternately sensitive and callous scribe who patiently listens to and cares for Johnny while cynically and self-consciously deciding just how much of Johnny's dying descent to include in the second edition of his biography. The novella thus assumes the guise of a metabiography and at the same time an unusual roman à clef evoking Charlie Parker's decline and cast of supporting characters, from session musicians and French music critics to female admirers and lovers.

Criticism of the story has tended to focus on the give-and-take between Bruno and Johnny as symptomatic of abstract ethical encounters between the calculating, savvy author and the brutalized savant, between critic and artist, self and other.[73] One interesting study argues that *El perseguidor* deserves a prominent place in Cortázar's body of work not because of its à clef treatment of Charlie Parker, but rather because of what the story has to say about the Argentine author's ontological claims for jazz.[74] In my view, though, the story's explicit biographical slant cannot be overlooked. The literary scholar Doris Sommer has suggested that Cortázar deconstructs traditional Argentine biography by replacing the "self-improving genre" centered on the lives of exemplary men with "a story that tracks the troubled afterthoughts about the very possibility of writing a life."[75] This, however, is too narrow a reading of *El perseguidor*, seeking as it does to place the story solely within the confines of Argentine literary and political history. The exemplary man in question, after all, is not Argentine, nor does the story take place anywhere near the Rio de la Plata. Instead, *El perseguidor* assumes the form of an intimate, self-conscious profile narrating the construction of an authorized jazz biography, written by a white non-Argentine about a black non-Argentine.

In a certain sense, *El perseguidor* reads more like an autobiography than it does a biography. Cortázar's fictional framework frequently gives Johnny room to speak for himself, even if each monologue comes wrapped in a critical aside in which Bruno underscores the musician's lack of logical coherence, sophistication, and even originality. Notwithstanding such disclaimers, Johnny's meanders emerge as bitterly skeptical, provocative critiques not just of jazz criticism but also of Western systems of knowledge more broadly.[76] The question of temporality is particularly important for the musician. Playing jazz, Johnny remarks, deepens his experience of the moment while removing him from the "mania" of conventional time.[77] Johnny's verbal assaults on quantifiable time are somewhat reminiscent of the primitivist typecasting of negritud that haunted Cortázar's early jazz writing. Yet they are also consistent with the thesis that the unique social conditions of early jazz musicians made temporality one of the central paradigms of jazz from its emergence in New Orleans in the late nineteenth and early twentieth centuries.[78]

In either case, Bruno's emphasis on the musician's chemical addictions and practical ineptitude severely undermine the authority of Johnny's metaphysical arguments. By characterizing Johnny's language as truncated, Bruno hints at the jazz musician's linguistic and intellectual inadequacy—the flipside of his creative virtuosity.[79] But he doesn't stop there. On a number of occasions, the critic resorts to out-and-out racism. In the middle of the musician's disquisition on time, Bruno likens Johnny physically to a chimpanzee; later, when Johnny is sitting naked before him, Bruno compares him to a "monkey in a zoo."[80] After listening to a recording of Johnny's tormented, brilliant interpretation of "Amorous," which the critic predicts will go down as one of the greatest moments in jazz history, Bruno is seized with a desire to purge himself of "that black formless mass without hands and without legs, that crazed chimp that runs his fingers over my face and smiles at me maniacally."[81]

In the end, Cortázar profoundly questions not just the mechanisms of biography or autobiography but also those of ethnography. In spite of his deep disdain for Johnny, Bruno also envies the musician's talent, which is "secret, irritating in its mystery, because it has no explanation."[82] The phrase is strikingly similar to Carlos Sandoval's 1936 declaration in *Swing* that the "enigma" of jazz required the interpretation of "cultured" music criticism only. The scholar George Yúdice has speculated that the creative intuition seen as endemic to primitive objects supplies modern capitalist societies with unadulterated cultural capital—what he calls a "prosthesis to reason."[83] Bruno acknowledges that just such an operation is afoot when he concedes that Johnny's seeming dependence on his phalanx of girlfriends, promoters, and hangers-on masks the opposite: "Deep down inside we are a bunch of egotists; under the pretext of caring for Johnny what we do is to safeguard our idea of him, to ready ourselves for the new pleasures Johnny will give us, to polish the statue we have erected amongst ourselves, and to defend it no matter what the cost."[84]

No doubt in part to ease the burden of his knowing exploitation of Johnny, Bruno repeatedly explains to himself and his readers why the musician needs him in the first place. In spite of his unrivaled musical talent, Johnny's "poor intelligence" prevents him from appreciating the full dimensions of his own exploits, thus fundamentally failing to qualify for what Bruno considers the universal standard of greatness.[85] If Bruno admires Johnny, it is only because the jazz virtuoso is a struggling "chimp that wants to learn."[86] When Johnny questions the fealty of Bruno's biography on the grounds that it gives an incomplete portrait of him, devoid of the man behind the music, Bruno comments defensively that Johnny's "mental age" prevents him from appreciating the book's subtle wordplay: "Creators, from the inventor of music right up to Johnny . . . , are incapable of extracting the dialectical consequences of their own work, of postulating the foundations and transcendence of that which they are writing or improvising."[87]

El perseguidor thus shows how the ethnographic authority of jazz criticism frequently justifies its own existence, claiming to pay back the unadulterated other on whom it depends by supplying (to invert Yúdice's turn of phrase) a sort of prosthesis to intuition. When in their discussions Johnny reveals insights into music and creativity, Bruno quickly writes them off either as naive, hackneyed, or confused. Not doing so would jeopardize Bruno's prescribed role as coherent intellectual and rational biographer. In short, the jazz critic cannot sanction Johnny as anything but a nonverbal primitive whose brilliant performance remains incomplete without the intervention of the white critic's higher consciousness. As in Cortázar's early music essays, jazz in *El perseguidor* is still largely presented as a vessel of absolute liberty, of a perpetual and ultimately fruitless search for a deeper essence beyond the surface of facile eroticism and sentimentalism.[88] Yet Bruno's case for reciprocal prosthesis depends on casting Johnny not as a universal, undifferentiated savage but rather as a fallible biographical subject who happens to be non-European and black: an uprooted, flesh-and-blood artist locked in an internal tug-of-war between the Parisian metropolis and the New World hinterlands—a bit like Cortázar himself.[89]

Given *El perseguidor*'s foregrounding of biography, some recent criticism of Cortázar's work has noted the story's loose resemblance to later biopics such as Bertrand Tavernier's *Round Midnight* (1986) and Clint Eastwood's *Bird* (1988). Osías Wilenski's fascinating adaptation of the novella (1965), meanwhile, has largely flown under the radar of jazz fans, critics, film historians, and academics, in spite of the film's considerable stylistic merits and creative divergences from the source material. Rather than delving into Cortázar's transnational politics, the neophyte Argentine director (himself a musician and composer) largely strips the novella of its ethnographic overlay by setting the story in Buenos Aires and focusing on the metaphysics of creation and self-destruction. Filmed in black and white in an art-house style that, like Godard's work from the early 1960s, relies heavily on the mood and iconography of Hollywood film noir, Wilenski's adaptation of *El perseguidor* nonetheless manages to creolize Cortázar's fiction under the guise of universality by eliminating virtually any mention of race, exile, or even national identity. While the many shots of decadent cityscapes would be readily familiar to porteños, Wilenski avoids populating the film with readily identifiable landmarks. Most importantly, though, Cortázar's Charlie Parker figure has been transformed into a white Argentine.

Once he has cleared the soundstage of obvious racial and national referents, Wilenski is free to unpack Cortázar's metaphysical fireworks unmolested.[90] The story's discourse on time is reduced to a brief though central discussion between Bruno and Johnny in which the racial and epistemological overtones of the novella are reduced to a simple difference of outlook attributable solely to Johnny's innate brilliance and mental and emotional instability. Likewise, Johnny's rejection of Bruno's petty pursuit of literary renown casts the musician as an artist in an existential crisis, without a meaningful political or economic subtext. Despite Wilenski's visual flair, an impressive soundtrack featuring solos by Gato Barbieri, and a stellar cast led by Sergio Renán (as Johnny), the simplification of Bruno and Johnny's world leaves little besides the ineffability of genius to distinguish the artist from the critic.

If Wilenski manages, at a price, to narrow the divide that separates Cortázar's two main characters, the director cannot risk playing the same game of evasion and subterfuge with spoken language. That a white Argentine jazz musician would call himself Johnny Carter to begin with forces the script to acknowledge the name as a foreign moniker. "If Juancito lived in another country, and was truly a Johnny," Wilenski's Bruno remarks, "then he would be the great star he deserves to be." "Johnny Carter" thus signifies a fictive stage name that could only be "true" elsewhere, even if Bruno also implies that such a metropolitan elsewhere is beyond the Argentine jazz musician's reach. At the same time, Wilenski (with an assist from screenwriter and former *vanguardista* Ulises Petit de Murat) suggests that Johnny cannot achieve celebrity status locally, either, presumably because the provincial jazz audiences of Buenos Aires are incapable of appreciating someone of his musical caliber.

Just as Buenos Aires masquerades as Paris or New York, so does Juan (with the help of Barbieri's canned solos) ape the hard bop style and psychological profile of a standard jazz virtuoso of the mid-1960s. That "Juancito" calls himself Johnny turns the character into a kind of ersatz jazzman and Bhabhian colonial mimic, "almost the same" as the North American original, "but not quite."[91] If such piecemeal imposture does not ultimately do justice to the Argentine musician's aspirations, it does manage to satisfy the imperial desires of Juan's social milieu. The scores of women and men who fawn over Johnny in Wilenski's adaptation obviously do not mistake him for an African American jazz musician. Yet it is precisely the incompleteness of Juan's mimicry that

Fig. 2.4. *El perseguidor* (dir. Osías Wilenski, 1965). In his adaptation of Cortázar's *The Pursuer*, Wilenski straddles the line between authenticity and believability. Casting a white actor as the tormented Johnny Carter—Cortázar's fictionalization of Charlie Parker—Wilenski struggles to keep the novella's existential content intact while relocating the jazz virtuoso from Paris to Buenos Aires.

enables his groupies to fawn. While he is devoid of the literary Johnny's racial core as well as his status as an expatriate, Juan certainly displays many of the superficial trappings of alterity—tortured genius, brilliant unpredictability, effortless nonconformism, and so forth. The porteño public, the film suggests, can only be fully seduced by a musical compatriot who *partially* embodies the otherness of jazz.

Oddly, in some ways Wilenski's work is closer in spirit to the pivotal body of Argentine jazz criticism of the 1930s and 1940s than it is to Cortázar's fictional work. With its ostensibly colorblind take on Johnny Carter, the film not only guts the novella of its vital racial content, it imagines contemporary Buenos Aires unperturbed by ethnic and racial nuance, a position consistent with the "repression and distortion" of *afro-argentinidad* and *mestizaje* historically used to safeguard the hegemony of whiteness.[92] This reversion to the nation's identitary status quo highlights the extent to which Cortázar in his novella labored in the opposite direction. While never mentioning Argentina by name, *El perseguidor* deconstructs the commonplaces of race and "intuitive" musicianship underlying not just Francophone jazz criticism since the 1920s but also much of the critical work of *Síncopa y Ritmo*, *Swing*, and *Jazz Magazine*. Specifically, the novella echoes and disrupts the arguments made by the likes of Juan José Hernández Arregui and Carlos Sandoval that the "ignorant wisdom" of *jazz negro* requires the interpretation of erudite critics such as themselves. In so doing, Cortázar interrogates notions of blackness and whiteness in ways that his compatriots—and even he himself—had never dared to do previously.

Lalo, Astor, and Gato

Despite Wilenski's almost absurdist flattening of Cortázar's Johnny Carter, the social milieu depicted in the film was not entirely fictitious. The years after the fall of Perón in 1955 ushered in a new generation of urban denizens and music fans who, much like Wilenski's Johnny, sought out new forms of socialization and rebellion often at odds with conventional emblems and institutions of argentinidad. In these heady years of economic and political instability, the historian Valeria Manzano writes, youth culture became "the carrier of sociocultural modernization *and* its discontents."[93] Feeling disenchanted with what were widely seen as the failed ideals and empty rhetoric of democratization, young, middle-class Argentines increasingly found inspiration in the rich assortment of transnational offerings at their disposal. And prior to the emergence of rock as a major cultural force later in the decade, jazz remained the sound and style of choice.[94]

Argentine jazz journals of the 1940s and 1950s chronicle the rise and fall of various jazz clubs (frequently sponsored by the magazines themselves) not only in Buenos Aires but also in smaller River Plate cities such as Rosario, Montevideo, and La Plata. The most significant of these venues was the Bop Club Argentino.[95] Founded in 1950, the Bop Club coalesced around a growing group of musicians, fans, and critics who opposed the reigning traditionalism of the Buenos Aires jazz scene. Having witnessed from afar the innovations of Parker and Gillespie, the new generation of enthusiasts—including such emerging musicians as Gato Barbieri, Mono Villegas, and Lalo Schifrin—championed jazz as a modern expression and "found in the new vocabulary a musical raison d'être."[96] Dizzy Gillespie's visit to Argentina in July 1956, part of a State Department tour, was an especially important catalyst for followers of bebop who, according to Sergio Pujol, were at the time still far outnumbered by hot jazz and swing proponents. At the same time, the fact that Gillespie performed with a big band assuaged the prejudices of the old guard. As Pujol puts it, the dynamic Gillespie arrived in Buenos Aires like a "modern jazz bomb in an orchestral format."[97]

Of all the young porteño musicians, it was Schifrin whose career was most transformed by Gillespie's live performances. Schifrin later recalled that he, Barbieri, and others had played privately for Gillespie after his concert. The famous trumpet player encouraged Schifrin to look him up if he was ever in the United States. Schifrin was clearly in awe of Gillespie, later comparing his musicianship and creative energy to Picasso's.[98] The young Argentine took Gillespie up on his offer shortly afterward, although his travel to the US was hindered, ironically, by the same State Department that had sponsored Gillespie's seminal performances in Argentina.[99] Eventually assuming the dual role of arranger-pianist in Gillespie's quintet, a role he held until 1962, Schifrin also shined as the composer of Gillespie's five-part "Suite Gillespiana." A critical and commercial success, the record led to a premier concert at Carnegie Hall, launching Schifrin's enduring and wide-ranging career as composer and arranger well beyond the world of jazz.

As important as bebop was to Schifrin and other young Argentine musicians of the period, it was not the only modern music to attract crowds in Buenos Aires. A pivotal live music venue in the early 1960s was Tucumán 676, where artists as diverse as the Modern Jazz Quartet, Stan Getz, João Gilberto, and Astor Piazzolla performed. El perseguidor's lead actor Sergio Renán also frequented the club, calling it a "generational touchstone" and a bridge between jazz and tango.[100] And indeed, it was here where new tango maverick Piazzolla met future collaborator and jazz vibes master Gary Burton, just to mention one musical encounter.[101] The newsmagazine *Primera Plana* went a step further in its assessment of the 676, praising the tiny club as a unique sanctuary where tango, Argentine folk music, and jazz at once competed and coexisted.[102] Buttressed by his Quinteto Nuevo's landmark records of the period—starting with *Nuestro Tiempo* (1962)—Piazzolla was the main attraction at the 676, the Jamaica Club, and other small tango clubs called *tanguerías* before moving on to larger venues later in the decade.

A cover story in *Primera Plana* (May 1965) positioned Piazzolla's work as both creatively ambitious and also socially divisive. While generally favorable, the article pointed out that Piazzolla's cult following had not yet translated into the kind of record sales still enjoyed by the likes of traditional tango stalwarts Carlos Gardel, Juan D'Arienzo, Osvaldo Fresedo, and Osvaldo Pugliese. The magazine strongly suggested that those who questioned the tango status quo were generally relegated to the fringes of the Argentine recording industry. Besides Piazzolla, one such artist was the jazz pianist Enrique "Mono" Villegas, who offered *Primera Plana* a provocative theory on the illusiveness of local celebrity: "There are two types of musicians: those who strive to improve each time they perform, right up until the moment they die; and those who perform, with great success, perfectly badly."[103]

If not yet universally famous, Piazzolla's notoriety at the time among young, middle-class audiences was such that he quickly became a fixture on Argentine television as well. Piazzolla's performances caught the attention of President Arturo Illia's government, which in 1965 promoted the quintet's well-received tour to Brazil, Uruguay, and the United States, including a televised concert on Mount Vernon.[104] At the same time, the *bandeonista* elevated his stature and gained a great deal of exposure through his much-publicized word-music collaboration with Jorge Luis Borges, resulting in the LP *El Tango*. Piazzolla had high regard for Borges and was flattered by the writer's keen interest in his innovations. In the *Primera Plana* profile, published during the rehearsal stage, Piazzolla boasted that Borges was enthusiastic about the idea of working together, stopping by his apartment every day with a poem or two in hand. "Imagine that! Borges!" he marveled.[105] When it came down to recording the project, though, stark differences and bitter disagreements emerged. After Borges exclaimed one day that Piazzolla simply did not understand tango, Piazzolla countered that Borges's notion of tango could only be attributed to his tone deafness, putting an end to the argument. "Piazzolla's knife was sharper," remarked Natalio Gorin.[106]

The heated exchange was highly emblematic of the period. Tango fundamentalists like Borges were almost invariably ambivalent about Piazzolla's work, if not downright hostile. Piazzolla, in turn, was always ready to joust vigorously with those who opposed him, whether they were internationally re-nowned writers or session musicians, poets or taxi drivers. His main message was simple enough: the tango could not afford to be relegated to "the canon of a permanent tradition."[107] What remains clear from literature of the period is that the main debate did not center on foreign influence so much as it did on the question of what exactly constituted tango. It was, in short, an ostensibly generic concern that provided cover for cultural nationalism. In this sense the Piazzolla controversy of the 1960s differed significantly from the bossa nova debate in Brazil, where (as I discuss at length in chapter 3) criticism hinged not just on a perceived affront to the sanctity of samba, but also fundamentally on the *bossanovistas'* supposedly alienated imitation of cool jazz.

The irony is that Piazzolla was arguably no less influenced by jazz than were musicians such as João Gilberto and Antônio Carlos Jobim. Although born in Argentina, Piazzolla spent most of his early childhood in New York, and was drawn back to the city periodically over the rest of his life. His binational upbringing came at a price. When as a boy in the 1930s he performed for a visiting Carlos Gardel, the legendary singer remarked that he played his ban-doneón like a *gallego* (foreigner).[108] Upon his return to Argentina in 1937 as a teenager, Piazzolla's English was considerably better than his Spanish. He later recounted that he had had little desire to return to Argentina; he soon missed his American friends from Greenwich Village, above all their regular jaunts to Harlem, where they would try to pass as adults just to watch Cab Calloway play.[109]

Piazzolla's passion for jazz remained unabated during his years in Buenos Aires and Paris in the 1940s and 1950s. In the late 1950s, temporarily back in New York in the hope of recording with Dizzy Gillespie and others, Piazzolla experimented with an ill-fated jazz-tango hybrid sound. After assembling a quintet made up of respectable if unremarkable jazz musicians, he recorded two sides with the Ti-Co label, *Take Me Dancing: The Latin Rhythms of Astor Piazola* [*sic*] *and His Quintet* and *An Evening in Buenos Aires.* Both recordings were widely considered failures; the second was apparently never released. Al-though the details are sketchy, in part because Piazzolla was reluctant to speak about the two recordings, it appears that Tito Puente and Johnny Pacheco may have participated in *Take Me Dancing.*[110] The title of the first record suggests that Ti-Co wished to take advantage of the mambo and cha-cha dance crazes still in vogue, and in fact Piazzolla had briefly supported himself in part by doing arrangements for Noro Morales's and Machito's bands. Although Azzi and Collier characterize both the Ti-Co records as "slightly above the level of muzak," *Take Me Dancing* (now readily available online in digital format) reveals flashes of innovation, particularly on the Piazzolla originals "Oscar Peterson" and "Boricua."[111] As a whole, though, the effort suggests an awkward attempt to place the bandeonista in a pan-Latin, popular setting rather than at the high crossroads of jazz and tango. As Piazzolla himself remarked years later, "It was a hybrid, although it had a seed of Piazzolla."[112] In any event, *Take Me Dancing* appears to have had little if any commercial or critical impact in the United States, and even less so in Argentina.

Of course, the so-called J-T sessions would not be Piazzolla's last incursion into the jazz world. After consolidating his reputation in Argentina and Uruguay in the 1960s, Piazzolla toured extensively in Brazil, Europe, and North America in the 1970s and 1980s. His international celebrity increased dramatically, and he recorded with such established jazz musicians as the baritone saxophonist Gerry Mulligan and the vibes player Gary Burton. In a 1975 interview with the French magazine *Jazz Hot* around the time of the Mulligan-Piazzolla release, *Summit*, Piazzolla declared that "the musicians [I love] are all jazz musicians, not tango musicians."[113] A number of critics, beginning with Piazzolla himself, have acknowledged his debt to jazz as regards instrumentation, harmonic progressions, and the ineffable quality of "swing." Piazzolla left no doubt as to how much he valued the latter. "Swing is everything," he told *Jazz Hot*. "If your music doesn't swing, you have nothing." Since "tango in-and-of-itself doesn't have swing," Piazzolla felt compelled to surround himself with jazz musicians, whether foreign or Argentine.[114] At the same time, he acknowledged that improvisation—so crucial to jazz performance since the emergence of bebop and free jazz—was barely compatible with his own tango-based compositional style. Perhaps due to this tension between the stylistic looseness intrinsic to his notion of swing and the Argentine composer's relatively rigid adherence to notation, Piazzolla in later comments softened his stance somewhat. "The one thing I could never stand was that the essence [of my music] might get lost. I wanted *tango* swing, not jazz swing or contemporary music swing. Piazzolla had to sound like Piazzolla."[115]

Beginning in the mid-1960s, Piazzolla received overwhelming critical praise from prestigious international publications such as the *New York Times*, *Down Beat*, and *Jazz Hot*. In 1965 *Times* critic Robert Shelton raved that Piazzolla's "vanguard tango" quintet, performing at an American Cancer Society benefit concert in Philharmonic Hall, sounded at different moments like an old-fashioned dance band, a Chico Hamilton-Fred Katz modern jazz combo, a classical chamber ensemble, and a bossa nova group. "In the last analysis," he reports, "Mr. Piazzolla's quintet sounded like nothing but itself, and that was quite enough."[116] Piazzolla reportedly treasured Shelton's review for the rest of his life as a bittersweet reminder that international listeners tended to accept and value his genre-defying music more than Argentine critics did.[117] Meanwhile, Piazzolla's increasingly numerous and open flirtations with jazz music and US jazz musicians, culminating in his recordings with Mulligan and Burton and performances in several jazz festivals, marked him as a genre-bending artist, perhaps as closely associated abroad with jazz as with tango.

Part of this association was encouraged by Piazzolla himself, who frequently distanced himself from the word "tango," particularly in the 1970s and early 1980s. In the 1975 *Jazz Hot* interview, for example, the Argentine musician made a point of refusing to label what he played tango, calling it "Buenos Aires music" instead. "Tango," he said provocatively, "c'est fini!"[118] In another long interview published three years later in the Argentine magazine *Buenos Aires Tango*, Piazzolla identified himself as a *tanguero* but once again asserted that his closest creative affiliations were with jazz musicians, since "they are open to all music and to study and to progress."[119]

Somewhat surprisingly, considering the extent to which he publicly identified with jazz, Piazzolla was generally critical of the most prominent Argentine jazz musician of the period: Gato Barbieri. When queried by *Jazz Hot* about his compatriot, Piazzolla quickly dismissed Barbieri as a phony who had been manipulated by his handlers into injecting Latin American folk elements into his music, presumably referring to the Impulse studio recordings released in 1973 and 1974—*Chapter One: Latin America*, *Chapter Two: Hasta Siempre*, and *Chapter Three: Viva Emiliano Zapata*. While acknowledging Barbieri's prodigious talents as a saxophonist, Piazzolla bemoaned his countryman's choice to stray from his calling as a jazzman in a supposedly commercially orchestrated effort to concoct a "mélange" of Argentine, Bolivian, and Brazilian music.[120]

Piazzolla's objection to Barbieri's folk-injected Latin jazz projects of the early 1970s is particularly revealing of the bandeonista's selective criticism of musical hybridity. Piazzolla dismissed contemporaneous Argentine rock artists (like Charly García) as complacent, mediocre, even laughable, imitators of US and British originals.[121] The fact that he criticized Barbieri for straying from his earlier adherence to the tenets of hard bop and free jazz—the Argentine had spent several years in the 1960s backing Don Cherry—foregrounds the inconsistency of Piazzolla's sharp-tongued appraisals of younger Argentine musicians. As an Argentine, apparently, one could and should be a pure jazzman, but not a pure rocker, much less a pure tanguero.

In fact, Gato Barbieri's drift toward internationalism in the late 1960s and early 1970s can in some ways be seen as analogous to Piazzolla's. Through the early and mid-1960s, Barbieri had garnered critical praise and professional respect for his "unaccented" collaborations with free jazz pioneer Don Cherry. As Karush suggests, Cherry's openness to global musical idioms and Third World radicalism made him something of a dissident to free jazz orthodoxy, in somewhat the same way that Dizzy Gillespie pushed the envelope for bebop in the 1940s through his innovative collaborations with Afro-Cuban musicians (a topic I explore in more detail in chapter 4). In any event, Cherry's tutelage provided an opening for Barbieri to rid himself of the race-based trappings of free jazz: as a non-black Latin American musician, Barbieri could only hope to garner honorary membership in the club to which he so ardently wished to belong.[122] It was not until the end of the decade that the Argentine found his niche injecting free jazz and hard bop with Latin American modalities on such LPs as *The Third World* (RCA Victor, 1969) and *Fenix* (RCA, 1971). Building on *Bolivia* (RCA, 1973), Barbieri's three Impulse sessions led him further away from modern jazz conventions and more and more into the realm of Latin fusion. Indeed, it is no exaggeration to say that Barbieri's set of early 1970s recordings, infused with political protest and *tercermundista* solidarity, sustained rhythmically by musicians as diverse as Airto Moreira and Luis Mangual, helped to set the stage for the global emergence of such artists as Irakere and Hermeto Pascoal later in the decade.

US jazz critic Nat Hentoff, one of Barbieri's most prominent advocates at the time, stated the significance of Barbieri's work in even stronger terms. Declaring the Argentine "the most original non-American jazz force since Django Reinhardt," Hentoff argued that Barbieri heralded "a new era of the internationalization of jazz."[123] Published in 1976, Hentoff's praise was prescient if somewhat premature. Barbieri's long, unremarkable descent into commercial fusion and smooth jazz beginning in the late 1970s no doubt diminished his standing in the modern jazz pantheon, eclipsing his own pathbreaking work of the late 1960s and early 1970s. It also made Piazzolla's misgivings about Barbieri's corporate handlers seem as prophetic as Hentoff's hyperbolic praise.

Seen from another angle, though, Gato Barbieri's shift to Latin jazz was an ambivalent response not just to the vagaries of the US and European music industries, but also to the rigidity of Argentine critical parameters. Barbieri himself admitted that he "did not listen to or understand" Argentine music early in his career, an oversight he clearly sought to rectify in his revolutionary phase.[124] Given the general climate of Argentine jazz criticism of the 1940s and 1950s, Barbieri's confession, and his early departure for foreign pastures, should come as little surprise. As we have seen, publications like *Jazz Magazine*

Fig. 2.5. This cover of *Chapter One: Latin America* (ABC/Impulse, 1973) shows how Gato Barbieri's carefully tailored sartorial presentation—a blend of pampas folk and nuyorican hip—reflected the shift in his musical and ideological profile from the 1960s to the 1970s.

actively supported and promoted local musicians and jazz scenes in Buenos Aires, Montevideo, Santiago, and elsewhere in the region. But ultimately the only truly "authentic" jazz musicians were black, hence the term jazz was often used interchangeably with *música negra* and *música negra americana*. Further, the only places where full jazz citizenship could be achieved were the United States and Europe (particularly Paris)—a bias expressed implicitly and explicitly in Wilenski's adaptation of *El perseguidor*. For a time, Barbieri's wife Michelle recalled, "Gato wanted very much to be a black jazz musician."[125] Only after realizing that he could be something other than white by appropriating folkloric styles associated with Latin America's rural poor did the saxophonist give up on his *jazz negro* dream.

Barbieri's desire for an identity makeover is all the more remarkable when we consider just how unviable the path to blackness or even mestizaje had been in Argentina for decades. As the historians Paulina Alberto and Eduardo Elena have noted, the prevailing "white exceptionalism" narrative in Argentina had been predicated since the nineteenth century on "the renegotiation of the boundaries of ethno-racial difference in socioeconomic and cultural terms," the result of both an elite desire for homogeneity and a popular wish for assimilation.[126] Even for an Afro-descendant musician like Oscar Alemán, achieving blackness in the long run proved strangely elusive and was largely dependent on the guitarist's evanescent status as a successful jazz musician.[127] Barbieri's late-blooming *latinidad* therefore can be seen as both a daring act of rebellion and a compromise: a self-conscious project of mitigated otherness made possible by a cultural and political climate somewhat more favorable to progressive Pan-Americanism and postnational aspirations, as reflected also in the 1960s work of Schifrin and Piazzolla.[128]

Barbieri's conversion to pan-Latin internationalism would take place, interestingly, only after striking up a friendship with the Brazilian filmmaker Glauber Rocha. The saxophonist identified strongly with Rocha's cinematic character António das Mortes, who first appears as the rugged agent of oppression in *Deus e o Diabo na Terra do Sol* (Black God, White Devil, 1964), only to switch sides and fight on the side of the oppressed peasants in *António das Mortes* (1969). The latter film struck a rebellious chord with Barbieri, so much so that it would inspire one of the four seminal tracks of *The Third World*. Even if by the late 1960s Barbieri was "not afraid any more of being Argentinian," he increasingly participated in musical projects that permitted him to embrace his national roots under the flag of Third World activism.[129] Barbieri's self-identification with undifferentiated Latin jazz and pop intensified in the 1970s. When asked about Piazzolla in a 1977 *Down Beat* interview, the saxophonist responded dismissively that "he doesn't play Latin music." His wife Michelle seconded him, arguing that tango was "a city product" made famous in Europe before Argentina.[130] The bitterness of their remarks suggests they were familiar with Piazzolla's *Jazz Hot* criticism of Barbieri as a talented sellout. Despite their simmering feud, though, in an important sense both Piazzolla and Barbieri pursued not just money and international recognition abroad but also the creative latitude the two musicians sorely lacked in Argentina. In different ways and at slightly different moments, both artists sought refuge in the more accommodating platform of the jazz industry, one now eager to freshen its portfolio through an eclectic assimilation of Latin American musical styles and musicians.

Syncopated Devotion

Early Argentine jazz criticism stands on its own as evidence of an increasingly complex appreciation of jazz in the region and also, just as importantly, evidence that such assessments should not be seen as purely aesthetic judgments. Jazz music's intimate entanglement with mass culture and ideologies of race reveals Latin American music criticism of the period to be an inherently political practice. Indeed, such a body of literature is indicative of the ways local intellectuals came to grips with the mass mediation of alterity during the two crucial decades prior to World War II. By insisting on blackness as a prerequisite to a jazz artist's authenticity, Argentine writers of the swing era implicitly qualified themselves as rational observers allied with "civilized" Continental criticism, while also sidestepping race in assessments of homegrown musicians like Paloma Efron and Oscar Alemán. The sheer abundance of Latin American jazz musicians in the 1930s and 1940s, as well as those immersed in analogous national idioms such as tango, choro, and rumba, belied claims that Latin America somehow stood beyond the native realm of "true" jazz. Yet it is precisely Argentine writers' forced othering of jazz that—in their own eyes, at least—safeguarded their own status as full-fledged intellectuals.

In subsequent decades, Cortázar's deconstruction of jazz essentialisms, Piazzolla's genre-bending experiments, and Barbieri's mestizo internationalism questioned the ways Argentines had grown accustomed to hearing jazz. However, this chapter's examination of jazz music's highly variable symbolism over the course of more than three decades, a span that marks the apex of jazz's popularity globally, reveals "syncopated" writers and intellectuals curiously out of step with the music's international profile. Many vanguard intellectuals had equated jazz with modern excess and elitist decadence precisely at a time (the 1920s and

1930s) when jazz in fact already had begun to reign supreme as a popular practice in North America and elsewhere. In the 1940s and 1950s a considerable
number of Argentine jazz critics (including Cortázar, initially) still viewed hot
jazz, early swing, and blues as the only legitimate forms of música negra americana, though they were hesitant to grant the Afro-Argentine Oscar Alemán
the same exalted status. By the 1960s, many critics had come to see jazz as an
emblem of bohemian counterculture, at a time when jazz was quickly becoming a middlebrow pursuit.

The commercial and critical success of artists such as Schifrin, Piazzolla,
and Barbieri challenged fans, critics, and even musicians themselves to reconcile hybrid musical practices with a shifting set of generic impositions tied to
global markets and fickle cultural politics imbued with competing commercial
and nationalist demands. Yet these recording artists' international prominence
also signaled a return to their motherland's deep ambivalence surrounding the
blackness of jazz. In their separate ways, Efron, Alemán, and Barbieri all felt
compelled to negotiate alterity in a nation whose racial politics worked cen-
tripetally to contain such "anti-white" impulses. The only viable alternative for
these musicians was to seek out the more spacious terrain of the transnational
aural sphere. To be considered authentic performers of jazz, in short, they were
compelled to defy or endure the tacit but strict parameters established by the
peculiar logic of Argentina's racial and cultural legacy.

3

The Anxiety of Americanization
Jazz, Samba, and Bossa Nova

The 1930 Brazilian premier of the Hollywood film *The King of Jazz* was a re-markable event on several accounts. Directed by John Murray Anderson and featuring Paul Whiteman and his orchestra, the high-budget musical had been something of a box-office flop in the United States, in part, no doubt, because of the timing of its release shortly after the stock market crash of December 1929.[1] The film nonetheless arrived in Brazil with considerable fanfare. Mindful of pleasing local audiences, Universal Studios had form-fitted the film's content, adding on-screen introductions to Whiteman's musical numbers in Brazilian Portuguese. The studio's choice of Brazilian Hollywood actors Lia Torá and Olympio Guilherme as the presenters of the augmented version was hardly haphazard. Neither actor ever achieved the international stardom expected of them—even the moderately successful Torá fell well short of the celebrity de-livered less than a decade later by Carmen Miranda. Yet they were at the time the most visible Brazilians in Tinseltown and as such quite well known among Brazilian film audiences of the late 1920s and early 1930s.[2] Torá and Guilherme were also of European descent, and therefore fitting emblems of the deeply contradictory racial politics on full display in Anderson's film, a fact made clear in Brazilian advertisements for the film.

Fig. 3.1. Appearing in the magazine *A Cena Muda*, this advertisement for *O Rei do Jazz* featured Brazilians Olympio Guilherme and Lia Torá on equal footing with the "King of Jazz," Paul Whiteman (1930).

The King of Jazz laid bare the biases of Hollywood in ways that can only be described as bizarre. The film overtly argues for the centrality of European music in the early evolution of jazz by crowning the white Whiteman as the top jazz bandleader and musician instead of such African American luminaries as Louis Armstrong and Duke Ellington. At the same time, the few black characters in *The King of Jazz* are relegated to virtual minstrel figures, simultaneously sexualized and infantilized, much in the manner of Josephine Baker.[3] Even more disturbing, the musical film's remarkable dearth of black performers belies the ostensible message that jazz is a symbol of the United States as a musical melting pot and international cultural force.

Hollywood's quickly evolving technical sophistication—*The King of Jazz* was the first full-length musical shot in Technicolor, and featured high-quality sound and innovative special effects—served to underscore the identity fables played out on the screen. In one remarkable scene, an animated caricature of Whiteman travels to Africa to hunt for big game, where through the magical power of each gunshot he manages to transform a lion into an entire jazz orchestra. One film historian has suggested that the episode represents an inversion of the widely held view that Africa was the main creative inspiration for jazz; here it was the other way around.[4] Another reading is that Whiteman symbolically "tames" (refines, adapts) the music's primitive source.[5] Whatever the case may be, the scene suggests that jazz, in the twilight of the Jazz Age, remained at once spellbinding and despotic: a metonymy of technological savvy and cultural conquest in the charge of a white, North American overseer.

For the most part, the film's colonialist overtones appear to have been lost on Brazilian critics of the time. Overwhelmed by the film's technical novelties, the magazine *Fon-Fon* wrote that *The King of Jazz* kept "the spectator riveted to his seat and submitt[ed] him to an agreeable torture of the senses." As for Whiteman, the same reviewer raved that the "great maestro" masterfully tamed the "crazy disharmony" and "musical hubbub" of jazz.[6] Rio de Janeiro film magazine *Cinearte*'s review was decidedly mixed. Editor and film reviewer Adhemar Gonzaga bluntly criticized *The King of Jazz*'s content as "common and vulgar." But he was also quick to highlight the film's technical polish and "marvelous" musical numbers, especially Whiteman's interpretation of Gershwin's "Rhapsody in Blue." Above all, Gonzaga praised Universal's unprecedented gesture of transposing segments of the early talkie into Brazilian Portuguese. Previous Hollywood talkies screened in Brazil had been shot in English or Spanish, so *The King of Jazz* was clearly unique: "Without a doubt, the Brazilian version should delight all [audiences] since, admittedly, it was well executed and, indeed, was tailor-made for us."[7]

Although Gonzaga was known to be a severe critic, his assessment of Paul Whiteman's role as the eponymous centerpiece of *The King of Jazz* was nothing short of glowing. Whiteman's orchestra, he wrote, was "undeniably one of the most formidable ever heard."[8] In spite of the film's prominent and highly problematic racial depictions, neither *Cinearte* nor *Fon-Fon* dared to touch the subject. Part of their lack of critical engagement with the specter of white-black relations was a function of editorial convention: "respectable" entertainment magazines of the period rarely took on such politically fraught issues, for fear of offending the moral sensibilities of their mostly middle-class readers. Yet these two reviews of *The King of Jazz* point to a telling peculiarity of Brazilian jazz criticism during the 1930s and 1940s. The interwar period gave birth to well-known journals like *Down Beat*, *Jazz Hot*, and *Metronome*, but also to under-the-radar but equally dynamic forums for jazz discourse such as the Argentine *Síncopa y Ritmo*, *Swing*, and *Jazz Magazine*. These journals and others like them catered to a growing body of devoted fans and served as promoters and gatekeepers of live jazz performance, record collecting, and radio listenership.

Such was not the case in Brazil during the same period. Popular jazz recordings did indeed make their way into record stores and private collections, particularly once big-band swing took hold in the mid-1930s. Even more so than in Argentina, though, government control of the airwaves and popular press under the first regime of Getúlio Vargas (1930–1945), especially after the declaration of the Estado Novo in 1937, discouraged the consumption and promotion of non-Brazilian music. Instead, the Estado Novo sought to hallow samba as the national music par excellence, one of the main vehicles for the unification of the nation under the democratic banner of *mestiçagem*—an ideological maneuver that cloaked the autocratic governance of the Vargas regime. Sociologist Renato Ortiz writes that Brazilian modernist intellectuals of the 1920s had drawn attention to urban cultural imports such as jazz thanks to the sheer scale of social change they encapsulated. In this sense, Vargas in turn harnessed and naturalized the newly unveiled power of mass culture, adapting already present notions of race to the "new demands of a 'modern' Brazil" first signaled by the modernists.[9]

To do so required using state supports and modern technology to transform samba—essentially an Afro-Brazilian practice centered in Rio de Janeiro— into a widely visible *mestiço* spectacle. It also meant muzzling the competition, or at least trying to. Since jazz posed the biggest challenge to samba in terms of record sales and airplay, the odd critical silence of the late 1930s and 1940s made perfect sense politically. Cultural nationalists were quick to accuse foreign-influenced artists and composers such as Radamés Gnattali of being sellouts, especially when their records were produced by Brazilian-based US figures like Wallace Downey (Columbia) and Leslie Evans (RCA Victor).[10] In such a climate, the kinds of specialized journals and "cult" fan clubs that dotted the urban landscape of Buenos Aires in the 1920s, 1930s, and 1940s were next to nonexistent in Rio de Janeiro and São Paulo until the 1950s.

As I will discuss in the first half of this chapter, the absence of sustained critical intervention had serious consequences for Brazilians' conceptual understanding of US popular music. Without either a wide selection of live performances to choose from or the mediation of an informed base of record collectors and aficionados, jazz as a concept all too often suggested a commercial catch-all and a blunt object of seduction or menace—and sometimes both at once—rather than a well-defined category of musical expression. Above all, jazz was for many Brazilians a key emblem of *americanização* (Americanization). This seemingly simple term provided cover for a complex set of concepts and emotions based on the preservation of national difference, a concomitant fear of cultural contamination, and an apprehension of Brazil's peripheral relationship to modern capitalism. As Ortiz has observed, americanização therefore did not just describe the United States per se. Rather, the term denoted the emerging global modernity ushered in by new technologies and the value system they harbored.[11]

For many Brazilians, jazz was not something just to be heard. In fact, for a time the music assumed the trappings of a cinematic subject.[12] This meant that the music reflected the commercial bent, racial ideology, and moral sensibilities of the US film industry. *The King of Jazz* was the first of scores of Hollywood films screened in Brazil and elsewhere in Latin America featuring music identified as jazz yet interpreted predominantly by white singers and musicians. In pictures such as *Swing Time* (1936), *Hollywood Hotel* (1937), *Birth of the Blues* (1941), *Orchestra Wives* (1942), and *Stage Door Canteen* (1943), performances by Benny Goodman, Tommy Dorsey, Glenn Miller, Kay Kyser, and others echoed the musical aspirations of white protagonists under the aegis of jazz (whether swing or otherwise) and blues. While black musicians and bandleaders like Cab Calloway, Armstrong, and Ellington did occasionally appear in narrative features of the period, they usually played narrow, "entertaining" roles extraneous to the main thrust of storyline and character development. As the scholar Krin Gabbard notes, filmgoers of the time "were much more likely to see white musicians holding the saxophones and drumsticks and snapping their fingers with hip insouciance."[13] As far as Brazilian spectators were concerned, the blackness of jazz had gone missing at one of the music's main ports of entry: cinema.

For a critic like Gonzaga to crown white North Americans as the legitimate torchbearers of jazz, then, was certainly problematic but hardly surprising. It is only natural that Brazilian movie audiences, intellectual or otherwise, should have conceived of jazz based on Hollywood's skewed representations of "authentic" musical performance and subjectivity. Such filtered perceptions were likely to weigh even more heavily on Brazilian audiences than on their North American counterparts, at least until the conclusion of the Second World War. The former typically had far more limited access to live performances by African American musicians—performances that might have lent depth and nuance to Hollywood's pale version of the jazz spectrum. Vargas's first departure from office in 1945 coincided with commercial big band's decline, a double aperture that opened up Brazilian markets to hot and Dixieland revivals and to bebop as well. This development rekindled jazz-samba debates begun decades earlier. Meanwhile, the sudden diversity in jazz offerings in Brazilian cities fostered exclusive yet vital fan clubs that would serve as laboratories not only for record collecting and critical literacy but also for transnational musical exchanges that laid the groundwork for bossa nova. Yet, as I will discuss in the second half of this chapter, even bossa nova would be subjected to intense interrogation as the deep anxiety over Americanization that characterized the jazz-samba debates continued unabated—even augmented—during the pitched cultural battles of the 1960s.

The Jazz-Samba Wars

Although initially lacking in publications dedicated to popular music analysis, Brazil in the 1920s and 1930s was not without its jazz critics. Despite its relatively small circulation and brief run, the pioneering journal *Phono-Arte* reached the economically powerful and swiftly growing demographic of literate record consumers and radio listeners, engaging intellectually with popular music and the recording industry at a time when both were still widely considered beneath the dignity of serious critical debate in Brazil and elsewhere.[14] Yet it quickly became apparent that the magazine viewed jazz as a venal menace. *Phono-Arte* downplayed the musical innovation of Ellington and others as a commercial assault facilitated by the sophistication of recording technology and the aid of Hollywood's growing mastery of sound technologies. *Síncopa y Ritmo* and other Argentine publications had largely chosen to ignore jazz's commercial legacy, thus ducking the loaded question of ideology. Due to its very mission, *Phono-Arte*, in a series of articles and editorials dating from the late 1920s and early 1930s, could ill afford to look beyond the culture industry that supported jazz. "The record, talking pictures, the dollar!" publisher José da Cruz Cordeiro wrote in the magazine's very first volume. "All at the service of American propaganda through one of its most accessible forms: music, therefore jazz."[15]

One of the most renowned and innovative Brazilian musicians of the 1920s, Pixinguinha, was the target of one of Cruz Cordeiro's best-known attacks. Focusing on two of the Orquestra Típica Pixinguinha-Donga's recordings of Pixinguinha's choros "Lamentos" and "Carinhoso," the young critic lamented that "our popular composer has come under the influence of the rhythms and melodies of jazz music." "Carinhoso" in particular seemed to get Cruz Cordeiro's goat. The song's introduction, the critic wrote, was "a veritable fox-trot," exhibiting all the hallmarks of "pure Yankee popular music."[16] Later, Cruz Cordeiro directed his wrath at a samba-maxixe, "Gavião calçudo," recorded with the same orchestra. Noting once again that the song "seems more like a fox-trot than a samba," the Brazilian critic saw the same pernicious source of foreign influence. "[The song's] melodies, its counterpoint, practically even its rhythm: everything is suffused with Yankee music."[17]

It was not unreasonable that Cruz Cordeiro would hear North American traces in Pixinguinha's music. To an even greater extent than other Latin American composers and bandleaders of the 1920s and 1930s, Pixinguinha freely vacillated between national and international idioms. His group the Oito Batutas can be seen as an emblem of the tricky cultural politics of the 1920s, when Afro-diasporic musical styles pulled Brazilian intellectuals in two different directions simultaneously. Elites such as Gilberto Freyre, Heitor Villa-Lobos, Mário de Andrade, and Benjamim Costallat, admirers of French high culture, felt compelled to emulate the City of Light's embrace of the *tumulte noir*. Yet these same intellectuals were prone to winnow Brazilian negritude from the chaff of African-rooted vernacular music generally, particularly North American forms such as jazz and blues that clearly bore the stigma of mass culture. The Oito Batutas brought such contradictions to the fore, since Pixinguinha's cohort mixed Afro-Brazilian music such as maxixe and choro with jazz while also making forays into other non-Brazilian forms such as tango. The group did so, moreover, on the vaunted European stage, winning the acclaim of the same "Parisian Brazilophiles" whom the "Francophilic" Brazilian intellectuals of the period so venerated.[18]

The oddly bitter condemnation of Pixinguinha's "Americanization" of choro in many ways anticipated the acrid samba-jazz debates of the 1940s and 1950s.[19] But by midcentury the cultural and political landscape of Brazil had changed considerably. Like many other Latin American nations, Brazil saw a veritable onslaught of big-band swing in the 1930s. Yet the swing craze did not just happen. As was the case in Argentina, radio and the recording industry played fundamental roles in the dissemination of such artists as Benny Goodman, Duke Ellington, Glenn Miller, and Tommy Dorsey. The historian José Geraldo Vinci de Moraes has noted that radio listenership in São Paulo exploded in number and diversity in the early 1930s as the city grew and stations shifted from educational to commercial programming. By the middle of the decade, jazz and tango were, after samba, the urban musical styles of choice, with stations like Rádio Record dedicating time slots to live swing orchestras and recordings.[20] Ample evidence of swing's penetration of major Brazilian markets can be found in the pages of *Fon-Fon*, one of the most important culture-and-society magazines of the period, which enjoyed a wide, mostly urban readership dating back to the Brazilian Belle Époque.[21] By the mid-1930s, a regular column ("Sopro-fon-fon") documented the constant arrival of new records by Tommy Dorsey, Benny Goodman, and others. The overlap between radio and Hollywood was not lost on the magazine's contributors. Citing the active participation of Hollywood film stars on US-based radio programs, *Fon-Fon* noted in 1937 that "film continues to exercise—and each day more and more—an enormous influence over the airwaves."[22]

The US film industry undeniably had a decisive impact on how jazz was seen and heard in Brazil in the 1930s. But the end of the decade witnessed a noticeable change in *Fon-Fon*'s somewhat frenetic coverage of radio and popular music recordings, even as film reviews and celebrity gossip columns continued unabated. At a time when swing increasingly invaded Hollywood sound stages, the magazine's coverage of jazz recordings and broadcasts oddly waned. In 1940, the Vargas government expropriated the already successful Rádio Nacional (previously owned by an international consortium), turning the station into a formidable promoter of Afro-Brazilian popular music.[23] Not surprisingly, radio reporting and music polls increasingly privileged samba above all others. Regular columns such as Juracy Araujo's "Novidades em discos" teemed with news about the latest Columbia and RCA Victor releases, no longer from the likes of Glenn Miller, Frank Sinatra, and Count Basie, but now from homegrown stars such as Francisco Alves, Carmen Miranda, and Ary Barroso.

The timing of *Fon-Fon*'s flagging interest in jazz was somewhat conspicuous, as it coincided with the establishment of the authoritarian Estado Novo in 1937, and with it samba's definitive ascent. The scholar Wander Nunes Frota views samba's rise in the 1930s as a unique by-product of dual desires: on one hand, middle-class Brazilians sought to buy into the dream of social ascension symbolized by the mass media, without which samba could not have achieved national prominence; on the other hand, they wished to offset their newfound elite status by remaining close to their "less noble origins."[24] Whatever its exact appeal, with vernacular origins and mixed-race pedigree, samba dovetailed well with Gilberto Freyre's articulation of mestiço nationalism as expressed in his watershed works *Casa grande e senzala* (1933) and *Sobrados e mucambos* (1936). The timing of Freyre's widely read studies could not have been more propitious. Vargas stepped up the state's relationship with samba from one of passive recognition to one of active promotion, helping to extend the music's reach to provincial capitals through the standardization of samba schools. From dedicated programs broadcast on Rádio Nacional to a National Exposition organized by the classical composer Heitor Villa-Lobos and featuring the music of Carmen Miranda, Almirante, and Donga, the Estado Novo for all intents and purposes made samba the official soundtrack of the nation's populist march toward the future.[25]

These efforts were not without deep internal contradictions. As late as 1933, for example, educators in the state of Minas Gerais actively discouraged the use of samba, maxixe, and tango in pedagogical exercises for young children, preferring the supposedly edifying, morally pure, citizenship-bestowing content of patriotic hymns over what one writer describes as the "fiery repository of vulgarity" displayed by popular urban music.[26] Such policies, frequently at odds with federal initiatives under Vargas, nevertheless shared with the normative logic of Freyrean mestiçagem an underlying reliance on eugenic discourses about race and hygiene.

Despite increasingly widespread if uneven acceptance that Afro-Brazilians belonged at the heart of state-sanctioned identity projects, by virtually all accounts racial prejudice was ubiquitous in the very cultural institutions underwriting samba's popularity. Pixinguinha later recalled that before the emergence of commercial radio in the late 1920s, the cinema had been one of the few public places where black musicians could earn money playing samba and choro, though only in the orchestra pit, never in the lobby.[27] The rise of Vargas and the end of the República Velha (1889–1930) did not rectify so much as attenuate the problems of social and racial inequities within the music industry. While Afro-Brazilian musicians made inroads in Rio, for example, radio work for blacks in São Paulo remained scarce until the 1940s.[28] The foundation of organizations such as the Sociedade Brasileira de Autores Teatrais (SBAT) and later the UBC (União Brasileira de Compositores) ultimately served to exacerbate the segregation of music labor between "artists" and rank-and-file musicians. Since they ultimately favored the interests of mostly white playwrights, composers, music executives, and marquee performers, the SBAT and to a lesser extent the UBC largely failed to protect the interests of most Afro-Brazilian *sambistas*.[29]

As both samba and big band reached the apex of their popularity during the last years of the Second World War, serious Brazilian jazz criticism began to emerge again after a ten-year hiatus. In a 1940 conference about musical expression in the United States, Mário de Andrade developed his ideas about jazz well beyond the heady days of the avant-garde journal *Klaxon*—and also in a different direction, emphasizing the music's national and folk origins over its high-art or modern-mass qualifications. Comparing a wide array of Latin American and North American musical idioms, Andrade contended that the former tended to be more individualistic than the latter, whose polyphony supposedly echoed the United States' democratic, collective ethos.[30] While he credited African American performers with leaving their indelible mark on the US mainstream, Andrade grouped jazz musicians together willy-nilly with Negro minstrels, criticizing both for allowing their state of "native purity" to yield to the falsity of "urban and semi-cultivated musicality."[31] Andrade's reassessment of jazz can be seen as a partial regression to the purity essentialism plaguing avant-garde discourse. His own writing from the 1920s—in which he championed the modern-savage hybrid of jazz as culturally exemplary— had gone against the grain of many of his vanguard contemporaries, including Freyre (see chapter 1).

Now, nearly two decades later, Andrade was in effect faulting the music for possessing the very same qualities. At once enviably democratic and menacingly venal—Andrade maintained—jazz simultaneously wove and soiled the national fabric of the United States. In a sense, Andrade had fallen victim to the overarching ethos of the times, one that permeated discourses on vernacular music during the 1930s and 1940s. The music scholar Ana María Ochoa Gautier has argued that the "aural public sphere" proved a pivotal arena for the elaboration of Latin American identity projects of the early twentieth century. Central to the construction of the region's distinctive modernity were the validation and consolidation of local musical practices made possible through the promotional heft of cultural elites, normally composers like Villa-Lobos or writers-folklorists such as Mário de Andrade. Highly influential public intellectuals who viewed music as a key to cultivating *brasilidade*, both men impacted cultural policy extensively during the first Vargas regime.[32] These sonic purifiers or "transculturators" (as Ochoa Gautier calls them) generally disapproved of overtly commercial styles like big-band swing that ostensibly violated identitary principles by introducing vulgarity to the pristine realm of the national-folkloric.[33]

Whatever may have been his motivation for giving jazz the cold shoulder, Andrade's newfound ambivalence previewed battles to come. The anthropologist Hermano Vianna has pointed out that accusations of Americanization leveled against Brazilian musicians did not heat up until samba had consolidated its position as the national music par excellence in the early 1940s, at which point critics began to "demand more symbolic coherence and authenticity" from performers such as Carmen Miranda.[34] Yet there were other contributing factors as well. For one thing, Vargas's nationalist hard line was undercut by Brazil's entry into the Second World War on the side of the Allies in 1942 and by the country's cooperation with Franklin Delano Roosevelt's Good Neighbor policy. The latter not only deeply involved Miranda, but also led to seemingly unlikely cultural collaborations such as those between Orson Welles and actor Grande Otelo, Leopold Stokowski and Pixinguinha, and Walt Disney and Ary Barroso.[35]

Closer ties with Washington certainly made it harder for the Estado Novo to keep the United States' main cultural exports completely out of the hearts and minds of Brazilians, as was demonstrated by a regular jazz column that surfaced in the entertainment magazine *A Cena Muda*.[36] Shortwave broadcasts produced by NBC and CBS in New York, made available through agreements between the Vargas government and Nelson Rockefeller's Office of the Coordinator of Inter-American Affairs (OCIAA), augmented North American musical content available to Brazilian radio listeners and included performances by the likes of the Harry James Orchestra.[37] Despite the newly intimate ties between the two nations—and to some extent because of them—the transnational components of popular music increasingly came under the scrutiny of critics.

The first major controversy about jazz's proper place in the Brazilian landscape emerged in 1941 in the political and cultural magazine *Diretrizes*. Cofounded in 1938 by Antônio José de Azevedo Amaral and Samuel Wainer, *Diretrizes* was initially nationalist and pro-Vargas in its orientation. But under Wainer's direction, the magazine emerged as thematically freewheeling and overtly anti-fascist. Featuring contributions by such A-list intellectuals as Raquel de Queiroz, Jorge Amado, José Lins do Rego, and Aníbal Machado, *Diretrizes*'s left-contrarian slant drew close scrutiny from the Estado Novo until its closure in 1944.[38] That did not, however, keep Wainer from persistently taking on controversial and timely subjects during his years at the helm. One such subject was jazz. In a survey designed by Villa-Lobos and consisting of eleven highly charged questions aimed at the magazine's readers, the celebrated composer asked if and why Brazilian popular music should be exposed to foreign influences. "Given all its original and excellent popular [music]," read question 3, "does Brazil really need the influence of foreign popular music?" Not satisfied with simply asking the question, Villa-Lobos gratuitously inserted arguments into several other questions that rendered question 3 a purely rhetorical one. "In the present moment, when Brazil is trying to use all of its spiritual and material resources to live on its own, should or shouldn't all that conspires to undermine its unifying traits be rejected?" As if there remained any doubt as to how readers should answer, Villa-Lobos made his point crystal clear in question 9, which strongly suggested that any Brazilians who chose not to respond to the survey "should be considered indifferent to patriotic initiatives," and question 10, which all but called for ostracizing dissenting resident-aliens from "our intellectual milieu."[39]

One month later, *Diretrizes* published an extensive rebuttal by Ary Barroso, perhaps the only public intellectual who could match Villa-Lobos's prestige as a composer—and a samba composer at that. Barroso focused on question 3 and used as an example the music (jazz) that Villa-Lobos never once mentioned by name, but against which his argumentative plebiscite was almost certainly aimed. As to whether foreign influence was necessary in Brazilian popular music, the composer of "Aquarela do Brasil" responded with a resounding yes. Although Barroso considered the fox-trot a poor style, lacking in any intrinsic value, the enviable technique and innovation of North American big bands managed to transform this dance rhythm into something noteworthy. It was precisely the extraordinary work and beneficial influence of North American swing bands, Barroso argued, that informed the orchestral arrangements of Radamés Gnatalli, for example, a fixture of Rádio Nacional and widely considered among the most sophisticated samba arrangers and bandleaders of the period. As for Villa-Lobos's suggestion that swing musicians should be considered undesirables in Brazil, Barroso responded with a soccer analogy: "Consider how ridiculous we would look if we considered a striker or any other foreign soccer player who had arrived here 'undesirable' for the simple fact that he had proved indifferent to Mr. Villa-Lobos's plebiscite."[40]

Perhaps the most damning element of Barroso's rebuttal was his indignation with Villa-Lobos's turgid linguistic register and insinuation that only those responding in writing to the survey should be considered true patriots. What was at stake, Barroso suggested, was not just correct nationalist sentiment but also the tacit exclusion of the poor and less educated from participating in the forum in the first place. Villa-Lobos's brand of patriotism, in short, was dogmatic and inherently elitist. To drive home his point, Barroso repeatedly claimed not to understand the convoluted language in which the survey questions were couched. "Patriotism is not the privilege of one class alone," he protested. "A decent person . . . faced with this questionnaire could well object, with sincerity and patriotism: 'I cannot respond. I don't understand what is written here.' And he would be right."[41]

The *Diretrizes* survey, while appearing to draw stark lines between jazz's enemies and defenders, ultimately complicated the terms of musical nationalism in Brazil, a tradition dating back to the late nineteenth century.[42] Despite his tone, Villa-Lobos was hardly consistent in his attitude toward Brazilian cultural politics or the question of Americanization over the course of his career. In the 1910s and 1920s, he was generally more than willing to play the "savage Brazilian" card, both in his compositions and when promoting his music at home and abroad. In the 1930s, as head of musical and artistic education in the Vargas administration, Villa-Lobos was expected to "revamp curricula and inculcate Brazilianness," a mandate to which he readily obliged.[43] By the early 1940s, however—shortly after the *Diretrizes* survey—the composer began to change his tune. Assuming the mantle of Pan-Americanism once Brazil had finally declared its allegiance to the Allied Powers, Villa-Lobos publicly renounced musical nationalism in favor of hemispheric universalism in a series of performances and lectures in the United States.[44]

Villa-Lobos's shifting views on the politics of Brazilian cultural production and the prickly topic of Americanization illustrate the deep complexities of the Pan-American paradigm in Latin America generally. Many critics and scholars have long considered the term, which first appeared in the late nineteenth century, to be vexed by the undercurrent of geopolitical dominance and cultural hegemony of the United States in hemispheric affairs. Yet as the scholar David Luis-Brown has rightly pointed out, Pan-Americanism, so often conflated with US imperialism, has in fact never been the exclusive dominion of US or even pro-US constituencies. Furthermore, the "grey zones of citizenship" have frequently emerged precisely within the framework of a critical Pan-Americanism.[45] Seen in this light, Villa-Lobos's project of universalism reveals not just vacillation or ambivalence but also adaptability to different modalities of hemispheric citizenship. In the immediate postwar era, without the ideological anchor of Vargas's Estado Novo or Roosevelt's Good Neighbor policy, Brazilian musicians and intellectuals struggled anew to reconcile nationalist goals with the evolving, sometimes unfriendly dynamics of inter-American relations.

If the Villa-Lobos-Barroso skirmish sounded the initial alarm about jazz, the first sustained attempt to come to terms with the music came in the pages of the venerable but short-lived *Revista da Música Popular* (1954–1956). In his first editorial, publisher Lúcio Rangel laid out the magazine's ambitious goal of publishing top-notch music criticism, interviews, and other fan-related material dealing primarily, but not exclusively, with Brazilian popular music. Much like *Phono-Arte* in the 1930s, *Revista da Música Popular* (RMP) precariously straddled the line between erudite journalism and populist-nationalist advocacy. Now, however, radio and the record industry were well-oiled music delivery systems. The RMP sought to exploit the massive reach of developing media without stooping to the commercial filler of such industry giants as *Revista do Rádio* and *Radiolândia*.[46] Along with like-minded contemporaries Almirante and Ari Vasconcellos, Rangel was highly instrumental at the time in promoting noncommercial samba through radio, print journalism, and *velha guarda* ("old guard," or revivalist) festivals. Such dedication, though, implicitly excluded other idioms from the conversation about Brazilian musical foundations.[47]

Nonetheless, Rangel also promised to dedicate space in each issue to jazz, "the great creation of North American Negroes." This was an impressive pledge given that jazz would be the only non-Brazilian music to receive extensive coverage at a time when mambo, bolero, and boogie-woogie, to name just a few styles, had also made inroads into Brazilian markets.[48] The magazine published a range of articles and record reviews by such writers as Jorge Guinle, Marcelo F. de Miranda, the Argentine Ortiz Oderigo, and Rangel himself. Guinle was the author of *Jazz Panorama* (1953), one of the first monographic studies on the subject in Brazil, and would soon emerge as a persuasive, anti-conservative voice in the RMP.[49] Yet initially the magazine's jazz editor and main contributor was the critic José Sanz. A staunch traditionalist, Sanz strove to sanctify jazz by placing it generically within the realm of folklore and culturally under the exclusive domain of Afro-descendant musicians of the US South. The Brazilian critic began the magazine's first essay on jazz with the stated goal of erasing confusion among Brazilian readers regarding jazz history. He thereby laid down a premise without which "whatever appreciation of jazz would lead, fatally, to fundamental errors." Jazz, he asserted, was "music created by the Negro from THE SOUTH of the United States, but more precisely New Orleans, and [had] its roots solidly planted in a certain region of Black Africa."[50]

By erecting rigid racial and geographic barriers around jazz, Sanz asserted that the music should not be confused with non-US, non-Africanized, nonfolkloric, or contemporary forms. His fundamentalism reached such extremes that he categorically declared jazz extinct, "never to be revived."[51] Real jazz, therefore, was culturally, spatially, and temporally out of reach for contemporary Brazilian fans, for whom Sanz—with echoes of both Adorno and Freyre—expressed open disdain. He declared his countrymen ignorant and deficient and therefore incapable of rationally judging the music's true merits and formal characteristics. "The 'cat' never leaves the realm of the senses," Sanz wrote, "and the deformity of taste can lead the individual even to like 'progressive jazz,' 'bebop' or 'cold jazz' [*sic*]."[52] It was a revealing rhetorical flourish. To disparage young Brazilian jazz fans, Sanz invoked an English slang term with class and race overtones ("cat"). In accusing such fans of being incapable of straying from their native "realm of the senses," Sanz implied a mutually exclusive distinction between erudite listenership and primitive fandom, the lettered minority and the vulgar mass.

Even among Brazilian critics who did not strike such an elitist pose, outright xenophobia was common. *Revista da Música Popular* featured a number of interviews with leading samba figures of the period as well as one fascinating poetic essay penned by Ary Barroso. In spite of his vigorous exchange with Villa-Lobos in defense of an open-minded approach to popular music the previous decade, Barroso now waxed nostalgic about traditional samba in much the same way Sanz bemoaned the passing of hot jazz. Samba used to be a simple, spontaneous expression, Barroso wrote, played on street corners rather than in concert halls, in a hardscrabble yet gilded time before fan clubs, slick promoters, and high-art pretensions robbed the music of its aboriginal purity. Although he did not mention it by name, one of the main samba corrupters was clearly jazz: "In the old days there were no 'American chords' in samba. And everyone understood it."[53] Never mind that Barroso himself had performed as a jazz pianist in the 1920s, or that he had profited handsomely from the commercialization and internationalization of samba, his song "Aquarela do Brasil" having been featured in Disney's Good Neighbor film *Saludos Amigos* (1942).[54] For the Brazilian composer, swept up by the revivalist wave of the late 1940s and early 1950s, samba music had not remained true to its Afro-Brazilian roots, and therefore had fallen irrevocably into decadence.

Not all samba composers took the same hostile attitude toward jazz. When asked in an interview if he liked jazz, Dorival Caymmi responded, "There is nothing more pure and spontaneous in our times than jazz. I love jazz improvisation, its instrumental virtuosity and creativity. Jazz, in my eyes, is the strongest musical expression of my era." As exuberant in his praise as he was, though, Caymmi too expressed a preference for the giants of previous decades— Morton, Waller, and Armstrong—and a pronounced distaste for bebop, which he wrote off as "musical Dadaism."[55] Even if he lauded jazz, Caymmi spoke of the "spontaneous" music of the United States as though it belonged to a distinct musical sphere from samba, temporally distancing hot jazz and early swing from postwar jazz by emphasizing the former's purity and discounting such contemporaneous artists as Dizzy Gillespie and Charlie Parker. Improvisation, virtuosity, and creativity may have been uniquely American qualities, in other words, but they were not readily accessible ones.

Both Barroso and Dorival Caymmi thereby fell into a seeming contradiction common to many sambistas of the 1940s and 1950s. Barroso the public intellectual, like Noel Rosa before him, tended to champion *samba do morro*—the stripped-down, "authentic" samba played by the mostly Afro-descendant residents of Rio's hillside (morro) favelas—as opposed to the slicker, more orchestrated sounds of the *samba da cidade* typically played in the city's whiter, middle-class neighborhoods.[56] All the while, Barroso the composer played a pivotal role in samba's increasing "refinement and sophistication" by way of commercialization. As the founder of the *samba-exaltação* (exaltation-samba) style, moreover, Barroso set patriotic lyrics awash in Freyrean racial democracy to lush, orchestral samba that freely borrowed musical ideas from sweeter strains of big-band jazz. Nurtured though not manufactured by Estado Novo–era nationalism, samba-exaltação thus celebrated "Afro-Brazilian culture as a source of national identity, albeit in a way that consigned Afro-Brazilians themselves to a folkloric, idealized and static past."[57]

Seen in such a context, jazz emerged as samba's kindred shadow for contributors of *Revista da Música Popular*. Barroso's odd lament essentially equated the iniquities of commercialization with US popular music: samba's *morro* purity ran the risk of being compromised by the venality and urban sophistication of the music industry, much as the forces of US mass culture had "ruined" jazz. Already decadent, jazz now threatened to infect samba in much the same way. As the historian Bryan McCann explains, the association of jazz with commercialization was due to a number of factors, ranging from the "white" traditionalism of early jazz imports to collaborations between US companies such as Coca-Cola and jazz-friendly samba bandleaders like Gnattali during the height of the Good Neighbor era.[58] To preserve samba as a pure national expression despite commercial and non-Brazilian influences (not all of them North American), sambistas and music critics of the 1950s assumed an ambivalent stance toward their long-standing rival. Largely dismissing its currency for Brazil, Sanz, Barroso, and Caymmi embraced jazz only insofar as it was cast as a mummified museum piece: a deceased distant cousin to vernacular samba. This fundamentally conservative posture was reinforced by a series of profile pieces penned by Marcelo de Miranda and the US jazz historian Fred Ramsey, articles that invariably focused on the canon of Dixieland, hot jazz, and blues. By cordoning off contemporary jazz music in such a way and specifically by discounting big band and bebop, these important critics and sambistas implicitly denied jazz's place in the national music scene.

In the summer of 1955, the RMP's music criticism temporarily took a back seat to a watershed event in the cultural landscape of Brazil: "With the death of Carmen Miranda," the magazine declared on its editorial page, "Brazil loses one of the most authentic expressions of its popular music."[59] Given the magazine's general stance in favor of tradition and against the "bad taste" of commercialism, the overwhelmingly favorable assessment of Miranda's artistry and career seemingly put the RMP at odds with its own platform. Culling eulogies and personal testimonies from a range of Brazilian writers and intellectuals, the special edition focused on Miranda's authenticity as a samba performer during her ascent to national stardom in the 1930s. When writers alluded to her subsequent Hollywood career, it was either to emphasize her role as "ambassadress" of Brazilian culture abroad or to allude to the pathetic self-destruction associated with her celebrity. At heart, she remained the same *pequena notável* (small, remarkable woman) that they remembered. Recalling her return to Brazil a year earlier, R. Magalhães Junior wrote that he felt sincere pity for the "nervous" actress who had "lost her joviality" and wept for no apparent reason.[60] In a similar vein, Augusto Frederico Schmidt (in an article appearing originally in *Correio da Manhã*) recalled a chance encounter with Miranda in a New York nightclub in which she had bemoaned missing yet another Carnival in Rio. "She seemed truly dispirited," Schmidt wrote. "Behind the mask of our star, who made friends with fame and achieved success in a great nation, I saw the old, *carioca* Carmen Miranda, the young girl whom we all knew so well, the one who was like family."[61]

The RMP's many eulogies masked a long-standing controversy and deep discomfort with Miranda's international celebrity among Brazilian intellectuals dating back to her rise to fame. Part of the debate predated the Brazilian singer's arrival in Hollywood. Even before Miranda appeared in her breakthrough picture *Down Argentine Way* (1940), for example, Renato de Alencar penned an editorial in *A Cena Muda* criticizing Hollywood's representation of Brazilian culture. Since US filmmakers consistently confused Brazil with Mexico and Argentina, Alencar wrote ironically, it might be best if they forgot about the country entirely. As for Miranda, still negotiating her contract with Fox, Alencar correctly predicted that her Hollywood roles would be limited to singing "those sambas done up in her Bahian outfit, exaggeratedly drowning in pearl necklaces and bracelets up to her armpits. What beautiful publicity for Brazil."[62]

Alencar's editorial was a strong indication that the road had already been paved for the strident cultural politics of Miranda's exotic spectacle. As a number of film scholars have pointed out, pictures like *Flying Down to Rio* (1933, starring Dolores del Río as the Brazilian Belinha de Rezende) had already signaled Hollywood's indifference to taking a veridical approach to national distinctions based on location, dress, language, and musical form.[63] Carmen Miranda's rising fame only intensified the debate in Brazil, since Hollywood's staging of her ethnicity almost completely ignored any notion of authentic representation so treasured by Brazilian intellectuals. Yet movie industry magazines, studio publicity, and even (at times) the films themselves identified Miranda as Brazilian.[64] Alencar, in another *A Cena Muda* piece titled "Carmen sem balangandãs," seized on the film star's use of sartorial extravagance as proof that she had let Hollywood grossly misrepresent Brazil. Typical of Miranda's critics of the period, part of Alencar's objection to Miranda lay in her supposed abuse of authenticity. By accepting roles of "anti-Bahian Bahian women," she had at once embraced and defiled Brazilian regional tropes—a liberty, he suggested, that should not have been taken by a Portuguese-born carioca. Yet Alencar's main objection had to do with taste. He criticized her turbans and *balangandãs* (Bahian baubles), therefore, but also "the imprudent theatrical vulgarities, the explosions of attacks of stupidity, the grotesque jealousy." In the end, it was not Miranda's misrepresentation that irritated the critic as much as it was her (and Hollywood's) "vulgar" exaggeration of Brazilian culture.[65]

Somewhat lost in the Carmen Miranda polemics of the 1940s—and indeed, in much of subsequent criticism of Miranda—was the question of her musical authenticity. The distortions of Brazilian national identity brought to bear through the scripted ambiguity of Miranda's pan-Latin-ness and meticulously outlandish wardrobe were accompanied by the hybridization of samba. Although Miranda, backed by her Rio-based Bando da Lua, sings and dances to straight sambas in several of her Hollywood films, most of her numbers feature elements of Caribbean music and, especially, big-band jazz. Miranda's reliance on non-Brazilian songs, as McCann points out, was due not just to studio pressures for her to internationalize her repertoire but also to Brazilian copyright laws, which were rigorously enforced by Columbia Records producer Wallace Downey in his role as representative of the Associação Brasileira de Compositores e Autores.[66]

Regardless of the reasons, many Brazilians were simply intolerant of what they saw and heard as Miranda's Americanization of the national patrimony. That the perceived defilement of samba played a central role in the controversy is evident from the way Miranda responded to the cold reception given to her at the

Cassino da Urca: through song. "Disseram que eu voltei americanizada" (They said I came back Americanized) (1940, written for Miranda by Luis Peixoto and Vicente Paiva) emphasizes samba do morro as a touchstone of her maligned Brazilian identity: To the claim that she had sold out, "That I can't stand the sound of the pandeiro any longer / And that I bristle when I hear a cuíca," the singer responds that, "I was born with samba and [still] live in the *terreiro* / playing that ancient rhythm all night long."

The song's lyrics resemble language used elsewhere by Cruz Cordeiro, José Sanz, and others to proclaim the supremacy of folk purism, reflecting a hidebound sensibility that flew in the face of the unstable, border-crossing nature of vernacular musics, whether jazz, samba, or any other modern idiom. My point here is not to demonstrate that Miranda was either a conservative throwback or a key musical innovator of a new hemispheric hybrid à la Pixinguinha, but rather that Brazilian accusations provoked by her music sounded much like objections typically leveled against postwar jazz. For Miranda's critics, the singer's transformation at the hands of the US film industry endangered the nation's frequently fragile sense of patriotism symbolized by samba. This was not because Miranda had diluted the samba music for which she was known in the 1930s, or at least not more than any other commercial sambistas had. Rather, it was because Hollywood gave global reach and audiovisual form to what some saw as a betrayal of Brazil's true essence. Armed with the self-righteous rhetoric of nationalist integrity and purist aesthetics, Brazilian intellectuals thus denigrated transnational mass spectacle under the guise of sober music criticism.

Only in the final year of *Revista da Música Popular*'s publication, once Marcelo de Miranda replaced Sanz as editor of the jazz section, did the magazine's fundamentalist slant come into question. In a devastating piece that must have shocked his editors, Jorge Guinle lambasted the "purely folkloric concepts" used by many Brazilian jazz critics, including Oderigo, Sanz, publisher Lúcio Rangel, and even Marcelo de Miranda himself, all of whom Guinle accused of being highly reductive and even superficial in their assessments of jazz: "There is no doubt that jazz [originally] looked to folklore for its themes and much of its 'manner.' As the music of Blacks, it couldn't help but to adopt many typical peculiarities. But contact with the city, the use of different instruments, the work of creative adaptation—which consisted of extracting its essence from folklore and giving it an instrumental character, the substitution of the strophic theme for the melodic motif and the harmonic development of the latter through improvisation—distinguished it from its origins."[67] Guinle's attack on jazz reductivism, while admitting the basis of some of its claims, pointed to undeniable facts generally ignored by the likes of Sanz and Miranda: namely, the rapidly changing urban environments that decades prior had brought New Orleans and Chicago musicians in touch with new instruments and influences, not to mention technological advances and commercial opportunities that facilitated the "creative adaptation" so central to the development of jazz.

Guinle's article could just as easily have been directed at the essentialism of samba criticism. As we have seen, "purely folkloric concepts" guided much of the *RMP*'s assessment of Brazilian music as well. In his article "Folcmúsica e música popular brasileira," the veteran music critic Cruz Cordeiro (author of the controversial Pixinguinha critique published in *Phono-Arte* some twenty-five years earlier) stressed the static, traditional elements of frevo, choro, maxixe, baião, and samba. In a clear effort to characterize most contemporary Brazilian music as not authentically national, Cordeiro also distinguished "folk" samba from "popular" samba. Although still alive, he lamented, folk samba was now limited mostly to carnival performances and *escolas de samba*. Popular samba, meanwhile, entered into decline soon after it left the hills for the flats in the 1930s, "and currently sounds more like bolero, blues, tango: anything but Brazilian samba."[68]

Evidence of a reaction within the ranks of *Revista da Música Popular*'s contributors against such conservative views can be found in Haroldo Costa's essay, "Os rumos da música popular brasileira," in which the young critic warned against prejudice and provincial stagnation among Brazilian musicians and composers. Far from being the enemy of the national patrimony, in other words, openness to change was fundamental to the continuing vitality of Brazilian popular music. Noting the recent influence of Stan Kenton and Dizzy Gillespie on national musical production, Costa praised the impact of improvisation and harmonic innovation on Brazilian technique. Why—he asked rhetorically—should the nation's music remain stuck in the 1930s? At the same time that Costa lauded the impact of contemporary jazz on samba, though, he warned against uncritical acceptance of foreign modalities. What was at stake, he maintained, was whether the essential Brazilian character of the nation's musical production could be preserved. "That's the crux of the matter," he wrote. "We should accept innovations, but only insofar as our music does not atrophy thematically or formally."[69]

In the final issue of *Revista da Música Popular*, perhaps to contest the moderate views of Costa and Guinle, Marcelo de Miranda made the magazine's main editorial thrust explicit in his review of one of Dizzy Gillespie's live concerts at Rio's Teatro República and two studio performances broadcast by Televisão Tupi in early August 1956. For Miranda, Gillespie's formidable skill as a soloist was eclipsed by his "limitless bad taste" as a bandleader. Commenting on the televised appearances, he wrote that it was "truly lamentable that a musician with the technical gifts of this affable Negro has stooped to performing such agitated and frenetic music, in an exhibition purely and simply of sharp strident notes and maneuvers of the valved instrument." What seemed to unnerve Miranda even more than Gillespie's well-executed "freneticism" was the way the band's "circus feats" were enthusiastically received by the live audience at the Teatro República. Berating the "screaming crowd that seemed to be dying of pleasure as it listened to such cacophony and pointless noise," Miranda used the occasion to criticize Brazilian jazz audiences generally. "It seems that they all walk around in a mental state suitable only for the formation of fan clubs."[70]

Much like his predecessor, José Sanz, Miranda thus demoted Brazilian concertgoers to the dubious status of fans. To achieve this end, he aggressively winnowed out vocal spectators from the larger category of jazz listeners. Yet the distinction was an artificial one: Miranda's disdainful censure of the audience's raucous expression of its delight suggested not just a difference of opinion but also class prejudice tinged with xenophobia. Indeed, his use of the word "fan" assumed all the social anxiety of an epithet, one that implied anger at spectators' ignorance and gullibility, since they had fallen for what the critic saw as Gillespie's ostentatious, trendy, pointless theatrics.

Dick Farney and the 1950s *Fã-Clubes*

Marcelo de Miranda and the raucous spectators at Dizzy Gillespie's show in Rio were distinguishable not so much by how they saw and heard the same performance, but rather by the different ways in which they expressed their reactions. Although the concertgoers Miranda wrote about were presumably more devoted followers of Gillespie and bebop than he was, all of the spectators at Gillespie's concert, including the critic himself, were arguably fans in a broader sense.[71] *Revista da Música Popular*'s jazz criticism, like that of *Síncopa y Ritmo* and other Argentine publications of the period, implicitly or explicitly affected a stance of beleaguered minority knowledge that in many ways made it difficult to distinguish articles and reviews from fan letters. Even writers such as Sanz and Miranda, who actively policed the boundaries of vernacular music, railing against the "limitless bad taste" of contemporary performers like Dizzy Gillespie and Charlie Parker, did so from a position of general advocacy and capitalist consumption of jazz music.

That said, there is a distinction to be made between fan-writers intent on consecrating jazz as a musical practice worthy of serious critical analysis, often under the pretext of locating jazz outside national boundaries, and the type of fans who filled the aisles of the Dizzy Gillespie concert. The latter were not limited to the ranks of noisy spectators or appreciative listeners alone. They also formed fan clubs. Beginning in the late 1940s, the first of several jazz societies emerged in Rio de Janeiro—the Sinatra-Farney Fan Club—to be followed soon afterward by the likes of the Glenn Miller Fan Club, the Stan Kenton Progressive Club, and the Dick Haymes–Lúcio Alves Fan Club. Answering a call made by radio announcer Luís Serrano on Rádio Globo for the creation of fan clubs with the idea of promoting records, three young cousins—Joca, Didi, and Teresa Queiroz—established a home base for the Sinatra-Farney Fan Club in the basement of the house their parents shared in the neighborhood of Tijuca. The group's name reflected the enterprising cousins' main interest: vocal jazz, particularly the big band-oriented crooning of Frank Sinatra and Dick Farney popularized by the Hollywood musicals and recordings of the period.[72]

Farney, whose birth name was Farnésio Dutra e Silva, had already made his mark in Brazil and the United States as a jazz pianist and crooner in the style of Bing Crosby. By the mid-1940s Farney was singing for Carlos Machado's orchestra at Rio's Cassino da Urca and performing on various radio programs, including the PRA-9 Rádio Mayrink Veiga show *Ritmos Americanos*.[73] Although Farney was widely praised for both his voice and piano technique, he was not without his critics in Brazil, some of whom were ambivalent about the seemingly imitative style of crooning at which Farney excelled. Much of the debate apparently revolved around exactly which North American singer the suave Brazilian most resembled: Bing Crosby, Ray Eberle, or Frank Sinatra. As early as 1942, *A Cena Muda* columnist Roberto Paulo Taborda questioned the quantity and quality of would-be jazz singers in Brazil and encouraged radio stations to give listeners a respite from the plague of homegrown crooners on the airwaves.[74] Taborda's criticism was not directed personally at Farney, for whom the journalist had nothing but praise. But the spectacle of a Brazilian singer performing a mostly English-language repertoire in a style that clearly emulated North American crooners could not help but unnerve musical nationalists.

Although Farney had made a name for himself in Brazil as a jazz singer, his moderately successful but relatively short-lived career in the United States was launched in response to the resounding impact of his samba-flavored hit "Copacabana" (1946). Once in the US under contract with NBC Radio, though, Farney returned to his straightforward big-band repertoire. The irony of Farney's status as foreign jazz star singing in English was not lost on the North American press. In a piece on the new generation of big-band crooners, *Time Magazine* included a brief profile on the "dark-eyed Brazilian baritone." Though not mentioning Farney's birth name, the article highlighted the singer's foreign origin and accent, and included an idiomatic quote ("I became the Beeng of Braseel") that echoed the pithy self-caricature for which Carmen Miranda had become known in her films and interviews.[75]

The parallels between the "Brazilian troubadour" and the "Brazilian bombshell" were not merely superficial. Whatever lack of critical consensus surrounded Farney's early career in Brazil, his temporary move to the US was met with much the same kind of excitement, anticipation, and—somewhat later—selective embellishment that greeted Miranda earlier in the decade. In an extensive article published in *A Cena Muda*, for example, Ramalho Neto listed off Farney's hit recordings in the US; featured photos of the singer posing with Sinatra, Nat King Cole, and Jimmy Dorsey; and recycled and augmented the "unanimous" praise of the North American press—including the *Time* piece published five years earlier. The piece also notably mythologized the story of Farney's seduction of NBC: "He sat at the piano and sang 'I Don't Know Why.' Since the loudspeakers were on, the music carried all the way to the NBC executive room; they were anxious to know who was the man behind the voice with such a unique *je ne sais quois*." [76]

Notwithstanding *A Cena Muda*'s exultant praise, Farney's star shone only modestly in the Northern firmament, and not for very long. Ramalho Neto's article was published more than three years after the crooner had returned to Brazil, and in a sense it reads like a eulogy disguised as a promulgation of Farney's international fame. In the annals of Brazilian conquests of the international culture industry, the Brazilian Troubadour's celebrity belongs somewhere between the Hollywood actor Olympio Guilherme's poetic obscurity of the late 1920s and early 1930s and Carmen Miranda's meteoric triumph ten years later. Nevertheless, Farney's brief success in the United States bought him a great deal of cultural cachet among a younger generation of jazz listeners interested in more than just Romantic swing ballads. Part of this was due to Farney's formidable talents on the piano, underused in his US big-band recordings but familiar to many Brazilian listeners who remembered his work in smaller formats dating back to the early 1940s.

The West Coast cool jazz sounds of Stan Kenton also captivated a number of aspiring musicians who frequented the club, including such future stars as Paulo Moura, Johnny Alf, João Donato, and Nora Ney, not to mention Farney himself. More than just a collection of jazz fans, then, Sinatra-Farney was a virtual laboratory for the next generation of Brazilian popular music, providing an informal, noncommercial space for jam sessions and a crucial forum for debates on music and culture. The fan club responded to more practical needs as well. It is worth noting that the group also included Cyl Farney (Dick's younger brother) and Carlos Manga, both of whom would go on to enjoy successful film and television careers in the 1950s and 1960s. Manga, one of the Sinatra-Farney founding members, appointed himself the club's "Sinatra imitator" and delighted in re-creating the atmosphere of a smoky American dive bar in the Queirozes' transformed basement. The visiting filmmaker Milton Rodrigues was apparently so impressed with the spectacle he witnessed there, in fact, that he hired Manga to work on one of his films; Manga talked Rodrigues into bringing aboard the Farney brothers as well.[77]

Yet it was in music circles that the Sinatra-Farney Fan Club would leave its most meaningful legacy. In an interview given decades later, pianist João Donato recalled his days at the club with fondness, citing how much he learned from playing and talking with Alf and Farney. The latter impressed Donato with his love of North American music and the extensive jazz record collection he kept in his house in the Santa Teresa neighborhood. In spite of the growing number of jazz enthusiasts in Brazil, Donato notes, many jazz imports were still very difficult to find even in Rio de Janeiro during the 1950s, never mind in remoter areas of the country.[78] Thus it was that the contacts fostered by the Sinatra-Farney Fan Club proved crucial in exposing younger artists like Donato to a wider, deeper, and less commercial swath of music than they would have had access to otherwise.

Farney in particular was a key broker between North American musicians and records (acquired by the singer during his stay in the United States) and Brazilian upstarts who still had relatively little access to either. Whether or not Farney's impact as a singer and musician matched his importance as a cultural icon and mediator is open to debate. He remained an important reference point in Brazilian jazz circles well into the 1960s. Perhaps due to Farney's continued visibility, in a controversial essay first published in 1966 the music critic José Ramos Tinhorão claimed that Farney constituted the nadir of slavish imitation and Americanization in Brazilian popular music. Farney's travel to the United States, he wrote, was the product of "the almost infantile belief that he could make a career for himself [in the US] singing American songs"—which of course he did, for a time. Still not satisfied, Tinhorão also wrote off Farney's return to Brazil on the grounds that the reconstituted crooner simply paid lip service to his national identity "by singing samba-canções imitating Bing in Portuguese in the whispery style of the blues." If the singer received any acclaim at all, it was only because—or so Tinhorão would have us believe—the Brazilian public of the 1950s and 1960s was as "alienated" as Farney.[79]

Much has been made of Tinhorão's aversion to cultural admixtures in Brazilian popular music, starting with Caetano Veloso's caustic denunciation of

Fig. 3.2. Cover of Dick Farney's LP *Jazz* (RGE Records, 1962). A formidable musician and singer and a key bridge between jazz and bossa nova, Dick Farney projected an image of cool elegance that seduced many Brazilian musicians and fans well into the 1960s, while drawing accusations of imitation and cultural alienation from critics such as José Ramos Tinhorão.

the critic in 1966. According to Veloso, the "hysterical" Tinhorão would only be satisfied if Brazil's widespread illiteracy remained intact, ensuring that the nation's only musicians were "authentic paupers singing authentic sambas."[80] Tinhorão's sustained attacks on jazz in many ways were a throwback to Cruz Cordeiro's evisceration of Pixinguinha's "virtual fox-trots" in the early 1930s. Yet his remark about Farney's "whispery" voice deserves somewhat closer scrutiny, and not just because the critic casually misattributed Farney's vocal style to the influence of the blues. José Estevam Gava has observed that whereas popular singers in midcentury Brazil tended to demonstrate their vocal virtuosity, emotion, and sonorous potency, Farney mastered a delivery that was "less dramatic, more relaxed." Gava notes that Farney's antecedents were not just Bing Crosby and Frank Sinatra but also Noel Rosa, Mário Reis, and somewhat later, Lupicínio Rodrigues, all of whom "sang and released records without worrying about sonorous potency, but rather privileged and propitiated intimate vocal inflections, with an almost spoken delivery."[81]

The fact that Gava finds Farney's vocal touchstone in his homeland may or may not be indicative of a desire to protect the singer's legacy from accusations of Americanization. In a certain sense his argument falls into much the same trap as Tinhorão's dismissive "blues" theory, although it seeks to do the opposite: place Farney safely within the domain of *Brazilian* musical tradition. As is often the case, the truth most likely lies somewhere between the two extremes. Farney was a product of the 1930s and early 1940s, a time when a range of local and foreign styles, responding to a complex array of political imperatives, played complementary roles in the invention of Brazilian popular music.[82] Regardless of Farney's intrinsic merits as a singer and performer or the national origins and antecedents of his vocal style, though, it was what he represented to his droves of "alienated" musicians and fans—in addition to the crucial cultural links he facilitated—that would have the greatest impact in the coming years.

Bossa Nova and Jazz

In "Balanço da Bossa Nova," an important essay first published in 1966 in *O Estado de São Paulo*'s literary supplement, Júlio Medaglia attributed the emergence of bossa nova in the late 1950s and early 1960s to a gap in the national musical landscape previously filled by jazz: "The inexistence of 'progressive' Brazilian music," Medaglia wrote, "led young musicians, thirsty for new experiences, to play jazz, since this was the only popular music that gave the musician complete freedom to invent, to improvise, to seek out sonority, harmony, and strange rhythms."[83] Due to already existing affinities between North American

and Brazilian music, Medaglia continued, the transformation of such musicians from obscure jazz fans and players into bossa nova all-stars was a relatively seamless one. Indeed, it was through collaborations and apprenticeships
fostered by the Sinatra-Farney Fan Club that young musicians who shaped
what came to be known as bossa nova—Johnny Alf, João Donato, and Emir
Deodato—established their careers. Although early bossa nova's two central
players, João Gilberto and Antônio Carlos "Tom" Jobim, had not been full-
fledged members of the seminal fan club, many of the performers championed
by the *sinatrafarnistas*—West Coast/cool jazz musicians such as Stan Getz,
Stan Kenton, Gerry Mulligan, Julie London, and Chet Baker—also happened
to be the favored international artists of the founding *bossanovistas*.

If bossa nova's foreign accent was beyond dispute, the problem of what to
call the new music was fraught with ideological tensions and interpersonal
rifts long before the legendary musical collaborations that turned Gilberto and
Jobim into household names abroad. From the beginning, the controversy centered on bossa nova's perceived resemblance to jazz. It did not help that João
Gilberto, whose 1958 recording of Vinícius de Morais and Jobim's composition
"Chega de saudade" heralded the new style, had precious little to say about
the matter. When he did comment on the subject, as he did in an interview in
Folha de São Paulo in the 1980s, he was characteristically unforthcoming, while
arguing against bossa nova as a generic category. What he and the others had
discovered, he said, was simply a new way of playing samba. The bossanovistas
were thus the latest in a long line of Brazilian analogues and borrowings. Whatever debt they owed to jazz also defined earlier Brazilian musicians, Gilberto
suggested, from Pixinguinha to Carmen Miranda.[84]

Bossa's defenders have tended to concur. In an article first published in 1966,
Caetano Veloso acknowledged that Brazilians' "crude imitations" of "the worst
American music" should indeed be considered evidence of cultural alienation.
But this was not the case with the best that bossa nova had to offer. For Veloso,
jazz was "nothing if not an enrichment of [Gilberto's] musical training, a lesson
in other sonic possibilities."[85] In his study *Bim bom*, Walter Garcia likens Gilberto's seeming vacillation with regard to jazz and samba to Mário de Andrade's
polemical stance three decades earlier, at a time when Pixinguinha was accused
of much the same crimes against Brazilian cultural purity. Just as Andrade's response had been to assert that jazz and choro were essentially two manifestations
of the same Afro-American matrix, Garcia argues that the guitarist was justified
in reducing the samba "cadence" to rhythms more akin to swing and cool jazz.
Jazz and samba, Garcia maintains, do not just share historical ties, but are also
bound by the same rhythmic principle of syncopation. Therefore, he writes, "João

Gilberto did not commit a grand heresy in employing jazz rhythmic procedures in stripping down samba's beat: he simply borrowed from a rich cousin."[86]

For all of Gilberto's status as a foundational figure of bossa nova, perhaps a more decisive factor in lending unity to the new music, as Castro has suggested, was the marketing savvy of composer, journalist, and promoter Ronaldo Bôscoli. After the success of the first annual "samba session" hosted in August 1959 by the College of Architecture at the Pontifical Catholic University of Rio de Janeiro (PUC-Rio)—an informal concert modeled after the recent Festival de Jazz at the Teatro Municipal, featuring headliners Gerry Mulligan and Herbie Mann—Bôscoli chose to promote the music of Jobim, Gilberto, and others as bossa nova (roughly, "new way") rather than Brazilian jazz, *sambalanço*, or *samba moderno*.[87] Bôscoli's strategic nomenclature placed the new music expertly but somewhat precariously between samba—with a nationalist-traditionalist connotation of Afro-Brazilian musicians and the morro—and jazz, a music that offered the cachet of modernity but also brought with it the undeniable whiff of foreign influence. Established figures like Ary Barroso, meanwhile, helped to win bossa nova wider acceptance within Brazil in the early 1960s by publicly endorsing the new musicians, going so far as to call Jobim "the greatest Brazilian composer of the last few decades."[88] Even singers as popular as Sílvio Caldas and Nelson Gonçalves, in a series of short interviews in *O Cruzeiro*, had mostly positive things to say about João Gilberto. Gilberto, though, was not nearly as charitable in his assessment of his Brazilian elders.[89]

Even as bossa nova musicians reaped the commercial benefits of their sexy moniker, the name itself was perennially thrown into question, and just as often from within. The lyrics of Carlos Lyra's "Influência do jazz" (1962), for example, openly played with the rhetoric of cultural contamination found in much Brazilian music criticism dating back to the 1920s:

> My poor samba
> It got mixed up
> It went modern
> It got lost
> Where's that sway of the hips?
> It's gone
> Where's that jig that shakes people up
> My poor samba, it changed all of a sudden
> The influence of jazz
>
> It has almost died
> It will end up dying, it's almost dead already

It didn't see
that samba swings from side to side
Jazz is different, back and forth
And samba, half dead, has gotten twisted around
The influence of jazz

It's gotten mixed up with Afro-Cuban [music]
It's going down the drain, yes it is.
It's getting all twisted up, and fast.
It's going, it's fading, it's falling off the swing.

My poor samba
Go back to the morro
And ask for help where you were born
So that you don't end up as a samba with too many notes
So that you don't end up crooked
Back and forth
You're going to have to turn around to free yourself
from the influence of jazz[90]

Lyra's lyrics offer a slightly ironic lament on samba's demise, a pessimism attributed to the corrupting influence not just of jazz but also Afro-Cuban forms. The scholar David Treece has remarked that the song served as a "musically enacted obituary for the traditional samba," and views it as part of Lyra's concerted effort to reaffirm his solidarity with the cultural matrix of the morro, thus "incorporating the technical innovations of the classical bossa nova style within a more socially conscious and critical idiom."[91] Be that as it may, "Influência do jazz" is at least as much a treatise on musical integrity in confronting the menace of jazz as it is an obituary for samba. For Lyra, traditional samba was under siege by the modern commercialism and musical impurities symbolized by jazz. At stake, in other words, was not the survival of samba per se but rather the stability of samba within the Brazilian imaginary.

Lyra's original recording of the song cuts against the almost plaintive tone of his lyrics. Far from being a testament to samba do morro unadulterated by foreign influence, his performance in many ways embodies such impurities, as samba cadences take a back seat to swing and even a hint of Cuban clave. Sardonically yet cheerfully, "Influência do jazz" celebrates in musical terms the very influences the lyrics seem to decry. For a putative protest song, Lyra's recording is highly ambivalent, encapsulating both a disavowal and an acceptance of jazz influence on Brazilian popular music, and particularly on bossa nova. The musician's partial misgivings about bossa nova echoed his rift with Roberto Menescal and Bôscoli. Lyra even coined the term "sambalanço" to distinguish his work from theirs, and hosted a "Sambalanço Night" at PUC-Rio on the same May evening in 1960 that Bôscoli promoted bossa with his "Night of Love, Smiles, and Flowers" at the School of Architecture at the Federal University of Rio de Janeiro (UFRJ).[92]

What makes Lyra's "Influência do jazz" all the more remarkable is that it debuted at the Carnegie Hall bossa nova concert of November 1962, a landmark event that featured performances by Gilberto, Jobim, Sérgio Mendes, and Roberto Menescal, among many others. Interestingly, the song's ambivalent touch anticipated the ways the concert itself would be assessed by many participants, spectators, and critics, even if the latter expressed themselves less with irony than with derision and sarcasm. Probably the most widely commented pan of the concert came from the *New York Times'* John S. Wilson, who berated the "monotonous mush" of the sound system and the inconsistent talent of the singers. Though Wilson praised the playing of guitarist Luis Bonfá and conceded that João Gilberto was "several notches" above the rest of the singers, he lamented that Gilberto' s "extremely intimate style was lost in Carnegie Hall."[93]

Brazilian critical response to the concert was, as Liliana Harb Bollos documents, both extensive and mostly secondhand.[94] The most notorious of the Brazilian reviews was probably *O Cruzeiro*'s, penned by stringer Orlando Suero but apparently based on loose reports by singer Sérgio Ricardo.[95] Declaring the concert "the biggest failure in [the history of] Brazilian music," the magazine emphasized the presence of international dignitaries, politicians, and assorted celebrities. Such an eminent and demanding audience, according to *O Cruzeiro*, witnessed an ostensibly Brazilian spectacle littered with non-Brazilians like Stan Getz and Lalo Schifrin playing non-Brazilian music. If the concert was supposed to present authentic bossa nova—already deemed a dubious representative of national identity—it had failed to accomplish even that. Above all, the article stressed the chaotic organization and amateurish presentation of the young Brazilian lions, "dwarfed by the grandiose stage" of Carnegie.[96]

O Cruzeiro's message was clear enough: the Carnegie show had misrepresented and maligned Brazilian popular culture on an international stage. Whatever its actual shortcomings might have been, though, the concert served as a springboard for the second, international phase of bossa nova's commercial success. Despite having being traumatized by the experience of singing in public for the first time, Roberto Menescal denied the Carnegie concert was a failure, and later claimed that once Brazilian critics had seen televised footage of the spectacle, the fiasco narrative spread by *O Cruzeiro* was thrown into question.[97] And even if the show was somewhat chaotic from an organizational standpoint, it launched the international careers of several of the participating musicians, including Menescal himself, Carlos Lyra, and Sérgio Mendes, and greatly elevated those of others, namely Jobim, Gilberto, and Bonfá. "After all that," Menescal concluded, "how could anyone say it was a failure?"[98]

The Carnegie Hall concert today is generally cited as emblematic of bossa nova's emergence as a global phenomenon. But in fact, the US recording industry and trade press had already taken notice of the movement prior to the performance, as shown by a full-page spread in *Billboard* in October 1962. Under the headline "Is the Bossa Nova the New Twist?," the series of short articles paid particular attention to the recordings of Charlie Byrd, Stan Getz, Herbie Mann, and Dizzy Gillespie. Noting the rapidly expanding radio and television coverage of the "new rhythm," *Billboard* painted a portrait of bossa nova as a Latin style already being quickly assimilated by US jazz artists. The magazine also correctly identified bossa's potential for breakout popular appeal, even if, as one writer noted, it had "no dance yet going for it."[99] Another piece acknowledged the foundational compositions of Jobim and Mendonça, though the writer curiously overlooked the role played by Brazilian musicians such as Gilberto.[100] If the tone of the spread was one of exploitation and fad potential, *Billboard*'s coverage documented the extent to which bossa nova had already established itself as a transnational idiom prior to the Carnegie Hall show and well before the celebrated 1964 *Getz/Gilberto* album.

Brazilian television and popular magazines were also instrumental in generating exposure and sales that led to the music's subsequent "discovery" in New York. Once again, Bôscoli would play a key part in laying the foundation for bossa nova's meteoric rise. As a journalist, he advocated for bossa nova's mainstream acceptance in a series of pieces for the popular magazine *Manchete*. In terms of television, *Dois no balanço* (Two on the Swing) (TV Excelsior, 1962), created by Bôscoli and Luis Carlos Miéle, was one of the most direct expressions of the movement. Bôscoli biographer Denilson Monteiro has characterized the short-lived program as "a Beco das Garrafas show with money," in reference to the alley off Rua Duvivier in Copacabana that served as ground zero for some of the most important bossa nova acts in the late 1950s and early 1960s.[101] Though particularly notable for its adherence to the tenets of the movement, *Dois no balanço* was just one of several Brazilian television programs to bring the bossa nova spectacle out of the bars and auditoriums of Rio de Janeiro and into living rooms across the country. Other shows that heavily featured bossa nova were Jobim's own *O bom Tom* (The Good Tom), which was broadcast on TV Paulista in 1959; *Musical Três Leões* (Three Lions Musical), also on TV

Paulista the same year, which featured regular performances by the likes of João Gilberto and a young Sérgio Mendes; and *Brasil 60*, a relatively ambitious show produced by São Paulo's TV Excelsior featuring live performances by Jobim, Gilberto, and Vinícius de Moraes.[102]

Bossa nova as a concept, meanwhile, would quickly assume extramusical dimensions. By 1960, the term would be picked up by director-screenwriter Victor Lima for a comedy (*Pistoleiro bossa nova*, or Bossa Nova Gunman) satirizing Hollywood Westerns; the plot had virtually nothing to do with the music. Popular Brazilian magazines like *O Cruzeiro* and *Manchete*, in addition to publishing a number of articles on the new music, frequently used bossa nova to describe anything new or unusual, particularly the strikingly modern: thus there were descriptions of "bossa nova judges" and "bossa nova prisons"; a hippopotamus born in the Rio de Janeiro zoo was named Bossa Nova. Advertisers followed suit. New designs in appliances, glasses frames, and shoes were said to be "bossa nova."[103] José Estevam Gava points out that consumerism centered on the musical movement before and after the Carnegie concert capitalized on the perceived eccentricity of the young musicians themselves. The associative connection forged between the term and "funny, ridiculous, or curious" situations drew in large part from the bossanovistas' supposed rupture with the accepted standards of consumption or traditional musical appreciation.[104] In other words, they were "bossa nova" in terms of their notoriety and also their consummate modernity.

As both a musical phenomenon and a cultural emblem of considerable resonance, bossa nova would take on new life through international film and television. Although the production of *Black Orpheus* (dir. Marcel Camus, 1959) very slightly predated the emergence of bossa nova, the film's Jobim-Moraes hits "O nosso amor" and "Felicidade" introduced a large international public to the duo's compositional style. Not only did *Orpheus* usher in newfound enthusiasm for things Brazilian in North America, Europe, and elsewhere, but the film's deft combination of high production values and on-location footage shot in Rio de Janeiro during Carnival also paved the way for the 1962 international production *Copacabana Palace* (The Girl Game). Directed by Steno (Stefano Vanzina), one of Italy's leading comedic directors, this film provides audiovisual documentation of a musical movement now in full bloom, featuring on-screen musical performances and minor acting roles by Jobim, Luis Bonfá, Gilberto, and the vocal group Os Cariocas in addition to a rendition of Jobim's "Samba do Avião" played during the opening credits. In case it were ever in doubt, Steno makes explicit his debt to *Black Orpheus* when one of the

Italian characters refers to Jobim as "that famous musician who composed the score to *Black Orpheus*."

With its focus on Rio's middle- and upper-class beach neighborhoods rather than on the city's largely Afro-Brazilian favelas, *Copacabana Palace* was a quintessentially bossa nova film in key ways that *Black Orpheus* was not. That Steno's Brazilian characters, reduced to minor roles, were white musicians closely associated with the movement lent the Italian film a racially skewed, revue quality similar in certain ways to Universal's *The King of Jazz* some thirty years earlier. In Camus's film, the music of Jobim, Moraes, and Bonfá was either played nondiegetically or interpreted on-screen by Afro-Brazilians. In *Copacabana Palace*, by contrast, there was virtually no attempt to foreground black or poor Brazilians' contributions to Rio's urban milieu other than as bikini-clad bodies or carnival dancers. Perhaps precisely because of Steno's emphasis on the frivolous escapades of European social elites, the Italian film did not have nearly the international impact of its celebrated predecessor.[105] It would be the last time during the period that foreign filmmakers would make a concerted attempt to cash in on bossa nova's trendy cachet.[106]

If cinema failed to fully capture the cultural significance of bossa nova, commercial television was another story. By the end of 1963, the venerable *Ed Sullivan Show* had showcased not just novelty dance acts such as Xavier Cugat's performance of "Blame it on the Bossa Nova" (with vocals by Eydie Gormé) but also the instrumental group Bossa Três (originally Samba Três)— "discovered" by a CBS producer at Rio's Bon Gourmet night club and flown to New York for the occasion.[107] But it was Astrud Gilberto's appearance on US television in 1964 in support of the landmark *Getz/Gilberto* album that would most emphatically put an international face on bossa nova. Initially, Astrud was not supposed to have appeared on the record. Her insistence on contributing vocals during the 1963 recording sessions convinced producer Creed Taylor and eventually her husband that a woman's voice, singing in English, was not a bad idea. Meanwhile, pressured by Taylor to reduce the length of the songs for commercial purposes, João Gilberto was essentially demoted to the auxiliary role of musical accompanist and secondary singer. Indeed, his Portuguese rendering of "Garota de Ipanema" was initially removed from the record for this very reason.[108]

The partial eclipse of João Gilberto in *Getz/Gilberto* pushed into the limelight the jazz specter always lurking in bossa nova. Even more significantly, Taylor's calculating shift in emphasis sent a message to non-Brazilian audiences that bossa nova was in some sense tribute music, or at best a novel adaptation of cool jazz. This impression was compounded by numerous US television appearances from 1964 onward, most of which took place after João Gilberto's estrangement from Astrud. The suppression of João Gilberto as the "inventor" and "father" of bossa nova—words routinely used to describe him in the Brazilian press—now made Astrud and Getz the headliners. The smashing commercial success of "The Girl from Ipanema" in effect turned Astrud into a personification of the song's inspiration, to the extent that television hosts of the period routinely introduced her as such even when she performed other songs.[109]

Like most of the performers associated internationally with Brazilian jazz, jazz-samba, and bossa nova, Astrud Gilberto also happened to be white. That she ultimately served as a kind of poster girl of bossa nova abroad intensified the contentious links between jazz, race, and nationalism foreshadowed by the Sinatra-Farney Fan Club in the late 1940s and early 1950s. Not surprisingly, one of bossa nova's most vociferous critics proved to be the same one who had mocked Dick Farney: José Ramos Tinhorão. In one of two essays first published in a special 1963 volume of the magazine *Senhor*, Tinhorão acerbically disparaged the bossanovistas as sellouts and cultural traitors. Framing his diatribe in the language of parentage and consanguinity, Tinhorão asserted that the mother of the "bastard daughter" was jazz itself. Having finally acknowledged having given birth to the "bossa half-breed," he wrote, jazz (and the US music industry for which it supposedly stood) had now decided to bequeath to the young Brazilian musicians a fabulous inheritance in royalties. On the pretext of deciding who the true father of the movement was, Tinhorão listed the leading suspects, highlighting their supposedly Americanized traits and other signs of cultural contamination: Johnny Alf was a "Brazilian mulatto with an American name." Vinícius de Moraes, "unknown" until his emergence as a bossa nova lyricist (a statement that was patently false, since Moraes was already a renowned poet in the 1940s), was pilloried for having written a single fox-trot in 1933 that "imitates North American rhythms." João Gilberto, Tinhorão wrote, would soon become a US citizen. Baden Powell, another turncoat, was further impugned for his name, "which comes from his father's alienated admiration" for British imperialism. And even Ronaldo Bôscoli, though lacking a Yankee address and moniker, was nevertheless held responsible for the "failure" of the Carnegie Hall show.[110]

Perhaps because the underlying irony of "Influência do jazz" simply fell beyond Tinhorão's grasp, the only figure mentioned in a relatively neutral light was Carlos Lyra. Meanwhile, the music critic insisted on dropping another name—Laurindo de Almeida—not normally associated with bossa nova. For

Tinhorão it was enough that Almeida was an "Americanized" musician who had spent the previous fifteen years in the United States playing with jazz musicians like Bud Shank, thus betraying his country at the same time that he violated the purity of samba. Like Carmen Miranda before him, it would seem, Almeida was a bossanovista avant la lettre. Yet even Tinhorão's suggestion of Almeida's tainted "paternity" served as a pretext to quote Almeida in English, which—Tinhorão reminded his readers—was "now his adopted language," as if *Down Beat* were expected to print its interview of the musician in Portuguese. In the end, Tinhorão refused to give any single man credit for siring the "bossa half-breed." "Everything that is bossa nova," he concluded, "whether it is Johnny Alf or Bud Shank, is American."[111]

In comparing the bossanovistas to mixed-race "bastards" from the *favela*, Tinhorão's essay exhibited casual racism that reached its nadir in another article from the same issue, "Bossa de exportação." Here the critic weighed in on the supposed fiasco of the Carnegie Hall concert, aiming his ire at what he considered the inappropriate appearance of the Afro-Brazilian singer and guitarist Bola Sete. "Physically . . . not so different from a gorilla," Tinhorão wrote, Bola Sete "monkeyed around" with his guitar in a way that "transformed Carnegie Hall for the first time in its history into a veritable 'zoo.'"[112] Tinhorão's two diatribes met with a great deal of criticism within Brazil, beginning with a terse rejoinder by editor Reynaldo Jardim in the same volume of *Senhor*.[113] In spite of the racist overtones of Tinhorão's comments, his objection to jazz was based largely on ham-handed nationalism: Afro-Brazilians were "gorillas" and "half-breeds" only when they strayed from what Tinhorão considered to be the correct parameters of Brazilian vernacular music. Perhaps the greatest irony of Tinhorão's posture was that it cost him an opportunity to more effectively interrogate bossa nova's defenders on legitimate grounds— namely, transnational racial politics, class privilege, and commercialism.

The touchy question of race would be thrust even more firmly into the limelight once bossa nova's foundational figures had settled abroad following the Carnegie Hall concert. The exodus, as we have seen, undermined the unsubstantiated claim by Tinhorão and others that the concert had been a monumental failure and therefore a national embarrassment. As one might have expected, though, bossa's success abroad also came with a price back home. Even before the Carnegie concert, a rift had been growing among bossanovistas, with some of the original group (Nara Leão, Carlos Lyra, Vinícius de Moraes) seeking to politicize music they felt had begun to drift into technical formula and lyrical banality. Lyra was the main dissident early on. His objective, he wrote later, was simple: "to take bossa nova to the streets and, above all, to bring the music of the people (Zé Keti, Cartola, Nelson Cavaquinho, João do Vale) to the middle class."[114] By 1963, the center of the controversy was Leão, the erstwhile muse of the movement, whose ocean-view apartment in Copacabana had served as one of the hubs of late-1950s musical creativity. In a highly charged essay-manifesto published in *O Cruzeiro*, Leão overtly and unapologetically renounced her role as kindly hostess and muse. Although she conceded that bossa nova had rescued Brazil from the tyranny of syrupy boleros and big-band jazz, she questioned those who had overused the lexicon of flowers and little birds in the pursuit of "pretty, pointless songs"—a clear allusion to João Gilberto's 1960 Odeon LP *O amor, o sorriso e o flor*. If the first generation of bossanovistas had made "samba for white people," Leão wrote, then it was time to bring the music back to its roots through collaborations with authentic Afro-Brazilian sambistas like Kéti and Cavaquinho. Leão left little doubt that one of the main culprits in bossa nova's current decadence was jazz. Specifically, she pointed the finger at singers and musicians whose foreign embellishments and affectations had revealed a "false notion" of Brazilian music, "performed in the name of modernism, which amounts to nothing more than a bad imitation of jazz from thirty years ago."[115]

Leão's first two LPs, *Nara* (1963) and *Opinião de Nara* (1964), added muscle to the new political wing of bossa nova. Striking a daring yet precarious balance between Zona Sul refinement and samba do morro, the records paved the way for subsequent recordings by Baden Powell, Vinícius de Moraes, and others. The polemics of politically engaged *participação* and race was raised another notch in a 1965 debate between Tinhorão, Luiz Carlos Vinhas, and Edu Lobo published in *Revista Civilização Brasileira*. Tinhorão had softened his stance very slightly since the aftermath of the Carnegie concert, going so far as to suggest that Nara Leão had saved samba from "alienated" bossanovistas like Jobim.[116] Ultimately, though, he found the political engagement of Nara Leão, Vinícius de Moraes, and Carlos Lyra futile, since the consumer costs of the music industry (record players, radios, televisions, and so forth) primarily served the upper classes in Brazil. "What the so-called participação movement proposes," he said, "is to speak nationalistically about national topics, [but] without renouncing its [American] accent."[117]

Although this last point of Tinhorão's was valid enough, he clearly lost an exchange with Edu Lobo on the subject of authenticity. Ever susceptible to making pithy declarative statements, Tinhorão asserted that the authenticity of Brazilian popular music consisted of a "conscious preoccupation with assimilating and incorporating ... rhythms, styles, and harmonies from foreign songs." Yet he quickly fell into his own trap when he conceded that Brazilian popular music had "always suffered foreign influence." The difference in the past, he argued, was that the "old choro bands" played waltzes and polkas in a way that "ended up giving them a Brazilian accent." Pixinguinha, then, was beyond reproach. But couldn't the same be said about bossa nova? Rather than countering Tinhorão from this angle, Lobo questioned the very validity of the term authenticity. "To present as negative the fact that bossa nova was influenced by jazz is comical," Lobo said, "because we must remember that samba bears an African influence. And thus we end up in chaos, without proving the authenticity of any music. So why should we bother saying one is authentic and the other isn't?"[118]

Despite the more famous recordings of such figures as Charlie Byrd, Stan Getz, and Frank Sinatra, it was black jazz musicians and singers like Billy Eckstine, Nat "King" Cole, Dizzy Gillespie, Sarah Vaughan, and Lena Horne who first took serious notice of bossa nova outside of Brazil. While performing in 1960 at the Copacabana Palace, Horne covered Gilberto's minor hit "Bim Bom," arranging to meet the innovative singer in her suite after the show.[119] Gillespie, meanwhile, followed up a visit to Brazil by recording "Desafinado" and "Chega de saudade" with his quintet in May 1962, the same month as the release of Getz and Charlie Byrd's *Jazz Samba* and several months before the Carnegie show; Gillespie later claimed that his were the first bossa nova pieces recorded in the United States.[120] Once the first wave of bossa took hold in the US, African American musicians seemed keen on staking a claim to the discovery of the Brazilian music and underscored bossa's Afro-Brazilian pedigree. In a 1962 interview with *Jet* magazine, jazz arranger and producer Quincy Jones, who had accompanied Gillespie to Rio de Janeiro, predicted the "Negro-created Brazilian rhythm" would soon take North America by storm.[121] In a 1964 profile of Dizzy Gillespie in *Ebony*, Allan Morrison wrote that Gillespie "grasped the beauty and vigor of the Brazilian *bossa nova* long before it became a fad."[122]

The recordings that garnered the most attention in both the United States and Brazil, though, were the collaborations between Gilberto, Getz, and Jobim, and later Jobim and Sinatra. The latter served as a bookend to classical bossa nova but also as a culmination to the productive cycle of North-South musical exchange initiated in Brazil by the Sinatra-Farney Fan Club. The Sinatra-Jobim sessions yielded tame pop recordings at a time when the airwaves and recording studios in Brazil and the US were trending toward the stridency and political and aesthetic radicalism of rock, soul, jazz fusion, and funk. In this sense, *Francis Albert Sinatra & Antonio Carlos Jobim* (1967) and to a lesser extent the later *Sinatra & Company* (1971) marked the end of an era. Even more so than the Getz-Gilberto collaborations, the Sinatra-Jobim recordings emphasized the asymmetrical nature of the jazz–bossa nova marriage.[123] Although the compositions were mostly Jobim's, the sessions were dominated by Sinatra's unique voice, rhythm, and musicality. The NBC-televised performances of some of the material recorded on the first LP revealed Jobim's delicate sensibility as a sideman, even if his sometimes frail singing voice and dubious pitch fell far short of matching Sinatra.[124] The taped performances also made clear who was in charge of the show. Indeed, the fact that Jobim had agreed to play the guitar (and not his true instrument, the piano) in the first place indicated the extent to which Sinatra and his handlers had dictated the terms of the collaboration: Jobim, as a Brazilian, needed to fill the stereotypical role of the Latin American musician in order for Sinatra to shine and the record to sell.

The slick elegance of the Sinatra-Jobim sessions laid bare the extent to which the artists had pared back the "Negro-created rhythms" that underlay Jobim's compositions and the hotter sound of Sinatra's earlier swing recordings. In this sense the sessions were emblematic of larger trends that characterized "adult" musical production of both nations in the mid- to late 1960s, a body of work that stood in contrast to the youth-oriented appeal of rock and related forms, including Tropicália in Brazil. The Brazilian proponents of commercial bossa nova largely turned their backs on the sonic experiments of such artists as Luiz Eça's Tamba Trio, not to mention the socially engaged work of Nara Leão, Baden Powell, and even Vinícius de Moraes. For a number of bossanovistas, the bossa-cool milestones of the 1960s were a kind of transhemispheric wish fulfillment, the culmination of the recognition and collaboration of some of the very US performers (Sinatra, Dave Brubeck, Charlie Byrd, Gerry Mulligan, and so forth) whose records the Brazilians had listened to and admired during their formative, Sinatra-Farney years.

At the same time, the commercial success of Jobim and the two Gilbertos effectively contributed to the whitening of jazz on the international stage. Given bossa's considerable debt to Afro-diasporic rhythms and instrumentation, this came as no slight irony. Backed by record executives, US jazz musicians saw in bossa nova an opportunity to enliven their music melodically, harmonically, and rhythmically. They also sought to bolster their careers at a time when rock and soul had displaced jazz and related forms such as mambo. This embrace of bossa nova allowed a more commercially viable wing of the jazz world to distance itself from the more challenging sounds of hard bop, progressive, and free jazz—especially as the latter, in particular, was increasingly associated with the political radicalism of Black Power. The fact that the most prominent bossa nova singers and musicians arrived on the shores of North America clean-cut and well-behaved (not to mention relatively fair-skinned) gave the industry the unthreatening Latin infusion it needed.

A Bossa Postmortem

Originally identified with bossa nova and jazz, artists such as Sérgio Mendes, Marcos Valle, João Donato, and Eumir Deodato began branching off in the mid- to late 1960s into areas that transcended generic boundaries. Part of the drift toward other musical pastures was because jazz had lost its status as a countercultural force to the loud, youthful rebellion of rock. In the early 1950s, as I have suggested, the reactionary position of many Brazilian critics inadvertently lent jazz oppositional capital the music might not have enjoyed otherwise in the eyes of younger fans and musicians. By the mid-1960s, most new jazz recordings in the United States had come to be considered prestige records, a turn that explained Verve's successful marketing of the Getz-Gilberto sessions as pop recordings. In Brazil, jazz's long-standing status as an emblem of cultural hegemony masked the music's slow demise. Around the same time that rock began to supplant jazz as the United States' predominant musical export, with a major assist from British groups like the Beatles and the Rolling Stones, Música Popular Brasileira (MPB) was emerging as a new cultural force in Brazil. Responding musically to the first phase of the military dictatorship (1964–68), without either paying obligatory tribute to samba or bearing the "excessive influence" of jazz, MPB initially did not constitute a wholesale substitute so much as it did a new, nationalist incarnation of bossa nova.[125]

Tropicália (or Tropicalismo, as it is also referred to) was the first popular movement to explicitly invoke Brazilian modernism as a creative model. Brazenly contesting the conservative rhetoric of influence, Caetano Veloso and other proponents of the movement used a multimedia attack, articulating their project though the printed word, painting, sculpture, performance art, televised spectacle, and finally through recordings and live performances that freely (and often playfully) drew from a diverse array of sources—from Louis Armstrong, Carmen Miranda, and Villa-Lobos to Afro-Cuban idioms, psychedelic rock, and bossa nova itself. The *tropicalistas* were not the only 1960s intellectuals to milk the sacred cows of the historical avant-garde. In their 1965 *O Senhor* debate, both Tinhorão and Edu Lobo cited Mário de Andrade to justify their positions. Lobo was the first to strike, quoting from Andrade's seminal "Ensaio sobre a música brasileira": "The reaction against what is foreign should be done cunningly through deformation or adaptation, not through repulsion," he wrote. "The artist shouldn't be exclusivist or unilateral." Tinhorão countered with his own quote from the same essay: "Anyone who creates international or foreign art, if he's not a genius, is useless, a nobody."[126] Bossa nova was thus labeled both a corrupting nemesis and an exemplar of musical nationalism, at once a useless copier and cunning adapter of jazz.

Writing for *O Estado de São Paulo*'s literary supplement the following year, Júlio Medaglia used Oswald de Andrade's complex, multilayered "Manifesto Antropófago" (1928) to resolve bossa nova's seeming contradictions. Medaglia argued that bossa nova constituted a new cultural practice by cannibalizing foreign influences such as jazz, "digesting and applying them creatively" instead of merely imitating them. His positive assessment of bossa's cultural value was more nuanced than Edu Lobo's. Medaglia stressed that the slow assimilation of influences, as opposed to a violent deformation, was bound not to *seem* to render a legitimately Brazilian product. Instead, brasilidade in musical and cultural terms was something that emerged a posteriori rather than a priori. Bossa nova therefore should be seen as a kind of precursor to Tropicália, one that actually "provoked the nationalization of Brazilian musical interests" by "reviving and reformulating" foreign and national influences and in so doing redefined what it was to be Brazilian.[127]

In spite of its impact on Lobo, Medalgia, and *tropicalistas* like Veloso, bossa nova largely failed to achieve deep resonance among Brazilian writers and intellectuals during the heady years of the 1960s and 1970s. This was partly due to the style's co-optation by global capitalism. But it certainly did not help that in spite of the efforts of Lyra, Leão, and others bossa nova as a musical idiom never managed to embody a cohesive national project based on liberatory ideals—an issue that acquired more urgency after the military dictatorship hardened its grip at the end of the 1960s.

The music's political insolvency is brilliantly revealed in Sérgio Sant'Anna's fictional work "O concerto de João Gilberto no Rio de Janeiro" (1982). Due to his notoriously high acoustic standards, Sant'Anna's Gilberto cancels a concert planned for a large venue in Rio. To fill the void, the narrator-journalist assigned to cover the event resorts to satirical flights of fancy emphasizing the singer's eccentric views, minimalist habits, and general megalomania. Upon his arrival in Rio from New York, Gilberto carries an empty cage (a gift to him from the composer John Cage) in which he places a "Bird of Perfection" (an *urubu*, or vulture) with which he has communicated in Morse code through the window of the airplane.[128] At the end of the story, frustrated by false leads and desperate for a denouement, Sant'Anna's journalist imagines a triumphant concert at Maracanã stadium by none other than Frank Sinatra. When the Dove of the

Holy Spirit and Cage's Bird of Perfection decide that Sinatra's time on earth is over, they dispense with the American crooner and summon Gilberto from the audience to take his place. Finally on stage, the fictional Gilberto leads the crowd through a rousing version of Ary Barroso's samba anthem "Aquarela do Brasil."

The fanciful ending reads like a tongue-in-cheek resolution to decades of fierce debate in the aural sphere, with Brazil finally winning the battle of musical nationalisms by vanquishing the foreign conqueror. But the truth was not so simple. Sant'Anna's depiction of Gilberto immersed in the self-indulgent trappings of international celebrity and utterly divorced from the national stage, much less political activism, accurately reveals an artist sectored off from the popular Afro-Brazilian culture that informs his music. While Gilberto was not the only bossa nova star to achieve iconic status in Brazil, his global stature, prickly public persona, and reclusive tendencies made him a ripe target for literary parody. Still, his musical legacy in Brazil and abroad was surely nothing to laugh at. As Veloso has argued, despite all the "lessons [Gilberto] learned" from jazz, the bossa pioneer was ultimately not a jazz performer.[129] This may be so. But even the "alienated" version of bossa nova epitomized by Gilberto and Jobim, later disowned by Leão and Lyra and mocked by Sant'Anna, played a central role in the latinization and globalization of jazz through its introduction of Afro-Brazilian rhythms into the repertoire. Jobim's major compositions— "Garota de Ipanema," "Insensatez," "Corcovado," "Wave"—quickly became jazz standards and remain so well into the twenty-first century. Given Brazil's long-standing anxiety about Americanization, it may have been simply too much to ask bossanovistas to identify themselves as jazz musicians. Yet in the greater Caribbean, a new generation of performers emerged after the Second World War whose complex, intimate ties with the United States would further challenge assumptions about jazz and its putative debt to Latin America.

4

The Hazards of Hybridity
Afro-Cuban Jazz, Mambo, and Revolution

¿Dónde comienza el jazz? ¿Dónde termina el mambo?
— NATALIO GALÁN, *Cuba y sus sones* (1983)

Music critics and historians from the United States, Europe, and Latin America have frequently treated postwar Afro-Cuban jazz and mambo as two sides of the same coin: the first as music that layered swing and later bebop harmonics and melodies with the complexity of Afro-Caribbean rhythms; the second as an essentially Cuban form that drew heavily from the big-band tonality and aggressive syncopation of jazz arrangers and bandleaders like Stan Kenton. Such distinctions have frequently typecast mambo as *música bailable*, or "danceable music." This was especially true as swing and big-band jazz lost popularity after World War II, with jazz itself increasingly associated with smaller ensembles and sedentary audiences. In a 1954 interview by *Down Beat*'s Nat Hentoff, for example, Tito Puente noted the emphasis in mambo of rhythm over harmonics. "The mambo itself," he said, "is basically a rhythm from Africa." The music's percussive force made mambo attractive to new styles such as bebop, which, Puente notes, sought to complement its harmonic strengths with the rhythmic sophistication of Afro-Cuban music. Yet the *timbalero* and bandleader goes on to remark that the syncopation common to mambo allied it more with jazz than rumba. If it was dance music, mambo was closer to jazz than were previously popular genres of música bailable.[1]

Puente's generic distinctions sum up what many other musicians, journalists, and jazz historians have written since mambo and Afro-Cuban jazz took shape amid a diverse miasma of musical idioms in the 1930s and 1940s. Jazz had benefited from the contact and influence of Afro-Cuban music since the first decades of the twentieth century—a testament to the vitality of Cuban popular music and the geographic proximity of the island to the United States. In some ways, such intimacy lent Cuba certain advantages over other Latin American countries. The nation was one of the first in the world to develop a viable radio industry, for example, and by the early 1930s dozens of stations across the island broadcast son, guajira, guaracha, and rumba to listeners of different social classes.[2] The very acuteness of economic and political ties with the United States during the 1930s, 1940s, and 1950s, though, left other Cuban cultural institutions, such as cinema and the recording industry, relatively impoverished when compared to some of the country's neighbors. Consequently, the island nation lacked the ability to channel its formidable musical acumen into pedagogical narratives of national identity of the sort cultivated by Mexico, Brazil, and Argentina during the same period.[3]

Although the United States cast an ominous shadow over the region in the early twentieth century, countervailing historical forces also shaped the remarkable mobility and adaptability of Afro-Caribbean musical expression, binding Cuban bodies and sounds to the whole region, as historian Lara Putnam has shown.[4] Together, Cuba's institutional handicaps and wayfaring acumen led many of the island's musicians to engage in international freelancing. By the 1930s, bandleaders, arrangers, and composers such as Xavier Cugat and Don Azpiazu were already making their mark on swing orchestras with their commercial adaptations of rumba and through compositions like Azpiazu's "El manisero" (The Peanut Vendor), destined to be a jazz standard for decades to come. Yet it was not until the mid-1940s, by which time bandleaders like Frank "Machito" Grillo and Arsenio Rodríguez and instrumentalists such as Mario Bauzá had begun to vigorously incorporate jazz elements into their New York–based *conjuntos*, when the jazz-Cuban fusion shifted into a different gear—the threshold, critic Gary Giddins writes, between "prewar Amero-Cuban pop and postwar Afro-Cuban jazz."[5] As I argue in this chapter, it took the arrival of two exceptional Cubans—percussionist Luciano "Chano" Pozo and bandleader Dámaso Pérez Prado—to induce the birth of what later came to be known as Latin jazz.

In the span of just over a year, Chano Pozo lent virtuoso chops and compositional creativity to Dizzy Gillespie's big-band ensemble. In so doing, the multitalented *conguero* changed the landscape of jazz forever by injecting the music with a rhythmic complexity it had rarely known before. The dynamic couplings that Pozo and Gillespie sparked initially provoked a great deal of resistance from US as well as Latin American music critics. At first sensationalized by US critics and musicians as an eccentric, primitive spectacle, 1940s big-band bebop sometimes found itself characterized as a Latin-tinged affair, which in many ways it was. Such depictions persisted as long as bebop could be safely written off as a flash in the pan. In time, though, as Parker and Gillespie's small-format innovations also proved to be seminal, central contributions to jazz, North American critics and historians tended to relegate the early Gillespie-Pozo collaborations to the status of a meaningful if fleeting sidebar and ethnic curiosity.

In a different but analogous way, the "American-tinged" qualities of mambo initially provoked considerable ambivalence among Latin American critics. Though the style was predominantly developed in Havana and New York City, the Mexican film industry quickly recognized mambo's commercial and symbolic potential, and featured Pérez Prado in a number of pictures beginning in the early 1950s. Rather than branding the music as an ominous sign of yanqui imperialism, the mambo comedies and melodramas performed a nifty balancing act—casting mambo as a modern if variably dangerous force through which normative Mexican and Latin American identities could be forged. In the same manner that bebop was ultimately integrated into the jazz canon disencumbered of its Afro-Cuban beginnings, so too was mambo rendered somewhat artificially into purely Latin music.

Why exactly did Cubop and mambo provoke such conservative responses from different coordinates of the Greater Caribbean? As we have seen, music critics since the 1920s had often fallen into the trap of celebrating jazz as an originary hybrid practice. In the interwar period, this apparently ecumenical take on the music's origins disguised a tendency to reduce jazz to an exclusive marriage of "sophisticated" European harmony and instrumentation and "intuitive" African rhythmic sensibility. As Deborah Pacini Hernandez has suggested, the dismissal of the Afro-Caribbean and other transnational modalities of jazz in the early twentieth century hinged in part on "bipolar racial imaginaries and hierarchies" prevalent in the US music industry.[6] Much the same was true for Cuban music criticism. Beginning in the 1920s, many Cuban intellectuals began to embrace danzón, son, and rumba as desirable Creole expressions, and also to defend them from the "contamination" of jazz at a time when the sounds of Whiteman, Baker, and Armstrong rang out insistently in Havana nightclubs and radio broadcasts, often blending with Cuban styles.[7]

In short, whenever newly consecrated musical amalgamations threatened to undergo major reconfigurations through global circulation and contact, cultural nationalists intervened to winnow the chaff of the exogenous from the grain of the nation. The critical disavowal of transnational hybridities characterized musical discourse on all sides of the Caribbean through much of the first half of the twentieth century, revealing the inherently reductive and even parochial basis of such positions. Literary scholar Joshua Lund's writing on the subject is particularly useful in this regard. Taking issue with what he considers to be a disregard for biopolitics undermining certain theories of cultural mixing in Latin America, Lund argues that state-sponsored hybrid projects such as mestizo nationalism have invariably mirrored the racial logic of "pure" genre, "which depends on [the] very exceptionalism [of hybridity] to maintain its legitimacy."[8] Discourses of cultural hybridity, in other words, have frequently and unwisely patterned themselves after the generic racial or national matrix on which they have depended historically, in effect protecting hallowed hybrids from new waves of hybridization.

The brave new world of Afro-Cuban jazz heralded by Bauzá, Machito, Pozo, Pérez Prado, and others would eventually receive wide critical acceptance and popular exposure. Nonetheless, Cuba's major role in jazz in the last half of the twentieth century remained paradoxical. The island nation continued to serve as a vital source of musical capital and jazz talent. As I will discuss in the second half of this chapter, this was true even after 1959, when a number of Cuban musicians remained absolutely central players in what became known as Latin jazz. At a time when the complex cultural politics of the Castro regime initially discouraged the jazz label in public discourse on ideological grounds, the informal jam sessions and formal institutional settings of Havana in the 1960s served as a fecund matrix of Cuban musicianship, launching the careers of such innovators as Arturo Sandoval, Gonzalo Rubalcaba, and the fusion band Irakere. The general reluctance of the revolution to acknowledge the yanqui provenance of Afro-Cuban jazz reflected not just anti-imperialist sentiment but also the persistence of generic biopolitical thinking that had initially greeted Cubop and mambo. In large part due to the stringency of a regime eager to police foreignizing nomenclature and the wayward transnational impulses of the island's cultural production, the new generation of Cuban musicians, composers, and critics were for many years unwilling or unable to claim their rightful place in jazz history.

Chano Pozo and the Inconvenience of *Cubanía*

Raised in hardscrabble tenement housing in Cayo Hueso, Luciano Pozo González (b. 1915) was a star in Cuba long before he moved abroad and sparked a musical revolution. Discovered, befriended, and by some accounts protected by the renowned singer Rita Montaner, Chano Pozo quickly established himself as an unusually talented *tamborero* (Afro-Caribbean drummer), dancer, and songwriter.[9] Besides Montaner, Pozo crossed paths with a number of famous Cuban figures early in his career. Most notable was the singer Miguelito Valdés, whom Pozo had known since their childhood together in Cayo Hueso and who introduced Pozo's signature songs "Blen blen" and "Parampampín" to a larger public through a stint with the prestigious Orquesta Casino de la Playa. Through his work in radio and on stage, Pozo also became acquainted with the trumpeter Félix Chappotín, sometimes called the "Cuban Louis Armstrong," and Mongo Santamaría, with whom Pozo performed at the Tropicana in the spectacle *Conga Pantera*, an odd marriage of Russian ballet and Afro-Cuban percussion in which Pozo and a young Santamaría played the roles of African tribesmen.[10] With the financial help and encouragement of such talented and influential figures, Pozo soon founded his own group, the Conjunto Azul, a new forum for his staggering virtuosity on the congas and at the same time a springboard for his popular compositions.[11]

Although Chano Pozo specialized at the time in rumba and son montuno, he also performed with the Havana Casino jazz band and as a soloist in Mario Santana's jazz quartet. For music historian Leonardo Acosta, this was a sign that the percussionist had already begun to adapt his skills to the jazz format before his later work with Machito and Dizzy Gillespie.[12] The most crucial contact Pozo made in Havana, however, was trumpeter Mario Bauzá, already a veteran of the New York swing scene, having played with the orchestras of Chip Webb and Cab Calloway. On a brief visit to Havana from Miami with Machito and His Afro-Cubans, Bauzá recommended that Pozo too come try his luck in New York. Eager to expand his musical horizons and his renown, Pozo listened. Within months of the tamborero's arrival in May 1946, Bauzá, at the insistence of Valdés, had put Pozo in touch with Dizzy Gillespie, assuring the bebopper that the Cuban percussionist was the missing piece for which he had been looking for years.[13] Between his first, spectacular collaboration with Gillespie and his big band at a Carnegie Hall concert in September 1947, and his death by gunshot at the hands of a petty drug dealer in December 1948, Pozo played in a number of landmark live shows with Gillespie and others. He made a central contribution with a series of seminal Afro-Cuban jazz recordings—including

"Cubano Be, Cubano Bop" (co-authored with Gillespie and George Russell), and his own "Manteca."

In his 1950 essay "Saba, samba y *bop*," the Cuban music historian Fernando Ortiz praised Pozo as a crucial link between Afro-Cuban traditions and North American jazz. By the early 1940s, Ortiz wrote, jazz music had won a hard-fought battle for recognition by metropolitan intellectuals. Then, just as jazz had achieved the status of a sophisticated art form, bebop arrived on the scene to complicate matters. As though it had been "possessed by spirits," in other words, jazz was "impetuously invaded by a new African freneticism." In his essay, Ortiz took pains to attribute the renovation of jazz to an infusion of Afro-Cuban musicality—a sensibility closer to the "undeniable African-ness" at the heart of jazz. Bebop, Ortiz contended, drew heavily from the polyrhythmic approach and stylistic explosiveness introduced by Pozo, as first-rate North American musicians such as Gillespie and Charlie Parker borrowed the unique technical skills of the Afro-Cubans to drive forward and complement their new, ambitious notions of harmony, tone, and velocity.[14]

Ortiz's pronouncement should not be read simply as wishful cultural nationalism. In fact, in casting Pozo as the key protagonist in Cuba's contributions to bop innovation, Ortiz drew extensively from Marshall W. Stearns's influential essay, "Rebop, bebop and bop," published in *Harper's Magazine* earlier the same year. In his article, Stearns took issue with Louis Armstrong's criticism that bebop offered "no beat to dance to" by arguing that bebop's rhythmic complexity was in fact its most valuable innovation. Moreover, Stearns wrote, bebop "went back to the good African earth for rhythmic inspiration" when Gillespie hired Chano Pozo.[15] Ortiz, though, put a patriotic spin on Stearns's assessment. Although agreeing that Pozo "was a revolutionary among jazz percussionists [who] infused North American jazz with a new and vigorous rhythmic energy," Ortiz ultimately stressed the tamborero's national profile as the latest in a line of Afro-Cuban musicians, many of them anonymous or unheralded, to plant the seed of change in metropolitan music industries. "Not only did Chano's ancestors speak through his drum; so did all of Cuba," Ortiz wrote. "We should remember his name so that it is not lost like so many anonymous artists who over the centuries have sustained the art of music with their genuine *cubanía* (Cuban-ness).[16]

Another prominent figure who clearly recognized Pozo's decisive impact on jazz and Cuban music, though from a substantively and culturally distinct perspective, was Gillespie. The trailblazing trumpeter considered Pozo central enough to his own career to devote the greater part of an entire chapter to the tamborero in *To Be, or Not . . . to Bop* (1979). Sensitive to accusations that he had simply co-opted Chano's novel rhythmic ideas and compositions, Gillespie was quick to note that he had transformed them with his own notions of structure and harmony. "Anytime you hear something that Chano and I wrote, that we were collaborators on, I didn't just gorilla myself in it, I contributed."[17] Gillespie's assertion would seem superfluous if he did not elsewhere praise Pozo as a singular talent and innovator, not to mention a decisive influence on his own subsequent work. The trumpeter pointed out that the pair's seminal recording of "Manteca" was "probably the largest selling record I ever had," and conceded that "Chano taught us all multi-rhythm; we learned from the master."[18]

Gillespie's equivocation over the question of influence is indicative of the fact that Afro-Cuban music and 1940s jazz did not merely engage in symmetrical, harmonious musical encounters to the mutual benefit of both traditions. Part of the tension could be explained in musical terms. Beneath Gillespie's and Bauzá's praise of Pozo, writes John Storm Roberts, "lay a certain ambivalence that goes to the heart of the weaknesses in the Gillespie/Pozo recordings. Gillespie was a leader in a revolutionary style whose innovations had a strong harmonic element; Pozo was a típico traditionalist." Roberts's suggestion of a correlation between divergences and "weaknesses" is debatable, yet he is right in identifying their collaboration as one based not just on musical affinity but also, conversely, on conflict and difference.[19] A number of musicians in Gillespie's orchestra were less than thrilled with Pozo's entry into the band. Bassist Ray Brown confessed later that he had never been completely comfortable with the rhythmic challenges posed by Pozo's playing. What is more, Brown admitted that in general the presence of conga players was disconcerting to mid-1940s rhythm sections made up of North American players. Although conceding that Pozo was not a distraction as long as he was playing "Latin tunes," when the Cuban percussionist was riffing over conventional jazz arrangements "it seemed to inhibit us."[20] Such encounters owed their productivity to divergences and syncopations that went beyond the purely musical. For starters, musicians like Pozo and Bauzá would have found inter- and postwar New York a place charged with both racial tension and xenophobia. Afro-Caribbean artists were routinely consigned to the status of others and outsiders by their ostensibly consanguine hosts. With linguistic barriers added to the mix, it is easy to see how Pozo's presence in Gillespie's orchestra rendered the sessions fruitfully inharmonious.[21]

Early media coverage of the Gillespie-Machito-Pozo performances helped to delegitimize the Afro-Cuban as a branch of jazz history. In a wide-ranging essay published in *Life* magazine highlighting Cuba's prominent place in the international music scene, Winthrop Sargeant struck an uneasy balance between genuine admiration and debasing mockery. He saw Pozo, "a big, flash-ily dressed Negro," as emblematic of the "homicidal musical limbo of Havana," a city that "floats somewhat indeterminately between two other worlds. One is the heaven of international success, money, New York nightclubs, and Hol-lywood fame to which good Cubans sometimes go in spite of themselves. The other is the underworld of African Cuba."[22] Although Sargeant praises the tal-ents of such composers as Eliseo Grenet and Ernesto Lecuona, he paints Pozo in cartoonish tones that emphasize personal vanity, venality, and violence over the percussionist's musical innovations. The "African Cuba" whence he comes is singled out for the wild, exotic religious practices seen as part and parcel of much of the island's musical heritage. Indeed, Sargeant maintains, "with few exceptions the instruments of Cuban music are constructed on native African models and are unquestionably the most primitive ones that have ever been used in civilized music."[23]

The era's leading jazz journals took much the same tack as Sargeant. *Down Beat*'s Michael Levin generally praised the September 1947 performance at Car-negie Hall and suggested that the warm reception given to "Cubano Be" was an indication that "there is much jazz can pick up on from the South American and Afro-Cuban rhythm styles." But Levin scolded Gillespie for exhibiting an excess of showmanship and took offense in particular at what he saw as the trumpeter's lewd dancing style, which the critic likened to that of "a bop buf-foon instead of a boff performer."[24] Reviewing a Gillespie-Pozo performance for *Jazz Hot*, André Hodeir semi-ironically foregrounded the Cuban percus-sionist's African heritage over his *latinidad*. While upbraiding fellow specta-tors for mocking Pozo with racist cries of "What a cannibal!" and "Go back to Timbuktu!" ("As if jazz came from St. Petersburg," Hodeir quipped), the critic praised the Cuban for bewitching the Parisian audience with his "disturbing eyes" and the sway of "each movement of his body." Hodeir should at least be credited for insisting on the swing-like qualities of Pozo's performance, which the critic saw as lending diversity to jazz rhythms and fitting into the "spirit of the new style." But his praise was double edged, as it used the supposedly disturbing theatrics of Pozo's performance to sell readers on the novelty of Gil-lespie's orchestra.[25]

Pérez Prado and the Politics of Mambo

At least initially, critical response to the Gillespie-Pozo-Bauzá collaborations among Cuban, Mexican, and Argentine music critics was negligible compared to the splash made in the North American press. If Chano Pozo's revolutionary turn in New York as a pioneer of Afro-Cuban jazz mostly flew under the radar of Latin American critics and intellectuals, however, figures such as Tito Puente, Pérez Prado, and Benny Moré were a different story. Their visibility was due largely to the meteoric rise of mambo and other *estilos bailables* beginning in the late 1940s and early 1950s, the widespread popularity of the Mexican film industry, and the gradual but steady rise of television, which by the end of the decade would rival radio as the dominant mass medium in Latin America.

Initially, though, it was cinema that would propel mambo into the international limelight. Hollywood's particularly tight hold on the Cuban public prior to the revolution was made possible not only by the island's proximity but also by its easy-access port cities, relatively well paid rural proletariat, and modern railway system, all of which enabled the dissemination of yanqui taste and consumption throughout the island, even across class and color lines.[26] Yet Hollywood pictures were not the only ones popular on the island. Mexican cinema was a big draw in the 1940s and 1950s, especially in smaller Cuban cities and towns where melodramatic celebrations of rural nostalgia, moral retribution, and social order appealed to the working classes.[27]

The scholar Josh Kun has observed that music performs a "delinquent" act in the sense that it "unsettles . . . the geopolitical boundaries of the nation state." For Kun, the unfettered movement of music across borders in the global era at once transcends and scrambles configurations of identity and power.[28] Of course, for some time this has hardly stopped many Latin American states from trying to harness music's power for patriotic ends. As we have seen, mid-twentieth-century populist regimes in Brazil, Argentina, and Mexico aggressively promoted pedagogical narratives of national unity, historical exceptionalism, and ideological orthodoxy through the productive overlap of popular music and film.[29] But unlike samba, tango, or even the bolero, mambo could not be so easily conscripted into national service. For starters, prerevolutionary Cuba did not have a film industry of sufficient strength with which to promote homegrown musical practices as unifying emblems of national identity. And the problem was not just a symbolic one. Thanks to the relatively chaotic state of prerevolutionary Cuba's cultural institutions, many innovative and ambitious Cuban musicians were compelled to look elsewhere for artistic and commercial fulfillment, namely Mexico and the United States.

There has been considerable debate over the years about mambo's true origins. As early as June 1948, in the Cuban weekly *Bohemia*, Odilio Urfé claimed the word first emerged in a musical context with the appearance of an eponymous danzón written by Orestes "Cachao" López and performed with the charanga orchestra Arcaño y sus Maravillas some eleven years earlier. In the last part of that piece, a coda or *montuno sincopado* was added that eventually evolved into an autonomous rhythmic style all its own.[30] Another key contributor to mambo's early development, as scholar David F. García has recently demonstrated, was conjunto innovator Arsenio Rodríguez, who by 1943 had begun to insert syncopated variations that he called *diablos* at the end of son recordings in order to challenge dancers. By 1947, García writes, such mambo moves had spread to big-band dances as well, becoming popular in both Havana and New York City.[31]

In spite of such important musical antecedents, there remains little doubt that mambo, as it had come to be known by 1950, depended primarily on the innovation, showmanship, and sheer good timing of Dámaso Pérez Prado. One of the main characterizing features of Prado's version of the mambo was the debt it owed to Stan Kenton and his progressive big-band sound. Cuban music criticism, especially since the triumph of the revolution, has tended to underplay Kenton's influence, perhaps because such an acknowledgment might well diminish the Cuban and Latin American credentials often applied to mambo ex post facto.[32] Composer and musicologist Ned Sublette has written convincingly of the centrality of Kenton's work to the development of the Pérez Prado sound. What the Cuban bandleader borrowed, Sublette argues, was not just a big-band attack, with its blistering saxophones and trumpets on either end of the register, but also a novel notion of jazz harmony and dissonance that "never sought to banish the tonal center, using dissonance instead as an extension of tonal harmony."[33] At the same time, Pérez Prado's Afro-Cuban sensibility brought to his orchestra a rhythmic intensity absent, at least initially, from Kenton's performances. Over time, the Prado-Kenton influence would prove mutual. Kenton had been incorporating Afro-Cuban elements into his big band since 1947, when for the first time he heard Noro Morales's and Machito's orchestras play in Harlem.[34] Pérez Prado released the single "Mambo a la Kenton" in 1950; Kenton would return the favor with his recording of "Viva Prado!" that same year.[35]

Although the Cuban bandleader had begun developing his signature style in Havana in the mid-1940s, Pérez Prado's sound and career would only come to full fruition in Mexico. This is explainable partly by the very uniqueness Pérez Prado brought to mambo—the "progressive" qualities Cuban producers and even other musicians at the time saw as technically difficult and eccentric.[36] One person who clearly recognized Pérez Prado's originality was the *vedette* Ninón Sevilla, who brought her compatriot on board as an arranger just as her star was rising in the Mexican film industry.[37] Within months of his arrival, Pérez Prado was making not only the records that had eluded him in

Cuba, but also numerous appearances in live music venues, radio, and theater.[38] He found in Mexico City, moreover, a vibrant Cuban expatriate community that included the singers Cascarita and Benny Moré, both of whom would record for Prado's new orchestra in the years to come. In March 1949, Pérez Prado recorded "Qué rico el mambo" for RCA Victor's international division, and the song became a hit throughout Latin America. Within two years of leaving Cuba, he had gone from making fifty dollars a week to around five thousand.[39] Pérez Prado's sudden popularity north of the border, meanwhile, was partly the product of good fortune. "Qué rico el mambo" was released by RCA just as the American Federation of Musicians went on strike, compelling its members to uphold a temporary ban on recording. RCA took advantage of the situation to push its "Latin" recordings in the North American market.[40]

The cinema was at least as important to Pérez Prado's rise as the recording industry, particularly in Latin America. While the Mexican film industry of the late 1940s and 1950s frequently featured mambo, however, this was not the only music heard on the soundstage. Directors such as Julio Bracho, Alberto Gout, Emilio Fernández, and Chano Urueta—in films ranging from urban melodramas to light musical comedies—regularly used jazz, boogie-woogie, and other popular styles of the period as signs of exotic modernity and licentiousness against which normative Mexican and Latin American identity could be elaborated, celebrated, and sometimes questioned. In Bracho's proto-noir, pre-mambo *Distinto Amanecer* (1942), big-band jazz and commercial rumba serve as the sonic backdrop to Mexico City's underbelly of corrupt politicians, organized crime, and prostitution. The film set the basic template for urban melodramas in years to come. US and Cuban nightclub music and dance, with mambo in the lead, would dominate the screen in subsequent films like *Aventurera* (dir. Alberto Gout, 1950), *Víctimas del Pecado* (dir. Emilio Fernández, 1951), and *Sensualidad* (dir. Alberto Gout, 1951), emerging as ambiguous metonymies of defiance, moral perdition, and cultural impurity. These so-called *cabaretera* or *rumbera* films used non-Mexican musical forms and dances to frame "dirty" urban spectacles often implicitly associated with the United States, scenes antithetical to the Mexican pastoral ideal featured in the competing genre of the *comedia ranchera*, with its nationalist celebration of traditional values. In *Aventurera*, the film's protagonist (played by Ninón Sevilla) descends into the underworld of Ciudad Juárez. The border town is visibly compromised by US urban culture in the same way—or so the film implies—that mambo is Latin American music compromised by big-band jazz arrangements and instrumentation. In Fernández's *Víctimas del Pecado*, also starring Sevilla, the iconic rumbera sings and dances coquettishly with Pérez Prado and his racially mixed orchestra, straddling the line between Afro-Caribbean authenticity and commercial music of the tourist variety.[41] Like *Aventurera* and *Distinto Amanecer* before it, *Víctimas del Pecado* equates North American–influenced musical styles with moral degeneration and the affected pochismo of Mexican gangsters.

Mexican cinema did not always invoke mambo as an emblem of menace and contamination. In most cabaretera pictures, in fact, Pérez Prado and his orchestra are consigned to auxiliary roles, interacting only fleetingly with the films' main characters during the dance numbers. In director Chano Urueta's social comedy *Al son del mambo* (1950), though, Pérez Prado takes center stage as a featured symbol of vital cultural inspiration and transnational coopera-tion. One of the film's key scenes introduces the Cuban bandleader not simply as a musician but as a "collector of sounds"—a primitive artist in need of the musical literacy of the white Mexican protagonist Roberto. The moment cap-tures the mediating role served by the Mexican film industry vis-à-vis unlet-tered Cuban performers. The fruit of the collaboration is mambo itself, which Roberto declares "A new rhythm created by Pérez Prado, created for every-one's pleasure. A different rhythm, formed by the simplest and most primitive elements of nature, one that excites and provokes happiness and praise alike. Let's spread it from city to city, town to town, to the remotest places on earth, proclaiming our idea with mambo as the example. And we will see that even the Eskimos will end up happy, dancing to the sound of mambo." In the various musical numbers that follow, the interspersion of mambos ("Quién inventó el mambo," "El ruletero") with the occasional Mexican number underscores the ostensible message of (asymmetrical) Cuban-Mexican fraternity.

If the film plays out like a party devoted to postwar pan-Latin solidarity, however, the specter of the United States is never far off. Urueta's exploitative use of Cuban culture and real and symbolic landscapes uncannily resembles the Cuba-as-primitive-playground ideology of so many Hollywood films of the 1940s, from the Carmen Miranda vehicle *Week-End in Havana* (1941) to *Holiday in Havana* (1949), starring Desi Arnaz. The liberating sound of the mambo, with its thick jazz accent, reflects the incorporation of US popular culture into the very mood and fabric of the island fiesta.

Chano Urueta's follow-up comedy *Del can-can al mambo* (1951) again casts Pérez Prado and his orchestra as lighthearted beacons of freedom and progress, this time pitting them against the social conservatism of Mexico's heartland. As the critic Carlos Monsiváis later observed, at the time of *Del can-can al mam-bo*'s release, the Mexican film industry was at war with the Liga de Decencia, an organization that actively sought whenever possible to remove "morally objec-tionable" films from theaters, and when this was not possible, to intimidate and even humiliate spectators who insisted on watching them. Monsiváis specifically cites *Del can-can al mambo* as an example of the film industry's resistance to such measures. Urueta's fictitious provincial city Tompiatillo, he writes, "is liberated by the intercession of the rhythm and arrangements of Pérez Prado which, in stripping bodies of their rigidity, destroys the paralysis imposed by the tyranny of 'decorum.'"[42] The film's final scene, in which even the rigid headmistress of a provincial boarding school finds herself caught up in the mambo frenzy, shows, however optimistically, that even the most reactionary elements of Mexican society harbored a potential for progress and tolerance. Pérez Prado's jazzed-up Latin American musical performance thus serves as a soundtrack and key backdrop to the temptations of transnational modernity: a siren song with the potential not just to corrupt and contaminate, but also to serve as a refuge from the rigidity of social norms and institutional models of Mexican identity during the presidency of Miguel Alemán (1946–1952).[43]

The moral subtext of *Al son del mambo* and *Del can-can al mambo* touched on ideological tensions that went well beyond the Liga de Decencia. In the late 1940s and early 1950s, when Pérez Prado's groundbreaking sound and dance spectacle first reached an international audience, a number of Latin American intellectuals stressed the connection between mambo and public morality. As early as 1948, the Cuban critic Manuel Cuéllar Vizcaíno, in an essay published in *Bohemia*, acknowledged that the "enemies of mambo" dismissed the music for its lack of elegance, a characteristic they attributed to its yanqui aggressiveness, introducing "prosaic movements and gestures that can in no way be reconciled to our [national] customs."[44] One such enemy was the Cardinal of Lima, Juan Gualberto Guevara. Responding to Pérez Prado's visit to Peru and the enthusiasm it generated, Gualberto Guevara roundly and publicly condemned the mambo, going so far as to deny absolution to anyone who dared to dance to the music. The infamous "mambo excommunication" was reported extensively not just in Latin America but also in the United States, from *Newsweek* to the Spanish-language daily *La Prensa* (New York).[45]

In an essay published in the Barranquilla newspaper *El Heraldo* in January 1951, a young Colombian journalist named Gabriel García Márquez ironically dismissed the verdict of erudite critics as elitist, and worse, apocalyptic: "Academics are throwing ashes over their heads and tearing apart their vestments. Yet vulgarity continues to be the best barometer. And I have the impression that more than a couple of academics will be dead and buried before the kid on the corner brings himself to accept that 'Mambo no. 5' is little more than a hodge-podge of barbaric chords, randomly strung together."[46] García Márquez's biblical overtones jibed perfectly not only with the real-life rhetoric of Latin American religious leaders, but also with the language employed by the provincial characters of *Del can-can al mambo*, who consistently refer to both mambo and the medium through which it first reaches local residents (television) as "diabolical" and "modern witchcraft."

For the Colombian writer, as for Urueta's Roberto, one of mambo's true values lay in its raw appeal to youth culture. A second article published later the same year chronicled Pérez Prado's celebrated arrival and performance in New York, the first leg of the orchestra's first US tour. García Márquez correctly predicted that "North American girls . . . will [soon] notice that there is something about Coca-Cola, blue jeans, and sneakers that proves particularly adaptable to Pérez Prado's devilish musical cataplasms." Yet here García Márquez took his "vulgarity as social barometer" argument one step further. Such visceral appeal to the North American public, he suggested, was also a dangerous one for cultural conservatives and nationalists, in the sense that the unusual hybridity of the new sound posed a threat to the status quo. For US music purists, even if some academics had argued that mambo was "a legitimate, displaced offspring of Harlem rhythms," mambo re-appropriated jazz in much the same reckless manner that jazz had often taken liberties with the sacred cows of classical music. Despite the "devilish" menace that Pérez Prado represented, his visit to the US metropolis was bound to leave a mark. Whether or not they approved of his music, García Márquez concluded, "[North Americans would] be left with a lasting memory [of his performance], without knowing for certain whether it [was] an homage, or a revenge."[47]

The subtle irony of García Márquez's position spoke well both to mambo's formal heterogeneity as a Latin American idiom that drew heavily on jazz harmony and instrumentation and to its deep symbolic ambiguity for US audiences. Interestingly, in a 1951 essay Alejo Carpentier wrote that the menace of mambo was due not to its vernacular inelegance, but rather the opposite. Alluding to the influence of Stan Kenton, Carpentier argued that mambo was the first genre of dance music to owe such a debt to harmonic approaches until recently belonging exclusively to composers considered modern. For the same reason, he says, such writers had "frightened away a large sector of the public."[48] Carpentier's position was typically iconoclastic in its expansion of what contemporaneous audiences may have perceived as menacing in mambo. Yet, like most Cuban criticism of the period, his essay still treated Pérez Prado largely as an exponent of national music. By contrast, García Márquez's essays fundamentally broke with debates over mambo's origins—debates that, though useful, tended to treat mambo as a purely musical phenomenon, as opposed to a transnational spectacle involving multiple sites of enunciation and mediation.

The Colombian writer was correct in predicting that Pérez Prado's music would eventually leave its mark on the US public. The scholar Alexandra Vásquez has recently remarked that mambo dovetailed with "the last postwar vestiges" of the Good Neighbor policy just as "cold war paranoia turned into policies of containment."[49] The politics of mambo were therefore politics of transition. But it would not be until the middle of the decade that mambo would fully arrive in the US in the sense that García Márquez predicted, as it had already arrived in Mexico and elsewhere in Latin America. Although Pérez Prado was already a recording star in the United States, his 1951 tour did not initially lead to such multimedia success.[50] His orchestra's second tour, in 1954, however, led to a May appearance on NBC's *The Spike Jones Show*, introducing mambo to hundreds of thousands of North American television viewers not yet familiar with Pérez Prado's RCA Victor recordings or live performances. The appearance cast the bandleader as more of a noisy clown than a serious maestro, setting the tone for the second, more decisive period of Pérez Prado's triumph in the United States.[51] Rather than playing the part of the erotic underworld soundtrack as it had in the cabaretera films, or serving as an emblem of moral laxity and creative liberty, as in the comedies of Chano Urueta, mambo in its North American phase would increasingly assume caricaturesque proportions in televised programs that ranged from *The Ed Sullivan Show* to *The Dinah Shore Show*.[52]

While Pérez Prado's first appearance in a Hollywood feature was in the drama *Underwater!* (dir. John Sturges, 1955), it was *Cha-Cha-Cha-Boom!* (dir. Fred F. Sears, 1956) that would push the Cuban bandleader into the cinematic spotlight. Like *Al son del mambo*, the Hollywood picture cast Cuba as a licensed and licentious enclave where white non-Cubans were free to express themselves in ways they would not have been inclined or permitted to otherwise.[53] As in Urueta's film, a semifictional Pérez Prado is discovered by an authoritative judge of local talent, his music championed at once as innovative and close to nature. *Cha-Cha-Cha-Boom!* features Pérez Prado's performance of his "Voodoo Suite," an ambitious composition that mingles mambo with bebop and guaguancó: a slice of urban modernity refreshed by its new contact with the tropics. Robert E. Kent's screenplay offsets Pérez Prado's over-the-top musical hybridity with reassurances from local characters that his orchestra is actually playing "native music, right from the heart of Cuba." Abandoning any pretense of historical accuracy, *Cha-Cha-Cha-Boom!* places tall, lean, white dancers in the place of curvy rumberas and injects their performance with an erotic violence that reads like an unchecked Northern fantasy of primitive excess.

Music critics and historians have usually defined mambo as an Afro-Caribbean form enlivened harmonically through its contact with progressive big-band jazz. Yet films like *Al son del mambo* and *Cha-Cha-Cha-Boom!* suggest the very opposite. In both pictures, mambo emerges rather as a kind of super-primitivized jazz, enhanced rhythmically and partially returned to its African roots, all without severing its link to modern life in North America. Political disparities between Mexican and US mambo pictures, meanwhile, highlight the symbolic versatility of mambo in articulating quite distinct national objectives and visions. *Del can-can al mambo* and *Al son del mambo* give voice to Mexico's vacillation in the face of progress even as they suggest an arriviste claim to a middling position within the hemispheric hierarchy of cultural citizenship: still one rung beneath the United States, but one or two above Cuba.

Breaking with the Good Neighbor code of racial ethics, Hollywood's mid-1950s treatment of Pérez Prado seemed to signal a partial return to the unrestrained stereotyping of the silent and early sound eras. Tinseltown's embodiment of Cold War cultural politics demanded of mambo an updated auxiliary role for Latin America that exaggerated the rest-and-relaxation typecasting already present in Carmen Miranda and Walt Disney films of the early to mid-1940s.[54] In *Underwater!* and *Cha-Cha-Cha-Boom!*, the Caribbean is not just a site of kindred cultures and quaint curiosities put on display for the benefit of gringo tourists and weekend ethnographers. Rather, it is a stereophonic, modern-savage space offering lurid ways and means to the acquisition of fortune, fun, erotic fulfillment, and creative inspiration: a crass, alloyed solution to the "burdens" of geopolitical leadership and modern capitalism.

The Un-jazz Revolution

Although mambo and cha-cha-chá gradually went out of style in the United States, eclipsed by dance forms spurred by the rapid ascent of rock and roll, Pérez Prado enjoyed a long and lucrative career as a bandleader in Mexico City. He also maintained an active, if sporadic, relationship with his native Cuba well after the triumph of the revolution in January 1959 despite his ambiguous association with global capitalism. He had achieved stardom through highly commercial recordings and decidedly "alienated" film and television appearances in the United States and Mexico. This did not prevent him from contributing to the soundtrack of one of revolutionary Cuba's most propagandistic documentary films: *Hasta la victoria siempre* (1967), Santiago Álvarez's ardently anti-imperialist tribute to Ernesto "Che" Guevara made shortly after his death. Although Pérez Prado's "Suite de las Américas," based loosely on a composition by the Brazilian classical composer Heitor Villa-Lobos, is hardly dance music, the piece's foundation in mambo and jazz lend it an unusual quality seemingly at odds with the film's subject matter—the revolutionary struggle between Bolivian peasants and CIA-sponsored terrorism, punctuated by footage of Guevara's later speeches. In some ways, the score resembles the Latin- and swing-inflected modernist experiments of such arrangers as Gil Evans, Chico O'Farrill, and early Lalo Schifrin. Álvarez, however, deftly capitalizes on the echoes of Hollywood and prerevolutionary Cuba implicit in Pérez Prado's sound, using the score's postmambo palette as both a sign of predatory capitalism and the soundtrack of its undoing. All the while, the Afro-Cuban strains of the recording remind the audience of Cuba's importance as a sponsor of peasant uprisings in the hemisphere.

Placed at the service of revolutionary resistance, "Suite de las Américas" thus stands as a truly remarkable follow-up to the "Voodoo Suite" from *Cha-Cha-Cha-Boom!* Now safely deglobalized and cocooned in a Latin American nation acceptable to Castro's ideological sensibilities, Pérez Prado was ripe for appropriation as a post-Cuban, postcapitalist performer whose sonic storehouse resonated with the sort of panhemispheric latinidad prized by the revolution. Yet in the end, Pérez Prado never fully conformed to the expectations of the industrial or national agents that sought to exploit him for monetary or ideological gain any more than mambo respected geopolitical borders. In short, the sui generis Cuban bandleader exemplified what the scholar José David Saldívar has termed an "outernational" cultural force.[55]

Pérez Prado's score for *Hasta la victoria siempre* illustrates the precariousness with which both the Cuban-born composer and Castro's cultural policy straddled the rift between vernacular authenticity and modern commercialism, Cuba and the world. Music historians and scholars have shown how revolutionary Cuba distanced itself from jazz and other US-identified musical expressions in the 1960s at the same time that such forms flourished in local musical venues. According to Leonardo Acosta, the revolution initially embraced jazz, or at least tolerated it. Prerevolutionary institutions such as the Tropicana, the Capri's Salón Rojo, and the Club Cubano de Jazz (CCJ) continued to host jazz musicians and jam sessions at the beginning of the new decade. One of the first official promoters immediately following the triumph of the revolution was the writer Guillermo Cabrera Infante, who organized a concert featuring several members of the CCJ including Acosta himself on tenor saxophone. Cabrera Infante planned to produce a televised history of jazz for the program *Lunes de Revolución* (produced by the magazine of the same name). Boycotted by the musicians' union and apparently undermined by the Castro regime, the show never made it to the air. Faced with growing hostility toward the United States and its signature music, Acosta published a defense of jazz in *Hoy* in which he pointed out that, far from being a voice of imperialism, jazz had in fact long symbolized the fight against socioeconomic bondage and racism in the United States.[56]

By 1963, however, a hardening line against jazz, rock, and dance music generally—what the scholar Robin Moore calls the revolutionary "politics of fun"—had altered the musical landscape of the island.[57] As *Hasta la victoria siempre* suggests, the cinema was one of the few media through which jazz and related forms could find expression in Cuba, in part because music's risky political connotations could be offset by the corrective of visual content. The first dramatic feature produced by the Instituto Cubano del Arte e Industria Cinematográficos (ICAIC), Julio García Espinosa's *Cuba baila* (1960), uses jazz and boogie-woogie performed by Bebo Valdés y su Cuarteto to underscore the venal decadence of the high bourgeoisie in prerevolutionary Havana. The film, as Michael Chanan has written, "works upon the characteristics of the social spaces, public, private, or semipublic, in which the different pieces of music that occur in the film are played and heard."[58] A swing dance sequence is presented as a dangerously seductive spectacle of the affluent. Ramón, an assistant manager at a cigar factory, is pressured by his arriviste wife to throw an equally lavish *quinceañera* for his daughter. He ultimately fails to raise the funds necessary to stage his own symbolic performance of upward mobility. Instead, he settles for a mixed-race, informal party held outdoors to the sounds of danzón.

Music plays an equally central role in *Soy Cuba* (I am Cuba, 1964), a Cuban-Soviet coproduction directed by Mikhail Kalatozov, and Sara Gómez's *Y . . . tenemos sabor* (1968). Ostensibly a four-part documentary about prerevolutionary Cuba, Kalatozov's highly experimental film features lush, delirious black-and-white cinematography and a soundtrack heavy on jazz and mambo. To an even greater extent than *Cuba baila*, music and image in *Soy Cuba* evoke the Batista era as beguiling yet ominous, sexy but tyrannical. In a key nightclub scene, first ominous and then cacophonous strains of hard bop and mambo punctuate the sexual exploitation of a young Cuban woman at the hands of foreign tourists. In Gómez's documentary short, meanwhile, jazz appears as the last of a series of didactic performances surveying popular instruments and dance music from guaguancó and son to cha-cha-chá. A voice-over introduces the final performance without identifying it as jazz: "These youths are working on something new, different, but retaining our *sabor*." A scatting Chucho Valdés and his small ensemble leave little doubt, however, that Afro-Cuban jazz is to be seen as the culmination—rather than antithesis—of a natural evolution of authentically Cuban musical idioms. Not surprisingly, *Y... tenemos sabor* has rightly been seen as a daring reaffirmation of dance music and jazz in the face of official opposition to both during the 1960s.

Acosta credits Gómez with safeguarding jazz from the wrecking ball of hardline cultural policies precisely by articulating the music's ties with Cuban popular music, not just in *Y... tenemos sabor* but also in the soundtracks of her other documentaries and the narrative feature *De cierta manera* (1974), the latter scored by the guitarist, percussionist, and composer Sergio Vitier, a former mainstay of the CCJ.[59] In fact, though, jazz never actually left the island. Even before the 1967 foundation of the Orquesta Cubana de Música Moderna (OCMM)—a veritable supergroup featuring such rising stars as Arturo Sandoval, Juan Pablo Torres, Paquito d'Rivera, and Chucho Valdés—combos such as Felipe Dulzaides's big band, Leopoldo "Pucho" Escalante's Noneto de Jazz, and the Free American Jazz Collective tirelessly gigged in hotel bars and small clubs. Even in the absence of larger venues and recording opportunities throughout most of the decade, such ensembles served as the "cohesive base" of improvisation and ever-evolving musicianship on the island.[60]

The 1970s saw a significant resurgence in the recognition accorded to jazz and mambo. Without a doubt the most important of Cuba's jazz critics and defenders was Acosta, who early in the decade began publishing a series of seminal magazine essays that served as the basis of his subsequent books. The key to Acosta's success in opening up discussion on the subject after a decade of virtual silence lay not only in his intimate, firsthand knowledge of jazz performance on the island, but also his rigorous approach to cultural criticism—an approach that combined a hard-nosed postcolonial perspective with an aversion to knee-jerk, orthodox essentialisms. Such dogmatic interventions were still the norm as late as 1972, when María Teresa Linares, in an essay published in Casa de las Américas' *Boletín de Música*, lamented that between 1930 and 1950 "our music was invaded by jazz bands" granted unfair global advantages by the US culture industry.[61] While Linares's assessment is not factually inaccurate, she nevertheless casts Cuba as an unfortunate victim of foreign musical influence and North American bullying rather than a major midcentury player in transnational give-and-take, however asymmetrical such exchanges may have been. What is more, her defense of Cuban music is posited on the deeply conservative premise that any outside or urban influence was necessarily a mercantilist sign of contamination at the hands of bourgeois mass culture. "Over the course of our history," Linares writes, "the process of neo-colonial cosmopolitanism and classist discrimination ... eliminated manifestations of popular expression."[62]

Acosta's critical innovation was to enable the reassessment of jazz and other urban musical forms in Cuba within an ideological framework that did not expurgate or minimize the crimes of the international culture industry. He did so by locating jazz at the margins of empire. In a seminal piece first published in *Revolución y Cultura* in 1976, Acosta argues that jazz emerged as a bold challenge to the musical and cultural status quo of the United States of the late nineteenth and early twentieth centuries, a period marked by social stratification, generic inflexibility, and a rigid separation between vernacular and erudite music, as well as between composer and musician. Jazz undercut such vertically imposed categories and hierarchies by blurring the traditional lines between notation and performance—a loosening of barriers that brought improvisation to the fore. "Similar to Cuban popular music (as well as Brazilian and others)," Acosta maintains, "written jazz presents the peculiarity of *not being able to be read literally*."[63]

In saying that jazz eludes the conventions of musical hermeneutics—that it should be regarded *other*wise—Acosta echoes historicist claims made by writers as diverse as Leonard Feather, Amiri Baraka, and, as we have seen, Julio Cortázar. Where he differs from these critics is in his insistence on attributing both the "illegibility" of jazz and the genealogical ties between jazz, son, and samba to a shared cultural matrix encompassing Africa, the Middle Passage, and postcolonial, postslavery conditions. These analogous musical practices, the Cuban stresses, allude not just to vague origins but also, more centrally, to still-evolving historical processes in the Americas. Acosta argues that "in practice, a jazz group acts like an African drum ensemble: both maintain basic common themes on which they improvise, establishing a 'dialogue' among the participants." At the same time, jazz depends on the interplay between musicians and an audience of "initiates," who together engage in a collective expression that stands in stark opposition to the stratified nature of Western erudite music, with its strict division of labor and segregation of artist and public.[64]

Acosta's emphasis on *africanidad* and collectivity, particularly in his earlier essays, did not seriously challenge revolutionary dictates. Yet he was the first post-1959 Cuban critic to systematically deploy the lexicon of decolonization in an effort to destigmatize jazz. Neither an emblem of individual freedom nor a symbol of savage capitalism, jazz for Acosta embodied an oppositional practice— a subversive, internal assault on the binary structure of bourgeois capitalism. If the claims the Cuban made came dangerously close to casting jazz as a representative of US exceptionalism, his views on mambo and Latin jazz from the period were just as revealing. In a 1976 profile of Orestes "Macho" López, who wrote and recorded the danzón "Mambo" in 1938, both Acosta and López suggested that Pérez Prado had not been the true inventor of mambo. López argued in the Acosta interview that by adding jazz orchestration, the so-called Mambo King had deprived the Cuban form of its traditional danzón origins. Acosta did not exactly come to Pérez Prado's defense. Although acknowledging the more famous bandleader's merits, Acosta ended his profile by writing that "a determinant factor in the international success [that Pérez Prado] achieved was that of the mass market publicity and media machinery at his disposal."[65]

Acosta was at the time in the midst of a creative outburst in which he regularly took aim at US mass media as long-standing agents of cultural exploitation; hence his ambiguous assessment of Pérez Prado (softened in comments made a decade later) was hardly surprising. To let the Mambo King completely off the hook ideologically would have contradicted Acosta's running hypothesis about the insidious dynamics of cultural imperialism. A more measured assessment of Pérez Prado's legacy came from Odilio Urfé. Though suggesting that the bandleader had simply "cosmopolitanized" the innovations of Orestes López, Arsenio Rodríguez, and other Cuban musicians, Urfé nonetheless located mambo and cha-cha-chá (as practiced by Enrique Jorrín and others) within a heroic narrative of Cuban cultural history. It is perhaps too predictable that Urfé, hailing from a family of *danzoneros*, should laud the two other idioms as essentially inventive elaborations of danzón rather than international hybrids drawing from diverse forms and traditions—from son, danzón, and rumba to swing, bebop, and even boogie-woogie—something the Mexican cabaretera films and mambo comedies clearly demonstrated. Yet Urfé also understood better than Acosta, at least at this point in time, that mambo served as evidence of the innovative potential of bourgeois transnationalism. Ingenious and deceptively inventive, Pérez Prado for Urfé was "without a doubt the most effective revolutionary that popular dance music has seen in the last [three decades]."[66]

If there was one figure Cuban intellectuals of the period could agree on, it was Benny Moré. As a singer and bandleader who had remained in Cuba after the triumph of the revolution only to die from liver failure in 1963, "el bárbaro del ritmo," (the Barbarian of Rhythm), as Moré has been known affectionately on the island since the latter part of his career, was certainly a safer emblem of official popular culture than was Pérez Prado. Relatively unblemished by US mass celebrity, Moré had nevertheless contributed to—and benefited from—many of the same cultural institutions and musical fashions that the internationally renowned bandleader had. Introduced in the late 1940s while both lived and performed in Mexico, Moré and Pérez Prado cut twenty-seven mambo recordings together between 1948 and 1950 alone, not to mention their appearances in cabaretera pictures.[67] Moré, however, returned to his native Cuba in 1950, where he used his versatile singing skills to earn a devoted following as an interpreter not just of mambos but also guarachas and boleros. Besides his charismatic personality, Moré's perceived loyalty to his rural Afro-Cuban roots formed the basis of his wide appeal on the island. "A *guajiro congo* from the center of the country," Sublette has observed, "[Benny] didn't come off like a *habanero* to the *santiagueros* [residents of Santiago de Cuba] or vice versa in Havana. He was the universal Cuban."[68]

Whatever the exact reasons, Benny Moré struck a chord with revolutionary intellectuals beginning in the mid-1960s. In a poetic eulogy written shortly after Moré's death, an incredulous Roberto Fernández Retamar lamented that the singer's "howled" words would "never return to the mouth / that now belongs to a bunch of unnameable animals." True to Sublette's claims, Retamar mentioned Moré's hometown by name: "Santa Isabel de las Lajas / that tremendous little hamlet in heat." Retamar saw Moré's personal appeal and impeccable popular credentials as inseparable from the authenticity of his live performances—music to which records could not do justice, contaminated as these were by the culture industry.[69] The venerable Afro-Cuban poet Nicolás Guillén mounted a more frontal attack in his own eulogy, published in the newspaper *Hoy*. Calling Moré's greatest merit his cubanía—the same word Fernando Ortiz had used more than a decade earlier to praise Chano Pozo—Guillén lauded not only the singer's Afro-Cuban roots and man-on-the-street demeanor but also his ability to make music "without giving in to the yanqui, or paying tribute to the false idol." The poet followed up his insinuation with a pointed clarification: "The reader knows [who I'm talking about]. Why name names? Everyone is aware of more than one prodigal native son who couldn't resist the temptation of capitalism, flying the coop for more 'solid' prospects abroad. Not Benny."[70] Another Cuban poet did name names. In a series of popular *décimas* dedicated to the late "Bárbaro del ritmo," Francisco Echazábal made a point of mentioning Moré's alliance with and subsequent "abandonment" of Pérez Prado in Mexico. Once the revolution arrived, the poet claimed, even as other Cuban artists fled or remained abroad, Moré turned down a lucrative recording contract since "he couldn't bear to desert the trenches" of revolutionary struggle.[71]

Guillén's and Echazábal's eulogies revealed a fondness for Moré's music, of course. But they also offered morality tales of fidelity through which correct versions of national cultural history could be shaped and defined. By following this narrative, revolutionary intellectuals consigned Pérez Prado to the role of capitalist sellout and exile. Cuban intellectuals, apprehensive of popular music's affective power to move large swaths of society, were keenly sensitive to the exploitative potential of the capitalist music industry. As Moore notes, this was especially true in cases where record companies molded Cuban forms to fit a commercial standard and "marketed [them] en masse to the country that served as [their] original source of inspiration."[72] Still, Guillén and Echazábal toed the party line with certain ambivalence. Pérez Prado had the same Afro-Cuban credentials as Moré, after all, and in any event had abandoned Cuba long before Castro came to power. Moreover, he eventually settled in Mexico—a country with which the revolution had long taken pains to maintain cordial, kindred relations. Yet Pérez Prado's long-standing associations with the international music industry certainly kept many revolutionary intellectuals from embracing him with open arms in the manner of Moré.

Although they never reached Moré's status as musical hero, Afro-Cuban jazz pioneers Machito and Chano Pozo received increasing attention from Cuban intellectuals and artists in the 1970s and 1980s. Acosta published an essay in *Revolución y Cultura* in 1986 in which he bemoaned Machito's anonymity in Cuba. Extolling his central role in the development of Afro-Cuban jazz, Acosta praised Machito as the "genuine father of Latin jazz and salsa."[73] Acosta, though, was playing catch-up, as Machito's resurgence elsewhere was in full gear by end of the 1970s. In 1973 the elder statesman of Cubop had recorded a successful follow-up to his 1940s collaborations with Dizzy Gillespie. In a 1976 issue devoted to Latin jazz, meanwhile, *Down Beat* featured an interview with Machito and Tito Puente.

Acosta followed *Down Beat*'s lead in privileging Machito's role as a more important innovator than either Pérez Prado or Chano Pozo. Yet it was the latter musician who ultimately had more appeal for the Cuban Revolution. Like Benny Moré, Pozo sported personal charisma, held working-class Afro-Cuban credentials, and died young. This last fact is worth emphasizing, since it allowed revolutionary intellectuals to champion the musical virtues of each without having to explain away a long and lucrative career outside Cuba after the triumph of the revolution—as was the case with Pérez Prado, Machito, and others. In Moré's case, a return to Cuba was spun as the singer's loyalty to his *guajiro* roots, while his demise could be attributed to insidious vices, namely alcohol, supposedly acquired during his years abroad. The violent circumstances surrounding Pozo's death, meanwhile, jibed with a standard revolutionary narrative of New York City as the tempting-yet-corrupt capitalist metropolis par excellence.

This image of the yanqui metropolis jumps to the foreground in the Cuban documentary short *Buscando a Chano Pozo* (1987), in which director Rebeca

Chávez depicts the famous tamborero's murder as the tragic consequence of his heroic refusal to be financially exploited by the local swindlers of the music industry. Chávez supports her central argument—that Pozo had a major hand in the invention of Latin jazz—by featuring several clips of an older Dizzy Gillespie not just exalting the percussionist-composer's unique talents but also acknowledging the debt North American jazz owed to Cuban music and musicians generally. In one of the film's last sequences, the appearance of a young Gonzalo Rubalcaba—a precociously talented pianist "discovered" by Gillespie in 1985, much like Chano Pozo four decades earlier—stresses Cuba's continuing centrality to jazz in spite of the island's relative isolation. Meanwhile, the director uses a montage of contemporary Cuban street scenes and interviews with fellow musicians to underscore the political currency of Chano Pozo's vernacular milieu and Afro-Cuban heritage. At once culturally authentic, proudly defiant, and internationally renowned, Pozo is cast as someone emblematic of the revolution itself.

Much the same message comes across in Josefina Rodríguez Olmo and Aristide Pumariega's graphic story *Mitos de la popularidad: Chano Pozo* (1994). Like *Buscando a Chano Pozo*, Rodríguez Olmo's text (in the prologue and captions) foregrounds the musician's rough childhood in Cayo Hueso, recounting how his musical talents garnered the attention of established Cuban artists Rita Montaner and Miguelito Valdés, and later Gillespie and Machito in New York. Yet Rodríguez is quick to stress the racial prejudice Pozo had encountered in both prerevolutionary Havana—the conga master could not find regular work at the Casino de la Playa, for example—and the Jim Crow South. Shortly before his death, we are told, Pozo put an end to a tour with Gillespie's orchestra because he "couldn't stand the treatment blacks received in the South."[74] To an even greater extent than Chávez's documentary, meanwhile, Rodríguez and Pumariega emphasize the dizzying verticality and seedy menace of wartime New York. In Pumariega's most arresting drawing (one featured on the cover), Pozo, conga in hand, exclaims "¡¡¡Coño!!!" (Fuck!!!) as he beholds the city's towering skyline for the first time. In his rendering of Pozo's murder, Pumariega resorts to hard-boiled stereotypes. The celebrated musician's assailant—in fact a disgruntled friend and Pozo's marijuana supplier, Eusebio Muñoz—is depicted as if he were a Mafia hitman.[75] Painting the great tamborero's demise in such broad strokes allows Rodríguez and Pumariega to characterize his death as inevitable given the supposedly insurmountable levels of poverty, racism, exploitation, and violence with which he had to contend, both in prerevolutionary Cuba and later in the United States.

Fig. 4.1. Cover of Josefina Rodríguez and Aristide Pumariega's graphic narrative *Mitos de la popularidad: Chano Pozo* (1994).

As in Chávez's documentary, Dizzy Gillespie appears as both a synecdoche of jazz celebrity and an authoritative judge of Pozo's remarkable talents. After representing the famous "battle of the bands" between Machito's and Stan Kenton's orchestras, in which Gillespie and Pozo performed as invited guests, Rodríguez and Pumariega sketch a brief exchange after the show in which Gillespie is asked what he thinks of "that Cuban." "Chano," the trumpeter answers, "will make jazz history."[76] Clearly one of the graphic book's objectives is to secure the Cuban percussionist's place in a Latin jazz canon still in its infancy and open to debate.

The rise of the supergroup Irakere in the 1970s posed a particularly revealing challenge to Cuban music critics. Formed in the ashes of the Orquesta Cubana de Música Moderna and headed by Chucho Valdés, Paquito d'Rivera, and Arturo Sandoval, Irakere quickly embarked in a bold new direction, trading in the modernist pretensions of OCMM for an innovative brand of music that was equal parts edgy jazz-funk fusion and traditional guaguancó, with hints of classical arrangements and Fania-style salsa. The band's sound was intellectually ambitious while still remaining música bailable, international and sophisticated without ever straying too far from Ortiz's notion of cubanía, and catchy without being overtly commercial. In a 1974 profile published in *Revolución y Cultura*, Adriana Belmonte lauded Irakere as the first Cuban jazz group to make a major splash abroad. Queried about the group's 1970 performance at Poland's prestigious Jazz Jamboree Festival, Valdés described how Dave Brubeck and other US musicians had arrogantly turned their backs while Polish and Swedish combos played before them. Eager to "savor [what they expected to be] the Cubans' failed and ridiculous performance," Brubeck and company watched dumbstruck as Irakere electrified the audience. Later, elated and apparently contrite, Brubeck and his cohorts introduced themselves and offered to disseminate the group's records in the United States.[77]

Valdés's charged narrative of aloof jazz titans taken aback by Irakere's brilliance functions at once as a condemnation of yanqui hubris, an illustration of Cuba's underdog status, and also, as in the case of Dizzy Gillespie's widely cited praise of Chano Pozo, an affirmation of ascendant talent by accepted masters of the idiom. It is also worth pointing out that Valdés's account cast white US jazz figures in the role of reluctant converts. Such a tactic would almost certainly have been riskier for Valdés and Belmonte had the festival's stars been African Americans. The fact that the headliners were Brubeck and Gerry Mulligan lends a subtly sinister tone to the pianist's account of the *norteamericanos'* initial disdain for the band's mostly Afro-Cuban musicians. The racial politics implicit in this characterization of Brubeck and company were especially ironic given the fact that, as Acosta points out elsewhere, Chucho Valdés's compositional and playing style owed a great deal to Lennie Tristano and, especially, Bill Evans—two of the most influential white jazz musicians of the period.[78]

In the 1970s and 1980s, however, Valdés and other musicians of his generation maintained an ambivalent stance toward jazz as a musical category. In Belmonte's profile of Irakere, the pianist expressed the truism that "a musician is a musician" even as he acknowledged jazz's crucial influence on his work as an arranger and improviser.[79] A decade later, in a polemical article published in the inaugural issue of the Cuban music magazine *Clave*, Armando Romeu and Gonzalo Rubalcaba went one step further. While criticizing the advocacy of creative stagnation in the name of musical nationalism—what Romeu called the "false standard of the national"—both Romeu and Rubalcaba also distanced themselves from the jazz label. Praising the harmonically and rhythmically innovative work of Valdés, Sandoval, Emiliano Salvador, Juan Pablo Torres, and José María Vitier, Romeu remarked that "what they do is evolved contemporary Cuban music, and not jazz." Rubalcaba applied a similar logic to his own work: "What I do is not jazz," he said, but rather "Cuban music with a new sense of improvisation; with a new way of using percussion and with a different structural conception."[80]

Rubalcaba and Romeu thus attempted to rechristen pioneering expansions of Cuban forms as *música cubana contemporánea*, or as Rubalcaba put it more baroquely, "a new type of contemporary, *avant-garde*, Cuban popular music."[81] The argument is much the same as that used by Ástor Piazzolla in the 1960s and 1970s, when the Argentine dubbed his innovations *nueva música urbana de Buenos Aires* (new urban music from Buenos Aires) and *música popular contemporánea de Buenos Aires* (contemporary popular music from Buenos Aires) as a way to eschew the traditionalist connotations of tango while preempting accusations of cultural imperialism provoked by the jazz appellation. In so doing, Rubalcaba and Romeu sought to defend the use of non-Cuban melodic influences and harmonic approaches against the censure of revolutionary orthodoxy and at the same time to duck accusations of being *extranjerizante* (foreignizing)—an epithet used by mudslinging nationalists across the hemisphere. Latin jazz, Rubalcaba reminded *Clave*'s readers, was a commercial construct. Yet unlike salsa, another catchall that emerged at about the same time in the 1960s, "Latin jazz" captured the kind of experimental, genre-expanding music to which artists like Rubalcaba aspired at the time. "We Cubans," he says, "are the most important promoters [and] creators not of the term in question, but rather of the musical practice as such."[82]

Cuban Curios

There is a deeply paradoxical quality to Rubalcaba's conceit, which rejects "Latin jazz" nomenclature even as it strives to safeguard the object to which the label refers. The pianist's hair-splitting reveals the abiding ambiguity of the jazz sign in Latin America generally. But it speaks above all to the particularly vexed cultural politics of revolutionary Cuba, where US popular music was for so long simultaneously embraced and rejected, celebrated and disavowed. Curiously, the model Rubalcaba cites as an exemplar of musical innovation is not Machito or Arsenio Rodríguez, Chano Pozo or Benny Moré, but rather Dámaso Pérez Prado. "A new form of Cuban musical expression," Pérez Prado for Rubalcaba symbolized true innovation and international popularity without either abandoning his cubanía (wherever he happened to be making his living) or carrying the "foreignizing" rubric of jazz.[83]

The recognition accorded to Pérez Prado seems belated, and odd given the silence often shrouding his name in Cuba since the triumph of the revolution. Yet Gonzalo Rubalcaba's declaration is representative of the delicate bind in which many Cuban musicians and intellectuals found themselves regarding the question of foreign influence. This was particularly true when the source was the United States—a country thoroughly despised by the revolution for having provided refuge to so many exiled capitalists and other defectors. In a pivotal essay published in 1971, Alejo Carpentier attempted to reconcile the specter of cultural imperialism with cultural nationalism by arguing that Cuban musical production was essentially based on resistance. The nation's strength, in this view, was predicated on the dimensions of the very invasive pressures that had assaulted the island throughout its history. Cuban music, he writes, was "resistant to all foreign influences that—due to some extent to the very force of outside currents—might have been able to dislodge it from its own realm."[84] Carpentier's theory thus explains the richness and resilience of Cuba's musical practices in part as an adaptation to the formidable waves of cultural invasion that it had absorbed over the centuries.

In a 1967 *Down Beat* interview, composer and arranger Chico O'Farrill remarked that he truly believed that "jazz ended up influencing Cuban music more than Cuban music influenced jazz."[85] To be fair, I should point out that O'Farrill made his comment before the full extent of Cuba's influence on jazz—and for that matter that of Brazilian and Puerto Rican musicians— had become self-evident. O'Farrill himself would contribute invaluably to the recognition of Afro-Cuban jazz in the 1970s when he returned to the studios with Dizzy Gillespie, Machito, and Mario Bauzá for the landmark recording

Afro-Cuban Jazz Moods (1975). As recently as 2000, however, critic Gary Giddins unearthed O'Farrill's earlier interview to justify his own almost complete exclusion of Afro-Cuban performers from an overview of twentieth-century jazz artists.[86] Given the late-century jazz contributions of such giants as Valdés, Sandoval, D'Rivera, and Rubalcaba, non-Cuban performers like Danilo Pérez and Miguel Zenón, whose work bears the mark of earlier Afro-Cuban jazz, not to mention countless other international artists who have incorporated Cuban compositions and styles into their repertoire, it is safe to say that O'Farrill's comment is no longer as convincing or as valid as it may have seemed at the time.

Many mainstream jazz historians, meanwhile, continue to ignore the facts at their own peril. Indeed, the scholar Jairo Moreno's claim that Afro-Cuban music has been only marginally integrated into jazz historiography seems borne out by the fact that Pozo, in recent accounts, is generally discussed only in passing.[87] In *The History of Jazz*, Ted Gioia dedicates scarcely two of nearly four hundred pages to Afro-Cuban jazz. What he does include reads like a reluctant acknowledgment of Pozo, Bauzá, and Machito's indelible contributions, at times framed in language that harkens back to midcentury essentialisms: Pozo was "an exciting conga player," if violent and illiterate; Bauzá and Machito, meanwhile, spearheaded an "exciting mix of traditions." Although Gioia acknowledges that each side felt constrained by the other's musical styles, he ultimately downplays Pozo's impact on jazz history as a composer. Despite the fact that Gillespie "wanted to draw on Pozo's instincts," in the end "much of the burden fell on Dizzy and his collaborators [Gil] Fuller and George Russell to transform Pozo's simple constructs into full-fledged pieces."[88]

In his equally ambitious *A New History of Jazz*, Alyn Shipton gives more emphasis than Gioia to Chano Pozo's role in shaping postwar jazz. Though drawing on much of the same source material, Shipton produces a more nuanced view of Pozo and Cubop generally. He credits the Cuban percussionist with changing big-band jazz forever by promoting overtly African modalities and rhythms within jazz, thus not only making an impression among New York-based musicians and listeners but also selling bebop to visiting European jazz musicians as a fundamentally international style.[89] At the same time, Shipton writes, "Cubano Be, Cubano Bop" (written for the Cuban's famous appearance with Gillespie at Carnegie Hall in 1947) prefigured the kind of modal improvisation made popular years later by the likes of Miles Davis and John Coltrane.[90] Shipton thus avoids the trap of relegating Pozo to the bit part of "exciting" musician and colorful jester in Gillespie's royal court. Even so, his insistence on banishing Afro-Cuban contributions to the cul-de-sac of "big-band bebop" suggests that Shipton is still not ready to give Cubop full citizenship within the postwar canon.

In more specialized jazz histories, coverage of the seminal Afro-Cuban jazz collaborations has been cursory at best. In *Bebop: The Music and Its Players*, Thomas Owens mentions Pozo in passing, virtually ignoring the relevant social factors while doing a formal analysis of "Manteca," a song set apart from most bebop by its "hint of Mixolydian [scale] and the syncopated Afro-Cuban rhythms of the theme and its accompanying ostinato."[91] Lewis MacAdams's *Birth of the Cool: Beat, Bebop, and the American Avant Garde* errs in the opposite direction, treating Chano Pozo's contributions as mostly anecdotal rather than musical. While giving some useful information on Pozo's cultural and religious background, MacAdams focuses above all on the visual spectacle of the Cuban's appearance at Carnegie Hall: "Naked to the waist, his upper body oiled to an ebony glow, Chano strutted the stage barefoot, pounding out rhythms, chanting in Yoruba, and driving the audience wild."[92]

Finally, and in my view most conspicuously given his stature as a pioneer of new jazz studies, Scott DeVeaux mentions Pozo only once in *The Birth of Bebop*, widely considered the most authoritative recent history of the style. This omission is puzzling in itself, considering Gillespie's unquestioned status as a foundational figure of bebop and the trumpeter's unequivocal declaration of Pozo's pivotal role in bebop's development. Interestingly, DeVeaux mentions the percussionist only when he wishes to underscore the sensationalism and racism of *Life* magazine's coverage of jazz music's newest renegades. Bauzá's and Machito's roles in the Gillespie-Pozo collaborations are completely ignored. While DeVeaux is correct in criticizing US mainstream media's initially reactionary stance toward bebop, he illustrates the shortcomings of his own analysis when he invokes Chano Pozo's name only to upbraid 1940s media outlets for misreading the new musical style. Why else, he suggests, would an Afro-Cuban musician be featured so prominently in *Life*'s article and photo spread? What DeVeaux implies is that Pozo was to be seen above all as an emblem of the sensationalism that distracted the public from the music's "real" (non-Cuban) foundations.

To safeguard the seriousness and police the nationality of the new sound, in other words, mainstream English-language jazz criticism and historiography, ever since the emergence of the commercial and critical category of Latin jazz, has tended to downplay the crucial interventions of Afro-Cuban performers during the foundational moments of the 1940s and 1950s. Not unlike its circum-Caribbean double, mambo, Cubop's "homicidal musical limbo" has compelled US critics to write the music off as something other than jazz altogether. With little to gain from claiming innovative Cuban-born musicians as anything but their own, musical nationalists in Cuba seconded this segregationist maneuver. What is more, the relegation of Chano Pozo and Dámaso Pérez Prado to the status of dancehall kings and ethnic curiosities outlasted even the first major revival of Afro-Cuban jazz in the 1980s. As evidenced not only by the wholesale de-latinization of jazz in Ken Burns's documentary, but also by the serious scholarly work of a number of contemporary critics and historians, the assertively non-US provenance and global practices of jazz continue to baffle both assailants and gatekeepers of "America's classical music."

5

Liberation, Disenchantment,
and the Afterlives of Jazz

llegué tarde : qué puedo hacer : salvo escuchar : como un tonto :
lo que ustedes hicieron cuando yo tenía : tres años
— HERMENEGILDO SÁBAT, *Scat: Una interpretación gráfica del jazz* (1974)

Jazz played both major and minor roles—and sometimes the villain—in the elaboration of collective identities in Argentina, Brazil, Mexico, and Cuba during key moments of the twentieth century. The prominence of jazz in the regional imaginary speaks not just to the long shadow cast by the United States, but also to the centrality of music generally to political and cultural debates in Latin America. The extent to which musicians, composers, novelists, critics, fans, and filmmakers echoed, questioned, and occasionally tangled with official discourses on musical nationalism is truly remarkable. As I have discussed in the last three chapters, such was the power of the aural public sphere during the middle decades of the century that vernacular music, whether samba or tango, rumba or mambo, frequently led or shaped discussions of national identity, race, and hemispheric citizenship.

What is surprising is that music did not initially enjoy quite the same political prestige in the United States. In spite of the international popularity of hot jazz and big-band swing from the 1920s to the 1940s, the US government did not exploit the symbolic capital of its greatest musical export nearly as much as one might have expected. This is not to say that US musicians, composers, and other intellectuals did not see the potential of jazz as an emblem of national creativity and cultural vitality. As early as 1924, in a survey of "prominent public men and musicians" published in the influential music magazine *The Etude*, the composer John Alden Carpenter had proclaimed jazz "the most important musical expression that America has achieved."[1] In the same survey, the conductor Leopold Stokowski called jazz "an expression of the times, of the breathless, energetic, super-active time in which we are living" and "the greatest hope in the whole musical world."[2] Yet in the same decade, even African American publications such as the *Chicago Defender*, sharing some of the same moral reservations as mainstream newspapers and cultural critics of the period, were generally reluctant to endorse the music of black jazz and blues artists.[3]

By the late 1930s jazz had finally gained some ideological traction in the United States. In the program notes to the landmark *From Spirituals to Swing* concert at Carnegie Hall (1938), James Dugan and John Hammond wrote that the hot jazz style of Armstrong, Bechet, Ellington, Basie, and others was "uniquely American, the most important cultural exhibit we have given the world."[4] During World War II, the Roosevelt administration, through the Office of the Coordinator of Inter-American Affairs (OCIAA), supported radio broadcasts and tours by classical orchestras and big bands in Latin America. Yet the persistence of racial segregation in traveling swing orchestras undermined attempts to use jazz as a brush with which to paint the United States as an exemplary democracy and alternative to fascism. To make matters worse, many of the most popular big bands of the period were white, and even goodwill performances by black musicians (including enlisted men) merely served to underscore the institutional racial prejudice back home—a fact not lost on Latin American audiences.[5] It did not help that Hollywood productions before the 1950s generally did not make jazz the musical and thematic centerpiece to the same extent that Argentine and Brazilian industries featured tango and samba. Even the OCIAA's large-scale attempts to build Pan-American bridges did not effectively capitalize on jazz. In what promised to counteract the long-standing dearth of black jazz performers and characters on the silver screen, Orson Welles collaborated with Duke Ellington on an ambitious film project (*The Story of Jazz*), to star Louis Armstrong as himself. Though cast and scripted, the film never made it to production.[6]

In the early Cold War era, however, the US government's jazz policy shifted dramatically. By the late 1950s, the administration of Dwight D. Eisenhower had concluded that jazz, then experiencing a temporary resurgence in popularity after a decade's decline, could help to quell anti-US sentiment in countries caught in the maelstrom of postwar politics. This was thought to be especially true after the US Supreme Court declared racial segregation unconstitutional in the landmark *Brown v. Board of Education* decision (1954). With the stain of institutional racism ostensibly removed, the US government reasoned that jazz performers would become agents of a new "freedom offensive," prompting the State Department to sponsor tours to Europe, Africa, Asia, and Latin America by such established figures as Duke Ellington, Dizzy Gillespie, Louis Armstrong, Dave Brubeck, and Woody Herman.[7] These racially integrated tours were buttressed by radio broadcasts, particularly Willis Conover's popular show *Music USA*, launched in 1955 on Voice of America. The performances indeed provided a highly effective counterpunch to the recurrent Soviet criticism of racial segregation and social inequality in the United States. In Venezuela and Peru, for example, Herman's band triumphantly performed in 1958 just three months after Vice President Richard Nixon had been forced to cut short his visits due to the open hostility of the crowds.[8] The verdict was crystal clear: jazz could now accomplish what conventional politics could not.

The music's newfound ideological muscle was not lost on contemporaneous journalists. As one *New York Times* article proclaimed at the time, jazz had become the nation's "secret sonic weapon"—a universal language and an emblem of individual expression from Tangier to Moscow. Lest readers be confused as to who possessed symbolic ownership of the music, however, the *Times* writer reminded them that "[jazz] knows no boundaries, but everybody knows where it comes from and where to look for more. . . . [N]obody plays jazz like an American."[9] The State Department's strategy proved crucial not only in sparking the interest of fans worldwide but also in paving the way for the international careers of Latin American musicians and composers profoundly influenced by jazz. Gillespie's tour of Argentina in the late 1950s, for example, exposed him to future collaborator Lalo Schifrin. A single jam session in Rio de Janeiro, meanwhile, was enough to bring the legendary trumpeter into contact with Antônio Carlos Jobim.[10]

The spike in jazz's commercial appeal would prove relatively short-lived. Rock and roll, along with other musical expressions such as soul, mambo, calypso, and—with the help of both Jobim and Schifrin—bossa nova soon eclipsed the music's popularity with younger consumers. It did not help that in their effort to hallow jazz as "America's art form," the US government and a good many jazz critics had endorsed experimental strains of the music unlikely to be confused with popular entertainment. In the late 1950s and 1960s, while Gillespie transitioned from bebop maverick to mainstream headliner, emerging musicians such as Ornette Coleman, John Coltrane, Eric Dolphy, and Cecil Taylor challenged not just traditional notions of jazz but also the very tenets of acoustic rectitude. Unsure of what exactly to do with the new music's challenging aesthetics and frequently prickly politics, ideological discourses in the United States "papered over" differences and "compressed stylistic and racial divisions" in an effort to project jazz as an emblem of national unity.[11]

In spite of such efforts, by the end of the 1960s jazz had permanently fallen off its throne as the monarch of the US music industry, therefore ostensibly dulling its power as an international symbol of freedom and democracy. Even so, two events assured that the jazz imaginary would survive the music's popular demise at home and abroad. The foothold provided by the US State Department and Voice of America renewed jazz's symbolic cachet in Latin America at precisely the time when nationalist populism had loosened or lost its grip on cultural policies in Argentina, Brazil, and Mexico. The weakening of protectionist institutions (including those of the film industry) that had played such a crucial role in the 1930s and 1940s opened the floodgates to foreign and transnational cultural currents in ways not seen since the 1920s. Thanks to increased access to jazz concerts, recordings, cinematic performances, and radio and television broadcasts, a new generation of free and avant-garde jazz-loving intellectuals recast jazz as an oppositional and anticommercial expression that would resonate in the region for decades to come. Indeed, the notorious unpopularity of free jazz performers such as Coleman, Archie Shepp, and Don Cherry held a special appeal for some Latin American countercultural projects of the 1960s precisely because these musicians seemed to turn their backs on the market, evincing the pursuit of an expression that embodied formal experimentation and revolutionary ideals of freedom.

At the same time, across Latin America jazz revivalist movements, record collecting trends, and cult fan practices already in place in the 1940s and 1950s spawned scores of narratives and activities that celebrated hot jazz and swing, frequently in ghostly tones. This was especially true in nations such as Brazil, Chile, Argentina, and Uruguay that suffered periods of acute political repression in the 1960s, 1970s, and 1980s. Beset by isolation and disenchantment, sometimes forced into exile, jazz-loving intellectuals saw in the music both the lineaments of personal expression and memory and, somewhat paradoxically, also the ruins of failed utopian projects. Such ardent hopes and bitter misgivings, what scholar Diana Sorensen has called "the twin rhythms of euphoria and despair," lent themselves especially well to literary expression, which returned front and center to Latin American jazz discourse beginning in the 1960s.[12] Avant-garde writers of the 1920s had championed jazz as an emblem of cosmopolitan currency and technological progress, popular vitality and social velocity, racial otherness and sexual transgression. As I will discuss in this chapter, some Cold War intellectuals in Latin America were drawn to the liberatory ethos of free jazz as a soundtrack to revolution unencumbered by conventional melody and harmony. Yet increasingly, writers and intellectuals across the region began to view jazz not as a futurist blueprint but rather, in a sense, as the opposite: a mapping device for geopolitical estrangement and poetic anachronism. By the 1970s and 1980s, having been recast as a nostalgic archive of private travails and no longer casting a spell over younger audiences, jazz acquired spectral dimensions that highlighted not just its temporal separation from the past but also its spatial isolation from idealized soundscapes.

Jazz Puzzles

Perhaps more than any other literary work, Julio Cortázar's *Rayuela* (Hopscotch, 1963) captured at once the unbridled artistic ambition and deep political disenchantment of a generation of Latin American intellectuals. The novel would also revive jazz as a model of neo-avant-garde production in the 1960s, garnering considerable attention as much for its unusual structure as for its story and narrative style. *Rayuela*'s plot centers on the struggling writer Horacio Oliveira and his gregarious, makeshift existence in Paris during the 1950s. After losing his lover, La Maga, Oliveira returns to his native Argentina, where he associates with characters who uncannily mirror the personal dynamics of his Parisian entourage. Tethered loosely to its cast of bohemian characters and their passions and conflicts, the novel does not ramble so much as it *riffs* on an assortment of philosophical, political, and cultural topics, including jazz and blues. The innovative texture of the novel extends to the table of contents, which Cortázar has replaced daringly with a "Table of Instructions" in which readers are told to choose their own version of the novel. In other words, *Rayuela* should either be read (a) linearly, from first chapter to last; (b) by following a scrambled, "hopscotch" sequence of chapters suggested by the author; or (c) by simply skipping through the book as one desires.[13]

The apparently open-ended format of the novel has led a number of critics to suggest parallels between Cortázar's narrative concept and the freewheeling or aleatory structures of jazz.[14] Cortázar himself lent credence to such views in interviews when he suggested a parallel between the improvised or "automatic" elements of jazz, surrealism, and his own fiction.[15] Such readings of *Rayuela* (including Cortázar's own) would seem to have the most validity if we view the novel's schematic mapping of itself as derivative not of the pure improvisation of free jazz but rather of something akin to the controlled chaos of modal jazz. First developed in the late 1950s and early 1960s by George Russell, Miles Davis, John Coltrane, and others, modal jazz sought to rid the music of its dependence on scripted chord progressions. This kind of radical structural innovation is a far cry from the kind of music actually listened to and debated by the novel's characters, beginning with Oliveira, who generally eschews Davis and Coltrane for previous generations of jazz and blues artists such as Bessie Smith, Bix Beiderbecke, and Louis Armstrong.

Oliveira's predilection for hot jazz, swing, and early bebop reflects Cortázar's own somewhat anachronistic musical inclinations during his first years in Paris in the 1950s, from which the novel draws its inspiration. Be that as it may, the novel's political take on jazz is not simply conservative or conventional. For starters, Cortázar thumbs his nose at official Cold War imperatives that paint jazz as a uniquely American art form. In one of the novel's most famous passages, jazz is described as

the only universal music of the century, something that brought men together more and better than Esperanto, UNESCO, or the airlines, a music primitive enough to prove universal and good enough to make its own history, with its rifts, renunciations, and heresies, its Charleston, its black bottom, its shimmy, its fox-trot, its stomp, its blues, to admit all types and labels, this style and that, swing, bebop, cool, the ebb and flow of romanticism and classicism, hot and cerebral jazz, a music-man, a music with history, so different from stupid, animalistic dance music, polka, waltz, zamba, a music that allowed people to recognize and respect themselves whether in Copenhagen or Mendoza or Cape Town.[16]

Here, jazz is not just a universalizing force; it is also a universal one. In the State Department's promotion of jazz in the 1950s, the supposedly transcendent qualities of jazz join the nation to the rest of the world while masking the primacy of the music's national provenance—proof of American supremacy in the cultural arena. Cortázar's view of jazz does not refute the utopianism implicit in the official US position. If anything, he accentuates it. In *Rayuela*, jazz alone includes and liberates; jazz alone transcends the "stupidity" of popular dance music to give listeners the gifts of self-knowledge and self-worth.

At the same time, though, *Rayuela* aggressively removes jazz from its narrowly imperial function as an emblem of the United States. Jazz, Cortázar writes, "is like a bird that migrates or emigrates or immigrates or transmigrates, a barrier-jumper, a customs-fooler, something that runs and spreads." Like the international performances of Ella Fitzgerald, Louis Armstrong, Kenny Clarke, and Oscar Peterson, jazz is "[ubiquitous and] inevitable, it is the rain and bread and salt, something absolutely indifferent to national rites, to inviolable traditions, to language and folklore: it is a cloud without borders, a spy of air and water, an archetypal form, something from before, from below, that reconciles Mexicans with Norwegians and Russians and Spaniards, reincorporating them into the obscure, forgotten central flame, clumsily and badly and precariously it returns them to a betrayed origin."[17] When he refers to jazz's indifference to "national rites" and "inviolable traditions," Cortázar's disdain for self-serving national politics is clear. Jazz, he implies, will not be reduced to playing the pawn in a Cold War chess match. And while it would not be difficult to infer from this passage a criticism of the way Latin American governments had frequently rallied around supposedly quintessential idioms such as tango and samba, Cortázar's manifesto goes well beyond the realm of the national.

In fact, *Rayuela* reads as a warning against cultural stagnation as much as it does an attack against instrumental uses of vernacular music. Above all, Cortázar would have us believe, jazz is a mobile unifier, a "barrier jumper" and a "customs fooler." Of course, the fact that he features jazz as uniquely symbolic of the desires and struggles of the novel's uprooted characters prevents Cortázar from staking claim to the music as a trope of normative national identity. And this is precisely the point. For the Argentine writer, jazz sets itself apart because it transcends the "national rites" that plague Latin America, serving instead as a "modest exercise in liberation" for the novel's displaced characters.[18] Ultimately, though, jazz serves as an emblem not of collective secular identities, even transnational ones, but rather as a ubiquitous trope of what Cortázar elsewhere in *Rayuela* calls the "kibbutz of desire": an ideal poetic realm poised between "body and soul" where life "could express itself by other compasses and other names."[19]

An obscure, though compelling, counterpoint to *Rayuela*'s use of jazz as displacement-and-desire, Mexican journalist Jaime Pericás's unsung oddity *Nuestro jazz* (Our Jazz, 1966) is a playful, eccentric work that echoes Cortázar's belief in jazz as a wide-ranging metaphor of liberation. Though hardly the international publishing juggernaut that *Rayuela* proved to be, *Nuestro jazz* likewise sprang from an intellectual and cultural milieu specific to a time and place in which jazz frequently served as a privileged muse for cultural production. Luc Delannoy has written that the apogee of the Mexico City jazz scene began in the late 1950s, after musicians Tommy Rodríguez and Chilo Morán founded the renowned Jazz Bar in the Condesa neighborhood. During this same period a number of US marquee jazz names visited the city, including Louis Armstrong, Benny Goodman, Stan Kenton, and Shorty Rogers.[20] After the initial triumph of the Cuban Revolution, jazz and other US styles had become synonymous with cultural imperialism. At the same time, Mexico City grew in stature as a center for jazz, thanks in part to the steady, mentoring presence of the influential composer and bandleader Chico O'Farrill, who for several years had been splitting his time between New York, Havana, and Mexico.[21]

To an even greater extent than Cortázar's Paris, Mexico City's literary culture of the long sixties was intimately intertwined with jazz. Alain Derbez and other historians and musicians have chronicled a wide array of jazz-oriented literary and art events, theatrical performances, and happenings in Mexico, particularly in the early to mid-1960s. In 1962, for example, artist Pedro Cervantes and photographer Nacho López organized an exposition, *Cincuenta Imágenes de Jazz*, that included local jazz musicians Chucho Zarzosa, Tino Contreras, and Mike Salas.[22] In 1963, Juan José Gurrola staged the poetic-theatrical spectacle *Jazz Palabra*, which blended the music of the Modern Jazz Quartet with the poetry of e. e. cummings, Dylan Thomas, Alfonso Reyes, and Octavio Paz.[23] That same year, jazz drummer and bandleader Tino Contreras brought an ambitious ballet-musical to Mexico City's Palace of Fine Arts, apparently with great success. Three years later, Contreras created a choral spectacle, *Misa en Jazz*. "Written out of devotion to the music," the work debuted in the Hermanos Josefinos convent, only later to appear at the Palace of Fine Arts.[24] That same year, composer Carlos Chávez gave a lecture and performance called *El Jazz* at the Colegio Nacional.[25]

Jazz's countercultural cachet in Mexico in the first half of the decade is revealed in a series of articles published in the highly influential magazine *S.NOB*. Despite lasting only seven issues (June–October 1962), *S.NOB* brought popular music and film into the forefront of cultural analysis for a new generation of readers and intellectuals. The magazine was founded and directed by Salvador Elizondo, an emerging poet and novelist who, along with José Agustín, Parménides García Saldaña, and others, would later be associated with the La Onda movement. *S.NOB* was one of the first "serious" Mexican publications to treat jazz as something other than aesthetically impoverished dance music or an emblem of cultural imperialism. The magazine consecrated jazz for intellectual consumption by characterizing the music as fundamentally an art of virtuoso soloists and "poetic" creators. In "Jazz y droga," the most provocative of the essays, Jomi García Ascot wondered whether drug use aided the genius of performers like Billie Holiday and Charlie Parker. "While the majority of addicts look to drugs in order to escape from something . . . , creators look to drugs in order *to find* something."[26] Comparing jazz performers to Baudelaire, Verlaine, and Thomas de Quincey, García Ascot partially echoed the sentiments of Bruno in Cortázar's *El perseguidor*. Yet unlike Bruno, the Mexican journalist did not write off drug addiction as a pathetic affliction but rather as the special privilege of the creative few. Indeed, García Ascot suggested, the achievements of Holiday and Parker gave other talented artists permission to indulge in 1960s vices—advice apparently heeded by many participants of La Onda later in the decade.

Another pivotal cultural publication of the period was the daily newspaper *Cine Mundial*. It was here that Pericás, along with José Luis Durán (organizer of the inaugural Festival Nacional de Jazz), wrote regular *crónicas* that would eventually serve as the basis for *Nuestro jazz*. As the book's title implies, though, *Nuestro jazz* is not content to enlist jazz as a general soundtrack for decentered modernity or a model for creative virtuosity. "For me," Pericás writes, "jazz is not just music; it is in all the arts and in all perfect things. It is in houses and towns, in cities and nations, in our planet and in the infinite. . . . All things, objects, places, colors, flavors, forms, and beings that please us have jazz."[27] Conversely, Pericás likens pollution, wars, and political corruption to out-of-tune keys of a piano and castigates people who suffer from a lack of spontaneity or grace, joy or honesty, as "antijazz."[28]

Despite framing jazz as a kind of universal benchmark, the writer's chief concern is clearly Mexico. *Nuestro jazz* attempts a semiserious rewriting of national history in which jazz serves avant la lettre as a metaphor for Mexico's striking pre-Columbian traditions as well as its modern achievements. In his view, both conquered Aztecs and conquering Spaniards had "jazz." There was "jazz in the poetry of Netzahualcóyotl" and in the "creative" vision of Columbus.[29] After the conquest, the nation's history followed the peaks and valleys of a "liberating" jazz solo: "shock during Independence, tears during the yanqui invasion, intrepid Mexicanism during the French occupation, and a spew of fire during the Revolution."[30] Contemporary Mexico, too, had its jazz. Pericás thus praises the sounds of Mexican factories and television studios as jazzlike. Even the pharmaceutical industry is exalted for enabling a greater appreciation of modernity—"with those marvelous pills of jazz," he writes, "man can better appreciate the beautiful things of life and realize that the noises that once damaged his ears are none other than music, and agreeable music, since it's pure jazz . . . our jazz."[31]

What is perhaps most salient about Pericás's strange revisionism is the extent to which he selectively expropriates jazz in the process. The United States, though "said to be where jazz was born," has begun to "go out of tune" as a society.[32] In short, the US could not claim to be jazzy any more than China or the Soviet Union, while Mexico was "super-endowed with the [kind of] jazz synonymous with progress, struggle, and harmony."[33] Pericás's slippage between using jazz as a sign of moral integrity or civilizational puissance and as a signifier of a specific cultural practice is apparent in the chapter "Malinchismo en jazz." The Mexican journalist sets his sights on international "traitors" such as Japan, for supposedly falsifying international trademarks, and Brazil, for stealing the musical spotlight from nations like Mexico. The members of the Brazilian group Tamba Trio, Pericás alleges, pass themselves off as jazz virtuosos when in fact they "hardly manage to master sleepy bossa nova."[34] For the Mexican writer, the main culprits are the snobs who "believe that jazz is only that which smells like the United States or Brazil, [and] remain pinned to their own ignorance, applauding to no end that guarded cold fish named Dave Brubeck."[35]

If *Nuestro jazz* represents the bizarre culmination of jazz-as-metaphor in the 1960s, the book is conspicuously short on *musical* analysis in Mexico or anywhere else. Jazz historian Géraldine Célélier Eguiluz has remarked that the book "is not in a strict sense a musicological text and does not offer greater information that could enrich our knowledge of Mexican jazz."[36] Indeed, after briefly mentioning the playing of Tino Contreras and activities of promoter José Luis Durán, Pericás withdraws to the comfort of a historically unspecified jazz imaginary for much of the rest of his book.

Shortly after the publication of *Nuestro jazz*, RCA Camden released a notable recording by the same title. A compilation of Mexican jazz musicians performing mostly original compositions, the record *Nuestro Jazz* featured liner notes by Pericás himself. While singing the praises of homegrown jazz talent such as Pablo Jaimes, Luis González, Nacho Rosales, Chinto Mendoza, and Jorge Ortega, Pericás seized the opportunity to make a case for jazz's unique capacity for assimilation and appropriation in any setting: "In its dizzying tour of the world, jazz has acquired naturalization papers in many countries, where it has been interpreted with all of its nuances, to which the peculiar tone of each people has been added."[37]

Yet jazz had still not been heard everywhere in "all of its nuances." The so-called New Thing had yet to take hold in Mexico in the mid-1960s, which may explain why Pericás failed to address avant-garde or free jazz any more than Cortázar had by that time.[38] The international performers who most often surface in Derbez's account of the period—Louis Armstrong, Duke Ellington, Dizzy Gillespie, Thelonious Monk, Charlie Byrd, Dave Brubeck—in fact differ little from *Rayuela*'s hallowed list of jazz references. Cortázar's initial resistance to cutting-edge jazz recordings was likely due more to disposition than access. As I have already suggested, there is a clear incongruity between the formal experimentalism of *Rayuela* and the mostly conservative views of jazz and blues espoused by the novel's cast of characters.

Cortázar's delay in embracing post-swing jazz came to an end with the publication of *El perseguidor* in 1959. Still, later works in which Cortázar profiles modern jazz musicians are marked by the same Johnny-come-lately celebration that plagues *Rayuela*. In his collection of essays *La vuelta al día en ochenta mundos* (Around the Day in Eighty Worlds), Cortázar obliquely acknowledges his anachronistic approach. Noting that nearly 15 years separated the original 1952 publication of a crónica inspired by one of Louis Armstrong's live performances ("Louis, enormísimo cronopio") and a similar profile of Thelonious Monk ("La vuelta al piano de Thelonious Monk"), Cortázar observes that the passage of time between the two accounts is hardly noticeable, since "whenever I talk about jazz I sound the same."[39]

Literary scholar Jean Franco has remarked that while Cortázar's embrace of jazz betrayed a utopian impulse to bridge the gap between popular and erudite cultures, spectators, and performers, he also typically favored "superseded forms" that allowed him to position himself and his characters as sophisticated archivists.[40] It is perhaps for this reason that Cortázar's jazz references, even those uttered from the heart of the Parisian metropolis, so often produce a sense of temporal isolation. Given his customary lag in literary appropriation, it is not surprising that the author's resistance to free jazz seemed to ease only in the later part of his career. In *La vuelta al día en ochenta mundos*, Cortázar coyly blames the "probable lack of information" in his prose on the fact that he had been spending his time "listening to Ornette Coleman and perfecting my trumpet playing."[41] In the self-referential poem "De lugar llamado Kindberg," from *Octaedro* (1981), he describes using an Archie Shepp record as a mantra to his solitary routines. Shepp's "brusque" playing interacts with him while he edits his latest writing, eats goulash, and reads Allen Ginsberg. The sound of the record softly resumes after dinner, a voice of nocturnal reassurance and continuity, tenderness and companionship:

> . . . and the Shepp cognac
> I have to think about the Shepp tomorrow
> I will not have lost you, Shepp[42]

Cortázar's delayed appreciation and eventual embrace of free jazz reflected a shifting political sensibility, not just on the Argentine's part but also for many other Latin American writers of his generation. But this shift also exemplifies the versatility of jazz's symbolic capital between the 1950s and the 1970s. As scholar E. Taylor Atkins has suggested, the universal value frequently attributed to jazz in the 1960s and beyond depended to some extent on the self-fulfilling prophecy of US jazz diplomacy of a decade earlier, in which the state apparatus reinforced the image of jazz as "America's inimitable gift to the world" through its sponsorship of high-profile international tours. These efforts had a carryover effect in the decades to come, as Latin American writers like Cortázar and Pericás built eccentric, even subversive jazz narratives upon foundations laid in part by the imperialist-universalist logic of the US State Department. "Precisely because it had originated among an oppressed group in the United States," Atkins writes, "jazz was a double-edged sword when brandished in postcolonial contexts and ideological skirmishes."[43] Jazz being jazz, in other words, it could be invoked as an emblem of revolutionary resistance just as easily as it could serve as a symbol of the "free world."

Liberation Adapted

The origins of the relationship between Latin America and what would later become known as the Black Power movement (and its cultural corollary, the Black Arts Movement) dates back to the late Eisenhower administration, when a young African American writer named LeRoi Jones toured a newly revolutionary Cuba under the aegis of the Fair Play for Cuba Committee (FPCC). The 1959 visits by Jones, Lawrence Ferlinghetti, and others signaled an intense mutual interest between the revolution and sympathetic writers from the United States.[44] Jones (who later changed his name to Amiri Baraka) was already widely considered a rising figure on the US literary scene, though still linked to white Beat writers such as Ferlinghetti, Allen Ginsberg, and Jack Kerouac. By the time of his arrival in Havana, one of Jones's poems had been published by the Cuban literary supplement *Lunes de Revolución*, whose editor, the novelist Guillermo Cabrera Infante, met with Jones during his stay.[45] Jones also made the acquaintance of the young writer Pedro Armando Fernández (who had translated his work for *Lunes de Revolución*) and the prominent Afro-Cuban poet Nicolás Guillén, with whom Jones conversed about Langston Hughes.[46] The Cuba visit made a lasting impression on Jones. On a train trip to the eastern part of the island to attend a July 26 celebration and hear a speech by Castro, the young American writer, referring to himself as an apolitical poet, was accused by a young Mexican woman of being a "cowardly bourgeois individualist."[47] Later Jones confessed that the spectacle of so many "already politicized" Latin American activists and intellectuals spurred him to integrate aesthetics and politics into his own life.[48]

LeRoi Jones's watershed books *Blues People* (1963) and *Black Music* (1967) had a decisive impact not just in defining jazz as African American music, but also specifically in resignifying jazz as a counterhegemonic banner of racial pride and liberation. Jones's message had considerable resonance beyond the United States. Archie Shepp remarked in a 1965 *Down Beat* interview that jazz was "against war; against Vietnam; for Cuba; for the liberation of the peoples of the world."[49] The Black Power movement was not all talk when it came to Cuba. Robert F. Williams, forced into exile in Cuba in the early 1960s, hosted a radio show there directed toward the United States (*Radio Free Dixie*). It was filled with black separatist speeches and the "way-out" sounds of Ornette Coleman and Max Roach, thus formulating "a new psychological concept of propaganda" aimed at the senses, "something similar to what is used in the churches."[50] In 1963, Williams also helped Leonardo Acosta and others organize a jazz festival on the island.[51]

Yet as the decade progressed, free jazz and the still incipient Black Power movement had difficulty gaining permanent traction either in Cuba or elsewhere in Latin America. Set to Lena Horne's controversial single "Now!," Santiago Álvarez's short documentary of the same name (1965) featured an innovative montage of still photos and archival footage from US civil rights protests. *Now* straddled the line politically between safe endorsement of passive resistance to imperial oppression and daring incitement to race-based revolution. While Álvarez's short paid homage to Martin Luther King Jr., the gunfire at the conclusion of the film, spelling out the title with bullet holes, suggested that armed resistance was the solution to racial discrimination in the United States. Still, Álvarez eschewed overt visual evocations of black nationalism. In this sense, the choice of Lena Horne's song was an interesting one. The straightforward populism of the song's lyrics and the singer's delivery surely appealed to revolutionary sensibilities.[52] Indeed, the inclusion of music more clearly aligned to the Black Arts Movement, such as free jazz, would likely have tilted Álvarez's statement of solidarity too far in the direction of radical separatism, as opposed to "merely" violent confrontation.[53]

Two years later, the Cuban writer Edmundo Desnoes edited a related volume, *Now: El movimiento negro en Estados Unidos*, featuring translated essays and fragments by the likes of Malcolm X, Martin Luther King Jr., James Baldwin, and Stokely Carmichael. The anthology also included LeRoi Jones's "Crítica de jazz e ideología," an adaptation of his 1960 essay "Jazz and the White Critic." In *Now*'s introduction, though, Desnoes glossed over the symbiotic relationship between free jazz and Black Power. What is more, he downplayed race consciousness in the movement as a mere precursor to a wider colonial consciousness that would unite oppressed peoples of the Americas and elsewhere. In other words, the Cuban writer attempted to paint Black Power as part of a broader Third World liberation front while assuring his readers (and censors) that "[US] blacks are moving from race consciousness to a consciousness of the colonized [subject]; they are against discrimination, underdevelopment—not against [US] whites."[54] That Desnoes sought to sand off Black Power's rougher edges in the name of internationalism reflected the hushed ambivalence of the Cuban government in matters of race, and specifically in relation to the capitalist-countercultural milieu whence Black Power arose.[55]

Revolutionary Cuba's reluctance to fully embrace or emulate African American militancy in the late 1960s may explain the lukewarm praise for free jazz in other parts of the region where official discourse was more openly hostile toward music associated with black separatism. In the case of Argentina, with a right-wing authoritarian regime in power and a long history of hostility toward blackness and *mestizaje* as viable categories of racial identity, it is no surprise that a music so strongly associated with the Black Arts Movement did not immediately find a sizable audience. But the same was also true in racially diverse Brazil, home of the largest Afro-descendant population in the Americas. The nation's first coordinated attempt to advocate for racial justice and representation through music centered on the dissident bossa nova *participação* movement of the early to mid-1960s. In spite of the involvement of such Afro-Brazilian musicians as Baden Powell and staunch advocacy on behalf of *samba do morro* musicians such as Nelson Cavaquinho and Zé Keti, though, participação amounted to a sort of minor black nationalist movement by white proxy, one that had more in common with King's "Freedom Now!" than Carmichael's Black Power.[56] By the late 1960s, the presence of a politically reactionary, socially intolerant military government in Brazil assured that any cultural expression of Black Power would be met with censorship or outright repression. It would not be until the mid-1970s that a musical alternative would emerge. As it turned out, though, it was North American funk and soul music, and not free jazz or samba do morro, that would serve as the main springboards for popular Afro-Brazilian political-cultural movements such as Black Rio and Ilê Aiyê.[57]

And yet, free jazz abided. Long after the music had waned as a political force and racial rallying cry in the United States and elsewhere in the world, a number of Latin American intellectuals besides Cortázar began to warm to the New Thing as a model of literary expression and personal, rather than collective or racial, liberation. In 1983, for instance, the Veracruz-born poet, musician, and essayist Alain Derbez published a unique chapbook of handwritten poems, *Para mirar el ruido* (To Look at Sound), featuring the illustrations of Jazzamoart (Javier Vásquez). Derbez and Jazzamoart's work found inspiration in Thelonious Monk and Billie Holiday, but the stronger influences were Dewey Redman, Cecil Taylor, Eric Dolphy, Archie Shepp, and Anthony Braxton. The tension between Vásquez's noisy, expressionistic visual style and Derbez's somber precision proved effective if at times somewhat unsettling. To a three-line poem ("improvisation / infinitude of a sea / that drowns us"), for instance, Jazzamoart juxtaposes a thumbnail portrait of the saxophonist Redman floating kite-like in the air, as if at odds with the sinking motion of Derbez's words.[58] The poem "Cae la noche," meanwhile, adeptly captures the particular contours of Shepp's music:

music
acid rain
   a fist of water
the slightest graze destroys the structure
sharp statues of salt
fearful of the wind
sustain the reality
on which we dance
the night falls
in the silence one hears everything[59]

The theme of silence is one Derbez turns to repeatedly in *Para mirar el ruido*. Of Anthony Braxton, Derbez asks:

how to narrate sounds
hollows of silence
big and rooouuund hooolloooows of silence
there's no doubt about it, Braxton, you owe me
an explanation on your tenor sax[60]

To illustrate the poet's bewilderment, Jazzamoart decorates the page with a serpentine figure that could pass for either a road and a saxophone, or neither. The puzzling image is likely a nod to the stubbornly cryptic diagrams found in many of Braxton's record covers and liner notes from the period. *Para mirar el ruido*'s illustrator thus conspires with Braxton against written interpretation and intelligibility generally. As if to defend the writer against such a joint assault, Derbez concludes his poem brazenly:

in the end
blacks like you

don't have the last word
honk, honk, honk!
there's no need[61]

We have heard a similar punch line before: in *El perseguidor,* Cortázar's Bruno makes a similar race-based, jazz-as-mystery argument to justify his work as Johnny's biographer. Yet Derbez and Jazzamoart do not sound half as convinced as Bruno that their intervention is all that necessary. Like many others in the *Para mirar el ruido* collection, the Braxton poem reads more like an emulative collaboration than a critical interpretation. Rather than pretending to offer a heuristic solution to the riddle of free and avant-garde jazz, in other words, Derbez and Jazzamoart, like respectful sidemen, seem content to play along in the same spirit of open-ended exploration.

Three years later the poems of *Para mirar el ruido* would re-appear in an extensive anthology of Latin American jazz poetry edited by Derbez. Though casting a much wider net than its predecessor, *Todo se escucha en el silencio* (In the Silence One Hears Everything, named after the line from Derbez's Archie Shepp poem) contains a number of pieces about the main proponents of free jazz and its various offshoots. Former *S.NOB* contributor Jomi García Ascot contributes a poetic eulogy to John Coltrane, praising "oh the sound oh the search" of the musician's later, extended solos, in which Coltrane "looked for the fixity of the river that never repeats itself."[62] Evodio Escalante's "La noche de Sun Ra," meanwhile, pays tribute to the recording artist's unique visual and musical style, cosmic aura, and Afrocentric themes:

Sun Ra, how to bite
the dead cranium of the Ozone
how to look twice at the same ecstatic Nile[63]

It is the Argentine saxophonist Gato Barbieri, though, who serves as the focus of one of the anthology's most memorable works. Given his relatively early involvement with free jazz and rising international fame in the 1970s, it should perhaps not come as a surprise that the "Latin Cat" should figure prominently in *Todo se escucha en silencio.* In a long paean to Eric Dolphy, Derbez appears to downplay the importance of Barbieri when he writes that "without dolphy / neither [Anthony] braxton nor barbieri / would be comprehensible."[64] Yet the very mention of Barbieri in such company suggests just how high his stature was in the global jazz scene of the late 1960s to late 1970s. In the poem "Gato," most likely based on the memory of a live performance,

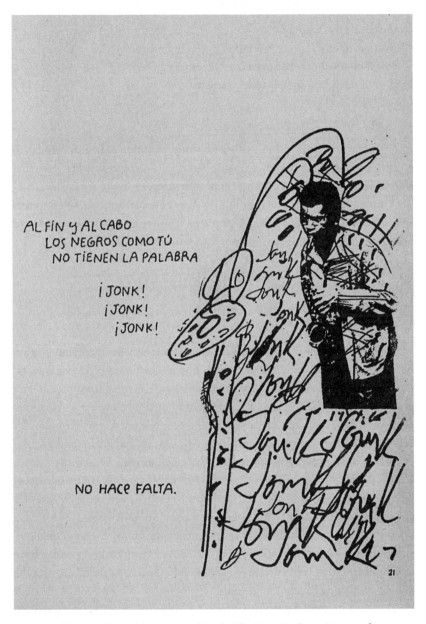

Fig. 5.1. Alain Derbez and Jazzamoart, "¡Jonk!," featuring Anthony Braxton, from *Para mirar el ruido* (1983).

Marcela Campos closely examines the subtle negotiations between the Argentine saxophonist's body and the notes produced in a solo:

> the humidity circulates
> wets your breath
> which tastes of the absent sound that sways you;
> the humidity you spit and which returns
> still less clean
> to your body[65]

Campos plays rather conventionally with tropes common to free jazz, and even recalls Cortázar's descriptions of Charlie Parker in *El perseguidor* when she writes that Barbieri is an arduous searcher for novelty who can "never retrace his steps." Yet Campos is unusually probing of the erotics of live performance and improvisation, both in terms of Barbieri's corporeal involvement with his instrument and also, finally, the musician's communication with his audience:

> before waking up again,
> you will wipe your saxophone clean with your shirtsleeve
> while you sense me
> and speak to me[66]

Campos's poem builds on the exaltation of one-way aural communication between jazz record and listener that we find in Cortázar's or Derbez's work, but with the inclusion of detailed visual and other sensorial information. Her study of Gato Barbieri is thus a narrative of fleshed-out interaction that goes far beyond the awed transcription of a radio broadcast or recorded music. Her version of Barbieri does not just play notes: he writhes and groans and spits; he "senses" and communicates nonverbally with his audience. On a broader level, "Gato" reveals just how ubiquitous live performances and filmed broadcasts of jazz had become by the 1980s.[67] The deeply holistic involvement captured by Campos's work no doubt reflects one fan's wishes for intimate contact with jazz celebrity. Yet the poem's emphasis on corporeal affect is somewhat anomalous. In fact, from Cortázar to Derbez, late twentieth-century Latin American literary tributes to free jazz were strikingly disembodied, a fact that suggests the abiding mediating function of records.

There is an essential paradox haunting utopian celebrations of improvised music, particularly free jazz. The very nature of recording technology would appear to deprive the music of its most salient formal features, namely its extemporaneity and unpredictability. A similar paradox applies to attempts to write about free jazz. Ana María Ochoa Gautier has called such procedures "entextualization," or "the act of framing the musical object to be studied through multiple modes of 'capturing' it." Ochoa Gautier has rightly underscored the similarities in this sense between writings about and recordings of traditional and popular music.[68] These parallels come into full view in cases where a record's functionality as a model of creative writing is made explicit, as in Silviano Santiago's *Keith Jarrett no Blue Note: Improvisos de Jazz* (Keith Jarrett at the Blue Note: Jazz Improvisations, 1996). A collection of semiautobiographical fiction focused thematically on homoeroticism and exile, *Keith Jarrett no Blue Note* consists of five stories named after the five tracks of Jarrett's live recording of the same name released by EMI in 1994. Using a precise prose style anchored by a second-person (*você*) narration that migrates freely through intricate layers of flashbacks, the five pieces mimic Jarrett's own palimpsestic approach to jazz standards. Like Jarrett and the rest of his trio (Jack DeJohnette on drums and Gary Peacock on bass), Santiago shifts fluidly between sentimental modes, from playful to plaintive to melodramatic. Straddling the continents, the stories echo Jarrett's vacillation between classical and jazz registers as well. As Santiago's narrator puts it, "Chopin and Art Tatum join hands and enter the river, rowing downstream, rowing upstream, in a musical canoe."[69]

Santiago's story "Autumn Leaves" draws especially deep correlations between fiction writing and Jarrett's performance. Playing his CD at home on a cold, rainy day in an unnamed northeastern US city, the solitary narrator enters into a reverie in which he recalls hearing the original version of the Prévert-Kosmas tune "Les feuilles mortes" (sung by Yves Montand) during his first stay in Paris decades earlier. "You are sure," he writes, "that Keith Jarrett is also listening to it [while he plays his version]."[70] Linking the two interpretations of the song are the narrator's meditations on dry leaves gathered on a walk to a local market—sentimental tokens recalling the autumnal leaves he had gathered on the banks of the Seine while living in Paris in the early 1960s—and the image of knives, which he associates with menace and also desire.[71] The narrator nostalgically recalls his stay—a detail that closely parallels Santiago's graduate studies in France during the same period—and in particular a romantic relationship with a young Mexican man, comparing his experience favorably to his present, lonely exile in the United States: "You did not feel like a stranger in Paris."[72]

The way Santiago's narrator cherishes his European memories echoes Jarrett's evocations of the original "Les feuilles mortes" in his jazz interpretation of "Autumn Leaves." But Santiago also evokes the pianist's conquest of European audiences in the 1970s, culminating in Jarrett's celebrated *Köln Concert* recording of 1975: "You remember [a *New York Times* critic saying] that Keith, despite having deep roots in American jazz and traditions, plays better in Germany and Scandinavian countries than in his native country."[73] Jarrett's notoriety as an expat jazz artist no doubt made him an attractive model for Santiago's narrative explorations of exile. Jarrett himself contributed to such a reputation. In a 1975 interview, when asked why he preferred giving solo concerts in Europe, Jarrett remarked that the prestige of jazz musicians in Europe was generally greater than in the United States, and very much on par with that of elite classical solo-ists.[74] Part of Europe's embrace of Jarrett's music in particular may have been due to the pianist's eclecticism, including his frequent tributes to the classical and popular traditions of the Continent, as well as his seemingly anticommercial stance against electric music.

Yet Jarrett's international, crossover appeal also hinged greatly on his uniquely charismatic stage presence, a visual style deeply rooted in rock counterculture that complemented the pianist's carefully cultivated image of a mystical genius. By the mid-1970s widespread footage of Jarrett's chanting and trance-like twisting and contorting had reinforced Jarrett's own assertion in liner notes, interviews, and elsewhere that during his solo improvisations, he served as a spiritual "channel for the Creative."[75] As David Ake puts it, the visually intensive "deep jazz" of Jarrett's solo concerts somewhat resembled a mass séance.[76] In "Autumn Leaves," Santiago alludes to the marketing gimmickry lurking behind Jarrett's cathartic visual language and apparently unbridled creativity. Writing that "you used to barely tolerate Keith's pretentious exhibitionism," the narrator comes to terms with the pianist's affectations only by writing them off as the "registered trademark" of a commercial artist working within the confines of the capitalist system. Thus he uses Jarrett as a point of departure for an extended meditation on a globalized US society caught in a cycle of consumption and waste.[77]

Literary critic Karl Posso has suggested that the "desirable imperfections of ambiguity and polysemy" of Santiago's "Autumn Leaves" at once reflect and benefit from the "undecidable freedom" of improvisation introduced to the story through the playing of Jarrett's music. What is more, the open-endedness of Jarrett's riffs as well as Santiago's mirror how the artifacts of capitalism itself—the porn magazines, matches, and strewn garbage described in the story—present endless choices to consumers.[78] Be that as it may, Santiago's narrator falls into a trap of his own making when he attempts to explain away Jarrett's antics as emblematic of dubitable commercial practices identified explicitly, and rather gloomily, with the United States, all the while exalting the pianist as a transnational conduit of memory whose music transcends the limits of the national marketplace.

One notable omission in *Keith Jarrett no Blue Note* is Santiago's lack of engagement with the racial politics of jazz. Much has been made by critics and musicians about Jarrett's phenotypic ambiguity. Though the pianist is of European descent on both sides of his family, Jarrett's kinky hair and swarthy appearance for many observers "whispered of other roots."[79] While such rumors have hardly damaged Jarrett's marketability, a more serious admonition was brought forth by German critic Joachim-Ernst Berendt, who in his 1976 article "Jazz and the New Fascism" accused Jarrett and other musicians, including Chick Corea and John McLaughlin, of stripping jazz of its social and political heritage.[80] To borrow Malcolm X's term, such bourgeois romanticism "bleached" the African American legacy of jazz.[81] Jarrett's musically eclectic virtuosity and apolitical countercultural stance certainly opened doors for the pianist. They also made Jarrett a useful model for writers in Latin America who sought to evoke the liberatory politics of jazz—in the case of Santiago's stories, grafting them onto the homoerotics of exile—without either sullying their hands with Black Power or severing symbolic ties to Europe.

Although it features ostensibly antihegemonic writing leveled against heterosexual societal norms, *Keith Jarrett no Blue Note* plays it curiously safe in its treatment of jazz. In this sense, an interesting counterpoint to Santiago's collection is César Aira's unusual story *Cecil Taylor* (1993). Rather than bypassing the eponymous musician's life to focus on his recorded work, as Santiago does with Jarrett, Aira strives for the opposite, framing his literary text à la Cortázar as a biography that questions the fictive strategies of conventional biographies. The biographies of famous musicians, he writes, tend to resemble thinly disguised hagiographies, in which an exalted "before" inevitably prefigures the artist's future success, the "afterward" offering "delicious consolations, all the more delicious for having been the object of spot-on prophecies."[82]

Openly aiming to break this mold, Aira focuses on Taylor's repeated and often ignominious failure to reach live audiences during the infancy of free jazz in the late 1950s. Taylor's early attempts to secure paid gigs, Aira tells us, condemned him to playing in inappropriate Manhattan venues, from dives in which music took a back seat to drugs and prostitution to stuffy, high-society parties. In both cases, Taylor's experiments with atonality were met with incredulity and derision. To pay rent in his squalid East Side apartment, which he shared with rats and cockroaches, he held numerous side jobs as a dishwasher, paint shop clerk, and so forth.[83] Like Santiago, Aira generally avoids foregrounding race. In this sense, the Argentine writer exhibits the telltale signs of a residual tendency to translate racial otherness into socioeconomic difference.[84] Yet his emphasis on Taylor's dire economic struggles at least acknowledges the poverty that has befallen so many African American jazz musicians, particularly those as creatively uncompromising as Taylor. As with the stories of *Keith Jarrett no Blue Note*, *Cecil Taylor* presents us with an unorthodox, probing tale resistant to easy consumption, the difficulty of the writing mirroring the challenge of the music itself. Here, though, the musician's life is revealed as materially challenging as well. Aira self-consciously recognizes the against-the-grain work of his endeavor: "Don't anecdotes also have to triumph, so that they are repeated?"[85]

In a way, Aira's story reads like an antidote to jazz-as-liberator narratives. Behind the intrepid searching of free and avant-garde jazz, Aira suggests, lie myriad dead ends, untold histories of struggle, failure, and social rejection. Unlike the linear narratives of most musical biographies, or the disembodied sounds of records and radio, the public lives of experimental jazz musicians like Taylor frequently mask narratives of racial prejudice, oblivion, and humiliation. "In truth failure is infinite," Aira writes, "because it is infinitely divisible, something that does not happen with success."[86] By restricting his imagination to the early years of Taylor's career and denying his readers the triumphant denouement they had come to expect from jazz biographies, Aira's fiction forces readers to come to terms with the dissonant social context from which aesthetic "freedom" is so often forged. The story thus functions politically as a comment on the mundane limits and banal failures hindering the monomaniacal pursuit of innovation. The critique is not without immediate political connotations. Unlike Cortázar's Johnny Carter, Aira's Taylor is not kept back by his own personal demons so much as by the tyrannical intransigence of musical audiences and convention. By revealing the labor and oppression behind the struggle for creative freedom, Aira—writing amid the ruins of utopian projects and reactionary violence in Argentina—ultimately unclothes revolutionary yearnings as bound to fail repeatedly.

Swing Time (Again)

By the 1980s and 1990s, a number of Latin American intellectuals had embraced contemporary strains of jazz at precisely the moment that such music struggled to reconnect with popular audiences in the United States, and to a lesser extent in Latin America. As I have suggested, writers such as Alain Derbez and Silviano Santiago downplayed or even dispensed entirely with the Black Power connotations of the New Thing and its offshoots, winnowing the potent aesthetics of improvisational jazz from its black nationalist, collectivist, and overtly political casings. By expanding jazz's generic and racial boundaries, Jarrett and Barbieri acted as attenuated messengers of the music's most radical exponents, a tendency laid bare by Aira's foregrounding of abject struggle in *Cecil Taylor*. Even so, by this time the liberatory capital of jazz in the region paled in comparison to other musical forms. For critics, rock and related expressions replaced jazz as the go-to metonymies of frivolous materialism, moral debauchery, and yanqui imperialism. Yet in Argentina and Brazil, foreign and domestic variations of rock and later funk provided the principal soundtracks to youth resistance movements just as military dictatorships hardened into violently repressive regimes in the late 1960s and early to mid-1970s.[87]

Displaced by more youthful and commercially successful musical expressions, jazz had become untimely. Perhaps sensing the anachronistic potential of the music amid the intense political theater of capitalism and authoritarianism, conflict and mourning, a number of Latin American writers collected and memorialized the ruins of jazz.[88] Even in the twilight of the Cold War, Latin American intellectuals were at least as likely to be fans of Louis Armstrong and Benny Goodman as they were to extol the virtues of Jarrett and Barbieri, much less Ornette Coleman and Don Cherry. Part of the seemingly dated quality of south-of-the-border jazz fandom was due to the uneven and sometimes glacial flow of information about the music. Even when "progressive" sounds made it ashore, as was the case of bebop in the 1950s, the music did not arrive all at once. Instead, experimental jazz tended initially to make small incursions within limited social circles, first winning over musicians and other aficionados in large urban areas. In the 1950s and 1960s, the peculiarities of Cold War politics compounded the problem, as the State Department generally gave preference to either consecrated or otherwise safe choices to represent the nation abroad. Shepp and Taylor were clearly not meant to be the global face of jazz.

Yet even mainstream headliners were often late in coming. Such was the case with Duke Ellington. Although by the 1940s virtually all Latin American jazz fans were familiar with the legendary bandleader, it was not until 1968 that Ellington and his orchestra toured South America. When they did arrive, they were met with throngs of adoring fans wherever they went. Ellington himself called the "generosity and enthusiasm" of audiences in Argentina, Uruguay, Chile, and Brazil "the inspiration of a lifetime—a virtual summit in my career."[89] Argentina, now ruled by an Onganía regime hostile to the youth culture associated with rock, seems to have been particularly welcoming of Ellington. At a performance at the US embassy, the Duke was regaled with a who's who of local jazz dignitaries, including Oscar Alemán, Louis Blue, and Enrique "Mono" Villegas. Besieged by autograph seekers virtually everywhere, whether in concert halls or hotels, streets or airports, Ellington "brought back a sense of jubilation missing since the 1950s" and inaugurated a new international phase in the Argentine jazz scene.[90]

The road to Ellington's late-career triumph in Latin America had been paved in previous decades by the stubborn persistence of hot jazz and swing fan clubs throughout the region. In the postwar period, Argentine and Uruguayan jazz discourse was unevenly split between traditionalists (*hoteros*) and modern jazz proponents (*boperos*), with the former outnumbering the latter. Founded in 1948, the Hot Club de Buenos Aires served as a meeting place for swing aficionados and hot revivalists. It sponsored live performances by like-minded local bands such as the Hot Jammers, the Guardia Vieja Jazz Band, and the Dixielanders. It also recorded many of these same local artists and hosted visits by touring international stars such as Louis Armstrong.[91] In Chile, too, traditional jazz enjoyed great popularity in the 1940s and 1950s thanks in part to the activities of the Club de Jazz de Santiago (founded in 1943), followed by similar clubs in Concepción, Valparaíso, and Viña del Mar. Like the Hot Club de Buenos Aires, the Club de Jazz de Santiago organized live performances and recording sessions for RCA Victor by local "hot" groups such as the Ases Chilenos del Jazz, the Chicagoans, and later the Retaguardia Jazz Band.[92]

The promotional activities of institutions like the Club de Jazz de Santiago trickled down to more popular venues. The Chilean writer Armando Méndez Carrasco incorporated hot jazz into a number of his fictional works from the 1940s, 1950s, and 1960s set in lower-class neighborhoods of Santiago. In the short story "El conventillo danza" (1949), a resident from one of the city's poor outlying neighborhoods sets out for the center of the city during carnival in search of medicine for his ailing wife. When he encounters a comparsa whose members mistake his actual rags for a costume, they pressure him to dance to hot jazz in a way befitting someone from the ghetto, "with his Negro moves."[93] In his later novel *Chicago Chico* (Little Chicago, 1962), Méndez Carrasco further chronicles traditional jazz's penetration of the streets and bars of Santiago's working class neighborhoods in the postwar period. *Chicago Chico* tells the coming-of-age story of a disaffected middle-class adolescent (Chicoco) who drops out of school, seduced by the seedy underworld of central Santiago. Over the course of the novel, Chicoco absorbs the language, manners, and mores of the roughhewn, generally dark-skinned, characters populating the neighborhood. As he assimilates to bohemian life, the small orchestras that play in the dives he frequents also begin to come closer to satisfying his high aesthetic standards, the local music evolving from the badly executed imitations of Dixieland to "sweet" jazz and finally to the hot Chicago sound Méndez Carrasco himself favored. Listening to bandleader Fernando Lecaros's new orchestra, Chicoco experiences a visceral transformation: "I understood, to my great satisfaction, that for the first time a [Chilean jazz] group had been formed that was a united, single voice that produced that indescribable thing that jazz musicians call, simply, swing."[94]

Chicoco, however, is not always so satisfied with what he hears. As a young boy in Valparaíso, a man "of American descent" had introduced him to the records of Louis Armstrong, Bix Beiderbecke, Gene Krupa, and Bunk Johnson.[95] Caught between international tastes acquired during his middle-class childhood and the Santiago underworld he has chosen to embrace as a young adult, the protagonist measures local musicians against the gold standard of the US jazz recordings with which he has grown familiar. A soundtrack of vice and struggle but also escape and mirth, hot jazz thus abides in *Chicago Chico* as a socially, nationally, and to a lesser extent racially coded dance music of critical importance in the postwar period. Jazz also serves as an emblem of the urban underclass's aspirations to bourgeois modernity and the object of envy of a local bourgeoisie disillusioned with native normative values. In short, Méndez Carrasco's Santiago occupies an intensely conflicted space of countercultural yearnings, social negotiation, and ambivalent nationalism.[96]

One of the hot jazz figures mentioned in *Chicago Chico*, the cornetist Bix Beiderbecke, had been celebrated in a consistently and particularly reverent manner since the first Latin American jazz journals appeared in the 1930s. While Latin American music critics had rarely failed to stress that Beiderbecke was white in a hot jazz scene where most of the major figures were not, Méndez Carrasco's fictionalized study "El trompetista de Harlem" (1958) signals an abiding interest in Beiderbecke's legacy. The story also reveals a particular fixation on the musician's skin color. From the tale's opening lines, Beiderbecke is identified as a white musician with a "black soul" who plays a "very white" trumpet convalescing in the "tenebrous hospital whiteness."[97] Taking a number of liberties with the musician's biography, Méndez Carrasco uses black musicians and performers like King Oliver, Louis Armstrong, and even Billie Holiday (whose career did not blossom until years after Beiderbecke's death in 1931) to consecrate Beiderbecke as a "miraculous" talent who had grown up on the streets of Harlem—never mind that he had in fact grown up in Davenport, Iowa. For Méndez Carrasco, Beiderbecke was destined to be a legend, though tragically consumed by his own devotion to jazz.[98] Even while foregrounding the musician's European descent and African American "ownership" of hot jazz, the Chilean writer appears intent on making Beiderbecke a case study of the music's universal promise, since "jazz imprinted on black people a constant desire: to forget about odious differences."[99]

The Uruguayan-born caricaturist Hermenegildo Sábat's unique work *Yo Bix, tú Bix, él Bix* (I Bix, You Bix, He Bix, 1972) pokes fun at some of the same narratives perpetuated by intellectuals like Méndez Carrasco. In the book's prologue, Sábat ironically lays down what he considers a number of misconceptions about the cornetist, such as that he was a "misogynist or shy or both"; that he had set out to "sweeten" the music's African roots; that he would have been nobody without the talent and celebrity of Paul Whiteman and Frankie Trumbauer; and that he was essentially a pathetic addict and amateur musician obsessed with money.[100] What follows is Sábat's attempt to playfully refute such notions through image. In the twenty caricatures that make up the book, Beiderbecke is cast as an undersized bohemian lothario surrounded by lanky, lascivious flappers whom he adroitly "plays" and seduces with his phallic instrument. In two particularly striking images, Sábat represents Beiderbecke as a satyr; in another, an angelic Bix towers over a number of male cohorts, their features effaced by dollar signs.[101] The book makes little attempt to tell Beiderbecke's life story in any cohesive way. Instead, Sábat uses record label reprints of a number of the musician's recordings as expressionistic signposts—Paul Whiteman's record "Because My Baby Don't Mean 'Maybe' Now!" accompanies the first of the satyr images, for example, while the angel-dollar tableau fleshes out the Trumbauer Orchestra's "A Good Man is Hard to Find." For the somber piano solo of "Bixology," meanwhile, Sábat portrays a later, alcoholic Bix, lovelorn and defeated.[102]

Yo Bix, tú Bix, él Bix lends "partial and arbitrary" graphic form (in Sábat's words) to a range of emotions suggested by the cornetist's original recordings while depicting a lifestyle mostly at odds with the conventional narratives about Beiderbecke's brief career. For all its parody and at times hallucinatory caricature, Sábat's work seriously aspires to capture the creative dynamism, venality, and moral contradictions of the Jazz Age. It also attempts to set the record straight about Beiderbecke, showing that "he lived legitimately, not as the protagonist of *The Bix Beiderbecke Story*."[103] Yet Sábat still celebrates the hot jazz era more in the manner of a fan-archivist than a contemporary critic willing to foreground his own experience as the consumer and scribe of a distant place and bygone time. In spite of the spectral pessimism of his drawings, he does not go so far as to assert (as he well could have) that his renderings of Bix's downward spiral echo the mood of early 1970s Argentina, immersed in a worsening cycle of political and social chaos, polarization, and finally violence and terror.

Perhaps mindful of the political timidity of *Yo Bix, tú Bix, él Bix*, Sábat broadens and sharpens his focus in *Scat: Una interpretación gráfica del jazz* (Scat: A Graphic Interpretation of Jazz, 1974). Organized chronologically

Fig. 5.2. Hermenegildo Sábat, "Bix Beiderbecke," from *Scat: Una interpretación gráfica del jazz* (1974).

beginning with Jelly Roll Morton and ending with Ornette Coleman, *Scat* ambitiously embarks on a multimedia retelling of jazz history in which Sábat complements his fanciful renderings with archival photographs and extensive free-verse accompaniment, including some revealing first-person references. Sábat's shift toward verbal expression adds further complexity to his drawings. Instead of offering the descriptive redundancy and dry narrative prose characteristic of so many early Latin American histories of North American jazz, *Scat* blends historiographical detail with personal anecdote: what matters, Sábat suggests, is not just the stories themselves but the way the author experiences jazz musicians' biographies and music. In the opening stanza of his profile of Jelly Roll Morton, for instance, Sábat foregrounds the difficulty of mounting an innovative tribute that pays appropriate homage to the groundbreaking pianist:

> Something will likely be lost
> in the translation
> but not much
> I should try it with a piano
> but my hands
> are unresponsive
> I detest organizing tributes
> I prefer
> to give monologues
> by myself
> . . . My rhythm
> can't desert me
> it consists
> of
> three
> words
> your music lives[104]

In spite of Sábat's eccentric pretensions to retell the entire story of jazz, an inordinate amount of *Scat* is dedicated to Dixieland, hot jazz, and swing. Even so, the book could hardly be called conventional. In describing Louis Armstrong's seminal work from the late 1920s, for example, Sábat writes:

> the New Orleans
> style
> is a proletarian monarchy
> where

anarchy
is squelched
and overthrows
are welcome[105]

As pithy as his assessments of early jazz are, the Uruguayan author does not limit himself to purely musical analysis any more than he adheres to the accepted norms of jazz biography or history. Employing a diverse set of poetic and narrative approaches, from the elegiac to the sardonic, from the popular register of yellow journalism to medical discourse and plaintive verse, Sábat's treatment of jazz constantly shifts shape. One moment he delivers a first-person eulogy to Louis Armstrong asking him to forgive "us" for misunderstanding him:

We thought we were listening well
but we didn't hear everything
that is our fault
forgive us this tango Louis Armstrong[106]

The next moment Sábat imagines himself carousing with and taking photos of Eddie Condon while the guitarist drinks bourbon:

While I watched him draw from his second
interminable glass, I understood
the differences that exist between
record collections and one miniscule
night alongside someone like Eddie[107]

Even while focused on the early twentieth century, Sábat foregrounds his own experience as a *rioplatense* fan in the 1970s. Drawings of Condon, Pee Wee Russell, Bud Freeman, and Muggsy Spanier, for example, are juxtaposed with contentious banter between Sábat and fellow aficionados over wine and dinner each Wednesday night.[108] In a "letter" to deceased pianist and composer Fats Waller, Sábat assumes the voice of a local businessman and record executive who announces his desire to found a "club of admirers" in Waller's name and reissue his hit songs. Sábat makes his pitch while strenuously denying any pecuniary interest.

What happiness it brings me, Fats
I am realizing the greatest
aspiration of my life
to produce records
without paying royalties[109]

The irony of Sábat's mock invitation is not just that it implicates Anglo-American and European exploitation of African American musicians and composers—a very common practice during the 1920s and 1930s—but that local capitalists and politicians in cities like Buenos Aires and Montevideo, with their deep ties to metropolitan capital, were all too often complicit in such arrangements. Latin American consumption of US popular music, Sábat implies, was never fully independent of such global systems of exploitation.

Sábat's recriminations against the commercialism of the jazz enterprise are not limited to musings about peripheral fandom. He is especially hard on figures that emerged during the modern and cool jazz vogue of the 1950s and early 1960s, as well as critics like Leonard Feather who helped to popularize them. With the Modern Jazz Quartet, Sábat writes, the popular New Orleans roots and blues modalities have given way to impeccable wardrobes, "tasteful" music, and savvy public relations.[110] While he accuses "professors" Dave Brubeck and Paul Desmond of creating antiseptic music in which there are no victims, only yawns, he saves his bitterest judgment for Stan Kenton. The "Kenton virus," he writes, "aggravates hypertension / in trumpets and trombones / generates vertigo" and ruptures eardrums, although the damage can be treated "with the vaccination of a Zoot Sims tenor sax."[111] For the opinionated Sábat, the legitimate heirs to Beiderbecke, Armstrong, and Ellington are musicians like Monk, Parker, Mingus, and Coleman, not just because of their virtuosity or originality but because their work appears to eschew the temptations of facile commercialism.

What sets *Scat* apart from so much other Latin American writing about jazz is Sábat's self-conscious ambivalence: his uncouth reverence and ironic self-effacement as a writer and illustrator in the presence of what he considers musical greatness. Comparing himself to an ailing Ella Fitzgerald, for instance, he writes that "my / systoles and / diastoles / are / a boring / routine / my heart . . . / could have been manufactured / in Switzerland / that's why, Dr. Catlett / I need / you to make me / live less long / produce imbalances / and eradicate / my underdeveloped / sense of rhythm."[112] To the musicians he most admires—Armstrong, Parker, Monk—Sábat frequently declares tender devotion while never seeking to downplay their human foibles. As for free jazz pioneers like Coltrane and Coleman, the Uruguayan confesses to an initial resistance, an attitude given graphic form by the scribbles emanating from their instruments. To fully appreciate the New Thing in jazz, Sábat had to clear away his own "forests of prejudice."[113]

Still, Sábat's real passion is for the anachronistic and the spectral. Like any good collector of memories (and records), he is focused, often mournfully so, on loss and recovery.[114] Not surprisingly, it is 1930s Harlem that elicits one of *Scat*'s most inspired moments. "Tourist of my own illusions," Sábat writes, "I visit my Harlem / yesterdaytodayalways." Embracing Langston Hughes on Lenox Avenue, imploring Ellington not to abandon the Cotton Club, necking with Billie Holiday, demanding private performances from Charlie Christian and Fletcher Henderson, the Uruguayan gleefully imagines himself rubbing shoulders with the stars. At the same time, he is painfully aware of the fact that "my Harlem is not Harlem." Rather than just a "milky way," Sábat writes, the Golden Age of jazz is a wall erected "by colleagues of my race / under the honest presumption / that every effort is too small / when it comes to avoiding infection / by the bacteria of beauty."[115] Harlem in the 1930s, in other words, is a utopia ultimately perpetuated by intellectuals to impose a safe distance between themselves and the "bacteria of beauty" generated by African American musicians, shielding them from the inherent "dangers" of the artists' world. This is especially true, Sábat suggests, for jazz music removed not just spatially but also temporally from the contemporary white jazz fan. The Uruguayan author's view is plainly pessimistic. It is as though all of his attempts to make contact with and, finally, insert himself into the lived-in space of idealized jazz production were destined to fail. Jazz-age Harlem, as both a real and imagined space, was simply out of reach.

The Militant and the Ghost

Metaphors of spectrality in cultural texts, as scholar Avery Gordon has suggested, reflect those "always incomplete forms of containment and repression" linked to social, emotional, or physical trauma.[116] This was certainly true in Latin America, where such tendencies dovetailed with social and geopolitical conditions of the 1960s, 1970s, and 1980s. Yet jazz as evoked in literary and visual texts from the late twentieth century did not function solely as a suture for the more extreme forms of political oppression or as a salve for the melancholy of exile. The unfolding failures of peripheral modernity and democratic governance in Cold War Latin America generated deep disillusionment with notions of progress and social justice that in many cases preceded the hardened dictatorships of the 1970s and 1980s. As a result, Jean Franco has argued, Latin American fictional narratives of the long sixties frequently assumed spectral dimensions: "Despite [writers'] espousal of modernity they were as haunted as their predecessors by the specter of anachronism, by the fact that they were thinking what others had done before them in Europe or North America."[117]

All the while, vernacular music produced what Franco calls "breaches" in the Lettered City. In bypassing the elite, masculinist protocols of the printed word, such points of entry lent access to the public sphere for a wider swath of Latin American citizens.[118] No longer strictly *música bailable*, jazz could not rival rock or funk's seductive power over disaffected youth in an age of political instability and turmoil any more than it could claim the homegrown status of such emerging forms as reggae, cumbia, and salsa. But jazz music's invocation of estranged freedom in vexed times, the high-low "universal" register of its appeal, and the expanding historical and spatial scope of its symbolism, proved enduringly meaningful to a relatively small but fiercely devoted group of Latin American writers and intellectuals. Of course, jazz's impact on Cold War writers and intellectuals was not merely acoustic. For this reason, the striking intermediality of works from Cortázar, Pericás, Sábat, and others should not be written off as merely incidental or anomalous.[119] As I have suggested earlier in this book, interwar and midcentury sonic imaginaries in Latin America were regularly enhanced by visual media, which served as delivery devices and affective adhesives.[120] It is fitting, then, that more recent writings about jazz reflect the mixed-media platforms through which the music had so often been experienced in the region.

Even so, jazz posed a challenge and an opportunity for late twentieth-century Latin American intellectuals quite different from those of the 1920s, 1930s, and 1940s. Jazz writing in the Cold War era mirrored the specters of anachronism long haunting Latin American modernity while also breaching the Lettered City through invocations of racial militarism and anti-market aesthetics. No longer the unparalleled symbol of youth and liberation that it once had been, nor the peerless sign of speed, urban mobility, and breezy Americanization, by the twilight of the century jazz embodied a new kind of paradox: an emblem of postcolonial radicalism and an idealized distillation of the recent past, with visible traces of the popular and the erudite, empire and its dissidents.

CONCLUSION. **The Cruelty of Jazz**

At the height of its popularity, jazz proved to be not just a cultural ambassador of Americanism but also a transnational emperor of the senses. Whether friend or foe, liberator or enslaver, slick modernizer or lewd seductress, jazz made its mark among Latin American listeners and consumers of the twentieth century in terms of feeling and not just meaning. The sheer visceral dimensions of vernacular music's appeal, David Hesmondhalgh writes, make it ideally suited to permeate various levels of human experience.[1] Key to this argument is the Aristotelian notion of human flourishing, or "the good life." Far from being merely an object of contemplative appreciation by intellectuals, organic or otherwise, music informs and sometimes defines public life as well, from the pleasures of dancing to the raw clashes of newspaper debates and political rallies. What makes music matter, in other words, is not just its ability to lend pleasure or happiness to individuals but its special aptitude for channeling collective impulses and facilitating shared freedom and social justice.[2]

For some Latin American urban dwellers of the 1920s and 1930s, jazz in the abstract encapsulated the rapaciousness of empire and the menace of social upheaval. But for many others jazz symbolized the best of modern life: the potential for social and artistic freedom, however provisional, supplied by the high-low cachet of African American musical practices and dance forms; a hybrid distillation of speed and progress ascribed to the technological wizardry of the Metropolis; and transgressive pleasure associated with the modern city's others. With the democratic, globe-trotting prestige of the jazz band, one that seemed to erase difference even as it celebrated strangeness, came the theoretical possibility of the belated acquisition of modern citizenship that had long eluded many Latin Americans.

The pursuit of transnational modernity soon tangled openly with resurgent populist agendas in Argentina, Brazil, Mexico, Cuba, and elsewhere in the region. In the strange theater of hemispheric nationalisms, where fascist-leaning discourses lived uncomfortably alongside fables of Pan-Americanism nurtured by Roosevelt's Good Neighbor policy, jazz alternately played the role of hip brother and venal villain. All the while, big-band swing, bebop, and cool jazz rarely remained discreetly within the confines of the acoustic. Instead, jazz of various kinds spilled into visual and print media, from newspaper accounts to theatrical revues, from cinema to early television. The added exposure only added to jazz's might. Popular music's peculiar affective potency, deeply embedded in other cultural practices, has rarely been purely musical.[3] But this was particularly true of jazz, whose wide performative spectrum radiated well beyond the aural sphere in the middle decades of the twentieth century.

Although jazz's saturation of cultural landscapes frequently provoked hostile reactions from nationalists, the very mobility and mutability of the music often blunted these very same attacks. The Cuba–Mexico–New York vector of big band, Cubop, and mambo in the 1940s and 1950s previewed the uncontainability of jazz within the opposing, traditional frameworks of nationalism and Pan-Americanism. From Chano Pozo and Pérez Prado to João Gilberto, Arturo Sandoval, and Gato Barbieri, the peculiarity of the music proved one step ahead of its time: eluding the biopolitical tidiness of state-sanctioned ideologies as well as the fraternal geopolitics of Pan-Americanism, which was so often predicated on benign folklore or high-culture pyrotechnics. Jazz thus worked within the fissures of US imperialism, operating in what David Luis-Brown has called the "contested gray zones" of hemispheric citizenship.[4]

Virulent antijazz discourse lost its grip the moment jazz ceased to be the poster child for market vulgarity, cultural invasion, and youth hysteria. "Good life" jazz narratives, meanwhile, given a temporary boost in the 1960s by the radical appeal of free jazz and Black Power, proved resilient in Latin American intellectual circles. These narratives held the advantage of an unknown future. In the last four decades of the century, as the region plummeted into a seemingly endless downward spiral of civil wars, bitter social divides, economic downturns, and political crises, jazz optimism became difficult to sustain except in the form of ghost stories. In the 1960s and 1970s, a new generation of Latin American avant-gardists, rather than entirely discarding the metaphorical capital of jazz, repurposed the music for different historical circumstances and political uses. In so doing, a handful of jazz-haunted writers converted a timely trope of massive appeal into something considerably more spectral and ambiguous, introspective and retrospective. In works like *Rayuela*, *Scat*, and *Keith Jarrett no Blue Note*, the recordings of Armstrong and Dolphy, Holiday and Jarrett hover inconclusively between an idealized past and an insecure, wartorn, neoliberal present.

Perhaps the persistent, seductive appeal of the remote and the estranged helps to explain the odd absence of "Latin jazz" from most Latin American cultural expressions of the late twentieth century. Outside of the occasional appearances of Chano Pozo and Gato Barbieri, south-of-the-border *jazzistas* are conspicuously absent from imaginative cartographies of jazz in Latin America. Then again, maybe the universalist basis of what the Mexican Jaime Pericás called "our jazz" precluded any need to incorporate Latin American jazz performers or styles into poetry and fiction of the period. The foundation laid by Pan-Americanism in the mid-twentieth century rendered jazz into a hemispheric subject and at the same time inoculated it from external, nationalist claims that threatened to sever the symbolic capital of jazz from the US body politic. Indeed, it could well be argued that the greatest threat to US jazz sovereignty came from within, in the form of the black separatist strains of free jazz. In any case, the menace was short-lived, as the liberatory capital of the New Thing was soon tamed and absorbed into subsequent mainstream jazz histories.

Even the seemingly expansive, integrationist category of Latin jazz has too often betrayed a reliance on national and ethnic exclusion that partially mimics the flawed logic of US exceptionalism.[5] Part of the problem has to do with the parameters that critics and their publishers have set for themselves by invoking a Latin label linked to both a recording industry and pan-Latino social movements first emerging in the United States during the 1960s and 1970s.[6] Indeed, though the answer to the question lies beyond the scope of this book, it is fair to ask whether "Latin jazz" in common parlance refers to *any* style of jazz performed by Latin American performers or rather only to the music of artists whose accomplishments have been staged mostly on US soil. At a time when the "postnational turn" in music has weakened the marketing potential of some nationally defined styles, scores of unincorporated Latin American musicians have continued to struggle for full-fledged jazz citizenship that has never been fully theirs for the taking.[7]

In the meantime, no other single musical idiom in the hemisphere has managed to follow in the giant footsteps of jazz. A protean embodiment of transracial cosmopolitanism, empire, modernization, militancy, and creative individualism, jazz during its apex was above all a highly adaptable expression. Among international musical styles, only rock has come close to rivaling jazz's once transcendent power in and beyond the hemisphere. It is no coincidence that rock has also been so closely identified with the United States. Surfing in the wake of US hegemony in the region, a path partly created by jazz, rock has appealed to generations of Latin Americans, supplying a ready-made soundtrack of urban middle-class rebellion in the 1950s, antiauthoritarian counterculture in the 1960s and 1970s, and (especially as punk, post-punk, and metal) youthful political and economic disaffection in the 1980s and beyond.[8] But rock's appeal has rarely conveyed the same degree of aspirational global citizenship that jazz did in the early to mid-twentieth century, nor has it channeled the postcolonial history or social yearnings of Afro-descendant communities in the Americas to the extent that jazz did at the various summits of its power.

Rock has had plenty of competition. Over the last several decades, imported soul, funk, and, somewhat later, R & B and hip-hop have enjoyed particular resonance with young Latin American audiences, especially among poorer, urban populations.[9] Of course, not all musical styles flooding south-of-the-border soundscapes have been unambiguously North American in origin. Since the 1960s, highly idiosyncratic, homegrown variations of US and British sounds have enraptured audiences from Mexico and Puerto Rico to Chile and Brazil. Meanwhile, reggae, salsa, and cumbia have all enjoyed considerable popularity, not just in the Americas but in other regions as well.[10] Cumbia is a particularly interesting case since, as Héctor Fernández-L'Hoeste and Pablo Vila note, it has managed to successfully mutate and "engender alternate national conditions" in Latin America in ways that rock has not, creating a promising new model of musical transnationalism in the process.[11] Yet despite their market-friendly accessibility and dynamic appeal to youth cultures—and maybe in some sense because of these very qualities—these idioms have not managed to engage intellectual, economic, and political elites in quite the way that jazz, samba, and tango once did.

Perhaps it is naive to expect anything quite as widely potent and provocative as jazz to inundate Latin American soundscapes anytime soon. Times have clearly changed since the music's heyday of the 1920s–1960s. For better or for worse, the current political configuration in the region lacks the centralized aural-intellectual sphere necessary to cultivate—and contest—singular musical nationalisms. What is more, global technologies and cultural flows have played increasingly decisive roles in the diversity, dissemination, and promotion of popular music. The rise of television in the second half of the twentieth century and the Internet-driven media convergences in the early twenty-first century have further weakened any one medium or idiom's ability to single-handedly represent a nation, a region, or even modernity itself. In short, political, technological, and economic conditions simply no longer favor the emergence of a new musical form that can fill the big, broad shoes of jazz.

The siren songs of Josephine Baker and Paul Whiteman, Louis Armstrong and Charlie Parker, meanwhile, have long since lost their ability to bewitch all but a relatively small, if devoted, audience of mostly middle- and upper-class enthusiasts in Latin America. Even so, the irreplaceability of jazz is ultimately not as disturbing as the unreachability of the dreams and goals the music once inspired. The persistent marginalization of Latin American musicians from the central symbolic terrain of jazz, Latin or otherwise, points to processes of promise and exclusion that go well beyond the musical realm. In her study *Cruel Optimism*, Lauren Berlant writes that in recent decades the fantasy of a good life has suffered from attrition in the sense that the concept has "become fantasmatic, with less and less relation to how people can live—as the blueprint has faded."[12] But narratives of flourishing were never the exclusive domain of wealthy liberal democracies, as Berlant seems to suggest.[13] Quite to the contrary: given the sheer distance in Latin America between consumer desires and economic and political access during the twentieth century, such narratives were more likely to materialize in Argentina, Brazil, Cuba, and Mexico than in relatively stable and prosperous nations such as the United States or France.

For many twentieth-century Latin Americans dazzled by the modern charms of jazz even as they struggled time and again with social oppression, vast economic disparities, and the unneighborly strains of hemispheric geopolitics, the yawning gap between fantasy and reality was especially cruel. In spite of their long and intense involvement with the world of jazz as musicians and composers, fans and critics, novelists and filmmakers, Latin Americans still have not managed to stake a lasting claim to the kind of democratic, metropolitan citizenship jazz once seemed to offer. As a primary agent and emblem of Americanization in the early to midcentury, jazz promised the good life to Latin Americans like few other cultural expressions could. As the decades have passed, the ever-changing music has continued to acquire new meanings and provoke new feelings. Still, while never losing its appeal to aficionados in Mexico City and Havana, São Paulo and Buenos Aires, jazz today resonates more with the past than it does with future, elegantly echoing the affective dissonances of history and the elusiveness of the good life in the global South.

Notes

Introduction

1. Pond, "Jamming the Reception," 11–12.

2. Burns's *Jazz* helped PBS and the Corporation for Public Broadcasting (CPB) reassert their relevance after the "culture wars" of the 1980s and 1990s, which culminated in withering attacks on public radio and television by a Republican-dominated Congress in 1994 and 1995. The federal appropriation of the CPB shrank from $285.6 million in 1995 to $250 million in 1999. By 2002 it had risen to $350 million, and it continued to rise for the next few decades. "CPB's Appropriations History," CPB, accessed November 16, 2013, http://www.cpb.org/appropriation/history.html.

3. George Lipsitz has argued that *Jazz* misses the boat politically for the same reason that it succeeds as entertainment, that is, by spinning a "fairy tale about cooperation, consent, and consensus," and thus responding adroitly "to the need of elites to recruit the populace to their political projects of triumphant nationalism and managerial multiculturalism" (*Footsteps in the Dark*, 81).

4. Ratliff, "Fixing," 32.

5. Meredith, "Latin Jazz," n.p.

6. A pioneering study in this regard is S. Frederick Starr's *Red and Hot: The Fate of Jazz in the Soviet Union* (1983), which underscores the paradox of "capitalist" music's popularity behind the Iron Curtain. Mike Zwerin's *Swing under the Nazis: Jazz as a Metaphor of Freedom* (1985) and Michael Kater's *Different Drummers: Jazz in the Culture of Nazi Germany* (1992) examine in different ways the singular menace, at once seductive and poisonous, that jazz represented during the Third Reich. Uta G. Poiger's *Jazz, Rock, and Rebels: Cold War Politics and American Culture in a Divided Germany* (2000) focuses on the postwar period, and in particular how jazz and early rock posed challenges to projects of national reconstruction. More recently, Jeffrey H. Jackson's *Making Jazz French: Music and Modern Life in Interwar Paris* (2003), George McKay's *Circular Breathing: The Cultural Politics of Jazz in Britain* (2005), Matthew F. Jordan's *Le Jazz: Jazz and French Cultural Identity* (2010), Jeremy Lane's *Jazz and Machine-Age Imperialism: Music, "Race," and Intellectuals in France, 1918–1945* (2014), and Tom Perchard's *After Django: Making Jazz in Postwar France* (2015) have filled out our understanding of vital areas of European contact with jazz. Everett Taylor Atkins's *Blue Nippon: Authenticating Jazz in Japan* (2001), meanwhile,

traces jazz's development in Japan, including the ambivalent embrace of swing music by wartime nationalists. Similarly, Andrew F. Jones's *Yellow Music: Media Culture and Colonial Modernity in the Chinese Jazz Age* (2001) studies the unique jazz hybrids in interwar China as well as the emergence of new urban forms supposedly stripped of "corrupting" foreign influence. Finally, Gwen Ansell's *Soweto Blues: Jazz, Popular Music, and Politics in South Africa* (2005) studies the social and cultural conditions that gave rise to South Africa's unique jazz scene over the course of the twentieth century; Steven Feld's *Jazz Cosmopolitanism in Accra* (2012) narrates the rich tapestry of Ghana's jazz and experimental music community; and Robin D. G. Kelley's *Africa Speaks, America Answers: Modern Jazz in Revolutionary Times* (2012) focuses on transnational encounters between US and African musicians during the 1950s and 1960s, cultural crossings that informed new identities and strategies of decolonization on both sides of the Atlantic.

7. Atkins, *Blue Nippon*, loc. 353.

8. The "Latin" label itself is the invention of a recording industry and pan-Latino social movements that emerged in the United States during the 1960s and 1970s, prevailing over earlier "Cubop" and "Afro-Cuban jazz" categories shortly after the triumph of the Cuban revolution (Washburne, "Latin Jazz," 97). Though to some extent born of a revolutionary climate, therefore, "Latin jazz" hews closely to what Claudia Milian calls the comfortable "structuring content" of US-centric *latinidad* (*Latining America*, 4).

9. US and Western European political theorists, journalists, and other intellectuals, Michael Billig points out, have frequently fallen prey to reductive impulses that consign nationalisms to "small sizes and exotic colors . . . located 'there' on the periphery, not 'here' at the center" (*Banal Nationalism*, 6). Given its persistent marginalization and invisibilization of Latin America in canonical jazz discourse, Burns's *Jazz* exemplifies what Billig has termed the "banal nationalism" of power-wielding Western democracies (8). This concept is somewhat akin to what Paul Gilroy calls "quiet cultural nationalism" or "crypo-nationalism," terms he uses to describe how even radical thinkers "are often disinclined to consider the cross-catalytic or transverse dynamics of racial politics" (*The Black Atlantic*, 4). For an analysis of the porosity of geopolitical borders when it comes to music, see Kun, *Audiotopia*, 21–22.

10. Early critics of jazz so frequently invoked "syncopated" and "syncopation" that the words often functioned as epithets. As Katherine Biers has suggested, North American and European assessments of ragtime music had initiated this tendency. While critics pointed to the bodily excitability supposedly produced by syncopated rhythms, ragtime's defenders argued that the music's skipped beats and sudden stops and starts expressed "the true American rhythm" ("Syncope Fever," 105–7).

11. Borrowing key concepts from the media scholar Jesús Martín-Barbero, the music theorist Jairo Moreno has used the expression "syncopated modernities" to identify the temporal and spatial dislocations that typify jazz music made by Latin Americans in the late twentieth and early twenty-first centuries. Such dislocations are "simultaneously sustain[ed] *and* challenge[d]" by the peculiarities of North-South geopolitics and hemispheric aural networks ("Past Identity," 98–99). As we will see, such inter-American syncopations are hardly endemic to the rise of Latin jazz in the 1960s and 1970s, having marked jazz since the early twentieth century.

12. See López, "Of Rhythms and Borders," 310–12. For a discussion of how Juan Perón frequently invoked the category "antipeople" as an oligarchist/imperialist catchall, see Beasley-Murray, *Posthegemony*, 504–21.

13. It is worth noting that an analogous "jazz picture" trend does not emerge on the same scale in the United States. Where it does, as Krin Gabbard has argued, it is usually in the form of "whitewashed" pictures, as in the case of Kay Kyser's RKO films featuring white performers and the most commercialized brand of swing (*Jammin' at the Margins*, 25–28).

14. "When music and dance are invoked as national discursive units of gestures, rhythms, and sounds," Ana M. López writes, "Bhabha's double-time becomes only too apparent. The rhythm must stand in as that which has *always* been a part of the national imaginary, but it must also serve as that which can *performatively* interpellate social actors into a community in the present" ("Of Rhythms and Borders," 311).

15. Beverly, *Latinamericanism after 9/11*, 27.

16. Radano, *Lying Up a Nation*, 11–12.

17. Although always in the background in debates about the origins of tango, race did not begin to be examined again in earnest until the 1980s, with the publication of Oscar Natale's *Buenos Aires, negros y tango*. It is significant that the venerable Argentine music scholar Néstor Ortiz Oderigo waited until 1988 to write *Latitudes africanas del tango*, though the study was not published until well after the author's death in 1996.

18. "Of all the great American vernacular musics," Gennari writes, "only jazz has cultivated intellectual discourse as a core element of its superstructure" (*Blowin' Hot and Cool*, loc. 292).

19. Gennari, *Blowin' Hot and Cool*, loc. 285–92.

20. See Rama, *Lettered City*, 17.

21. The postwar period witnessed a flowering of collaborations between prestige writers and challenging music (particularly bebop) increasingly divorced from the dance floor. See Lopes, *Jazz Art World*, 4–8.

22. Here it would be prudent to make a distinction between Jazz Critics (in the sense of a regular vocation) and *informal critics of jazz*, the latter a much broader category that included, over the course of the twentieth century, politicians, folklorists, musicologists, composers, fiction writers, filmmakers, and film and cultural critics from all corners of the globe.

23. Gennari, *Blowin' Hot and Cool*, loc. 230.

24. Ochoa Gautier, "Social Transculturation," 396.

25. Ochoa Gautier, "Social Transculturation," 397.

26. Radano and Olaniyan, *Audible Empire*, loc. 233. Rather than focus simply on the "audibility of dominance," Radano and Olaniyan propose "to inquire into ways in which imperial structures help to modify and produce qualities of hearing and to make a 'music' discernible in the first place" (loc. 233–40).

CHAPTER ONE. *La Civilizada Selva*

The epigraph to this chapter translates as "In the civilized jungle / the cat-like eyes of automobiles do battle."

1. Menanteau, *Historia del jazz*, 27.

2. Pujol, *Jazz al Sur*, 38.

3. Garrido, "Recuento integral," 40–41, 65–66. In his candid accounts, written in the mid-1930s for the Santiago magazine *Para Todos*, Garrido was nothing if not self-effacing. Though he characterized his forays into sweet jazz a decade earlier as misguided, he now declared that his "only deity" was Duke Ellington.

4. Balliache, *Jazz en Venezuela*, 15–16.

5. Vedana, *Jazz em Porto Alegre*, 18.

6. *Discografía de Francisco Canaro*, 9–24.

7. Pujol, *Jazz al Sur*, 33–35.

8. Serna, *Making Cinelandia*, 65.

9. Serna, *Making Cinelandia*, 65, 80.

10. Nieto de Herrera, "Cómo baila el jazz," 4.

11. "El baile de moda," *El Universal* (Caracas), January 12, 1918, 4.

12. "La danza a la moda," *El Universal* (Caracas), December 9, 1919, 4.

13. "El mundo baila pero no está contento con lo que baila," *Crítica* (Buenos Aires), May 5, 1921, 4.

14. "Pedirán al Sr. Presidente la reglamentación del jazz y del shimmy," *El Universal* (Mexico), May 6, 1921, 14.

15. "El 'jazz,' música de interés," *La Prensa* (San Antonio, TX), May 2, 1924, 3.

16. "Ocupaciones raras," *El Universal* (Mexico), March 12, 1922, 3–5.

17. "Dansas modernas e jazz-band," *Estado de São Paulo*, July 1, 1922, 2. *O Estado de São Paulo* leaned heavily on an article penned by William Wills Davies, a frequent contributor to Latin American newspapers of the period. Published in *La Nación*, Davies's missive apparently referred to the same sermon reported on in a *New York Times* article quoting Percy Grant: "Jazz is retrogression. It is going to the African jungle for our music. It is a savage crash and bang. It rings the bell for full steam astern. Its effect is to make you clatter, and, as Voltaire said, 'to go on all fours,' to which I would add— and to whisk your tail around a tree" ("Rector Calls Jazz National Anthem," January 30, 1922, 9).

18. Appiah, *Cosmopolitanism*, 112.

19. Kennaway, *Bad Vibrations*, 121–24; Radano, "Hot Fantasies," 474.

20. Stepan, *Hour of Eugenics*, 167.

21. Radano defines "descent" in temporal terms, as "the evolutionary myth of origins, which had cast black music as a primordial cure for the ills of a civilized and increasingly modernized society." By contrast, "displacement" refers to the tendency among modernist intellectuals to view African Americans as "out of place" in the modern world, with the concomitant fears of danger and contamination that this social, cultural, and demographic shift entailed. Thus, musical "hotness," culminating in hot jazz, "articulated a pairing of racialized extremes, one temporally preceding and the other spatially exceeding the plain view of white common sense" ("Hot Fantasies," 460–61).

22. Such appeal was highly engineered, made possible by Hollywood's grip on film production, distribution, and exhibition in the 1920s; sustained by the US culture industry's micromanagement of the celebrity sign through a diverse array of publicity channels; and facilitated by the complicity of journalistic star discourse. For a discussion of the latter, see deCordova, *Picture Personalities*.

23. García Canclini, *Hybrid Cultures*, 47. Along similar lines, but somewhat less mindful of historical conditions specific to coloniality, Hartmut Rosa observes that functional differentiation and basic lack of "integrating temporal authority" have lent modernity a desynchronized quality characterized by a "mosaic of temporal ghettos" ("Social Acceleration," 104).

24. Denning, *Noise Uprising*, 40. Here and elsewhere, I use terms such as "popular music," "vernacular forms," and "hybrid styles" as ways to locate jazz among analogous musical practices. Particularly in the crucial context of the 1920s and 1930s, however, I agree with Denning that it is best to think of emerging forms like jazz as vernacular idioms or practices rather than popular genres: vernacular (rather than popular) because the former term avoids pigeonholing jazz or any other such expression as the product of a certain "folk" or national tradition; and idiom (rather than genre) given the fluidity of "everyday common musicking" across geographical borders. I am thinking specifically of jazz's tendency to mingle with other practices such as tango, samba, rumba, and so forth during the interwar period. As Denning writes, "A musician raised in one vernacular did not effortlessly 'speak' another, though many 'bilingual' musicians emerged, and 'translations' of songs from one idiom to another abounded" (106–7). That being said, the word "popular" in English carries with it a strong connotation of market politics that I wish to emphasize in certain contexts where the mainstream commercialization of vernacular dance music takes center stage, as is often the case during the big-band era.

25. Jordan, *Le Jazz*, 44.

26. Jordan, *Le Jazz*, 40.

27. For a revealing discussion of the cross-pollination and generic confusion between danzón and early jazz, see Madrid and Moore, *Danzón*.

28. Seigel, *Uneven Encounters*, 84.

29. Seigel, *Uneven Encounters*, 85.

30. Seigel, *Uneven Encounters*, 91.

31. Cited in Wisnik, *O coro dos contrários*, 45.

32. After Nazareth's death in 1934, Mário de Andrade praised him as an admirable composer and the most representative exponent of the maxixe, in the same breath criticizing the maxixe as a bourgeois adaptation in which "one perceives the grotesqueness of the white European wanting to adapt himself to the Negro" (*Música e jornalismo*, 135).

33. Milhaud, *Notes without Music*, 63.

34. Cendrars would himself travel to Brazil in 1924. For an extensive study of Cendrars's pivotal encounters with the Brazilian modernists, see Amaral, *Blaise Cendrars*.

35. Siqueira, *Ernesto Nazareth*, 135.

36. Seigel and others have recounted that Cendrars claimed that Donga (Ernesto Joaquim Maria dos Santos) asked him to tell Milhaud that he thanked him for the tribute, and would return it in kind with a samba called "O boi na Torre Eiffel" (Seigel, *Uneven Encounters*, 114).

37. Cited in Braga Martins, *Os Oito Batutas*, 108; italics added.

38. Seigel, *Uneven Encounters*, 90.

39. Cited in Braga Martins, *Os Oito Batutas*, 110.

40. "The camaraderie between [US and Brazilian] musicians took hold to such an extent," Alves commented in an interview given upon the Batutas' return to Brazil, that North American drummers often accompanied Brazilian instrumentalists with their "extravagant, fiendish" drum sets. Cabral, *Pixinguinha*, 80.

41. Cabral, *Pixinguinha*, 97–100.

42. Cabral, *Pixinguinha*, 99–100.

43. "The symbolic role in 1920s Paris," as Bernard Gendron puts it, "was decisively affected by the way [jazz] circulated as a signifier in debates among modernists, and between modernism and traditional culture" (*Between Montmartre*, 95, 98). Interestingly, Blaise Cendrars engaged in "samba" slumming in Rio de Janeiro's favelas during his stay in Brazil, intrepid urban meanders that brought the Frenchman in touch with Donga (Vianna, *Mystery of Samba*, 72–73).

44. In an essay first published in *Carteles* ("Bajo el cetro del blues"), Carpentier celebrated jazz and blues as consanguine models of redemptive alterity, the collective expression of "a strongly marked race, [one] that has come to [Cuba] in order to freshen the modern sensibility with the deep poetry of its blues and the incipient manifestations of a miraculously intuitive art form" (182). Carpentier's early essay was remarkable for the way it labored mightily to present black North American music as a modern variation of a shared cultural heritage, in effect postulating *le primitif* as the common link of all modern Western dance music, from the waltz and contradanza to tango, son, and jazz. Specifically, Carpentier saw jazz not just as the object of intuitive genius but also as a sophisticated idiom of special relevance to Latin America, given the region's analogous histories of slavery, colonial oppression, and *fin-de-siglo* migrations to burgeoning urban centers.

45. Carpentier, "Temas de la lira," 538.

46. The tendency among Francophone critics to describe African American popular music as a hybrid of technological panache and "naive" savagery dates back to the prewar, ragtime era. A 1912 article penned by a French illustrator and commentator, for example, attributed the uniqueness of fashionable dances like the grizzly bear and turkey trot to the mechanized gaiety and "electricity" of the "Yankee race" and also the merry antics and "innocent passion for movement" of Negroes (Blake, *Le Tumulte Noir*, 55). Early jazz criticism centered similarly on a doubly exalted version of US blacks, who were seen as hybrid symbols of Yankee technological ingenuity and "native" African vitality.

47. Coeuroy and Schaeffner's 1926 monograph *Le Jazz* essentialized jazz as a subcategory of "strangely" homogeneous African and Afro-diasporic musical expressions, all linked by a common denominator of "unnerving" simplicity and "aggressive" adaptability (14). Writing initially for such publications as the journal *Jazz-Tango* in the early 1930s, Hugues Panassié soon cofounded (with Charles Delaunay) the seminal jazz journal *Jazz Hot*. In a brash, provocative style that alienated many fellow jazz critics (including Coeuroy), the young Panassié wrote of a unique symbiosis between white and black jazz musicians in the United States, one combining the polish of Europeans' "superior culture" and musicianship while retaining "that wild Negro spontaneity" (Panassié, *Le Jazz Hot*, 29). Matthew F. Jordan has pointed out that Panassié was especially pivotal in making pithy jazz criticism focused on individual recordings the norm in France. Other critics, such

as Coeuroy, however, accused Panassié of being divisive, dogmatic, and even narcissistic (Jordan, *Le Jazz*, 168–69).

48. Gendron, *Between Montmartre*, 110; Jordan, *Le Jazz*, 70.

49. Goffin, *Aux frontières du jazz*, 14.

50. Peiró, *White Gypsies*, 114; Gubern, "Ruido, furia y negritud," 284–85. De Torre's collection *Hélices* (1923) would feature a number of poems that exhibit what one critic has called the "indissoluble muddle of primitivism and ultramodernity" typical of Spanish writing about jazz during the 1920s (Herrero Senés, "El arte nuevo," 326).

51. A. Saraiva, *Modernismo brasileiro*, 172. While Ferro's flamboyance was shocking to some, it could not have come as a complete surprise to local audiences. Upon his arrival in Brazil, he was already fairly well known among Brazilian intellectuals as an author of polemical essays (such as his "Teoría da indiferença," 1920) and experimental fiction (*Leviana*, 1921), although it was primarily due to Ferro's work as a playwright and theater critic that he was invited to the country in the first place.

52. A. Saraiva, *Modernismo brasileiro*, 173–77.

53. Ferro, *A idade do jazz-band*, 60–61.

54. Ferro, *A idade do jazz-band*, 62.

55. Ferro, *A idade do jazz-band*, 65.

56. Huyssen, *After the Great Divide*, 53.

57. Ferro, *A idade do jazz-band*, 51, 60.

58. Ferro, *A idade do jazz-band*, 68–69.

59. Ferro, *A idade do jazz-band*, 69–70. Ferro's intoxication with the creatively destructive, "furnace" elements of jazz foreshadowed his fascist-leaning future, as he later served in various capacities in Salazar's Estado Novo, returning to Brazil a number of times.

60. Menotti del Picchia, "Arte moderna," 230.

61. M. Andrade, "Klaxon," 264.

62. A. Saraiva, *Modernismo brasileiro*, 175.

63. Cited in A. Saraiva, *Modernismo brasileiro*, 566.

64. C. Andrade, "A alma tumultuosa," 551–53.

65. Vianna, *Mystery of Samba*, 84.

66. Freyre, *Tempo de aprendiz*, 155.

67. Vianna, *Mystery of Samba*, 59.

68. Freyre, *Tempo de aprendiz*, 156–57.

69. By contrast, the major Spanish American vanguard publications of the mid- to late 1920s (e.g., *Contemporáneos*, *Martín Fierro*, *Amauta*, and *Revista de avance*) were generally more collaborative, less purely nationalist vehicles than Brazilian journals like *Klaxon* and *Revista de antropofagia*. Whereas periodicals like the Argentine *Martín Fierro* regularly dialogued with the rest of Latin America, including Brazil, the internationalist aspects of Brazilian vanguard journals tended to limit themselves to the Brazil-Europe axis (Schwartz, *Vanguardia y cosmopolitismo*, 76–77).

70. D. Borges, "Afro-Brazilian Symbols," 71–72.

71. Vianna, *Mystery of Samba*, 62.

72. Nancy Leys Stepan observes that Freyre's opposition to scientific racism "did not constitute a fundamental break with the past," in the sense that his elaboration of a harmonious

"luso-tropical" civilization was ultimately predicated on racialist claims that smacked of eugenics, such as the claim that Portuguese colonists and African slaves—and their offspring—were particularly suited to thrive in Brazil's tropical climate (*Hour of Eugenics*, 166–68).

73. Kennaway, *Bad Vibrations*, 121.

74. Sevcenko, *Orfeu extático na metrópole*, 278–79.

75. A. Williams, *Covarrubias*, 12–13; Navarrete, *Miguel Covarrubias*, 8–10.

76. A. Williams, *Covarrubias*, 14–15, 19–20.

77. Cited in A. Williams, *Covarrubias*, 40.

78. Covarrubias's international influence had become considerable by end of the decade, when he provided Hughes with a pivotal letter of introduction to José Antonio Fernández de Castro, editor of *El Diario de la Habana*, during the author's trip to Cuba (Ramperstad, *Life of Langston Hughes*, 177). By the late 1930s Covarrubias's clout was such that Nelson Rockefeller sought the artist's influence to help persuade the Cárdenas government to support a 1939 exhibit on Mexican culture at New York's Museum of Modern Art, for which Covarrubias served as curator (Indych-López, *Muralism without Walls*, 165n229).

79. Tablada, "Miguel Covarrubias," 412–13, 415.

80. A. Williams, *Covarrubias*, 9.

81. Leblanc, "Nuestros músicos opinan," 18–19.

82. For a discussion of Mexican intellectuals' ambivalent response to US silent cinema, and in particular to Hollywood's frequently stereotypical depictions of Latin Americans, see García Riera, *México visto*.

83. Filmador, "El elogio del jazz," 26.

84. Dalevuelta, "El jazz en México," 23. It should be noted that by 1925 jazz and associated dances had already made their mark on popular theater revues in Mexico. A few examples are "Su majestad el Shimmy" (Teatro Lírico, 1920; restaged at the Teatro Iris in 1922); "Tenga su fox" (Teatro Arbeu, 1923); and "El rizo de la Flapper" (Teatro Principal, 1924). See Moreno Rivas, *Historia de la música*, 77–78.

85. According to Luis Mario Schneider, Maples Arce drew inspiration for his theory of sound and music from the Italian Futurist Luigi Russolo (Schneider, *El Estridentismo*, 102).

86. Maples Arce, "Jazz=XY," 15.

87. Maples Arce, "Jazz=XY," 44.

88. Néstor García Canclini, taking his lead from the Brazilian literary scholar Roberto Schwarz, has written that foreign or "out of place" ideas filled the heads of Latin American vanguard writers, whose aesthetic pretensions in most cases did not correspond to the socioeconomic realities of the peripheral modernity in which they lived (*Hybrid Cultures*, 48–50). In inverse fashion, Radano evokes the phrase "out of place" to describe the fears of white modernist intellectuals in the United States faced with seductive, unnerving, or "displacing" hot sounds of jazz and other black musical styles of the early twentieth century, sounds associated with actual demographic shifts, as African Americans and immigrants "encroached on" and thus altered the physical landscape of US cityscapes ("Hot Fantasies," 469–71).

89. Rose, *Jazz Cleopatra*, 24.

90. Rose, *Jazz Cleopatra*, 20.

91. The connection between jazz and minstrelsy has been made convincingly by Simon Frith, who notes that in minstrelsy "black Americans became coded as the 'other' of lower-middle-class relaxation, a source of musical access to one's heart and soul less daunting than bourgeois concert forms," a process later to be repeated in the consumption of jazz (*Music for Pleasure*, 49).

92. Artundo, *Mário de Andrade*, 81. Like *Klaxon* several years earlier, *Verde* itself had jazz-inspired beginnings. The journal's first incarnation, according to *Verde*'s manifesto, was a "rag" (*jornaleco*) called *Jazz-Band*. Mineiro filmmakers Geraldo and Renato Santos Pereira later characterized *Jazz-Band* as "tremendously irreverent, insolent, the worst kind of loose tongue" (Lara, "A 'alegre e paradoxal' revista," 2). *Verde* remained true to its trans-atlantic jazz origins by publishing, in French, a playful four-verse poem by Blaise Cendrars, who in turn pays homage to the previous Brazilian vanguard publication as well: "Tango vient de tanguer / Et jazz vient de jaser / Qui importe l'etymologie / Si ce petit klaxon m'amuse" ("Aux jeunes gens," 11).

93. Fingerit, "Josefina Baker," 8. Jazz-mania among vanguardistas encouraged contact with just the kinds of morally suspect recording industries, venues, and performers frequently perceived to be as sick as the "patients" themselves. This paradox comes to the fore in the Cuban writer Francisco Ichaso's unusual crónica "Terapéutica de jazz," first published in 1928 in the short-lived journal *Musicália*. Warned by a doctor not to continue exposing himself to the plaintive airs of Chopin played by a sickly, tubercular young girl "with blond locks and blue hands," Ichaso moves to an apartment facing a music hall where he takes in the frenetic yet therapeutic and "hygienic" sounds of drums, violins, and saxophones. While careful to remain safely outside the physical confines of the music hall (with the bodily and social contact that the space implied), the Cuban author still benefits at a distance from the waves of modern sounds wafting up to his elegant balcony ("Terapéutica de Jazz," 95–96).

94. Writing about early twentieth-century Latin America, the music scholar Thomas Turino has identified an international shift in which a concern for elite-oriented practices and spectacles gradually gave way to a modernist privileging of "reformist-popular" or folkloric styles—what he calls the "modular processes of post-colonial musical nationalism" ("Nationalism," 1–2).

95. Martín-Barbero, *De los medios*, 188–89.

96. The literary scholar Fernando Rosenberg writes that Latin American avant-garde intellectuals were "especially attuned to the reverberations between the new art and the logic of the commodity because both shared, from the standpoint of the peripheries of capitalism, the affective aura of modernity as identified with an elsewhere" (*Avant-Garde and Geopolitics*, 7).

97. Vallejo, "Poesía nueva," 190.

98. Ortiz de Montellano, "Motivos negros," 109–10, 112.

99. Baker's paradoxical allure for the avant-garde has been noted by scholar Samir Dayal, who writes that "in modernity's contradictory logic, blacks were simultaneously threateningly hypersexualized and 'infantilized,' and therefore rendered insupportable or invisible as subjects" ("Blackness as Symptom," 41).

100. Peña Barrenechea, "Elogio," 20.

101. Mariátegui makes explicit his own aversion to jazz in his article "Arte, revolución y decadencia," first published in *Amauta* in 1926. "There are poets," Mariátegui writes dismissively, "who believe that the 'jazz-band' is a herald of revolution" (4).

102. Adán, "Nota polémica," 21.

103. Adán, "Nota polémica," 21.

104. Pujol, *Jazz al Sur*, 22–23, 46–47; Peralta, "Josephine Baker"; Shaw, "Baiana," 94.

105. J. Brown, *Babylon Girls*, 254–56. Jennifer Anne Boittin has argued that given the presence of thousands of Africans and Antilleans, not to mention untold numbers of white French citizens whose lives and livelihoods had been touched by the nation's massive overseas network, interwar Paris was a "colonial space . . . in which the specter of 'empire' guided the self-identification of its residents as well their social and political interactions." This climate encouraged white women and colonial migrants to negotiate their way through the creative "manipulation" of race and gender politics (*Colonial Metropolis*, xiv–xv).

106. J. Brown, "From the Point of View," 175.

107. Wood, *Josephine Baker Story*, loc. 2800; Gasió, *Yrigoyen en crisis*, 251–52.

108. Tálice, *100.000 ejemplares*, 361.

109. Pujol, *Jazz al Sur*, 48–49.

110. Baker and Bouillon, *Josephine*, 79–80.

111. Baker and Bouillon, *Josephine*, 80; Gasió, *Yrigoyen en crisis*, 252. Baker in her memoirs recalls the uproar happening at her inaugural performance. Gasió, however, cites three different newspapers confirming the near-riot as occurring on June 6. While Baker remembers the protests coming from both sides, meanwhile, *Crítica* reports that they came mostly from the right, with shouts of *¡Viva Yrigoyen!* and *¡Viva la Iglesia!* aimed at the singer (Tálice, *100.000 ejemplares*, 363). Baker later remarked bitterly, "What did I care about Argentine politics? I didn't know the slightest thing about them" (Baker and Bouillon, *Josephine*, 80).

112. Gasió, *Yrigoyen en crisis*, 252–53.

113. Wood, *Josephine Baker Story*, loc. 2813.

114. Cited in Seibel, "La presencia afroargentina," 202.

115. Rinke, "Las torres de Babel," 176.

116. González and Rolle, *Historia social*, 509–10.

117. As Camilo Bustos Montoya writes, public diversions in Chile had long been seen by elites as a cause and touchstone of problems suffered by the poor. This was especially true for Indian migrants and *rotos* ("broken ones," shorthand for the mestizo masses), routinely associated with the moral and material degradation of modernity in late nineteenth-century Santiago and other developing cities " 'De rotos, chinas y futres,' " 124–31).

118. "Josefina Baker viene a Chile," *Zig-Zag* (Santiago), 1929.

119. Mistral, "Primer recuerdo," 220–22, 223.

120. "It is extraordinary," Fiol-Matta writes, "that Mistral acted as if she had never known of the black populations of Latin America prior to her travels to the Caribbean in the 1930s and that she responded to the black subject with stereotypical white responses: anxiety, sexualization, and pathologization" (*Queer Mother*, 35–36).

121. Mistral, "Primer recuerdo," 220–22.

122. Cited in Rinke, "Las torres de Babel," 175–76.

123. For a broad overview of Hollywood's initial impact on Latin American intellectuals, see Borge, *Latin American Writers*.

124. As has been noted, the Peruvian poet Enrique Peña Barrenechea had already highlighted Baker's supposedly androgynous features in his 1928 tribute to the performer in the avant-garde magazine *Amauta*. If anything, skeptics were even more likely to take aim at the dancer's femininity. Shortly before Baker's arrival, for example, the Buenos Aires daily *La Razón* wrote: "Is it a woman? Is it a man? . . . Her voice is piercing, shaken by an incessant tremor, mercurial, epileptic; her body twists like that of a reptile, or more exactly, it resembles a moving saxophone. . . . Is she horrible? Is she charming? Is she black? Is she white? Does she have hair or is her scalp painted black? No one knows" (cited in Hering Coelho, "Os músicos transeuntes," 230–31).

125. Pelligrinelli, "Separated at 'Birth,'" 41–42.

126. Rodrigues, "A 'Vênus negra,'" 109.

127. Rodrigues, "A 'Vênus negra,'" 108–9.

128. Rodrigues, "A 'Vênus negra,'" 108–9.

129. "Josephine Baker no Rio," *Cinearte* 5, no. 213 (1930): 33.

130. Boaventura, *O salão e a selva*, 144.

131. Rodrigues, "A 'Vênus negra,'" 109.

132. Rodrigues, "A 'Vênus negra,'" 110. *Progresso*'s boastful depiction of Baker's visit to São Paulo reflected the sometimes rosy view of Brazilian race relations characteristic of middle-class Afro-Brazilian publications during the 1920s. As George Reid Andrews has written, given black paulistas' difficult economic and political circumstances, this view should be taken with a grain of salt, expressive more of a desire for racial democracy than any real conviction that it had been achieved (*Blacks and Whites*, 126–29, 139). Notably, a few Afro-Brazilian writers, though generally in agreement that prejudice against blacks was greater in the United States, also praised what they perceived as the strength and defiance that such prejudice had produced in African Americans (136–37).

133. Rodrigues, "A 'Vênus negra,'" 111–12.

134. Melo Gomes, *Um espelho no palco*, 288.

135. Seigel, *Uneven Encounters*, 117.

136. Melo Gomes, *Um espelho no palco*, 294.

137. Davis, *White Face, Black Mask*, 211.

138. As Marc A. Hertzman has pointed out, Alves was considered by some, such as the Afro-Brazilian journalist Francisco Guimarães (Vagalume), to be something of a poacher and diluter of black styles and compositions (*Making Samba*, 128). Still, the singer's popularity was unrivaled, reaching its peak in the swing-influenced samba "Aquarela do Brasil" (1939), composed by Ary Barroso and arranged by Radamés Gnattali.

139. Andrews, *Blackness*, 74–76. By the 1940s, Baker's influence was so widespread in Uruguay that she had become a stock character in the Montevideo carnival's Desfile de Llamadas (Lille, *Equipoise*, 14).

140. Carpentier, "Moisés Simons," 65.

141. Carpentier, "Moisés Simons," 69.

142. Carpentier, "Don Azpiazu," 557.

143. As late as 1940, for instance, Afro-Colombian writer Jorge Artel cites Baker and Whiteman as the dual emblems of jazz in his poem "Dancing": "Josephine Baker, / black

morning star of the century, / your legs toying / with civilization! / Paul Whiteman, / imperial wizard of Fox / the world belongs to both of you!" (Cited in Prescott, *Without Hatreds or Fears*, 142; translation mine.)

144. Carpentier, "Don Azpiazu," 558.

145. Carpentier, "Don Azpiazu," 558–59.

146. Acosta, *Cubano Be, Cubano Bop*, 50–51.

147. Collier, *Carlos Gardel*, 197.

148. Guillén, "Josefina Baker en Cuba," 90; IMDb's page for *Princesse Tam-Tam* (http://www.imdb.com/title/tt0026891/).

149. Loaeza and Granados, *Mi novia, la tristeza*, n.p.; Baker and Chase, *Josephine*, 279. Although it was apparently a case of unrequited love, Lara considered the friendship "eternal" and professed great admiration for Baker as a performer and humanitarian (cited in Loaeza and Granados, *Mi novia, la tristeza*, n.p.). In 1952, Baker opened her own nightclub—the Chez Josephine Baker—on Mexico City's Paseo de la Reforma ("Jo Baker Opens New Nitery in Mexico City," *Jet*, April 10, 1952, 56).

150. Baker and Bouillon, *Josephine*, 153, 155–57. Chile, where the Charleston remained a fixture on the *revista* and variety-show circuit, witnessed a major revival of the dance form following Baker's second tour of the region in the 1940s (González and Rolle, *Historia social*, 550–52).

151. Baker and Bouillon, *Josephine*, 188; Hammond and O'Connor, *Josephine Baker*, 197. Perhaps it was fitting that the Latin American city that had originally greeted La Baker with the most hostility—Buenos Aires—gave her the biggest welcome the second time around, in 1952. Gone or silenced were most of the conservative politicians, clerics, and intellectuals who had plagued her first visit. In their place was Juan Perón, recently bereft of his wife Eva. Inspired by the Peróns' populist social platform, Baker appeared on stage in clothing made by Evita's favorite designers, worked behind the scenes for the deceased diva's charitable foundation, and joined the newly reelected president in fighting racism and strenuously criticizing the United States. Once widely reviled by newspapers and magazines, Baker was now praised in the Peronist press (Guterl, *Josephine Baker*, loc. 1211–35).

152. Baker and Bouillon, *Josephine*, 185.

153. Baker and Bouillon, *Josephine*, 158, 171. Perhaps the most fitting testimony to Baker's renewed celebrity in Cuba was Rita Montaner's controversial imitation of the vedette in the 1951 revue *Los pecados de Salomé*. As one critic wrote, "Only notable [artists like Baker] deserve the honor of caricature and imitation" (cited in Fajardo Estrada, *Rita Montaner*, 339).

154. Ngô, *Imperial Blues*, 4–5.

CHAPTER TWO. **Dark Pursuits**

1. Rossi, *Cosas de negros*, 35.

2. J. L. Borges, "Ascendencias del tango."

3. Cited in Rossi, *Cosas de negros*, 102. In typical ambiguous fashion, Borges praised Rossi's descriptions of candombe and, "his errors notwithstanding," correctly predicted the Uruguayan writer would be rediscovered one day (9).

4. Rossi, *Cosas de negros*, 226–27.

5. The full title appearing on the cover of the second edition (1926), included in facsimile in the Taurus edition of 2001, was *Cosas de negros: rectificaciones y revelaciones de folklore y de historia* (33).

6. The scholar Alejandro Solomianski acknowledges the "naturalized" negation of blackness in late twentieth-century and early twenty-first century Argentina, according to which the nation's African-descendant legacy has come to be viewed as antithetical (even absurdly so) to normative identities and narratives (*Identidades secretas*, 16–17). Solomianski argues that the national imaginary, particularly in the nineteenth and early twentieth centuries during Argentina's foundational and modernizing stages, depended systematically on the "repression and distortion" of afro-argentinidad in order to safeguard the pairing of national identity with whiteness (14).

7. Branche, *Colonialism and Race*, 215.

8. Peter Wade has argued that since "nationalisms work between homogeneity and heterogeneity, then the presence of people who identify themselves and others as belonging to different racial categories" constitutes "a possible threat to putative national purity," while also potentially serving as the basis for a more diverse, inclusive basis of future national identities (*Music, Race, and Nation*, 14–15).

9. Garramuño, *Primitive Modernities*, 18, 33. Such intellectuals sought to "expel the savage and exotic primitivism that [was] not recognized as one's own in favor of a more familiar one." Garramuño thus describes "a cultural process whereby the primitive will no longer be considered or valued as exotic but rather for finding in itself a certain affinity and consonance with the meaning of the modern for the Argentine and Brazilian cultures" (33).

10. Though acknowledging some overlap between mainstream fandom and cult fandom, Matt Hills defines the latter as distinctly "tautological" (regularly using idiosyncratic or "cult" discourses), "temporal" (enduring), and "affective" (bearing the characteristics of "an intensely felt experience") (*Fan Cultures*, x–xi).

11. Cummings, "Collectors, Bootleggers," 97–99.

12. Pujol, *Jazz al Sur*, 84–85.

13. According to the jazz historian Ted Gioia, the claim to be the first fully dedicated jazz magazine belongs to Sweden's *Orkester Journalen*, founded in 1932, two years earlier than *Le Jazz Hot*, *Down Beat*, and *Síncopa y Ritmo* (*History of Jazz*, 171).

14. Pujol, *Jazz al Sur*, 74–75.

15. Iriberri, "El jazz y los discos," 2.

16. Iriberri, "El jazz y los discos," 2.

17. Petit de Murat, "Autenticidad en la inspiración," 6–7.

18. In Petit de Murat's racial reading of jazz, he distanced himself from a 1927 article, published in the Argentine avant-garde journal *Martín Fierro*, in which he had downplayed jazz's geographical and racial origins, denouncing an unnamed European critic who had purportedly reduced the new music to Negro dancing and "unharmonious stridence." On the contrary, Petit de Murat wrote, jazz was characterized as much by sophistication, unpredictability, and economy of expression as it was by sheer exuberance ("Afirmación del jazz-band," 4).

19. Porter, *What Is This Thing*, 47. As Michael Jarrett has observed, "Instead of considering that authenticity might be a question of politics—an effect of hegemony—jazz discourse has repeatedly concerned itself with essential matters, that is, with erecting and policing real/fake distinctions" ("Four Choruses," 346).

20. Álvarez Nájera, "Música negra," 37.

21. Álvarez Nájera, "Música negra," 37.

22. Solomianski identifies as *afroargentinos* not just the early interpreters, composers, and lyricists of milongas and tangos, but also many of the renowned *payadores*, including the most celebrated of all, Gabino Ezeiza (*Identidades secretas*, 28). In spite of the manifest centrality of racial otherness (whether black or Indian, *pardo, moreno*, or mestizo) in modern Argentine history, however, discourse on Argentine whiteness "either tends to ignore Argentine blackness, consign it to the period of colonial slavery, or if race is mentioned, it is often embedded in an unacceptable line of reasoning" (58).

23. In his influential study *Le Jazz Hot* (1934), Panassié wrote that African American jazz musicians combined Europeans' "superior culture" with "that wild Negro spontaneity" (29).

24. Hernández Arregui, "Sentido social del jazz," 29–30.

25. In *Decline of the West*, volume 2, Spengler writes that "the Age has itself become vulgar, and most people have no idea to what extent they are themselves tainted. . . . Jazz and Negro dances as the spiritual outlet in all circles of society, women painted like prostitutes, the efforts of writers to win popularity by ridiculing in their novels and plays the correctness of well-bred people, and the bad taste shown even by the nobility and old princely families in throwing off every kind of social restraint and time-honored custom: all of these go to prove that it is now the vulgar mob that gives the tone" (99).

26. Hernández Arregui, "Ensayo anti-sentimental," 5–6. Of course, even Hernández Arregui's praise of the benefits of African American musicians' "ardent instinct" is problematic, since it uncritically associates rhythm with sexuality, and, moreover, identifies both as inherently African qualities. As Simon Frith has pointed out, "One can begin to see clearly why 'African' and 'European' are somewhat arbitrary labels. The musical differences at issue (the focus on performative participation; the emphasis on structural cognition) are really differences between ideologies of *listening*" (*Performing Rites*, 142).

27. Roth, "De las composiciones de jazz," 4–5.

28. "Perspectivas del jazz," *Swing* 1, no. 3 (1937): 1.

29. Sandoval, "La verdadera misión," 8.

30. Horvath, *Memorias y recuerdos*, 33.

31. Sandoval, "Los pianistas de jazz," 25.

32. Pujol writes that Lois Blue's given name, Lucy Bolognini Míguez, had been traded in for her "catchy and musical" pseudonym to attract a larger radio audience, as in the case of Efron. Although Míguez overshadowed her predecessor in terms of vocal talent and fame, it was Efron who set the blueprint for Argentine performance of "jazz negro," according to Pujol. "Blackie's biggest contribution to Argentine jazz was to have accentuated the Afro side of a music that, thanks to commercialization, had strayed from its original identity" (*Jazz al Sur*, 90–92).

33. Sandoval, "Las tres gracias," 48.

34. In his *Síncopa y Ritmo* essay "El jazz y la música moderna," for example, Klimovsky briefly traces what he calls some "interesting and honorable points of contact" between jazz music and contemporaneous classical composers such as Stravinsky (11).

35. It seems that Efron's own father also saw her lack of intimate familiarity with African American culture as a professional liability. In the late 1930s she embarked on a trip to New York City, where her brother studied. There, for several years she steeped herself in black literature, folklore, and of course jazz and blues (Deutsch, *Crossing Borders*, 102).

36. Sandoval, "Blackie realiza un sueño," 24.

37. Karush, *Musicians in Transit*, 18–25.

38. "Oscar Alemán: El músico argentino más famoso en el mundo del jazz," *Síncopa y Ritmo* 71 (April 1941): 5.

39. Pujol, *Jazz al Sur*, 133–34.

40. Using Vicente Rossi's *Cosas de negros* as a point of departure, Jorge Luis Borges in an essay published in *Martín Fierro* argues that the tango has set its "blemished" roots in the lowly suburbs of Buenos Aires, and not in the Afro-Uruguayan population of Montevideo, as Rossi maintains. It is worth noting, however, that Borges does not contest Rossi's factual claim as much as he does the premise of what it means to "have roots" in the first place. Tango is essentially porteño, Borges reasons, simply because the people of Buenos Aires "recognize themselves" in the music, whereas residents of Montevideo, "ever nostalgic of gauchos," do not ("Ascendencias del tango," 6).

41. Karush, *Culture of Class*, 58.

42. Karush, *Culture of Class*, 45–46.

43. Karush, *Culture of Class*, 60–61.

44. Simon Collier has documented the enthusiastic reception of Gardel's films not only in Buenos Aires but also in such far-flung places as Barcelona, New York's Spanish Harlem, and Guatemala City (*Carlos Gardel*, 183).

45. Collier, *Carlos Gardel*, 204.

46. "La música americana va en camino de desplazar al tango," *La Canción Moderna* 360 (1935): 1.

47. Acede, "'Jazz' y tango," 42.

48. "Tango versus jazz," *Síncopa y Ritmo* 2, nos. 16–17 (1935): 28.

49. "Tango versus jazz," 32.

50. "Tango versus jazz," 33.

51. "Tango versus jazz," 32.

52. Gómez de la Serna, *Ismos*, 182.

53. "Tango versus jazz," 32.

54. Karush has noted that in the 1940s and 1950s such publications as *Sintonía* and *Jazz Magazine* also frequently criticized Oscar Alemán for his commercialism, and in particular his penchant for non-jazz music and entertainment gimmickry (*Musicians in Transit*, 35–36).

55. Ortiz Oderigo, "Notas sobre blues," 2.

56. Karush, *Culture of Class*, 200.

57. Pujol, *Jazz al Sur*, 106.

58. Karush, *Culture of Class*, 200–201.

59. Gioia, *History of Jazz*, 255–66.

60. Pujol, *Jazz al Sur*, 179–80.

61. Ortiz Oderigo, *Historia del jazz*, 256–57.

62. Pujol, *Jazz al Sur*, 188–91. In a detailed and insightful review of Villegas's work published in *Jazz Magazine* in December 1953, Jorge Otero Santa María noted the influence of stride pianists like Art Tatum while also comparing "Mono's" phrasing to that of Gillespie, Miles Davis, Charlie Parker, and even Argentine folk musicians ("El mensaje jazzístico," 11–12). Above all, Otero stressed Villegas's personalized, "abstract" approach to jazz and praised his work as one of the few non–North American musicians who have managed to forge their own independent style (8).

63. Fragments of Goffin's seminal book *Aux frontières du jazz* (1931), for example, were featured in a number of issues of *Síncopa y Ritmo*, beginning with a profile of Duke Ellington in September 1934.

64. Fiore, "Dizzy Gillespie," 16–17.

65. Di Baja, "Enfoques y reflexiones (II)," 5.

66. Ortiz Oderigo, *Historia del jazz*, 256.

67. Cortázar, "Soledad de la música," 139.

68. Cortázar, "Elogio del jazz," 210, 214.

69. Cortázar, "Elogio del jazz," 212, 213; italics in the original.

70. Specifically, Cortázar anticipated Amiri Baraka's 1963 assertion that it was pointless for critics to engage in technical comparisons of jazz and classical notation. For Baraka, the secret to nonessentialist jazz criticism was an increased emphasis on the complex social and intellectual contexts of US popular music production: "The notator of any jazz solo . . . has no chance of capturing what in effect are the most important elements of the music. . . . A printed musical example of an Armstrong solo, or of a Thelonious Monk solo, tells us almost nothing except the futility of formal musicology when dealing with jazz" ("Jazz and the White Critic," 181–82).

71. In a recent critical analysis of Cortázar's musical poetics, Nicholas Roberts has compared the Argentine author's celebration of jazz's "ontological unity" among composer, performer, and audience to Antonin Artaud's quest for a radical closing of the gap between theatrical authorship and performance ("Subverted Claims," 733–35).

72. Cortázar, "Elogio del jazz," 215. Such purist notions were not limited to music. In fact, they were frequently invoked with regard to silent film as well. Latin American proponents of *cinéma pur* frequently invoked Benedetto Croce's notion of an optimally direct relationship between artist and object (Borge, *Latin American Writers*, 77–79). As much as he tried to distance himself from conventional aesthetics, Cortázar in his early writing made a similarly Crocean argument with which to secure jazz poetics from the rational realm.

73. Saúl Sosnowski, for example, emphasizes Bruno's exploitative transposition of Johnny's miserable life through the vehicle of popular biography. Rather than a true critic, Bruno is thus an opportunistic capitalist who makes sure that "Johnny is canned and placed on a shelf with a fancy label" ("Pursuers," 165, 161). For Héctor Mario Cavallari

and Graciela P. García, the fact that Bruno fetishizes Johnny lays bare the circular reciprocity perpetuated by a bourgeois society that "represses what it pursues and pursues what it represses" ("Escritura y desfetichización," 269). Such an unstable relationship between the bourgeois subject and its excluded-yet-sought-after other, Doris Sommer notes, indicates an "agonistic" tension between two supposedly oppositional characters and categories, but ultimately signals "a refusal to overcome difference" ("Pursuing a Perfect Present," 223).

74. N. Roberts, "Subverted Claims," 744.

75. Sommer, "Pursuing a Perfect Present," 222.

76. Christopher Harlos has observed that jazz autobiographies, particularly those that emerge beginning in the 1970s such as Charles Mingus's *Beneath the Underdog* (1971) and *Miles: The Autobiography* (1989), frequently reveal musicians' deep dissatisfaction with music critics and jazz writing generally. Harlos maintains that such ambivalence leads to a "discourse of distrust" in which the African American autobiographical subject frequently disavows the "storywriting" role of the literary author in favor of a guise of oral authenticity, or "storytelling" ("Jazz Autobiography," 134–35, 159–60).

77. Cortázar, *El perseguidor*, 91, 98.

78. Charles B. Hersch has made a compelling case that early New Orleans jazz constituted a temporal "emancipation" of mostly black and Creole musicians who, as exploited laborers in the Jim Crow south, subverted employers' monopolization and regimentation of their labors by refashioning time after hours in the bars and brothels of New Orleans, "a new kind of time, or a new experience of time . . . not anchored to the insistent, predictable rhythm of everyday routine" (*Subversive Sounds*, 621).

79. Cortázar, *El perseguidor*, 92.

80. Cortázar, *El perseguidor*, 94, 100.

81. Cortázar, *El perseguidor*, 124. Significantly, Bruno unleashes perhaps the most vicious of his primate metaphors precisely when he feels most cornered by the musician—after Johnny compares the first edition of the biography to a mirror image that is somehow "lacking in something." Pressed for details, Johnny becomes more and more severe in his judgment, eventually accusing Bruno of the ultimate sin of omission for a biographer: that he simply didn't capture the essence of his subject. "Jazz is not only music," he says, "[And] I am not just Johnny Carter" (142). Panicked, Bruno worries that the "savage monkey" might go so far as to criticize his biography publicly (136).

82. Cortázar, *El perseguidor*, 121.

83. Yúdice, "Postmodernity and Transnational Capitalism," 13. Yúdice connects the quest for unadulterated cultural capital to avant-garde practices such as surrealism by drawing a parallel between geographical and psychological referents, whereby "primitivism is not just a matter of collecting exotic objects from the outer reaches of the empire, it is a source of 'still unalienated' cultural capital that will enable aesthetics . . . to open up heretofore untapped regions of the psyche and facilitate their colonization in the process" (13).

84. Cortázar, *El perseguidor*, 109.

85. Cortázar, *El perseguidor*, 109.

86. Cortázar, *El perseguidor*, 127.

87. Cortázar, *El perseguidor*, 137–38.

88. Cortázar, *El perseguidor*, 111.

89. One of the few literary critics to examine *El perseguidor* in political terms, however circumspectly, Noé Jitrik argues that jazz, not unlike classical Greek mythology, does not belong to any one community or nation in particular, hence "all of us—legitimately—can concern ourselves with jazz" ("Crítica satélite y trabajo crítico," 337–38). At the same time, the jazz subject in Cortázar assumes the form of a real person who, similar to the "universal" writer Cortázar, "[embodies] the conflict between the local and the universal and even seems to resolve [such a conflict]" (338).

90. As I have already suggested, this is what most literary critics have tended to do with the novella as well, tackling the text's conundrums in an environment uncluttered by identity politics.

91. Bhabha, *Location of Culture*, 122.

92. See Solomianski, *Identidades secretas*, 14; Geler, "African Descent and Whiteness," 213–18, 236.

93. Manzano, *Age of Youth in Argentina*, 3.

94. Another Argentine film of the period that featured Barbieri was Rodolfo Kuhn's *Los jóvenes viejos* (The Old Young Ones, 1962). Composed by Sergio Mihánovich, the film's score used the "universal" sounds of hard bop, cool jazz, and lounge pop to paint a portrait of alienation and Americanization crippling the middle-class youth of Buenos Aires. As Manzano writes, *Los jóvenes viejos* became closely associated with "a generation marked by Peronism and the frustrated projects geared toward overcoming its legacies" (*Age of Youth in Argentina*, 38).

95. As Robert Farris Thompson points out, another important club of the time for jazz and tango, though perhaps even more as a preserver of black rioplatense forms like candombe, was the Shimmy Club, located in the ground floor and basement of 254 Rodríguez Peña in the Centro from the 1940s to the 1970s (*Tango*, 137–39).

96. Pujol, *Jazz al Sur*, 188.

97. Pujol, *Jazz al Sur*, 192.

98. Gillespie, *To Be, or Not*, 433. "From my late teens onward," Schifrin later recalled in his memoirs, "every time I left the house I would say to my mother, as a joke, 'If Dizzy Gillespie calls, tell him I'm not here!' " (Schifrin, *Mission Impossible*, 43).

99. Schifrin, *Mission Impossible*, 44.

100. Fischerman and Gilbert, *Piazzolla, el mal entendido*, 200–201.

101. Pujol, *Jazz al Sur*, 215.

102. "La sinfonía de Buenos Aires," *Primera Plana* 3, no. 133 (May 25, 1965): 50.

103. "La sinfonía de Buenos Aires," 52.

104. Azzi and Collier, *Le Grand Tango*, 89.

105. "La sinfonía de Buenos Aires," 51.

106. Gorin, *Astor Piazzolla*, 166–67.

107. Azzi and Collier, *Le Grand Tango*, 80.

108. Azzi and Collier, *Le Grand Tango*, 16.

109. D. Piazzolla, *Astor*, 96.

110. Azzi and Collier, *Le Grand Tango*, 72; Karush, *Musicians in Transit*, 82–83.

111. Azzi and Collier, *Le Grand Tango*, 71–72.

112. Gorin, *Astor Piazzolla*, 133.

113. A. Piazzolla, interview by Laurent Goddet, 2.

114. A. Piazzolla, interview by Laurent Goddet, 4.

115. Gorin, *Astor Piazzolla*, 58; italics added.

116. Shelton, "Argentine Music at Philharmonic," 28.

117. Azzi and Collier, *Le Grand Tango*, 89.

118. A. Piazzolla, interview by Laurent Goddet, 4.

119. A. Piazzolla, "Balada para un cuerdo," interview by Horacio del Prado, 4.

120. A. Piazzolla, interview by Laurent Goddet, 4.

121. Piazzolla and Gorin, *Astor Piazzolla*, 148–49.

122. See Karush, "Reinventing the Latin," 5–9.

123. Hentoff, *Jazz Is*, 241.

124. Hentoff, *Jazz Is*, 244.

125. Hentoff, *Jazz Is*, 247.

126. Alberto and Elena, "Shades of the Nation," 7.

127. Karush observes that Alemán found himself in a peculiar situation upon returning to Argentina after his swing-era stint in Europe: "Alongside his commercial and critical success in Europe, Alemán's blackness gave him instant jazz credibility. At the same time, the inverse was also true: it was his association with jazz that made his blackness so visible" ("Black in Buenos Aires," 88). When by the 1960s Alemán had lost his jazz celebrity, he "became yet another invisible Afro-Argentine" (*Musicians in Transit*, 38).

128. Lea Geler has argued that the underlying problem of race in Argentina has to do not just with blackness or whiteness per se, but rather with what she terms the "impossibility" of Argentine mestizo identity since the nineteenth century, due (paradoxically) to narratives of "whitening" through miscegenation ("African Descent and Whiteness," 213–18, 236). However, Eduardo Elena notes that the combination of massive rural-urban migration, tercermundista currents, and the spectacle of anti-Peronist racism in the 1960s led to a certain acceptance of nonwhiteness, particularly among left-wing Peronist intellectuals and activists. While in some ways a belated answer to Latin American mestizo nationalism of earlier decades, the new, more favorable climate of racial nuance—what Elena calls the "browning" of Peronism—was both less utopian and less totalizing than Mexican and Brazilian versions ("Argentina in Black and White," 192–93, 200–201).

129. Hentoff, *Jazz Is*, 246.

130. Barbieri and Barbieri, "Gato Barbieri," 46.

CHAPTER THREE. **The Anxiety of Americanization**

1. Barrios, *Song in the Dark*, 333.

2. The build-up to the film's October premier at Rio's Pathé-Palace was covered extensively by *Cinearte*, the leading Brazilian film magazine of the time. *Cinearte* had followed Torá and Guilherme's "budding" Hollywood careers closely, with Guilherme having contributed numerous *crônicas* and other missives from Los Angeles. Torá's most notable role was as the lead in Emmett J. Flynn's *The Veiled Woman* (1929). For a detailed account of Guilherme's years in Hollywood, which included a number of secondary roles as well as

the directorship of a semiautobiographical picture, see Borge, "Olympio Guilherme" and *Latin American Writers*.

3. Gabbard, *Jammin' at the Margins*, 13.

4. Berrett, *Louis Armstrong and Paul Whiteman*, 91.

5. Seen in this way, the scene was a precursor to Disney's subsequent attempts to colonize otherness through animation—indeed, the scene may well have been influenced by Disney's earliest "Silly Symphonies," which date back to 1929.

6. "O rei do jazz," *Fon-Fon*, November 10, 1930, 54.

7. Gonzaga, "*O Rei do Jazz*," 30.

8. Gonzaga, "*O Rei do Jazz*," 30.

9. R. Ortiz, *Cultura brasileira e identidade nacional*, 40, 43.

10. McCann, *Hello, Hello Brazil*, 130–40.

11. R. Ortiz, *Mundialização e Cultura*, 122.

12. McCann, *Hello, Hello Brazil*, 137.

13. Gabbard, *Jammin' at the Margins*, 20.

14. For an insightful analysis of *Phono-Arte*'s enduring impact and importance, see Nunes Frota, *Auxílio luxuoso*, 91–98.

15. Cruz Cordeiro, "Jazz," 2.

16. Cabral, *Pixinguinha*, 122–23.

17. Cabral, *Pixinguinha*, 123.

18. Seigel, *Uneven Encounters*, 113.

19. As José Adriano Fenerick has observed, the attacks on Pixinguinha exemplified a pervasive "critical procedure [in Brazil] that rejects *a priori* any possibility of the use of foreign musical elements" (*Nem do morro*, 50).

20. Vinci de Moraes, *Metrópole em sinfonia*, 74–77.

21. See C. Oliveira, *As pérfidas salomés*.

22. *Fon-Fon* 11 (March 13, 1937), 37.

23. McCann, *Hello, Hello Brazil*, 34–35.

24. Nunes Frota, *Auxílio luxuoso*, 150.

25. Vianna, *Mystery of Samba*, 90–92. As early as 1932, Mário de Andrade recognized the importance of music in Vargas's political vision. "[The dictator] is a highly musicalized being," he wrote. "Music obsesses him" (*Música, doce música*, 267).

26. F. Oliveira, "Orpheonic Chant," 52–54.

27. Borges Pereira, *Cor, profissão e mobilidade*, 222.

28. Borges Pereira, *Cor, profissão e mobilidade*, 228–29; Vinci de Moraes, *Metrópole em sinfonia*, 92.

29. Hertzman, *Making Samba*, 14–15, 192–95.

30. M. Andrade, *A expressão musical*, 8.

31. M. Andrade, *A expressão musical*, 13. Andrade's comparison of jazz and the minstrel tradition is essentialist, though not without some basis in cultural history. Simon Frith has noted that in minstrelsy "black Americans became coded as the 'other' of lower-middle-class relaxation, a source of musical access to one's heart and soul less daunting than bourgeois concert forms," a process later to be repeated in the consumption of jazz (*Performing Rites*, 49).

32. As early as 1932, Villa-Lobos served as the director of Vargas's Superintendência de Educação e Artística (Vianna, *Mystery of Samba*, 133n43). In 1937 he composed the score for Humberto Mauro's iconic film *O descobrimento do Brasil*, a patriotic product of the Instituto Nacional do Cinema Educativo (National Institute of Educational Film; INCE) (D. Williams, *Culture Wars in Brazil*, 71–72). In 1940 he presided over state-sponsored samba rehearsals in the Quitungo favela (Vianna, *Mystery of Samba*, 92). Though his relationship with the Estado Novo was considerably more strained than Villa-Lobos's, Mário de Andrade also held prominent positions in the 1930s, for example, directing São Paulo's Department of Cultural Expansion (Stroud, *Defence of Tradition*, 137).

33. Ochoa Gautier, "Social Transculturation," 395–98.

34. Vianna, *Mystery of Samba*, 84, 94.

35. For a general overview of Roosevelt's Good Neighbor policy, including ample treatment of Brazil, see Sadlier, *Americans All*. For an analysis of Orson Welles's Brazilian project, see Benamou, *It's All True*.

36. Perhaps mindful of not straying too far from *estadonovista* nationalism, the columnist Roberto Paulo Taborda announced in his first column that he would be discussing "jazz groups from this country and others, as well as small *crônicas* comparing our 'crooners' with those abroad, drawing comparisons [between the two]" ("Jazz no cinema [i]," 10).

37. Tota, *Seduction of Brazil*, 47.

38. Duque Filho, "Política internacional," 12–16; Ferrari, "Diretrizes," 2–5.

39. Villa-Lobos, "Villa-Lobos lança um plebiscito," 12.

40. Barroso, "Não compreendi o plebiscito," 9.

41. Barroso, "Não compreendi o plebiscito," 9.

42. By two accounts, Brazilian musical nationalism emerged just as popular idioms such as the maxixe, choro, and tango brasileiro distinguished themselves from European polkas and other styles. Jairo Severiano highlights Henrique Alves de Mesquita's successful compositions "Olhos matadores" (1868) and "Ali Baba" (1872) as seminal pieces that gave rise to the tango brasileiro, "a mixture of habanera and Spanish tango with elements of polka and lundu" (*Uma história da música*, 28–29). Gerard Behague, meanwhile, lists Brasílio Itiberê da Cunha, Alexandre Levy, and Alberto Nepomuceno as the three most important composers of the early or "transitional" nationalist period. In particular, he cites Itiberê da Cunha's piano piece "A Sertanjeja" (1869) as a key erudite expression of urban popular music. Interestingly, Behague dismisses Carlos Gomes's highly successful Italian operas as having little to do musically with Brazil (*Beginnings of Musical Nationalism*, 9–10). As Tracy Devine Guzmán points out, however, this did not mean that Gomes's *Il Guarany* (1870, based on José de Alencar's celebrated 1857 novel *O guarani*) did not inspire considerable nationalist sentiment in imperial Brazil (*Native and National*, 69–71).

43. Hess, *Representing the Good Neighbor*, 85–90, 97–98.

44. Hess, *Representing the Good Neighbor*, 131–33.

45. While acknowledging Pan-Americanism's frequent dependence on imperialist institutions and discourses, Luis-Brown points out that in the early twentieth century alone, a number of Latin American and US-based antiwar protesters, labor activists, and women's organizations worked under the aegis of Pan-Americanism, appropriating the term for their own ends. "Hemispheric citizenship was perhaps practiced most fully," Luis-Brown

writes, "in the various Pan-American and Inter-American social movements that emerged within, alongside, and in outright opposition to the US-initiated, state-sponsored versions of Pan-Americanism that promoted the interests of US capital. . . . Thus despite its efforts, the US State Department never succeeded in putting a lid on the tendency of Pan-Americanism to generate contradictory meanings and practices" (*Waves of Decolonization*, 26–28).

46. Wasserman, "'Abre a cortina,'" 81–82.

47. Stroud, *Defence of Tradition*, 21.

48. Rangel, Editorial, 25.

49. Guinle's *Jazz panorama* appeared in print the same year as Sérgio Porto's *Pequena história do jazz*, a book heavily influenced by Ortiz Oderigo's work.

50. Sanz, "Gato por lebre," 38.

51. Sanz, "Gato por lebre," 39.

52. Sanz, "Gato por lebre," 40.

53. Barroso, "Decadência," 7.

54. Seigel, *Uneven Encounters*, 100. See also Cabral, *No tempo de Ari*, 35–37. Explaining his early dalliance with jazz piano, Barroso commented ironically in a 1930 interview, "When jazz began its invasion of our land, I was its first victim" (cited in Fenerick, *Nem do morro*, 158).

55. Caymmi, "Dorival Caymmi," 4.

56. José Adriano Fenerick points to Noel Rosa and also to the journalist Vagalume (Francisco Guimarães) as two seminal figures who mapped out what would become commonplace distinctions between samba do morro ("idyllic space of the spontaneous sambista") and samba da cidade ("the space of the adulteration of samba, guided by the purely mercantilist logic of the culture industry") (*Nem do morro*, 244). As McCann has pointed out, however, the two spaces in reality were never fully separate, since "there were always intermediaries absorbing the styles of both camps, carrying messages between them and fostering mutual influence" (*Hello, Hello Brazil*, 58).

57. McCann, *Hello, Hello Brazil*, 78.

58. The curious marriage of Coca-Cola and samba was brokered by US advertising firm McCann Erickson. Coca-Cola's sponsorship of the Rádio Nacional show *Um milhão de melodias* beginning in 1943 proved commercially beneficial. Since Gnattali (the show's orchestral director) insisted on playing only Brazilian music (though with a jazz twist), it also served the interests of musical nationalism. According to Bryan McCann, Americanization thus "represented no danger, because as the American way of life was imported it became Brazilianized" (*Hello, Hello Brazil*, 225–27).

59. Rangel, Editorial, 389.

60. Magalhães, "Êxito que mata," 402.

61. Schmidt, "Sucesso de fato," 442.

62. Alencar, "O Brasil na tela," 1.

63. Ana M. López has noted that Hollywood was simply not interested in "mimetic relationships." Rather than "[representing] ethnics and minorities," classical Hollywood "creates them and provides its audience with an experience of them" ("Latins from Manhattan," 68).

64. In *The Gang's All Here*, for example, Miranda's character on more than one occasion is identified as the "Brazilian bombshell," a moniker coined in Hollywood that blurred the line between Miranda and the roles she was playing.

65. Alencar, "Carmen sem balangandãs," 3.

66. McCann, *Hello, Hello Brazil*, 146.

67. Guinle, "Jazz," 43.

68. Cruz Cordeiro, "Folcmúsica e música popular," 8, 40.

69. Costa, "Os rumos da música," 19.

70. Miranda, "Dizzy Gillespie no Rio," 42.

71. See in particular Fiske, "Cultural Economy of Fandom," and Sandvoss, *Fans*. Building on Fiske's seminal work on the subject, Sandvoss has noted that fandom draws from the whole spectrum of Bourdieu's hierarchy of taste, and that even so-called fan subcultures frequently reproduce hegemonic attitudes on gender, race, and the like. The crux of fandom therefore hinges on how fan objects are interpreted differently by distinct social and cultural groups, rather than the "external signification" of the objects themselves (38).

72. Castro, *Chega de saudade*, 36–37.

73. Taborda, "Melodias e ritmos," 6.

74. Taborda, "Jazz no cinema [ii]," 22.

75. "Radio: Languor, Curls and Tonsils," *Time Magazine*, September 15, 1947, n.p.

76. Ramalho Neto, "Dick Farney cantor internacional," 25.

77. Castro, *Chega de saudade*, 44. For the next two decades, Cyl would be a fixture in Brazilian cinema, particularly in the popular genre known as *chanchadas* and usually playing the suave romantic lead. The jam sessions in the Queirozes' basement came in handy. In a dream sequence from Manga's *Carnaval Atlântida* (1952), the Farney brothers appear in full "dive bar" mode. In the upbeat jazz number, Cyl—who has a central role in the film—rattles off a bop-inflected drum solo while Dick shows off his impeccable piano technique.

78. Donato, *Songbook João Donato*, 14.

79. Tinhorão, *Música popular*, 58.

80. Veloso, *Alegria, alegria*, 1.

81. Gava, *A linguagem harmônica*, 40–41.

82. By at least one account Farney was not particularly fond of traditional Brazilian popular music. In an interview he gave with *Diário da Noite* in 1952, he went so far as to say that Brazilian music would only improve once it had abandoned the pandeiro altogether (Cabral, *Antônio Carlos Jobim*, 120).

83. Medaglia, "Balanço da Bossa Nova," 107.

84. W. Garcia, *Bim bom*, 97–98.

85. Veloso, *Alegria, alegria*, 4.

86. W. Garcia, *Bim bom*, 101.

87. Bôscoli, *Eles e eu*, 63–65.

88. Castro, *Chega de saudade*, 245.

89. "O que eles pensam deles," *O Cruzeiro*, September 10, 1960, 4–5.

90. "Pobre samba meu / Foi se misturando / Se modernizando / E se perdeu / E o rebolado cadê? / Não tem mais / Cadê o tal gingado, que mexe com a gente / Coitado do meu samba, mudou de repente / Influência do jazz

"Quase que morreu / E acaba morrendo, está quase morrendo / Não percebeu / Que o samba balança de um lado pro outro / O jazz é diferente, pra frente, pra trás / E o samba meio morto, ficou meio torto / Influência do jazz

"No afro-cubano, vai complicando / Vai pelo cano, vai / Vai entortando, vai sem descanso / Vai, sai, cai . . . do balanço!

"Pobre samba meu / Volta lá pro morro / E pede socorro onde nasceu / Pra não ser um samba com notas demais / Não ser um samba torto / Pra frente e pra trás / Vai ter que se virar pra poder se livrar / Da influência do jazz"

91. Treece, "Guns and Roses," 15–16.

92. Treece, *Brazilian Jive*, 123; Bôscoli, *Eles e eu*, 64–65. In his memoirs, Bôscoli did not mince words about the competition with Lyra. Though he was not looking for "direct confrontations," he writes, it was no coincidence that the UFRJ bossa show took place on the same night as Lyra's sambalanço concert at PUC-Rio (64).

93. Wilson, "Brazilian Musicians," 51. This view was echoed by *Down Beat*'s Bill Coss, who also praised Gilberto while accusing the production of a distinct lack of professionalism (Dunn, "Por entre máscaras," 264). *Billboard*, meanwhile, quoted at length from one of the show's sponsors, who maintained that the audience's reaction to the concert was "extremely good," even if the large number of musicians involved in the show, many of them last-minute bookings, made for a somewhat crowded—and expensive—spectacle (Chase, "Saga of the Bossa," 16).

94. Harb Bollos's exhaustive survey of Brazilian periodicals suggests that negative reviews of the concert were focused as much on Wilson's *Times* piece as the show itself. Of the eyewitness accounts, the most authoritative was probably that of *O Globo* jazz writer Sylvio Tullio Cardoso. According to Cardoso, the concert, even if "far from perfect," was nevertheless a "most significant success" (Harb Bollos, *Bossa Nova e crítica*, 181–82).

95. Castro, *Chega de saudade*, 329–30.

96. Suero, "Bossa Nova desafinou," 6–10.

97. Menescal, *Coleção Gente*, 52–54.

98. Menescal, *Coleção Gente*, 53.

99. Rolontz, "After Start in Jazz," 4.

100. "Brazilians Did It All," *Billboard*, October 13, 1962, 4.

101. D. Monteiro, *A bossa do lobo*, 209.

102. Castro, *Chega de saudade*, 218, 248, 276–77. All of these shows would serve as preludes to one of the most successful programs of the decade, TV Records' *O Fino da Bossa*, which reigned supreme during the mid- to late 1960s. Relying on the singing talent and charisma of Elis Regina, the show paired her with crooner Jair Rodrigues, backed by the jazz- and bossa-based Zimbo Trio. As Castro argues, though, *O Fino da Bossa* did not so much sustain bossa nova as hasten its demise (405–6).

103. Gava, *A linguagem harmônica*, 74–75, 78.

104. Gava, *A linguagem harmônica*, 78.

105. According to *Billboard*, *Copacabana Palace* did not open in the United States until early 1963, by which time bossa nova's popularity had begun to grow considerably (International News Reports, *Billboard*, January 12, 1963, 30).

106. Perhaps not as surprising, given the music's toxic association with the bourgeoisie, Brazilian Cinema Novo filmmakers generally failed to make hay with bossa nova. The lone attempt to fully exploit the music was Leon Hirszman's *Garota de Ipanema* (1967), according to one film historian a "swan song" documenting a transitional moment in the nation's history when "sensuality yielded to promiscuity, and grace [gave way to] violence" (Pessoa Ramos, *Mas afinal*, 360). The film featured a virtual who's who of Brazilian popular music composers and performers, from Moraes, Jobim, Ary Barroso, and Dorival Caymmi to Pixinguinha, Luis Eça, Elis Regina, and Chico Buarque.

107. Cabral, *Antônio Carlos Jobim*, 203.

108. Castro, *Chega de saudade*, 336–37.

109. In her initial appearance on *The Hollywood Palace* in September 1964, Astrud Gilberto yielded the stage to Getz as well. That same year, the two also performed together in the Hollywood film *Get Yourself a College Girl* (dir. Sidney Miller) and the made-for-television movie *The Hanged Man* (dir. Don Siegel). Astrud's television appearances in the United States and Europe continued sans Getz throughout the decade and even into the next. She performed on *The Ed Sullivan Show* as late as 1970 and *The Mike Douglas Show* in 1971 (IMDb).

110. Tinhorão, "Bossa-Nova vive um drama," 20–21.

111. Tinhorão, "Bossa-Nova vive um drama," 21.

112. Tinhorão, "Bossa de exportação," 12.

113. "Influence is a not a plague," Jardim wrote. "It is a necessary chapter in the history of art. Jazz's influence on bossa nova does not humiliate anyone. Jazz and Wall Street are two different things. Jazz is the truest, most compelling musical expression of the American people. It is the music of the Negro" ("Bossa participante," 28).

114. Lyra was careful to include a disclaimer: "Despite considering myself politically a 'proletarian,' I could not escape the fact that I was economically a *petit bourgeois*. And worse: aesthetically an aristocrat" (*Eu e a bossa*, 60).

115. Leão, "Nara de Nara," 7.

116. Coutinho, "Confronto," 306.

117. Coutinho, "Confronto," 310.

118. Coutinho, "Confronto," 312.

119. Castro, *Chega de saudade*, 318.

120. Gillespie, *To Be, or Not*, 517.

121. "Quincy Jones Sees Bossa Nova Rhythm as New Craze," *Jet* 22, no. 19 (August 30, 1962): 58.

122. Morrison, "Man behind the Horn," 149.

123. It is worth noting that while Sérgio Cabral's biography of Jobim dedicates an entire chapter to his collaborations with Sinatra, in Michael Freedland's *All the Way: A Biography of Frank Sinatra*, Jobim merits only a short paragraph in which the biographer lauds Sinatra's "swinging in perfect harmony with the smooth tones of Jobim's acoustic guitar" (335–36).

124. The performances were taped in October 1967 and broadcast the next month as part of a Sinatra special called *A Man and His Music + Ella + Jobim* (Gioia, *Jazz Standards*, 73).

125. Castro, *Chega de saudade*, 377.

126. Coutinho, "Confronto," 309, 311.

127. Medaglia, "Balanço da Bossa Nova," 107–8.

128. The urubu in this context has a number of rich connotations besides the obvious. The "Urubu Malandro" (referred to elsewhere in Sant'Anna's story) is the name of a choro first recorded in 1914, later to be made famous by Pixinguinha (Efegê, *Figuras e coisas*, 266; Cabral, *Pixinguinha*, 91). Antônio Carlos Jobim recorded an album in 1976 titled *Urubu*.

129. Veloso, *Alegria, alegria*, 7.

CHAPTER FOUR. **The Hazards of Hybridity**

1. Hentoff, "The Mambo!!," 52.

2. Moore, *Nationalizing Blackness*, 102–4.

3. López, "Of Rhythms and Borders," 311. Although in the early sound era film producers, distributors, and exhibitors throughout Latin America found themselves at a deep disadvantage in competing with Hollywood imports, by the end of the 1930s Mexico, Argentina, and to a lesser extent Brazil had established robust industries. Although in 1933 only 6 Argentine narrative features made it to the box offices, by 1939 this figure had grown to 50. In 1938 the Mexican film industry produced 57 features; after a brief dip in production, the industry grew even more prolific in the following decade, topping off at 107 features in 1949 (King, *Magical Reels*, 38, 47, 53, 56–57). Many Argentine, Mexican, and Brazilian films of the period were musicals. By comparison, only 12 narrative features were produced in Cuba in the entire decade of the 1930s. By the end of the 1940s, this figure had risen to approximately 2–3 narrative features per year, a number of them Mexican-Cuban and Argentine-Cuban coproductions (Douglas, *Catálogo del cine cubano*, 153–79).

4. Putnam has demonstrated how Cuba in the 1920s and 1930s exported its popular music and musicians not just to the United States but also to the English- and Spanish-speaking West Indies, such that "the tens of thousands of Jamaicans returning to Jamaica from Cuba, Costa Rica, Panama, and beyond in the 1920s and 1930s were coming back from musical environments saturated with multiple varieties of ragtime and swing as well as multiple varieties of *son*" (*Radical Moves*, 170, 194–95). At the same time, what Putnam calls the embodied, raced, "supranational" dimensions of circum-Caribbean performance made port cities like Panama City, Kingston, and Port of Spain, not to mention Havana, obligatory stops for US touring groups and other performers (14, 173).

5. Giddins, *Visions of Jazz*, 325.

6. Pacini Hernandez, *¡Oye cómo va!*, 18.

7. Moore, *Nationalizing Blackness*, 105, 120–21. According to Moore, particularly instrumental to the consecration of Afro-Cuban culture were the publications and public comments of intellectuals such as Fernando Ortiz, Juan Marinello, and Emilio Roig de Leuchsenring, for whom "Afrocuban forms had the potential to serve as a barrier to national disintegration and the possibility of cultural subsumption by the United States" (127). At the same time, beginning in the late 1920s and early 1930s, the rising international popularity and prestige of jazz helped to promote *afrocubanismo* in both popular and intellectual circles (133).

8. Lund, *Impure Imagination*, 8–9, 15.

9. At the time, it was widely rumored that Pozo was also involved romantically with Montaner (Delannoy, *¡Caliente!*, 123–24; Padura Fuentes, "Chano Pozo," 210). Montaner's son Alberto later claimed these rumors were false, however, and insisted that Pozo saw Montaner as a sincere friend and musical partner, as well as a kind of surrogate mother (Fajardo Estrada, *Rita Montaner*, 229).

10. Delannoy, *¡Caliente!*, 125–26, 129. Acosta writes that the hybrid "supershow" *Conga Pantera* combined on one stage the talents of Pozo, Rita Montaner, Ignacio Villa (Bola de Nieve), Roderico Neyra (later to become famous as the cabaret dancer and choreographer Rodney), and finally the Russian ballet choreographer David Lichine, as well as two of his leading dancers (*Cubano Be, Cubano Bop*, 66–67). "This encounter," Acosta writes, "would be for the world of show business in Cuba as important as the one between Chano and Dizzy Gillespie was for Afro-Cuban jazz or Cubop some years later" (67).

11. Austerlitz, *Jazz Consciousness*, 72; Delannoy, *¡Caliente!*, 127.

12. Acosta, *Cubano Be, Cubano Bop*, 68.

13. Salazar, *Mambo Kingdom*, 45–46.

14. F. Ortiz, "Saba, samba y *bop*," 251, 252–53.

15. Stearns, "Rebop, Bebop, and Bop," 93–94.

16. F. Ortiz, "Saba, samba y *bop*," 253–54. First published in the Cuban periodical *Mensuario de Arte, Literatura, Historia y Cultura* shortly after Pozo's early, violent death, Ortiz's essay was republished twenty-five years later in the journal *Signos*. Since then it has been recycled in numerous Cuban tributes, articles, and other works on Chano Pozo, evolving into a doctrinal touchstone for Chano Pozo's symbolic importance to the latter-day revolution as a musician and native son. The essay has also served as an authoritative comment on the many international exponents of Afro-Cuban musical performance whose "authenticity" ultimately engaged—and transformed—the supposedly ominous forces of the "bourgeois" culture industries of Europe and the United States.

17. Gillespie, *To Be, or Not*, 319, 321.

18. Sublette has noted that in personal conversations, Gillespie interviewer Robert Palmer frequently remarked that Gillespie was frustrated with the way mainstream jazz critics tended to write off his collaborative work with Pozo, "as if it were an eccentricity or a sideshow, when to Dizzy it was the most important thing he'd done" (Sublette, *Cuba and Its Music*, 537).

19. J. Roberts, *Latin Jazz*, 77.

20. Shipton, *Groovin' High*, 201.

21. As Jairo Moreno has argued, Pozo and Bauzá's landmark collaborations with US jazz musicians can be seen as part of a "tense and dynamic syncopation of sonic and social histories and temporalities" ("Bauzá-Gillespie-Latin/Jazz," 178).

22. Sargeant, "Cuba's Tin Pan Alley," 151.

23. Sargeant, "Cuba's Tin Pan Alley," 152. The aura of the savage and the occult carries over into a subsequent bebop piece, also published in *Life*. One caption describes how Pozo "whips beboppers into fever with a Congo beat" ("Bebop," 140); in another the conguero was said to be "shouting inherently" while he played (141). The "offbeat" followers of the new "cult" of bebop, meanwhile—which include such celebrities as Mel Tormé and

Ava Gardner—are cast above all as uniformly eccentric dressers with a taste for frenzied, "discordant" music (139).

24. Levin, "Despite Bad Acoustics," 1, 3.

25. Hodeir, "Dizzy Gillespie à Paris," 7.

26. Pérez, *On Becoming Cuban*, 287.

27. Chanan, *Cuban Cinema*, 77–80.

28. Kun, "Against Easy Listening," 288–89.

29. López, "Of Rhythms and Borders," 311.

30. Urfé, "La verdad sobre el mambo," 31–33. David García notes that the generally accepted date for Arcaño y sus Maravillas' performance of "Mambo" is 1938, although it was not actually recorded until 1951 ("Going Primitive," 521n).

31. D. García, "Going Primitive," 507–8.

32. Even Leonardo Acosta, generally so clearheaded in his analysis, has fallen into this trap. While attempting to repudiate assertions that Pérez Prado was influenced by Stan Kenton, Acosta nonetheless ends up constantly invoking Kenton's name in his discussion of Pérez Prado's style (*Elige tú*, 32–33).

33. Sublette, *Cuba and Its Music*, 559.

34. Sparke, *Stan Kenton*, 59.

35. Yanow, *Afro-Cuban Jazz*, 60.

36. Pérez Firmat, *Life on the Hyphen*, 77, 209n.

37. Martínez, *Cubanos en la música*, 72.

38. Sublette, *Cuba and Its Music*, 561.

39. Pérez Firmat, *Life on the Hyphen*, 77.

40. Powell, *Tito Puente*, 148.

41. Such issues of race, morality, and national identity cannot be fully understood without unpacking some of mambo's racial baggage. Robin Moore has pointed out that Cuban music of the 1940s and 1950s underwent a "blackening" or "re-Africanizing." Previous Afro-Cuban forms denigrated by the cultural elites (such as the percussion-heavy, noncommercial rumba) were recovered. In much the same way, jazz underwent a transformation as bebop musicians like Charlie Parker and Dizzy Gillespie attempted to wrest it away from commercial swing bands dominated by white musicians. "Blackening" therefore followed "whitening" in both Cuban and US contexts (*Nationalizing Blackness*, 110, 178–79).

42. Monsiváis, "Censura," n.p.

43. Carl J. Mora has argued that the cabaretera film epitomized widespread disenchantment with the corruption associated with the Alemán administration, while also suggesting a breakdown of traditional values expressed in the comedia ranchera (*Mexican Cinema*, 84–85).

44. Cuéllar Vizcaíno, "La revolución del mambo," 24.

45. Tyler, *Music of the Postwar*, 63; D. García, *Arsenio Rodríguez*, 76–77. As the historian Juan Gargurevich writes, if "thousands and thousands [of *limeños*] were sent to Purgatory because of the mambo," the church's condemnation only served to heighten the music's appeal among the excommunicated (*La prensa sensacionalista*, 213).

46. García Márquez, "El mambo," 19.

47. García Márquez, "Mambo de Nueva York," 21–22.

48. Giro, "Todo lo que usted," 14.

49. Vásquez, *Listening in Detail*, 145–46.

50. See Adler, "Mambo and the Mood."

51. In his interview on the show, the bandleader responded to Jones's questions in Spanish only. At one point the host implored him to stop his "enchilada" gibberish, provoking the arrival of two "interpreters" (a giant and a little person, Spike Jones regular Billy Barty), neither of whom spoke Spanish. The linguistic impasse quickly led to a challenge and subsequent battle of the bands: Pérez Prado's Orchestra versus Jones's satirical house band, the City Slickers, whose dissonant incompetence made a mockery of the competition itself while also poking fun at Pérez Prado's trademark sound. It seems that mambo's flamboyance was not to be taken too seriously. For more criticism in the same vein, see Mrs. Arthur Murray's "What the Heck Is the Mambo?"

52. Somewhat disturbingly, Pérez Prado's US television appearances signaled Hollywood's return to an early tendency to relegate Latin American actors and performers to highly stereotyped, often denigrating roles. For a critical overview of Hollywood's troubled history of Latin American and Latino stereotyping, see Berg, *Latino Images in Film*. For a more detailed history of Mexico's particularly fraught relationship with the early US film industry, see García Riera, *México visto por el cine extranjero*.

53. Such national typecasting was employed in other Hollywood pictures of the period, perhaps most notably in *Guys and Dolls* (dir. Joseph Mankiewicz, 1955).

54. While Good Neighbor films hardly put an end to such representations—for proof, one need look no farther than the Miranda vehicle *Week-end in Havana* (dir. Walter Lang, 1941)—they at least softened their edges and went to some lengths to avoid pegging cultural bias to overarching narratives of racial inferiority and social backwardness.

55. Saldívar, *Trans-Americanity*, xiii–xiv.

56. Acosta, *Cubano Be, Cubano Bop*, 174–75, 176.

57. Moore, *Music and Revolution*, 66, 108–10, 282n.

58. Chanan, *Cuban Cinema*, 151.

59. Acosta, *Cubano Be, Cubano Bop*, 168.

60. Acosta, *Cubano Be, Cubano Bop*, 186.

61. Linares, "Sobre nuestra tradición cultural," 6.

62. Linares, "Sobre nuestra tradición cultural," 4.

63. Acosta, "La música afroamericana," 17; italics in the original.

64. Acosta, "La música afroamericana," 17–18.

65. Acosta, "¿Quién inventó el mambo?," 75.

66. Urfé, "Danzón, mambo y cha-cha-chá," 57.

67. Sublette, *Cuba and Its Music*, 560.

68. Sublette, *Cuba and Its Music*, 566.

69. Fernández Retamar, "Oyendo un disco," 29–30.

70. Guillén, "Benny," 80.

71. Echazábal, "Benny Moré," 156. The revolution's canonization of Benny Moré continued into the 1970s and beyond. Sergio Giral's short biographical film *Qué bueno canta usted* appeared in 1973. This was followed by a number of generally anecdotal crónicas and essays, beginning with Eduardo Robreño's "Mis recuerdos del Benny," published in

Bohemia in August 1974; and Acosta's "Elige tú que canto yo," first published in *Revolución y Cultura* in 1978, which would later serve as the basis of a book of the same title. For a selection of Cuban texts on Moré from the 1960s to the early twenty-first century, see Félix Contreras's *Yo conocí a Benny Moré.*

72. Moore, *Music and Revolution,* 21–22.

73. Acosta, *Elige tú,* 55.

74. Rodríguez and Pumariega, *Mitos de la popularidad,* 7. Although probably not the only reason Pozo did not rejoin Gillespie, the Cuban's alleged aversion to the US South was entirely possible, given the many linguistic and racial barriers he would have had to confront there at the time (Sublette, *Cuba and Its Music,* 540).

75. Rodríguez and Pumariega, *Mitos de la popularidad,* 14, 22. Such images are strikingly similar to those of interwar Chicago and Havana in Juan Padrón's animated film *¡Vampiros en la Habana!* (1985), in which a mambo- and jazz-inspired soundtrack sets the mood for the film's allegorical farce and outlandish underworld violence.

76. Rodríguez and Pumariega, *Mitos de la popularidad,* 17.

77. Belmonte, "Grupo Irakere," 72.

78. Acosta, "Un gran músico," 16.

79. Belmonte, "Grupo Irakere," 72.

80. Suco, "¿Jazz latino o música cubana?," 19–20.

81. Suco, "¿Jazz latino o música cubana?," 22.

82. Suco, "¿Jazz latino o música cubana?," 19, 22. Lise Waxer has observed that the word "catchall" could well be applied not just to New York–based salsa of the 1960s but also to the earlier umbrella term "Latin music," which was frequently used to denote danceable styles from different parts of Latin America beginning in the 1930s. Both "Latin music" and the musically more specific "salsa," in spite of their original association with Cuba and Puerto Rico, "have evolved into [musical expressions] with multiple sites of articulation" ("Situating Salsa," 5–6).

83. Suco, "¿Jazz latino o música cubana?," 22.

84. Carpentier, "La música popular cubana," 12.

85. O'Farrill, "Well-Rounded Writer," 23.

86. Giddins, *Visions of Jazz,* 325.

87. Moreno, "Bauzá-Gillespie-Latin/Jazz," 178.

88. Gioia, *History of Jazz,* 222–23.

89. Shipton, *¡Caliente!,* 384.

90. Shipton, *¡Caliente!,* 382.

91. Owens, *Bebop,* 21.

92. MacAdams, *Birth of the Cool,* 69. That Scott Yanow's *Bebop* foregrounds Pozo and Machito's work to a greater degree than Owens and MacAdams is not surprising, given the fact that Yanow has devoted a separate volume to Afro-Cuban jazz. Although written as more of a popular reference guide than a scholarly history, Yanow's book on bebop, like the others I have mentioned, nonetheless misses an opportunity to make the argument that Pozo and others were not simply engaged in "[fusing] Cuban folk music with Bebop" (*Bebop,* 171) but rather were instrumental in the genesis of bebop itself.

CHAPTER FIVE. **The Afterlives of Jazz**

The epigraph translates as "I arrived late / what can I do / except listen / like a fool / to what all of you did when I / was / three years old."

1. *The Etude*, August and September 1924. Reprinted as "The Jazz Problem," in *Keeping Time: Readings in Jazz History*, ed. Robert Walser (New York: Oxford University Press, 1999), 41–54.

2. *The Etude*, "The Jazz Problem," 52.

3. Garrett, *Struggling to Define a Nation*, loc. 1443–45. In a series of 1928 *Defender* columns, Dave Peyton bemoaned the supposed lack of musicianship among black jazz performers and "mushy, discordant jazz music" generally, exhorting African American musicians to emulate the "smoothness" and precision of white orchestras (Peyton, "Black Journalist Criticizes Jazz," 58–59).

4. Dugan and Hammond, "Jazz at Carnegie Hall," 102.

5. Pike, *FDR's Good Neighbor Policy*, 123–24, 254.

6. In 1941, Welles and Duke Ellington began collaboration on the episode, intended to be part of a larger Pan-American film project called *It's All True*, which was to include other episodes based in Mexico and Brazil. Both Ellington and Armstrong were eager to participate in the project, which was ultimately bogged down by lack of organization and hindered by Welles's conflicts with RKO Pictures (Benamou, *It's All True*, 27–31, 58, 65–66).

7. Penny M. Von Eschen has noted that in spite of Eisenhower's conviction, Gillespie's watershed 1956 tour of South America was in fact the product of a confluence of interests, including civil rights activists, musicians and industry promoters, and cultural critics. Still, the president's involvement in jazz diplomacy would be decisive. Irked by accusations of hypocrisy in the area of race and democracy, Eisenhower ultimately realized that jazz, given its historical roots in and close association with the United States, lent the nation a comparative advantage over European and Soviet critics. While the United States could never hope to stand toe-to-toe with Europe in the cultural realm of classical music or ballet, jazz was another story (*Satchmo Blows Up the World*, 4–6, 40).

8. Anderson, *This Is Our Music*, loc. 423–36, 444–61.

9. Belair, "America's 'Secret Sonic Weapon,'" 42.

10. Von Eschen, *Satchmo Blows Up the World*, 40.

11. Anderson, *This Is Our Music*, 279–92.

12. Sorensen, *Turbulent Decade Remembered*, 3.

13. Cortázar, *Rayuela*, 3.

14. The literary critic Jaime Alazraki, for example, writes that *Rayuela*'s structure responds to a conception of the novel as essentially open-ended and aleatory, lending itself to the participating reader's "combinatorial analysis" ("Rayuela," 631). In his focus on the importance of jazz to *Rayuela* at both formal and thematic levels, Saúl Yurkievich argues that jazz in Cortázar's work constitutes an "inspirational numen, and an aesthetic model that he seeks to transfer to his writing" ("La pujanza insumisa," 667). Working against the grain of logocentric order, jazz in *Rayuela* assumes "orgiastic" and "despotic" proportions (668).

15. González Bermejo, *Revelaciones de un cronopio*, 119.

16. Cortázar, *Rayuela*, 67–68.

17. Cortázar, *Rayuela*, 68–69.

18. Cortázar, *Rayuela*, 47.

19. Cortázar, *Rayuela*, 170–71.

20. Delannoy, *Convergencias*, n.p.

21. Delannoy, *¡Caliente!*, 187–91.

22. Tibol, *Pedro Cervantes*, 57–58; Derbez, *El jazz en México*, 51–53. In the exposition's catalog, the photographer López defended jazz against accusations of fashion and snobbery. The music, he wrote, "suited the rhythm of this dislocated city, [piercing] the sensibility of its tense citizenry" (Tibol, *Pedro Cervantes*, 58).

23. Derbez, *El jazz en México*, 55.

24. T. Contreras, *Mi amor, el jazz*, 51–52, 57.

25. Derbez, *El jazz en México*, 24.

26. García Ascot, "Jazz y droga," 24.

27. Pericás, *Nuestro jazz*, 19–20.

28. Pericás, *Nuestro jazz*, 24, 98–99.

29. Pericás, *Nuestro jazz*, 42–43.

30. Pericás, *Nuestro jazz*, 52.

31. Pericás, *Nuestro jazz*, 66–67.

32. Pericás, *Nuestro jazz*, 28.

33. Pericás, *Nuestro jazz*, 90.

34. Pericás, *Nuestro jazz*, 79.

35. Pericás, *Nuestro jazz*, 84.

36. Célélier Eguiluz, "Jazz mexicano," 337.

37. Derbez, *El jazz en México*, 62.

38. In terms of recorded music, a good indication of the typical jazz repertoire in Mexico in the 1950s and 1960s can be gleaned from the composer Alberto Domínguez's long-running show *"Mister Jazz"* on the radio station XEW (Moreno Rivas, *Historia de la música*, 173).

39. Cortázar, *La vuelta al día*, 13.

40. Franco, *Critical Passions*, 165, 504.

41. Cortázar, *La vuelta al día*, 144.

42. Derbez, *Todo se escucha*, 116.

43. Atkins, "Toward a Global History," loc. 190.

44. Todd F. Tietchen has written that FPCC's work led to a sympathetic "subgenre of Beat travel narrative" that he dubs "Cubalogues," texts such as Ferlinghetti's "Poet's Notes on Cuba," LeRoi Jones's "Cuba Libre," and Mark Schleifer's "Cuban Notebook" (*Cubalogues*, 2). Jones's awed description of train travel across the island in his essay "Cuba Libre" is seen by Tietchen as evidence of how "stock features of Kerouacian fiction—such as the cross-country train ride and aural epiphany—took on new roles in a transnational political drama" (72).

45. Baraka, "Cuba Libre," 128.

46. Baraka, *Autobiography of LeRoi Jones*, 244.

47. Baraka, "Cuba Libre," 147.

48. Baraka, *Autobiography of LeRoi Jones*, 245.

49. Cited in Mazzola and Cherlin, *Flow, Gesture, and Spaces*, 4.

50. Tyson, *Radio Free Dixie*, 288.

51. Acosta, *Cubano Be, Cubano Bop*, 176.

52. Cultural populism is central to Álvarez's work of the 1960s. As Michael Chanan remarks, Cuban revolutionary cinema was not merely a didactic expression, but "also a celebration of . . . expansive popular culture" (*Cuban Cinema*, 21, 204–5).

53. It was not until the short documentary *LBJ* (1968) that Álvarez would openly address the Black Power movement. Although the film includes footage of a speech by Stokely Carmichael, the fragment is hardly incendiary, as Carmichael emphasizes the "civilizing" function of Black Power over its revolutionary calling.

54. Desnoes, *Now*, 15, 20.

55. It is telling, for instance, that Afro-Cuban playwright Tomás González later claimed that his position as the unofficial figurehead of the Cuban Black Power movement led to accusations of racial separatism by the Castro regime (Howe, *Transgression and Conformity*, 79–80).

56. As black activist organizations like the Sociedade de Intercâmbio Brasil-África (SINBA) were quick to point out, the main agents of participação were white, middle-class musicians such as Vinícius de Moraes, Nara Leão, and Carlos Lyra. Although the "hard bossa" bands of the decade included some Afro-descendant musicians, Brazil in the 1960s clearly lacked a cadre of black, politically committed avant-garde performers of the stature of Coleman, Shepp, and Sun Ra.

57. As Paulina L. Alberto points out, a seminal event for Black Rio was a screening of the US documentary *Wattstax* at the Museu de Arte Moderna. The film featured extended footage of a 1972 soul and funk concert held in the Watts neighborhood of Los Angeles as a kind of black Woodstock. Sponsored by the Instituto de Pesquisas das Culturas Negras (IPCN), a splinter group of SINBA, the screening attracted thousands of jubilant favela residents to one of the main symbols of elite Rio culture (*Terms of Inclusion*, 276–77).

58. Derbez, *Para mirar el ruido*, 10.

59. Derbez, *Para mirar el ruido*, 23.

60. Derbez, *Para mirar el ruido*, 20.

61. Derbez, *Para mirar el ruido*, 21.

62. Derbez, *Todo se escucha*, 108.

63. Derbez, *Todo se escucha*, 112.

64. Derbez, *Todo se escucha*, 109.

65. Derbez, *Todo se escucha*, 122.

66. Derbez, *Todo se escucha*, 123.

67. The State Department–sponsored tours of the 1950s, and later the emergence of a number of homegrown jazz festivals in the 1960s and 1970s, exposed much larger audiences to a wider swath of live jazz performance than ever before. Throughout the 1960s, the journalist José Luis Durán organized jazz festivals and other shows, including performances by Stan Kenton and his orchestra (Derbez, *El jazz en México*, 74–75). In fall 1966, what was billed as the first Festival Nacional de Jazz was held at the main auditorium at the Universidad Nacional Autónoma de México (UNAM). *Billboard* characterized attendance as "good, considering the limited jazz interest here," though also acknowledging, contradictorily, that "many performers record [in Mexico]." The magazine also noted that Pericás's book *Nuestro jazz* was sold during all the festival's performances ("First Mexican Jazz Fest Gets a

'Good' Reception," *Billboard*, October 8, 1966, 32). By many accounts, the first large-scale jazz festival in Brazil was the Festival de Jazz de São Paulo. First held in September 1978, the inaugural festival was broadcast on TV Cultura (Leal Filho, *Atrás das câmaras*, 49). Featuring prominent international figures such as John McLaughlin and Chick Corea as well as fast-rising national artists like Hermeto Pascoal, the festival's contemporary (and electric) slant was a big hit with Brazilian audiences (Bahiana, "Música instrumental," 64).

68. Ochoa Gautier, "Social Transculturation," loc. 10438–43.

69. Santiago, *Keith Jarrett*, 33.

70. Santiago, *Keith Jarrett*, 26.

71. In Portuguese, *folha* means "leaf" as well as "sheet of paper" and "knife."

72. Santiago, *Keith Jarrett*, 33.

73. Santiago, *Keith Jarrett*, 33.

74. Elsdon, Köln Concert, 27.

75. Elsdon, Köln Concert, 40–41.

76. Ake, *Jazz Cultures*, 109.

77. Santiago, *Keith Jarrett*, 18–25.

78. Posso, *Artful Seduction*, 84.

79. Carr, *Keith Jarrett*, 46.

80. Elsdon, Köln Concert, 34.

81. Anderson, *This Is Our Music*, 1994.

82. Aira, *Cecil Taylor*, 18.

83. Aira, *Cecil Taylor*, 24–26, 32.

84. See Alberto and Elena, "Shades of the Nation," 7.

85. Aira, *Cecil Taylor*, 67.

86. Aira, *Cecil Taylor*, 74.

87. For an enlightening discussion of the role that rock played in mobilizing Argentine youth resistance to military regimes in the late 1960s and early 1970s, see chapters 5 and 6 of Valeria Manzano's *The Age of Youth in Argentina*.

88. Avelar, *Untimely Present*, 2–5, 20–21.

89. Dance, *World of Duke Ellington*, 274.

90. Pujol, *Jazz al Sur*, 243–44.

91. Pujol, *Jazz al Sur*, 179–81.

92. Menanteau, *Historia del jazz en Chile*, 54–57, 72–77, 83.

93. Méndez Carrasco, *Dos cuentos de jazz*, 26.

94. Méndez Carrasco, *Chicago Chico*, 182–83. Fernando Lecaros was an important figure in Chilean music during the 1930s and 1940s. As Méndez Carrasco suggests, Lecaros was a versatile, ever-evolving talent whose dance orchestra was equally at home playing foxtrots, waltzes, boleros, rumbas, guarachas, and mapuchinas—a mixture of Chilean indigenous music and bolero (Menanteau, *Historia del jazz en Chile*, 41). Lecaros was the uncle of Roberto Lecaros, who in the 1960s and 1970s would become one of the key innovators of Chilean jazz and popular music generally. Associated at a young age with the Club de Jazz de Santiago, Roberto Lecaros played with Omar Nahuel's well-regarded quartet. He would later become an important music educator, forming an influential jazz workshop in his house in 1978 (Menanteau, *Historia del jazz en Chile*, 101–2).

95. Méndez Carrasco, *Chicago Chico*, 39–40.

96. Méndez Carrasco has generally received short shrift from literary critics. One notable exception is the novelist, critic, and performance artist Diamela Eltit, who has praised him for "[politicizing] a space of otherness" at a time when mainstream Chilean literature and other official discourses generally ignored Méndez Carrasco and the "nocturnal nomadism" and "complex, paradoxical" existences he chronicled (Eltit, "Chicago Chico," n.p.).

97. Méndez Carrasco, *Dos cuentos de jazz*, 9–10.

98. Méndez Carrasco, *Dos cuentos de jazz*, 10, 16.

99. Méndez Carrasco, *Dos cuentos de jazz*, 14.

100. Sábat, *Yo Bix*, 1.

101. Sábat, *Yo Bix*, 13, 16–17, 43.

102. Sábat, *Yo Bix*, 24–25.

103. Sábat, *Yo Bix*, 1.

104. Sábat, *Scat*, 8.

105. Sábat, *Scat*, 29.

106. Sábat, *Scat*, 39.

107. Sábat, *Scat*, 53.

108. Sábat, *Scat*, 47.

109. Sábat, *Scat*, 59.

110. Sábat, *Scat*, 129.

111. Sábat, *Scat*, 130, 134.

112. Sábat, *Scat*, 99.

113. Sábat, *Scat*, 142.

114. See Avelar, *Untimely Present*, 4.

115. Sábat, *Scat*, 73.

116. Gordon, *Ghostly Matters*, xvi.

117. Franco, *Decline and Fall*, 8–9.

118. Franco, *Decline and Fall*, 10, 182–83.

119. As I have mentioned, Jaime Pericás's *Nuestro jazz* featured the "naive" illustrations of Ignacio Navarro. Cortázar's sketches of Armstrong and Monk in *La vuelta al día en ochenta mundos* are accompanied by archival photos of both musicians. Alain Derbez's chapbook *Para mirar el ruido* features handwritten poems (several of which would be included typewritten in his anthology *Todo se escucha en silencio*) juxtaposed with small and full-page renderings by the painter Jazzamoart.

120. See Ahmed, "Happy Objects," loc. 395, and Gibbs, "After Affect," loc. 2624, 2787. In general terms, I am thinking of Sarah Ahmed's notion of the "stickiness" of affect, "or what sustains or preserves the connection between, ideas, values, and objects" (loc. 395).

Conclusion

1. Hesmondhalgh, *Why Music Matters*, 2, 4.

2. Hesmondhalgh, *Why Music Matters*, 17–18, 20.

3. Hesmondhalgh, *Why Music Matters*, 23–24. Cinema, writes Anna Gibbs, is particularly powerful in that it facilitates mimesis (a key agent of "affect contagion"), thereby

"[binding] spectators into complex forms of sociality, including story, cinematic spectatorship, and audience membership" ("After Affect," loc. 2624, 2787).

4. Such gray zones are endemic to imperial spatialities and the "partly denationalized" zones they create. "If the phrase *hemispheric citizenship* sounds like a contradiction in terms," Luis-Brown writes, "that is because citizenship has traditionally been associated with legal and political rights promised within the space of a single nation-state. But in the context of the geographically 'stretched out' character of social relations under imperialism and neocolonialism, citizenship acquires new meanings" (*Waves of Decolonization*, 21, 25).

5. In a recent study, Claudia Milian employs "Latinity" and "Latinities" instead of *latinidad* precisely because, she says, the "structuring content" of the latter "is unquestionably tied to a collective ethos located no further than its surrounding US Latino and Latina criterion" (*Latining America*, 4).

6. The musician and scholar Christopher Washburne has suggested that the concept "Latin jazz" began to prevail over the earlier "Cubop" and "Afro-Cuban jazz" categories during the 1960s, when pan-Latin social movements gained traction in the United States. Like pan-Africanism, Washburne writes, pan-Latinismo was "fueled largely by political and economic pressures, promoting common unity for empowering a minority or marginalized group with mass mobilization toward a common goal" ("Latin Jazz, Afro-Latin Jazz," 97).

7. See Corona and Madrid, "The Postnational Turn," 3–11.

8. For an overview of rock's dispersion, impact, and various appropriations in the hemisphere, see Pacini Hernandez, Fernández-L'Hoeste, and Zolov's introduction to the essential volume *Rockin' Las Américas*.

9. Recent years have witnessed a number of groundbreaking studies of Latin American hip-hop, including Derek Pardue, *Ideologies of Marginality in Brazilian Hip Hop*; Christopher Dennis, *Afro-Colombian Hip-Hop: Globalization, Transcultural Music, and Ethnic Identities*; and Marc D. Perry, *Negro Soy Yo: Hip Hop and Raced Citizenship in Neoliberal Cuba*.

10. For studies that encompass the global and historical dimensions of salsa, see Waxer, "Situating Salsa: Latin Music at the Crossroads"; Christopher Washburne, *Sounding Salsa: Performing Latin Music in New York City*; and Juliet McMains, *Spinning Mambo into Salsa: Caribbean Dance in Global Commerce*.

11. Fernández-L'Hoeste and Vila, *Cumbia!*, 17–18.

12. Berlant, *Cruel Optimism*, 11.

13. Berlant, *Cruel Optimism*, 15.

Acede. "'Jazz' y tango." *Síncopa y Ritmo* 7 (February 1935): 42.

Acosta, Leonardo. *Cubano Be, Cubano Bop: One Hundred Years of Jazz in Cuba*. Translated by Daniel S. Whitesell. Washington, DC: Smithsonian Institution, 2003.

———. *Elige tú, que canto yo*. Havana: Letras Cubanas, 1993.

———. "La música afroamericana: Integración y reinterpretación." *Revolución y Cultura* 48 (August 1976): 8–19.

———. "¿Quién inventó el mambo? Entrevista con Orestes López." *Revolución y Cultura* 42 (February 1976): 70–75.

———. "Un gran músico y 88 teclas." *Revolución y Cultura* 74 (October 1978): 15–19.

Adán, Martín. "Nota polémica: Contra Josefina Backer [*sic*]." *Amauta* 13 (1928): 21.

Adler, Barbara Squires. "The Mambo and the Mood." *New York Times Magazine*, September 16, 1951.

Adorno, Theodor W. "Perennial Fashion—Jazz." In *Prisms*, translated by Samuel and Shierry Weber. Cambridge, MA: MIT Press, 1981.

Ahmed, Sara. "Happy Objects." In *The Affect Theory Reader*, edited by Melissa Gregg and Gregory J. Seigworth, loc. 391–733. Durham, NC: Duke University Press, 2010. Kindle edition.

———. *Strange Encounters: Embodied Others in Post-coloniality*. London: Routledge, 2000.

Aira, César. *Cecil Taylor: Con ilustraciones de El Marinero Turco*. Buenos Aires: Mansalva, 2011.

Ake, David. *Jazz Cultures*. Berkeley: University of California Press, 2002.

Alazraki, Jaime. "*Rayuela*: Estructura." In Julio Cortázar, *Rayuela: Edición crítica*, edited by Julio Ortega and Saúl Yurkievich, 2nd ed., 629–38. Madrid: ALLCA XX, 1996.

Alberto, Paulina L. *Terms of Inclusion: Black Intellectuals in Twentieth-Century Brazil*. Chapel Hill: University of North Carolina Press, 2011.

Alberto, Paulina L., and Eduardo Elena, eds. "Introduction: The Shades of the Nation." In *Rethinking Race in Modern Argentina*, edited by Paulina L. Alberto and Eduardo Elena, 1–24. New York: Cambridge University Press, 2016.

Alencar, Renato de. "Carmen sem balangandãs." *A Cena Muda* 21, no. 1073 (October 14, 1941): 3.

———. "O Brasil na tela." *A Cena Muda* 19, no. 985 (February 6, 1940): 1.

Álvarez Nájera, Pablo. "Música negra y música de 'jazz.'" *Síncopa y Ritmo* (1938): 37–38.

Amaral, Aracy A. *Blaise Cendrars no Brasil e os modernistas*. São Paulo: Martins, 1970.

Anderson, Iain. *This Is Our Music: Free Jazz, the Sixties, and American Culture*. Philadelphia: University of Pennsylvania Press, 2007. Kindle edition.

Andrade, Carlos Drummond de. "A alma tumultuosa de Antônio Ferro." In *Modernismo brasileiro e modernismo português: Subsídios para o seu estudo e para a história das suas relações*, edited by Arnaldo Saraiva, 551–53. Campinas, SP: Editora da UNICAMP, 2004.

Andrade, Mário de. *A expressão musical nos Estados Unidos*. Rio de Janeiro: Leuzinger, 1941.

———. "Klaxon." In *Las vanguardias latinoamericanas: Textos programáticos y críticos*, edited by Jorge Schwartz, 262–64. Mexico City: Fondo de Cultura Económica, 2002.

———. *Música, doce música*. 2nd ed. São Paulo: Livrari Martins Editora, 1976.

———. *Música e jornalismo: Diário de S. Paulo*. Edited by Paulo Castagna. São Paulo: HUCITEC/EDUSP, 1993.

———. "Regionalismo." In *Las vanguardias latinoamericanas: Textos programáticos y críticos*, edited by Jorge Schwartz, 516–17. Mexico City: Fondo de Cultura Económica, 2002.

Andrade, Oswald de. "Idéias-novas: A arte e a literatura do Brasil moderno." In *Modernismo brasileiro e modernismo português: Subsídios para o seu estudo e para a história das suas relações*, edited by Arnaldo Saraiva, 567–68. Campinas, SP: Editora da UNICAMP, 2004.

Andrews, George Reid. *Blackness in the White Nation: A History of Afro-Uruguay*. Chapel Hill: University of North Carolina Press, 2010.

———. *Blacks and Whites in São Paulo, Brazil, 1888–1988*. Madison: University of Wisconsin Press, 1991.

Ansell, Gwen. *Soweto Blues: Jazz, Popular Music, and Politics in South Africa*. New York: Continuum, 2004.

Appiah, Kwame Anthony. *Cosmopolitanism: Ethics in a World of Strangers*. New York: W. W. Norton, 2006.

Arnedo-Gómez, Miguel. *Writing Rumba: The Afrocubanista Movement in Poetry*. Charlottesville: University of Virginia Press, 2006.

Artundo, Patricia. *Mário de Andrade e a Argentina: Um país e sua produção cultural como espaço de reflexão*. Translated by Gênese Andrade. São Paulo: Editora da USP, 2004.

Atkins, E. Taylor. *Blue Nippon: Authenticating Jazz in Japan*. Durham, NC: Duke University Press, 2001. Kindle edition.

———. "Toward a Global History of Jazz." In *Jazz Planet*, edited by E. Taylor Atkins, loc. 64–362. Jackson: University Press of Mississippi, 2003. Kindle edition.

Austerlitz, Paul. *Jazz Consciousness: Music, Race, and Humanity*. Middletown, CT: Wesleyan University Press, 2005.

Avelar, Idelber. *The Untimely Present: Postdictatorial Latin American Fiction and the Task of Mourning*. Durham, NC: Duke University Press, 1999.

Azzi, María Susana, and Simon Collier. *Le Grand Tango: The Life and Music of Astor Piazzolla*. Oxford: Oxford University Press, 2000.

Bahiana, Ana Maria. "Música instrumental—o caminho do improviso à brasileira." In *Anos 70: Ainda sob a tempestade*, edited by Adauto Novaes, 61–69. Rio de Janeiro: Aeroplano/Editora Senac Rio, 2005.

Baker, Jean-Claude, and Chris Chase. *Josephine: The Hungry Heart*. New York: Cooper Square Press, 2001. Kindle edition.

Baker, Josephine, and Jo Bouillon. *Josephine*. Translated by Mariana Fitzpatrick. New York: Harper and Row, 1977.

Balliache, Simón. *Jazz en Venezuela*. Caracas: Ballgrub, 1997.

Baraka, Amiri [LeRoi Jones]. *The Autobiography of LeRoi Jones*. Chicago: Lawrence Hill Books, 1997.

———. *Blues People: Negro Music in White America*. New York: William Morrow and Company, 1968. Orig. pub. 1963.

———. "Cuba Libre." In *The LeRoi Jones/Amiri Baraka Reader*, edited by William J. Harris, 125–60. New York: Thunder's Mountain Press, 2000.

———. "Jazz and the White Critic." In *The LeRoi Jones/Amiri Baraka Reader*, edited by William J. Harris, 179–85. New York: Thunder's Mountain Press, 2000.

Barbieri, Leandro, and Michelle Barbieri. "Gato Barbieri: The Argentine Eclectic." Interview by Larry Birnbaum. *Down Beat* 44 (April 21, 1977): 15–16, 46–47.

Barrios, Richard. *A Song in the Dark: The Birth of the Musical Film*. New York: Oxford University Press, 1995.

Barroso, Ary. "Decadência." *Revista da Música Popular* 9 (1955): 7. Reprinted in *Revista da Música Popular: Edição completa em facsímile*, 463. Rio de Janeiro: Funarte, 2006.

———. "Não compreendi o plebiscito de Villa-Lobos." *Diretrizes*, June 12, 1941, 9.

Beasley-Murray, Jon. *Posthegemony: Political Theory and Latin America*. Minneapolis: University of Minnesota Press, 2010.

"Bebop." *Life* 25, no. 15 (October 11, 1948): 138–42.

Behague, Gerard. *The Beginnings of Musical Nationalism in Brazil*. Detroit: Information Coordinators, 1971.

———. *Discografía de Francisco Canaro*. Buenos Aires[?]: n.p., 1964.

Belair, Felix, Jr. "America's 'Secret Sonic Weapon.'" *New York Times*, November 4, 1955, 1, 42.

Belmonte, Adriana. "Grupo Irakere: Un ritmo con raices populares." *Revolución y Cultura* 24 (August 1974): 68–72.

Benamou, Catherine L. *It's All True: Orson Welles's Pan-American Odyssey*. Berkeley: University of California Press, 2007.

Berg, Charles Ramírez. *Latino Images in Film: Stereotypes, Subversion and Resistance*. Austin: University of Texas Press, 2002.

Berlant, Lauren. *Cruel Optimism*. Durham, NC: Duke University Press, 2011. Kindle edition.

Berrett, Joshua. *Louis Armstrong and Paul Whiteman: Two Kings of Jazz*. New Haven, CT: Yale University Press, 2004.

Beverly, John. *Latinamericanism after 9/11*. Durham, NC: Duke University Press, 2011.

Bhabha, Homi. *The Location of Culture*. London: Routledge, 2004.

Biers, Katherine. "Syncope Fever: James Weldon Johnson and the Black Phonographic Voice." *Representations* 96, no. 1 (2006): 99–125.

Billig, Michael. *Banal Nationalism*. London: Sage, 1995.

Blake, Jody. *Le Tumulte Noir: Modernist Art and Popular Entertainment in Jazz-Age Paris, 1900–1930*. University Park: Pennsylvania State University Press, 1999.

Blanco, María del Pilar, and Esther Peeren. "Introduction: Conceptualizing Spectralities." In *The Spectralities Reader: Ghosts and Haunting in Contemporary Cultural Theory*, edited by María del Pilar Blanco and Esther Peeren, loc. 207–856. New York: Bloomsbury, 2013. Kindle edition.

Boaventura, Maria Eugenia. *O salão e a selva: Uma biografia ilustrade de Oswald de Andrade*. Campinas: Editora UNICAMP, 1995.

Boittin, Jennifer Anne. *Colonial Metropolis: The Urban Grounds of Anti-imperialism and Feminism in Interwar Paris*. Lincoln: University of Nebraska Press, 2010.

Borge, Jason. *Avances de Hollywood: Crítica cinematográfica en Latinoamérica, 1915–1945*. Rosario, Argentina: Beatriz Viterbo, 2005.

———. *Latin American Writers and the Rise of Hollywood Cinema*. New York: Routledge, 2008.

———. "Olympio Guilherme: Hollywood Actor, *Auteur* and Author." *Luso-Brazilian Review* 44, no. 1 (2007): 158–76.

Borges, Dain. "The Recognition of Afro-Brazilian Symbols and Ideas, 1890–1940." *Luso-Brazilian Review* 32, no. 2 (1995): 59–78.

Borges, Jorge Luis. "Ascendencias del tango." *Martín Fierro* 4, no. 37 (1927): 6, 8.

Borges Pereira, João Baptista. *Cor, profissão e mobilidade: O negro e a rádio de São Paulo*. 2nd ed. São Paulo: Editora da Universidade de São Paulo, 2001.

Bôscoli, Ronaldo. *Eles e eu: Memórias de Ronaldo Bôscoli*. Rio de Janeiro: Nova Fronteira, 1994.

Braga Martins, Luiza Mar. *Os Oito Batutas: História e música brasileira nos anos 1920*. Rio de Janeiro: Editora UFRJ, 2014.

Branche, Jerome C. *Colonialism and Race in Luso-Hispanic Literature*. Columbia: University of Missouri Press, 2006.

Brown, Jayna. *Babylon Girls: Black Women Performers and the Shaping of the Modern*. Durham, NC: Duke University Press, 2008.

———. "From the Point of View of the Pavement: A Geopolitics of Black Dance." In *Big Ears: Listening for Gender in Jazz Studies*, edited by Nichole T. Rustin and Sherrie Tucker, 157–79. Durham, NC: Duke University Press, 2008.

Brown, Lee B. "Marsalis and Baraka: An Essay in Comparative Cultural Discourse." *Popular Music* 23, no. 3 (2004): 241–55.

Bustos Montoya, Camilo. " 'De rotos, chinas y futres': Discriminación social y protesta popular en el Chile tradicional, 1850–1900." In *Historias de racismo y discriminación en Chile*, edited by Rafael Gaune and Martín Lara, 123–51. Santiago de Chile: Uqbar Editores, 2009.

Cabral, Sérgio. *Antônio Carlos Jobim: Uma biografia*. Rio de Janeiro: Lumiar Editora, 1997.

———. *No tempo de Ari Barroso*. Rio de Janeiro: Lumiar Editora, 1993.

———. *Pixinguinha: Vida e obra*. Rio de Janeiro: Lumiar Editora, 1997.

Caldeira, Jorge. *A construção do samba*. São Paulo: Mameluco, 2007.

Calderón, Alfonso. *Toca esa rumba, Don Azpiazu*. Santiago: Editorial Universitaria, 2001. Orig. pub. 1970.

Carpentier, Alejo. "Bajo el cetro del *blues*." In *Ese músico que llevo dentro*, vol. 2, 181–85. Havana: Letras Cubanas, 1980.

———. "Don Azpiazu en París." In *Ese músico que llevo dentro*, vol. 2, 554–59. Havana: Letras Cubanas, 1980.

———. "La consagración de nuestros ritmos." In *Ese músico que llevo dentro*, vol. 2, 528–32. Havana: Letras Cubanas, 1980.

———. "La música popular cubana." *Signos* (Havana) 2, no. 3 (May-August 1971): 7–12.

———. "Moisés Simons y el piano Luis XV de Josephine Baker." *Social* 16, no. 12 (December 1931): 52, 65, 69.

———. "Temas de la lira y el bongó." In *Ese músico que llevo dentro*, vol. 2, 537–44. Havana: Letras Cubanas, 1980.

Carr, Ian. *Keith Jarrett: The Man and His Music*. New York: Da Capo, 1992.

Carroll, Noël. "The Specificity Thesis." In *Film Theory and Criticism: Introductory Readings*, edited by Leo Braudy and Marshall Cohen, 5th ed., 322–28. New York: Oxford University Press, 1999.

Castro, Ruy. *Chega de saudade: A história e as histórias da Bossa Nova*. São Paulo: Companhia das Letras, 2008.

Cavallari, Héctor Mario, and Graciela P. García. "Escritura y desfetichización: En torno a 'El perseguidor' de Julio Cortázar." *Revista de Crítica Literaria Latinoamericana* 22, nos. 43–44 (1996): 267–77.

Caymmi, Dorival. "Dorival Caymmi fala sobre pintura, literatura e música." Interview by Paulo Mendes Campos. *Revista da Música Popular* 4 (1955): 2–4. Reprinted in *Revista da Música Popular: Edição completa em facsímile*, 182–84. Rio de Janeiro: Funarte, 2006.

Célélier Eguiluz, Géraldine. "Jazz mexicano: El encuentro con su historia." In *La música en México: Panorama del siglo XX*, edited by Aurelio Tello, 324–94. Mexico City: Fondo de Cultura Económica, 2010.

Cendrars, Blaise. "Aux jeunes gens de Catacazes." *Verde* 3, no. 1 (November 1927): 11.

Chanan, Michael. *Cuban Cinema*. Minneapolis: University of Minnesota Press, 2004.

Chase, Sam. "Saga of the Bossa Bath at Carnegie: Musicians Cost a Lot of Cruzeiros." *Billboard*, December 22, 1962, 16.

Clifford, James. "On Ethnographic Surrealism." *Comparative Studies in Society and History* 23, no. 4 (1981): 539–64.

———. *The Predicament of Culture: Twentieth-Century Ethnography, Literature, and Art*. Cambridge, MA: Harvard University Press, 1988.

Coeuroy, André, and André Schaeffner. *Le Jazz*. Paris: Editions Claude Aveline, 1926.

Collier, Simon. *The Life, Music, and Times of Carlos Gardel*. Pittsburgh: University of Pittsburgh Press, 1986.

Contreras, Félix. *Yo conocí a Benny Moré*. Havana: Ediciones Unión, 2002.

Contreras, Tino. *Mi amor, el jazz*. Mexico City: Ediciones del Gobierno de Chihuahua, 1986.

Copland, Aaron. "Jazz Structure and Influence" [1927]. In *Aaron Copland, A Reader: Selected Writings, 1923–1972*, edited by Richard Kostelanetz, 83–87. New York: Routledge, 2004.

Corona, Ignacio, and Alejandro L. Madrid. "Introduction: The Postnational Turn in Music Scholarship and Music Marketing." In *Postnational Musical Identities: Cultural Production, Distribution, and Consumption in a Globalized Scenario*, edited by Ignacio Corona and Alejandro L. Madrid, 3–22. Lanham, MD: Lexington Books, 2008.

Cortázar, Julio. "Elogio del jazz: Carta enguantada a Daniel Devoto." In *Obra crítica*, edited by Saúl Yurkievich, 204–16. Barcelona: Galaxia Gutenberg, 2006.

———. *El perseguidor*. In *Las armas secretas*, 85–150. Madrid: Cátedra 1993.

———. *La vuelta al día en ochenta mundos*, vol. 1. 10th ed. Madrid: Siglo XXI de España, 1976.

———. *Rayuela: Edición crítica*. 2nd ed. Edited by Julio Ortega and Saúl Yurkievich. Madrid: ALLCA XX, 1996.

———. "Soledad de la música." In *Obra crítica*, edited by Saúl Yurkievich, 135–40. Barcelona: Galaxia Gutenberg, 2006.

Costa, Haroldo. "Os rumos da música popular brasileira." *Revista da Música Popular* 13 (1956): 18–19. Reprinted in *Revista da Música Popular: Edição completa em facsímile*, 682–83. Rio de Janeiro: Funarte, 2006.

Coutinho, Henrique. "Confronto: Música popular brasileira." *Revista Civilização Brasileira* 1, no. 3 (July 1965): 305–12.

Covarrubias, Miguel. *Negro Drawings*. New York: Knopf, 1927.

Crouch, Stanley. "Putting the White Man in Charge." *JazzTimes*, April 2003. http://jazztimes.com/articles/19802-putting-the-white-man-in-charge.

Cruz Cordeiro, José da. "Folcmúsica e música popular brasileira." *Revista da Música Popular* 7 (1955): 6–8, 40–41. Reprinted in *Revista da Música Popular: Edição completa em facsímile*, 342–44, 376–77. Rio de Janeiro: Funarte, 2006.

———. "Jazz." *Phono-Arte* 2, no. 27 (September 15, 1929): 1–2.

Cuéllar Vizcaíno, Manuel. "La revolución del mambo." In *El mambo*, edited by Radamés Giro, 23–30. Havana: Letras Cubanas, 1993.

Cummings, Alex. "Collectors, Bootleggers, and the Value of Jazz, 1930–1952." In *Sound in the Age of Mechanical Reproduction*, edited by David Suisman and Susan Strasser, 95–114. Philadelphia: University of Pennsylvania Press, 2010.

Dalevuelta, Jacobo [Fernando Ramírez de Aguilar]. "El jazz en México." *El Universal Ilustrado*, July 3, 1924, 23, 44.

Dance, Stanley. *The World of Duke Ellington*. New York: Da Capo, 2000.

Davis, Darien. *White Face, Black Mask: Africaneity and the Early Social History of Popular Music in Brazil*. East Lansing: Michigan State University Press, 2009.

Dayal, Samir. "Blackness as Symptom: Josephine Baker and European Identity." In *Blackening Europe: The African American Presence*, edited by Heike Raphael-Hernández, 35–52. New York: Routledge, 2004.

deCordova, Richard, *Picture Personalities: The Emergence of the Star System in America* Champaign: University of Illinois Press, 2001.

Delannoy, Luc. *¡Caliente! Una historia del jazz latino*. Translated by María Antonia Neira Bigorra. Mexico City: Fondo de Cultura Económica, 2001.

———. *Convergencias: Encuentros y desencuentros en el jazz latino*. Translated by José María Ímaz. Mexico City: Fondo de Cultura Económica, 2012.

de Miranda, Marcelo F. "Dizzy Gillespie no Rio." *Revista da Música Popular* 14 (1956): 42. Reprinted in *Revista da Música Popular: Edição completa em facsímile*. Rio de Janeiro: Funarte, 2006.

Denning, Michael. *Noise Uprising: The Audiopolitics of a World Musical Revolution*. London: Verso, 2015.

Dennis, Christopher. *Afro-Colombian Hip-Hop: Globalization, Transcultural Music, and Ethnic Identities*. Lanham, MD: Lexington Books, 2011.

Derbez, Alain. *El jazz en México: Datos para una historia*. Mexico City: Fondo de Cultura Económica, 2001.

———. *Para mirar el ruido*. Mexico City: La Flor de Otro Día, 1983.

———. *Todo se escucha en silencio: El blues y el jazz en la literatura*. Mexico City: Alebrije, 1987.

Desnoes, Edmundo. *Now: El movimiento negro en Estados Unidos*. Havana: Instituto del Libro, 1967.

Deutsch, Sandra. *Crossing Borders, Claiming a Nation: A History of Argentine Jewish Women, 1880–1955*. Durham, NC: Duke University Press, 2010.

Devine Guzmán, Tracy. *Native and National in Brazil: Indigeneity after Independence*. Chapel Hill: University of North Carolina Press, 2013.

Di Baja, A. César. "Enfoques y reflexiones (II)." *Jazz Magazine* (Buenos Aires) 43 (December 1953): 4–6.

Dinerstein, Joel. *Swinging the Machine: Modernity, Technology, and African American Culture between the World Wars*. Amherst: University of Massachusetts Press, 2003.

Domingues, Petrônio. "A 'Vênus negra': Josephine Baker e a modernidade afro-atlântica." *Estudos Históricos* 23, no. 45 (January–June 2010): 95–124.

Donato, João. *Songbook João Donato*. Edited by Almir Chediak. Rio de Janeiro: Lumiar Editora, 1999.

Douglas, María Eulalia. *Catálogo del cine cubano, 1897–1960*. Havana: Ediciones ICAIC, 2008.

Duffy, Enda. *The Speed Handbook: Velocity, Pleasure, Modernism*. Durham, NC: Duke University Press, 2009. Kindle edition.

Dugan, James, and John Hammond. "Jazz at Carnegie Hall" [1938]. In *Keeping Time: Readings in Jazz History*, edited by Robert Walser, 101–5. New York: Oxford University Press, 1999.

Dunn, Christopher. "Por entre máscaras cool, twists mornos e jazz fervente: A bossa nova no cenário norte-americano, 1961–64." In *João Gilberto*, edited by Walter García, 251–69. São Paulo: Cosac Naify, 2012.

Duque Filho, Alvaro Xavier. "Política internacional na revista *Diretrizes*." Master's thesis, São Paulo, UNESP/Assis, Faculdade de Ciências e Letras, 2007.

Echazábal, Francisco. "Benny Moré: El Bárbaro del Ritmo." *Signos* 17 (May–December 1975): 156.

Efegê, Jota. *Figuras e coisas do carnaval carioca*. Rio de Janeiro: Funarte, 1982.

Elena, Eduardo. "Argentina in Black and White: Race, Peronism, and the Color of Politics, 1940s to the Present." In *Rethinking Race in Modern Argentina: The Shades of the Nation*, edited by Paulina L. Alberto and Eduardo Elena, 184–210. New York: Cambridge University Press, 2016.

Elsdon, Peter. *Keith Jarrett's* The Köln Concert. New York: Oxford University Press, 2013.

Eltit, Diamela. "Chicago Chico." *La Nación* (Chile), January 14, 2006. Accessed online July 3, 2013.

Evans, Nicholas M. *Writing Jazz: Race, Nationalism and Modern Culture in the 1920s*. New York: Garland, 2000.

Fajardo Estrada, Ramón. *Rita Montaner: Testimonio de una época*. Havana: Casa de las Américas, 1997.

Feather, Leonard, and Ira Gitler. *The Biographical Encyclopedia of Jazz*. New York: Oxford University Press, 1999. Kindle edition.

Feld, Steven. *Jazz Cosmopolitanism in Accra: Five Musical Years in Ghana*. Durham, NC: Duke University Press, 2012.

Fenerick, José Adriano. *Nem do morro nem da cidade: As transformações do samba e a indústria cultural, 1920–1945*. São Paulo: Annablume/Fapesp, 2005.

Fernández, Raúl. *Latin Jazz: The Perfect Combination*. San Francisco: Chronicle Books/ Smithsonian, 2002.

Fernández L'Hoeste, Héctor, and Pablo Vila, eds. *Cumbia! Scenes of a Migrant Latin American Music Genre*. Durham, NC: Duke University Press, 2013.

Fernández Retamar, Roberto. "Oyendo un disco de Benny Moré." *Historia antigua*, 29–30. Havana: La Tertulia, 1964.

Ferrari, Danilo Wenseslau. "Diretrizes: A primeira aventura de Samuel Wainer." *Histórica: Revista Eletrônica do Arquivo Público do Estado de São Paulo* 4, no. 31 (June 2008). Accessed online November 16, 2015. http://www.arquivoestado.sp.gov.br/site/assets /publicacao/anexo/historica31.pdf.

Ferro, Antônio. *A idade do jazz-band*. 2nd ed. Lisbon: Portugalia, 1924.

Filmador, Sánchez [Gustavo F. Aguilar]. "El elogio del jazz." *El Universal Ilustrado*, July 3, 1924, 26.

Fingerit, Marcos. "Josefina Baker." *Verde* 4, no. 1 (December 1927): 8.

Fiol-Matta, Licia. *Queer Mother for the Nation: The State and Gabriela Mistral*. Minne- apolis: University of Minnesota Press, 2002.

Fiore, Edgardo. "Dizzy Gillespie." *Jazz Magazine*, 1946, 16–17.

Fischerman, Diego, and Abel Gilbert. *Piazzolla, el mal entendido: Un estudio cultural*. Buenos Aires: Edhasa, 2009.

Fiske, John. "The Cultural Economy of Fandom." In *The Adoring Audience: Fan Culture and Popular Media*, 30–49. London: Routledge, 1992.

Franco, Jean. *Critical Passions: Selected Essays*. Durham, NC: Duke University Press, 1999.

———. *The Decline and Fall of the Lettered City: Latin America in the Cold War*. Cam- bridge, MA: Harvard University Press, 2002.

Freedland, Michael. *All the Way: A Biography of Frank Sinatra, 1915–1998*. New York: St. Martin's Press, 1997.

Freyre, Gilberto. *Tempo de aprendiz*. Vol. 1. São Paulo: IBRASA, 1978.

Frith, Simon. *Music for Pleasure: Essays in the Sociology of Pop*. New York: Routledge, 1988.

———. *Performing Rites: On the Value of Popular Music*. Cambridge, MA: Harvard University Press, 1996.

Gabbard, Krin. "Introduction: Writing the Other History." In *Representing Jazz*, edited by Krin Gabbard, 1–8. Durham, NC: Duke University Press, 1995.

———. *Jammin' at the Margins: Jazz and the American Cinema*. Chicago: University of Chicago Press, 1996.

Gabilliet, Jean-Paul. "A Disappointing Crossing: The North American Reception of Asterix and Tintin." In *Transnational Perspectives on Graphic Narratives: Comics at the Crossroads*, edited by Daniel Stein, Shane Denson, and Christina Meyer, 257–70. London: Bloomsbury, 2013.

Galán, Natalio. *Cuba y sus sones*. Valencia: Pre-Textos, 1983.

García, David F. *Arsenio Rodríguez and the Transnational Flows of Latin Popular Music*. Philadelphia: Temple University Press, 2006.

———. "Going Primitive to the Movements and Sounds of Mambo." *Musical Quarterly* 89, no. 4 (winter 2006): 505–23.

Garcia, Tânia da Costa. *O "it verde e amarelo" de Carmen Miranda (1930–1946)*. São Paulo: Annablume, 2004.

Garcia, Walter. *Bim bom: A contradição sem conflitos de João Gilberto*. São Paulo: Paz e Terra, 1999.

García Ascot, Jomi. "Jazz y droga." *S.NOB* 7 (October 15, 1962): 21–24.

García Canclini, Néstor. *Consumers and Citizens: Globalization and Multicultural Conflicts*. Translated by George Yúdice. Minneapolis: University of Minnesota Press, 2001.

———. *Hybrid Cultures: Strategies for Entering and Leaving Modernity*. Minneapolis: University of Minnesota Press, 1995.

García Márquez, Gabriel. "El mambo." In *El mambo*, edited by Radamés Giro, 19–20. Havana: Editorial Letras Cubanas, 1993.

———. "Mambo de Nueva York." In *El mambo*, edited by Radamés Giro, 21–22. Havana: Letras Cubanas, 1993.

García Riera, Emilio. *México visto por el cine extranjero, 1: 1894–1940*. Guadalajara: Ediciones Era, 1987.

Gargurevich, Juan. *La prensa sensacionalista en el Perú*. Lima: Fondo Editorial, 2002.

Garramuño, Florencia. *Primitive Modernities: Tango, Samba, and Nation*. Translated by Anna Kazumi Stahl. Stanford: Stanford University Press, 2011.

Garrett, Charles Hiroshi. *Struggling to Define a Nation: American Music and the Twentieth Century*. Berkeley: University of California Press, 2008. Kindle edition.

Garrido, Pablo. "Recuento integral del jazz en Chile." *Para Todos* (Santiago) 4, no. 30 (June 10, 1935): 40–41, 65–66. Accessed December 31, 2015. http://www.memoria chilena.cl/602/w3-article-82691.html.

Gasió, Guillermo. *Yrigoyen en crisis 1929–1930*. Buenos Aires: Corregidor, 2006.

Gates, Henry Louis, Jr. "King of Cats." *New Yorker*, April 8, 1996, 70–81.

Gava, José Estevam. *A linguagem harmônica da Bossa Nova*. 2nd ed. São Paulo: Editora UNESP, 2002.

———. *Momento Bossa Nova*. São Paulo: Annablume, 2006.

Geler, Lea. "African Descent and Whiteness in Buenos Aires: Impossible *Mestizajes* in the White Capital City." In *Rethinking Race in Modern Argentina: The Shades of the Nation*, edited by Paulina L. Alberto and Eduardo Elena, 213–40. New York: Cambridge University Press, 2016.

Gendron, Bernard. *Between Montmartre and the Mudd Club: Popular Music and the Avant-Garde*. Chicago: University of Chicago Press, 2002.

Gennari, John. *Blowin' Hot and Cool: Jazz and Its Critics*. Chicago: University of Chicago Press, 2006. Kindle edition.

Gibbs, Anna. "After Affect: Sympathy, Synchrony, and Mimetic Communication." In *The Affect Theory Reader*, edited by Melissa Gregg and Gregory J. Seigworth, loc. 2557–2833. Durham, NC: Duke University Press, 2010. Kindle edition.

Giddins, Gary. *Visions of Jazz: The First Century*. Oxford: Oxford University Press, 1998.

Gillespie, Dizzy, with Al Fraser. *To Be, or Not . . . to Bop*. Minneapolis: University of Minnesota Press, 2009. Orig. pub. Doubleday, 1979.

Gilroy, Paul. *The Black Atlantic: Modernity and Double Consciousness*. Cambridge, MA: Harvard University Press, 1993.

Gioia, Ted. *The History of Jazz*. Oxford: Oxford University Press, 1997.

———. *The Jazz Standards: A Guide to the Repertoire*. New York: Oxford University Press, 2012.

Giro, Radamés. "Todo lo que usted quiso saber sobre el mambo . . ." In *El mambo*, edited by Radamés Giro, 5–18. Havana: Letras Cubanas, 1993.

Goffin, Robert. *Aux frontières du jazz*. 4th ed. Paris: Sagittaire, 1932.

———. *Nouvelle Histoire du jazz: Du Congo au bebop*. Brussels: L'Ecran du Monde, 1948.

Gómez de la Serna, Ramón. *Ismos*. Madrid: Biblioteca Nueva, 1931.

Gonzaga, Adhemar. Review of *O Rei do Jazz*. *Cinearte* 5, no. 242 (October 15, 1930): 30.

González, Juan Pablo, and Claudio Rolle. *Historia social de la música popular en Chile, 1890–1950*. Santiago: Ediciones Universidad Católica de Chile, 2005.

González Bermejo, Ernesto. *Revelaciones de un cronopio: Conversaciones con Cortázar*. 2nd ed. Montevideo: Ediciones de la Banda Oriental, 1986.

Gordon, Avery F. *Ghostly Matters: Haunting and the Sociological Imagination*. 2nd ed. Minneapolis: University of Minnesota Press, 2008.

Gorin, Natalio. *Astor Piazzolla: A Memoir*. Translated by Fernando González. Portland, OR: Amadeus Press, 2001.

Groensteen, Thierry. *Comics and Narration*. Translated by Ann Miller. Jackson: University Press of Mississippi, 2013.

Gubern, Román. "Ruido, furia y negritud: Nuevos ritmos y nuevos sones para la vanguardia." In *Vanguardia española e intermedialidad: Artes escénicas, cine y radio*, edited by Mechthild Albert, 273–302. Madrid: Iberoamericana Vervuert, 2005.

Guillén, Nicolás. "Benny." In *Yo conocí a Benny Moré*, edited by Félix Contreras, 79–81. Havana: Ediciones Unión, 2002.

———. "Josefina Baker en Cuba." In *Prosa de prisa (1929–1985)*, 88–90. Havana: Ediciones Unión, 2002.

Guinle, Jorge. "Jazz: Críticos e estilos." *Revista da Música Popular* 13 (1956): 42–43. Reprinted in *Revista da Música Popular: Edição completa em facsímile*, 706–7. Rio de Janeiro: Funarte, 2006.

———. "Os fatores essenciais da música de jazz." *Revista da Música Popular* 3 (1954): 44–47. Reprinted in *Revista da Música Popular: Edição completa em facsímile*, 172–75. Rio de Janeiro: Funarte, 2006.

Guterl, Matthew Pratt. *Josephine Baker and the Rainbow Tribe*. Cambridge, MA: Belknap Press, 2014. Kindle edition.

Haddock, Mable, and Chiquite Mullins Lee. "Whose Multiculturalism? PBS, the Public, and Privilege." In *Art, Activism, and Oppositionality: Essays from Afterimage*, edited by Grant H. Kester, 136–47. Durham, NC: Duke University Press, 1998.

Hajdu, David. "Not Quite All That Jazz." *New York Review of Books*, February 8, 2001, n.p. http://www.nybooks.com/articles/archives/2001/feb/08/not-quite-all-that-jazz/.

Hammond, Bryan, and Patrick O'Connor. *Josephine Baker*. London: Jonathan Cape, 1988.

Harb Bollos, Liliana. *Bossa Nova e crítica: Polifonia de vozes na imprensa*. São Paulo: Annablume, 2010.

Harlos, Christopher. "Jazz Autobiography: Theory, Practice, Politics." In *Representing Jazz*, edited by Krin Gabbard, 131–66. Durham, NC: Duke University Press, 1995.

Hentoff, Nat. *Jazz Is*. New York: Random House, 1976.

——. "The Mambo!! They Shake A-Plenty with Tito Puente." In *DownBeat—The Great Jazz Interviews: A 75th Anniversary Anthology*, edited by Frank Alkyer, Ed Enright, Jason Koransky, Aaron Cohen, and Jeff Cagle, 51–52. New York: Hal Leonard, 2009.

Hering Coelho, Luís Fernando. "Os músicos transeuntes: De palavras e coisas em torno de uns batutas." Ph.D. dissertation, Program in Social Anthropology, Universidade Federal de Santa Catarina. Florianópolis, 2009.

Hernández Arregui, Juan José. "Ensayo anti-sentimental sobre la esclavitud negra (y nuevos aportes para una interpretación más profunda del jazz)." *Síncopa y Ritmo* 15–16 (October–November 1935): 4–6.

——. "Sentido social del jazz." *Síncopa y Ritmo* 12 (July 1935): 28–30.

Herrero Senés, Juan. "El arte nuevo y el jazz: El cifrado del siglo XX." In *Vanguardia española e intermedialidad: Artes escénicas, cine y radio*, edited by Mechthild Albert, 317–30. Madrid: Iberoamericana Vervuert, 2005.

Hersch, Charles B. *Subversive Sounds: Race and the Birth of Jazz in New Orleans*. Chicago: University of Chicago Press, 2007.

Hertzman, Marc A. *Making Samba: A New History of Race and Music in Brazil*. Durham, NC: Duke University Press, 2013.

Hesmondhalgh, David. *Why Music Matters*. Maldon, MA: Wiley Blackwell, 2013.

Hess, Carol A. *Representing the Good Neighbor: Music, Difference, and the Pan American Dream*. New York: Oxford University Press, 2013.

Hills, Matt. *Fan Cultures*. London: Routledge, 2002.

Hobsbawm, Eric. *The Jazz Scene*. New York: Pantheon Books, 1993.

Hodeir, André. "Dizzy Gillespie à Paris." *Jazz Hot* 21, no. 14 (March 1948): 6–7.

Homer, Sean. *Jacques Lacan*. London: Routledge, 2005.

Horvath, Ricardo. *Memorias y recuerdos de Blackie*. Buenos Aires: Todo es Historia, 1979.

Howe, Linda S. *Transgression and Conformity: Cuban Writers and Artists after the Revolution*. Madison: University of Wisconsin Press, 2004.

Huyssen, Andreas. *After the Great Divide: Modernism, Mass Culture, Postmodernism*. Bloomington: Indiana University Press, 1986.

Ichaso, Francisco. "Terapéutica de Jazz." *Musicalia* 3 (1928): 95–96.

Indych-López, Anna. *Muralism without Walls: Rivera, Orozco, and Siqueiros in the United States, 1927–1940*. Pittsburgh: University of Pittsburgh Press, 2009.

Iriberri, Fernando. "El jazz y los discos." *Síncopa y Ritmo* 1, no. 1 (1934): 2.

Jackson, Jeffrey H. *Making Jazz French: Music and Modern Life in Interwar Paris*. Durham, NC: Duke University Press, 2003.

———. "Making Jazz French: The Reception of Jazz Music in Paris, 1927–1934." *French Historical Studies* 25, no. 1 (2002): 149–70.

Jardim, Reynaldo. "Bossa participante." *Senhor* 5, nos. 50–51 (April–May 1963): 28–29.

Jarrett, Michael. "Four Choruses on the Tropes of Jazz Writing." *American Literary History* 6, no. 2 (1994): 336–53.

Jay, Martin. *The Dialectical Imagination: A History of the Frankfurt School and the Institute of Social Research, 1923–1950*. Boston: Little, Brown, 1973.

Jeanneret, Albert. "El negro y el jazz." *Revista de avance* 1, no. 12 (September 1927): 314.

Jitrik, Noé. "Crítica satélite y trabajo crítico en 'El perseguidor' de Julio Cortázar." *Nueva Revista de Filología Hispánica* 23, no. 2 (1974): 337–68.

Jones, Andrew F. *Yellow Music: Media Culture and Colonial Modernity in the Chinese Jazz Age*. Durham, NC: Duke University Press, 2001.

Jordan, Matthew F. *Le Jazz: Jazz and French Cultural Identity*. Urbana: University of Illinois Press, 2010.

Karush, Matthew B. "Black in Buenos Aires: The Transnational Career of Oscar Alemán." In *Rethinking Race in Modern Argentina*, edited by Paulina L. Alberto and Eduardo Elena, 73–98. Cambridge: Cambridge University Press, 2016.

———. *Culture of Class: Radio and Cinema in the Making of a Divided Argentina, 1920–1946*. Durham, NC: Duke University Press, 2012.

———. *Musicians in Transit: Argentina and the Globalization of Popular Music*. Durham, NC: Duke University Press, 2017.

———. "Reinventing the Latin in Latin Jazz: The Music and Career of Gato Barbieri." *Journal of Latin American Cultural Studies* 25, no. 3 (2016): 379–96.

Kater, Michael H. *Different Drummers: Jazz in the Culture of Nazi Germany*. New York: Oxford University Press, 1992.

Kelley, Robin D. G. *Africa Speaks, America Answers: Modern Jazz in Revolutionary Times*. Cambridge, MA: Harvard University Press, 2012.

Kennaway, James Gordon. *Bad Vibrations: The History of the Idea of Music as Cause of Disease*. Farnham, UK: Ashgate, 2012.

King, John. *Magical Reels: A History of Cinema in Latin America*. New ed. London: Verso, 2000.

Klimovsky, León. "El jazz y la música moderna." *Síncopa y Ritmo* 14 (September 1935): 11.

Kraniauskas, John. "From the Archive: Introduction to Mariátegui." *Journal of Latin American Cultural Studies* 10, no. 3 (2001): 303–4.

Kun, Josh. "Against Easy Listening: Audiotopic Readings and Transnational Soundings." In *Everynight Life: Culture and Dance in Latin/o America*, edited by Celeste Fraser Delgado and José Esteban Muñoz, 288–309. Durham, NC: Duke University Press, 1997.

———. *Audiotopia: Music, Race, and America*. Berkeley: University of California Press, 2005.

Lane, Jeremy. *Jazz and Machine-Age Imperialism: Music, "Race," and Intellectuals in France, 1918–1945*. Ann Arbor: University of Michigan Press, 2014.

Lara, Cecília De. "A 'alegre e paradoxal' revista VERDE de Cataguases." *Verde: Revista Mensual de Arte e Cultura*. Fascimile ed. Edited by Henrique de Resende, Martins Mendes, and Rosário Fusco. Cataguazes, Minas Gerais: Metal Leve, 1978.

Leal Filho, Laurindo. *Atrás das câmaras: Relações entre cultura, estado e televisão*. 2nd ed. São Paulo: Summus Editorial, 1988.

Leão, Nara. "Nara de Nara." *O Cruzeiro*, August 3, 1963, 7.

Leblanc, Oscar. "Nuestros músicos opinan sobre la trascendencia musical del jazz." *El Universal Ilustrado*, July 3, 1924, 18–19.

Ledbetter, James. *Made Possible By . . . : The Death of Public Broadcasting in the United States*. London: Verso, 1997.

Levin, Michael. "Despite Bad Acoustics, Gillespie Concert Offers Some Excellent Music." *Down Beat* 14, no. 22 (October 22, 1947): 1, 3.

Lille, Dawn. *Equipoise: The Life and Work of Alfredo Corvino*. New York: Rosen Book Works, 2010.

Linares, María Teresa. "Sobre nuestra tradición cultural." *Boletín de Música* 22 (1972): 4–8.

Lipsitz, George. *Footsteps in the Dark: The Hidden Histories of Popular Music*. Minneapolis: University of Minnesota Press, 2007.

Loaeza, Lupe, and Pável Granados. *Mi novia, la tristeza: El recuento biográfico más completo, informado y original que se haya escrito sobre Agustín Lara*. Mexico City: Grupo Océano, 2008. E-book.

Lopes, Paul. *The Rise of a Jazz Art World*. Cambridge: Cambridge University Press, 2002.

López, Ana M. "Are all Latins from Manhattan? Hollywood, Ethnography and Cultural Colonialism." In *Mediating Two Worlds: Cinematic Encounters in the Americas*, edited by John King, Ana M. López, and Manuel Alvarado, 67–80. London: British Film Institute, 1993.

———. "Of Rhythms and Borders." In *Everynight Life: Culture and Dance in Latin/o America*, edited by Celeste Fraser Delgado and José Esteban Muñoz, 310–44. Durham, NC: Duke University Press, 1997.

———. "Tears and Desire: Women and Melodrama in the 'Old' Mexican Cinema." In *Multiple Voices in Feminist Film Criticism*, edited by Diane Carson, Linda Dittmar, and Janice R. Welsch, 254–70. Minneapolis: University of Minnesota Press, 1994.

Luis-Brown, David. *Waves of Decolonization: Discourses of Race and Hemispheric Citizenship in Cuba, Mexico, and the United States*. Durham, NC: Duke University Press, 2008.

Lund, Joshua. *The Impure Imagination: Toward a Critical Hybridity in Latin American Writing*. Minneapolis: University of Minnesota Press, 2006.

Lyon, James. "'Rhymes with Lust': The Twisted History of Noir Comics." In *A Companion to Film Noir*, edited by Andrew Spicer and Helen Hanson. Malden, MA: Wiley Blackwell, 2013.

Lyra, Carlos. *Eu e a bossa: Uma história da bossa nova*. Rio de Janeiro: Casa da Palavra, 2008.

MacAdams, Lewis. *Birth of the Cool: Beat, Bebop, and the American Avant-Garde*. New York: Free Press, 2001.

Machado, António de Alcântara. *Pathe-Baby* [1926]. Facsimile ed. São Paulo: Imprensa Oficial do Estado de São Paulo, 1982.

Madrid, Alejandro L., and Robin D. Moore. *Danzón: Circum-Caribbean Dialogues in Music and Dance*. New York: Oxford University Press, 2013.

Magalhães Júnior, R[aimundo]. "Êxito que mata." *Revista da Música Popular* 8 (1955): n.p. Reprinted in *Revista da Música Popular: Edição completa em facsímile*, 402–3. Rio de Janeiro: Funarte, 2006.

Manzano, Valeria. *The Age of Youth in Argentina: Culture, Politics, and Sexuality from Perón to Videla*. Chapel Hill: University of North Carolina Press, 2014.

Maples Arce, Manuel. "Jazz=XY." *El Universal Ilustrado*, July 3, 1924, 15, 44.

Marechal, Leopoldo. "Jazz Band." *Martín Fierro* 3, nos. 27–28 (1926): 3.

Mariátegui, José Carlos. "Arte, revolución, y decadencia." *Amauta* 3 (November 1926): 3–4.

Marín, Juan. *Looping*. Santiago, Chile: Nascimento, 1929.

Marsalis, Wynton. "Why We Must Preserve Our Jazz Heritage." *Ebony* 46 (November 1990): 159–62, 164.

Marshall, P. David. *Celebrity and Power: Fame in Contemporary Culture*. Minneapolis: University of Minnesota Press, 1997. Kindle edition.

Martín-Barbero, Jesús. *De los medios a las mediaciones: Comunicación, cultura y hegemonía*. Mexico City: G. Gili, 1987.

Martínez, Mayra A. *Cubanos en la música*. Havana: Editorial Letras Cubanas, 1993.

Mazzola, Guerino B., and Paul B. Cherlin. *Flow, Gesture, and Spaces in Free Jazz: Towards a Theory of Collaboration*. Berlin: Springer, 2009.

McCann, Bryan. *Hello, Hello Brazil: Popular Music in the Making of Modern Brazil*. Durham, NC: Duke University Press, 2004.

McKay, George. *Circular Breathing: The Cultural Politics of Jazz in Britain*. Durham, NC: Duke University Press, 2005.

McMains, Juliet. *Spinning Mambo into Salsa: Caribbean Dance in Global Commerce*. Oxford University Press, 2015.

Medaglia, Júlio. "Balanço da Bossa Nova." In *Balanço da Bossa, e outras bossas*, edited by Augusto de Campos, 5th ed., 67–123. São Paulo: Editora Perspectiva, 2003.

Melo Gomes, Tiago de. *Um espelho no palco: Identidades sociais e massificação da cultura no teatro de revista dos anos 1920*. Campinas: Editora da UNICAMP, 2004.

Menanteau, Álvaro. *Historia del jazz en Chile*. 2nd ed. Santiago: Ocho Libros, 2006.

Méndez Carrasco, Armando. *Chicago Chico*. 18th ed. Santiago: Ediciones Juan Firula, 1967.

———. *Dos cuentos de jazz*. Santiago: Luis Rivano, 1963.

Menescal, Roberto. *Coleção Gente: Roberto Menescal*. Edited by Luiz Carlos Lisboa. Rio de Janeiro: Editora Rio, 2002.

Menotti del Picchia, Paulo. "Arte moderna." In *Vanguarda européia e modernismo brasileiro: Apresentação dos principais poemas, manifestos, prefácios e conferências vanguardistas, de 1857 até hoje*, edited by Gilberto Mendonça Teles, 4th ed., 227–33. Petrópolis: Vozes, 1977.

Meredith, Bill. "Latin Jazz: The Latin Tinge." *Jazz Times*, November 1, 2007. http://jazztimes.com/articles/19036-latin-jazz-the-latin-tinge.

Milhaud, Darius. *Notes without Music: An Autobiography*. Translated by Donald Evans. London: Dennis Dobson, 1952.

Milian, Claudia. *Latining America: Black-Brown Passages and the Coloring of Latino/a Studies*. Athens: University of Georgia Press, 2013.

Mistral, Gabriela. "Primer recuerdo de Isadora Duncan." In *Materias: Prosa inédita*, 220–25. Santiago: Editorial Universitaria, 1978.

Monsiváis, Carlos. "Censura: La eternidad de las costumbres." *El Universal* (Mexico City), November 18, 2001. http://archivo.eluniversal.com.mx/editoriales/11235.html.

Monteiro, Denilson. *A bossa do lobo: Ronaldo Bôscoli*. São Paulo: Leya, 2011.

Montero, Julio, and María Antonia Paz. "Ir al cine en España en el primer tercio del siglo XX." In *Ver cine: Los públicos cinematográficos en el siglo XX*, edited by José-Vidal Pelaz and José Carlos Rueda, 91–136. Madrid: Ediciones RIALP, 2002.

Moore, Robin D. *Music and Revolution: Cultural Change in Socialist Cuba*. Berkeley: University of California Press, 2006.

———. *Nationalizing Blackness: Afrocubanismo and Artistic Revolution in Havana: 1920–1940*. Pittsburgh: University of Pittsburgh Press, 1997.

Mora, Carl J. *Mexican Cinema: Reflections of a Society*. Rev. ed. Berkeley: University of California Press, 1989.

Moreno, Jairo. "Bauzá-Gillespie-Latin/Jazz: Difference, Modernity, and the Black Caribbean." In *The Afro-Latin@Reader: History and Culture in the United States*, edited by Miriam Jiménez Román and Juan Flores, 177–86. Durham, NC: Duke University Press, 2010.

———. "Past Identity: Guillermo Klein, Miguel Zenón, and the Future of Jazz." In *Music and Youth Culture in Latin America: Identity Construction Processes from New York to Buenos Aires*, edited by Pablo Vila, 81–105. Oxford: Oxford University Press, 2014.

Moreno Rivas, Yolanda. *Historia de la música popular mexicana*. Mexico City: Editorial Patria, 1989.

Morrison, Allan. "The Man behind the Horn." *Ebony* 19, no. 8 (June 1964): 143–51.

Murray, Albert. *The Omni Americans: Some Alternatives to the Folklore of White Supremacy*. New York: Da Capo, 1970.

———. *Stomping the Blues*. 2nd ed. New York: Da Capo, 2000. Orig. pub. 1976.

Murray, Mrs. Arthur. "What the Heck Is the Mambo?" *Down Beat* 20, no. 24 (December 1, 1954): 2.

Natale, Oscar. *Buenos Aires, negros y tango*. Buenos Aires: Pena Lillo, 1984.

Navarrete, Sylvia. *Miguel Covarrubias: Artista y explorador*. Mexico City: Dirección General de Publicaciones del Consejo Nacional para la Cultura y las Artes, 1993.

Ngô, Fiona I. B. *Imperial Blues: Geographies of Race and Sex in Jazz Age New York*. Durham, NC: Duke University Press, 2014.

Nieto de Herrera, Carmela. "Cómo baila el jazz: Descripción de la última novedad en cuestión de baile." *El Mundo* (Havana), December 15, 1917, 4.

Nunes Frota, Wander. *Auxílio luxuoso: Samba símbolo nacional, geração Noel Rosa e indústria cultural*. São Paulo: Annablume, 2003.

Ocampo, Victoria. *Testimonios: Primera serie, 1920–1934*. Buenos Aires: Sur, 1981.

Ochoa Gautier, Ana María. "Social Transculturation, Epistemologies of Purification and the Aural Public Sphere in Latin America." In *The Sound Studies Reader*, edited by Jonathan Sterne, 388–404. New York: Routledge, 2012. Kindle edition.

O'Farrill, Chico. "The Well-Rounded Writer." Interview by Helen Dance. *Down Beat* 34, no. 3 (February 23, 1967): 6, 23.

Oliveira, Cláudia de. *As pérfidas salomés: A representação do pathos do amor em Fon-Fon! e Para todos . . . —1907–1930*. Rio de Janeiro: Fundação Casa de Rui Barbosa, 2008.

Oliveira, Flávio. "Orpheonic Chant and the Construction of Childhood in Brazilian Elementary Education." In *Brazilian Popular Music and Citizenship*, edited by Idelber Avelar and Christopher Dunn, 44–63. Durham, NC: Duke University Press, 2011.

Ortiz, Fernando. "Saba, samba y *bop*." In *Estudios etnosociológicos*, 248–54. Havana: Pensamiento Cubano, 1991.

Ortiz, Renato. *Cultura brasileira e identidade nacional*. 5th ed. São Paulo: Brasiliense, 2006.

———. *Mundialização e Cultura*. São Paulo: Brasiliense, 1994.

Ortiz de Montellano, Bernardo. "Motivos negros." *Contemporáneos*, September–December 1928, 109–12.

Ortiz Oderigo, Néstor R. *Historia del jazz*. 2nd ed. Buenos Aires: Ricordi Americana, 1952.

———. *Latitudes africanas del tango*. Caseros: EDUNTREF, 2009.

———. "Notas sobre blues." *Jazz Magazine* (Buenos Aires), October 2, 1945.

Otero Santa María, Jorge. "El mensaje jazzístico de Enrique Villegas." *Jazz Magazine* (Buenos Aires) 43 (December 1954): 8–12.

Owens, Thomas. *Bebop: The Music and Its Players*. New York: Oxford University Press, 1995.

Pacini Hernandez, Deborah. *¡Oye cómo va! Hybridity and Identity in Latino Popular Music*. Philadelphia: Temple University Press, 2010.

Pacini Hernandez, Deborah, Héctor Fernández-L'Hoeste, and Eric Zolov, eds. *Rockin' Las Américas: The Global Politics of Rock in Latin/o America*. University of Pittsburgh, 2004.

Padura Fuentes, Leonardo. "Chano Pozo, la cumbre y el abismo." *El viaje más largo*, 207–15. Havana: Ediciones Unión, 1994.

Panassié, Hugues. *Le Jazz Hot*. Paris: Editions R.A. Corrêa, 1934.

Panish, Jon. *The Color of Representation: Race and Representation in Postwar American Culture*. Oxford: University of Mississippi Press, 1997.

Pardue, Derek. *Ideologies of Marginality in Brazilian Hip Hop*. Palgrave Macmillan, 2008.

Peiró, Eva Woods. *White Gypsies: Race and Stardom in Spanish Musicals*. Minneapolis: University of Minnesota Press, 2012.

Pelligrinelli, Lara. "Separated at 'Birth': Singing and the History of Jazz." In *Big Ears: Listening for Gender in Jazz Studies*, edited by Nichole T. Rustin and Sherrie Tucker, 32–47. Durham, NC: Duke University Press, 2008.

Peña Barrenechea, Enrique. "Elogio a Miss Backer [*sic*]." *Amauta* 13 (1928): 20–21.

Peralta, Gonzalo. "Josephine Baker, bailarina exótica: La Diosa de Ébano que conquistó Chile." *The Clinic Online*, June 20, 2014. Accessed June 8, 2017. http://www.theclinic.cl/2014/06/02/josephine-baker-bailarina-exotica-la-diosa-de-ebano-que-conquisto-chile/.

Perchard, Tom. *After Django: Making Jazz in Postwar France*. Ann Arbor: University of Michigan Press, 2015.

Pereda Valdéz, Ildefonso. "A Josefina Baker." *Toda la poesía negra*, 17–18. Montevideo: Índice Mimeográfica, 1979.

———. "La esencia del arte negro." *Síntesis* 9 (1928): 317–21.

Pérez, Louis A. *On Becoming Cuban: Identity, Nationality, and Culture.* Chapel Hill: University of North Carolina Press, 1999.

Pérez Firmat, Gustavo. *Life on the Hyphen: The Cuban-American Way.* Rev. ed. Austin: University of Texas Press, 2012.

Pericás, Jaime. *Nuestro jazz.* Mexico City: B. Costa-Amic, 1966.

Perrone, Charles A., and Christopher Dunn. " 'Chiclete com Banana': Internationalization in Brazilian Popular Music." In *Brazilian Popular Music and Globalization*, edited by Charles A. Perrone and Christopher Dunn, 1–38. Gainesville: University Press of Florida, 2001.

Perry, Marc D. *Negro Soy Yo: Hip Hop and Raced Citizenship in Neoliberal Cuba.* Durham, NC: Duke University Press, 2015.

Pessoa Ramos, Fernão. *Mas afinal . . . o que é mesmo documentário?* São Paulo: Editora Senac, 2008.

Petit de Murat, Ulises. "Afirmación del jazz-band." *Martín Fierro* 4, no. 43 (1927): 4.

———. "Autenticidad en la inspiración musical negra." *Síncopa y Ritmo* 3 (October 1934): 6–8.

Peyton, Dave. "A Black Journalist Criticizes Jazz" [1928]. In *Keeping Time: Readings in Jazz History*, edited by Robert Walser, 57–59. New York: Oxford University Press, 1999.

Piazzolla, Astor. "Astor Piazzolla: Balada para un cuerdo." Interview by Horacio del Prado. *Buenos Aires Tango* 21 (October 1978): 2–7.

———. Interview by Laurent Goddet. *Jazz Hot* 315 (April 1975): n.p.

Piazzolla, Astor, and Natalio Gorin. *Astor Piazzolla: A Memoir.* Translated by Fernando González. Portland: Amadeus Press, 2001.

Piazzolla, Diana. *Astor.* Buenos Aires: Corregidor, 2005.

Pike, Fredrick B. *FDR's Good Neighbor Policy: Sixty Years of Generally Gentle Chaos.* Austin: University of Texas Press, 1995.

Poiger, Uta G. *Jazz, Rock, and Rebels: Cold War Politics and American Culture in a Divided Germany.* Berkeley: University of California Press, 2000.

Pond, Steven F. "Jamming the Reception: Ken Burns, 'Jazz,' and the Problem of 'America's Music.' " *Notes*, 2nd Series, 60, no. 1 (September 2003): 11–45.

Porter, Eric. *What Is This Thing Called Jazz? African American Musicians as Artists, Critics, and Activists.* Berkeley: University of California Press, 2002.

Posso, Karl. *Artful Seduction: Homosexuality and the Problematics of Exile.* Oxford, UK: Legenda, 2003.

Powell, Josephine. *Tito Puente: When the Drums Are Dreaming.* Bloomington, IN: AuthorHouse, 2007.

Prescott, Laurence E. *Without Hatreds or Fears: Jorge Artel and the Struggle for Black Literary Expression in Colombia.* Detroit: Wayne State University Press, 2000.

Pujol, Sergio. *Jazz al Sur: La música negra en la Argentina.* Buenos Aires: Emecé Editores, 1992.

Putnam, Lara. *Radical Moves: Caribbean Migrants and the Politics of Race in the Jazz Age.* Chapel Hill: University of North Carolina Press, 2013.

Quiroga, Horacio. "Jazz-band latina." *Repertorio Americano*, September 17, 1927, 173.

Radano, Ronald. "Hot Fantasies: American Modernism and the Idea of Black Rhythm." In *Music and the Racial Imagination*, edited by Ronald Radano and Philip V. Bohlman, 459–80. Chicago: University of Chicago Press, 2000.

———. *Lying Up a Nation: Race and Black Music*. Chicago: University of Chicago Press, 2003.

Radano, Ronald, and Tejumola Olaniyan. "Introduction: Hearing Empire—Imperial Listening." In *Audible Empire: Music, Global Politics, Critique*, edited by Ronald Radano and Tejumola Olaniyan, loc. 121–606. Durham, NC: Duke University Press, 2016. Kindle edition.

Rama, Ángel. *The Lettered City*. Translated by John Charles Chasteen. Durham, NC: Duke University Press, 1996.

Ramalho Neto, [A.]. "Dick Farney cantor internacional . . ." *A Cena Muda* 32, no. 18 (May 1, 1952): 15, 32.

Ramperstad, Arnold. *The Life of Langston Hughes*. Vol. 1. New York: Oxford University Press, 1988.

Rangel, Lúcio. Editorial. *Revista da Música Popular* 8 (July–August 1955): 1. Reprinted in *Revista da Música Popular: Edição completa em facsímile*, 389. Rio de Janeiro: Funarte, 2006.

Rasula, Jed. "Jazz as Decal for the European Avant-Garde." In *Blackening Europe: The African American Presence*, edited by Heike Raphael-Hernández, 13–34. New York: Routledge, 2004.

Ratliff, Ben. "Fixing, for Now, the Image of Jazz." *New York Times*, January 7, 2001, AR1, 32.

Rinke, Stefan. "Las torres de Babel del siglo XX: Cambio urbano, cultura de masas y norteamericanización en Chile, 1918–1931." Translated by Mónika Contreras Saiz. In *Ampliando miradas: Chile y su historia en un tiempo global*, edited by Fernando Purcell and Alfredo Riquelme, 159–94. Santiago: RIL Editores, 2009.

Roberts, John Storm. *Latin Jazz: The First of the Fusions, 1880s to Today*. New York: Schirmer Books, 1999.

Roberts, Nicholas. "Subverted Claims: Cortázar, Artaud, and the Problematics of Jazz." *Modern Language Review* 104, no. 3 (July 2009): 730–45.

Robreño, Eduardo. "Mis recuerdos del Benny." In *Yo conocí a Benny Moré*, edited by Félix Contreras, 47–52. Havana: Ediciones Unión, 2002.

Rodrigues, Petrônio. "A 'Vênus negra': Josephine Baker e a modernidade afro-atlântica." *Estudos Históricos* (Rio de Janeiro) 23, no. 45 (January–June 2010): 95–124. http://www.scielo.br/scielo.php?script=sci_arttext&pid=S0103-21862010000100005.

Rodríguez, Linda. "Tropical Interludes: The Rumbera in Mexican Cine." *ReVista: Harvard Review of Latin America* 7, no. 1 (fall 2007): 44–47.

Rodríguez Olmo, Josefina, and Aristide Pumariega. *Mitos de la popularidad: Chano Pozo*. Havana: Pablo de la Torriente, 1994.

Rolontz, Bob. "After Start in Jazz, Fad Breaks in Pop." *Billboard*, October 13, 1962, 4, 43.

Rosa, Hartmut. "Social Acceleration: Ethical and Political Consequences of a Desynchronized High-Speed Society." In *High-Speed Society: Social Acceleration, Power, and Modernity*, edited by Hartmut Rosa and William E. Scheuerman, 77–112. University Park: Pennsylvania State University Press, 2009.

Rose, Phyllis. *Jazz Cleopatra: Josephine Baker in Her Time.* New York: Doubleday, 1989.

Rosenberg, Fernando J. *The Avant-Garde and Geopolitics in Latin America.* Pittsburgh: University of Pittsburgh Press, 2006.

Ross, Andrew. *No Respect: Intellectuals and Popular Culture.* New York: Routledge, 1989.

Rossi, Vicente. *Cosas de negros.* Buenos Aires: Taurus/Alfaguara, 2001. Orig. pub. 1926.

Roth, Albert H. "De las composiciones de jazz—Diferencias con las de música clásica— Importancia de la interpretación." *Swing* 1, no. 6 (July–August 1937): 4–5.

Sábat, Hermenegildo. *Scat: Una interpretación gráfica del jazz.* Buenos Aires: Instituto Salesiano de Artes Gráficas, 1974.

———. *Yo Bix, tú Bix, él Bix.* Buenos Aires: Editorial Airene, 1972.

Sabella, Andrés. "Prólogo síncopado por las nostalgias." In Armando Méndez Carrasco, *Dos cuentos de jazz*, 5–7. Santiago: Luis Rivano, 1963.

Sadlier, Darlene J. *Americans All: Good Neighbor Cultural Diplomacy in World War II.* Austin: University of Texas Press, 2012.

Salazar, Max. *Mambo Kingdom: Latin Music in New York.* New York: Schirmer Trade Books, 2002.

Saldívar, José David. *Trans-Americanity: Subaltern Modernities, Global Coloniality, and the Cultures of Greater Mexico.* Durham, NC: Duke University Press, 2012.

Sampayo, Carlos. *Memorias de un ladrón de discos.* Buenos Aires: Grupo Editorial Norma, 1999.

Sampayo, Carlos, and José Muñoz. *Billie Holiday.* Translated by Katy MacRae, Robert Boyd, and Kim Thompson. Seattle: Fantagraphics Books, 1993.

Sandoval, Carlos. "Blackie realiza un sueño." *Síncopa y Ritmo* 2, nos. 21–22 (1936): 24.

———. "Las tres gracias argentinas del jazz." *Síncopa y Ritmo* 1, no. 7 (1935): 47–49.

———. "La verdadera misión del crítico." *Swing* 1, no. 2 (November 1936): 8.

———. "Los pianistas de jazz en la Argentina y su clasificación." *Síncopa y Ritmo* 1, no. 9 (1935): 25–26.

Sandvoss, Cornel. *Fans: The Mirror of Consumption.* Malden, MA: Polity, 2005.

Sant'Anna, Sérgio. *O Concerto de João Gilberto no Rio de Janeiro: Contos.* São Paulo: Ática, 1982.

Santiago, Silviano. *Keith Jarrett no Blue Note: Improvisos de Jazz.* Rio de Janeiro: Rocco, 1996.

Sanz, José. "Gato por lebre." *Revista da Música Popular* 1 (1954): 38–40. Reprinted in *Revista da Música Popular: Edição completa em facsímile*, 60–62. Rio de Janeiro: Funarte, 2006.

Saraiva, Arnaldo, ed. *Modernismo brasileiro e modernismo portugués: Subsídios para o seu estudo e para a história das suas relações.* Campinas, SP: Editora da UNICAMP, 2004.

Saraiva, Joana. "Da influência do *jazz* e outras notas: Discursos sobre a cena musical de Copacabana dos anos 50." In *Leituras sobre música popular: Reflexões sobre sonoridades e cultura*, edited by Emerson Giumbelli, Júlio Cesar Valladão Diniz, and Santuza Cambraia Naves, 83–97. Rio de Janeiro: 7Letras, 2008.

Sargeant, Winthrop. "Cuba's Tin Pan Alley: From Havana's Shabbiest Cabarets and Voodoo Lodges Pours an Endless Flood of Sultry Rhythms, Which Are Danced to All Over the World." *Life*, October 6, 1947, 146–57.

Schifrin, Lalo. *Mission Impossible: My Life in Music.* Edited by Richard Palmer. Lanham, MD: Scarecrow Press, 2008.

Schmidt, Augusto Frederico. "Sucesso de fato." *Revista da Música Popular* 8 (1955): n.p. Reprinted in *Revista da Música Popular: Edição completa em facsímile*, 442. Rio de Janeiro: Funarte, 2006.

Schneider, Luis Mario. *El Estridentismo, o una literatura de la estrategia.* Mexico City: Letras Mexicanas, 1997.

Schwartz, Jorge. *Vanguardia y cosmopolitismo en la década del veinte: Oliverio Girondo y Oswald de Andrade.* Rosario, Argentina: Beatriz Viterbo, 1983.

Seibel, Beatriz. "La presencia afroargentina en el espectáculo." In *El negro en la Argentina: Presencia y negación*, edited by Dina V. Picotti, 199–207. Buenos Aires: Editores de América Latina, 2001.

Seigel, Micol. *Uneven Encounters: Making Race and Nation in Brazil and the United States.* Durham, NC: Duke University Press, 2009.

Serna, Laura Isabel. *Making Cinelandia: American Films and Mexican Film Culture before the Golden Age.* Durham, NC: Duke University Press, 2014.

Sevcenko, Nicolau. *Orfeu extático na metrópole: São Paulo, sociedade e cultura nos frementes anos 20.* São Paulo: Companhia das Letras, 1992.

Severiano, Jairo. *Uma história da música popular brasileira: Das origens à modernidade.* São Paulo: Editora 34, 2008.

Shaw, Lisa. "'What Does the Baiana Have?': Josephine Baker and the Performance of Afro-Brazilian Female Subjectivity on Stage." *English Language Notes* 49, no. 1 (spring/summer 2011): 91–106.

Shelton, Robert. "Argentine Music at Philharmonic: Cancer Society Benefit Is a Part of 'Cultural Panorama.'" *New York Times*, May 27, 1965, 28.

Shipton, Alyn. *Groovin' High: The Life of Dizzy Gillespie.* New York: Oxford University Press, 2001.

———. *A New History of Jazz.* London: Continuum, 2001.

Silva, Marilia T. Barboza da, and Arthur L. de Oliveira Filho. *Filho de Ogum Bexiguento.* Rio de Janeiro: Funarte, 1979.

Siqueira, Baptista. *Ernesto Nazareth no música brasileira: Ensaio histórico-científico.* Rio de Janeiro: Aurora, 1967.

Solomianski, Alejandro. *Identidades secretas: La negritud argentina.* Rosario, Argentina: Beatriz Viterbo, 2003.

Sommer, Doris. "Pursuing a Perfect Present." In *Julio Cortázar: New Readings*, 211–36. Cambridge: Cambridge University Press, 1998.

Sorensen, Diana. *A Turbulent Decade Remembered: Scenes from the Latin American Sixties.* Stanford: Stanford University Press, 2007.

Sosnowski, Saul. "Pursuers." In *The Final Island: The Fiction of Julio Cortázar*, edited by Jaime Alazraki and Ivar Ivask, 159–67. Norman: University of Oklahoma Press, 1978.

Sparke, Michael. *Stan Kenton: This Is an Orchestra!* Denton, TX: University of North Texas Press, 2010.

Spengler, Oswald. *The Decline of the West.* Vol. 2. Translated by Charles Francis Atkinson. New York: A. A. Knopf, 1928.

Starr, S. Frederick. *Red and Hot: The Fate of Jazz in the Soviet Union, 1917–1991.* Updated edition. New York: Limelight Editions, 2004.

Stearns, Marshall W. "Rebop, Bebop, and Bop." *Harper's Magazine* 200, no. 1199 (April 1950): 89–96.

Stepan, Nancy Leys. *The Hour of Eugenics: Race, Gender, and Nation in Latin America.* Ithaca: Cornell University Press, 1991.

Stroud, Sean. *The Defence of Tradition in Brazilian Popular Music: Politics, Culture and the Creation of* Música Popular Brasileira. Aldershot: Ashgate, 2008.

Sublette, Ned. *Cuba and Its Music: From the First Drums to the Mambo.* Chicago: Chicago Review Press, 2004.

Suco, Adalberto. "¿Jazz latino o música cubana?" *Clave* 1, no. 1 (1986): 16–22.

Suero, Orlando. "Bossa Nova desafinou no EUA." *O Cruzeiro*, December 8, 1962, 6–13.

Tablada, José Juan. "Miguel Covarrubias: El hombre que descubrió a los negros en los Estados Unidos. La belleza en donde nadie la había visto" [1924]. In *Obras-VI: Arte y artistas*, edited by Adriana Sandoval, 410–15. Mexico City: UNAM, 2000.

Taborda, Roberto Paulo [Bob Hill]. "Jazz no cinema e no radio [i]." *A Cena Muda* 22, no. 1105 (May 26, 1942): 10.

———. "Jazz no cinema e no radio [ii]." *A Cena Muda* 22, no. 1113 (July 21, 1942): 22.

———. "Melodias e ritmos no cinema y no rádio." *A Cena Muda* 22, no. 2 (January 12, 1943): 6.

Tálice, Roberto A. *100.000 ejemplares por hora: Memorias de un redactor de* Crítica*, el diario de Botana.* Buenos Aires: Corregidor, 1977.

Taylor, Charles. *Modern Social Imaginaries.* Durham, NC: Duke University Press, 2004.

Thiers, Walter. *El Jazz criollo y otras yerbas, 1950–1995.* Buenos Aires: Corregidor, 1999.

Thompson, Robert Farris. *Tango: The Art History of Love.* New York: Vintage Books, 2006.

Tibol, Raquel. *Pedro Cervantes.* Mexico City: Sep/Setentas, 1974.

Tietchen, Todd F. *The Cubalogues: Beat Writers in Revolutionary Havana.* Gainesville: University Press of Florida, 2010.

Tinhorão, José Ramos. "Bossa de exportação." *Senhor* 5, nos. 50–51 (April–May 1963): 12.

———. "Bossa-Nova vive um drama: Não sabe quem é o pai." *Senhor* 5, nos. 50–51 (April–May 1963): 20–21.

———. *Música popular: Um tema em debate.* 3rd ed. Rio de Janeiro: Editora 34, 1997.

Titlestad, Michael Frank. " 'The Artist Gathers the Bones': The Shamanic Poetics of Jazz Discourse." In *Music, Popular Culture, Identities*, edited by Richard Young, 301–17. Amsterdam: Rodopi, 2002.

Torres, Vicente Francisco. *La novela bolero latinoamericana.* Mexico City: UNAM, 1998.

Tota, Antônio Pedro. *The Seduction of Brazil: The Americanization of Brazil during World War II.* Translated by Lorena B. Ellis. Austin: University of Texas Press, 2009.

Treece, David. *Brazilian Jive: From Samba to Bossa and Rap.* London: Reaktion, 2013.

———. "Guns and Roses: Bossa Nova and Brazil's Music of Popular Protest, 1958–68." *Popular Music* 16, no. 1 (January 1997): 1–29.

Turino, Thomas. "Nationalism and Latin American Music: Selected Case Studies and Theoretical Considerations." *Latin American Music Review* 24, no. 2 (2003): 169–209.

Tyler, Don. *Music of the Postwar Era.* Westport, CT: Greenwood Press, 2008.

Tyson, Timothy B. *Radio Free Dixie: Robert F. Williams and the Roots of Black Power*. Chapel Hill: University of North Carolina Press, 1999.

Unruh, Vicky. *Latin American Vanguards: The Art of Contentious Encounters*. Berkeley: University of California Press, 1994.

Urfé, Odilio. "Danzón, mambo y cha-cha-chá." *Revolución y Cultura* 77 (January 1979): 54–57.

———. "La verdad sobre el mambo." In *El mambo*, edited by Radamés Giro, 31–35. Havana: Letras Cubanas, 1993.

Vallejo, César. "Poesía nueva." In *Las vanguardias literarias en Hispanoamérica*, edited by Hugo J. Verani, 3rd ed., 190–91. Mexico City: Fundo de Cultura Económica, 1995.

Vásquez, Alexandra T. *Listening in Detail: Performances of Cuban Music*. Durham, NC: Duke University Press, 2013.

Vedana, Hardy. *Jazz em Porto Alegre*. Porto Alegre: L&PM, 1987.

Veloso, Caetano. *Alegria, alegria*. Rio de Janeiro: Pedra Q Ronca, 1977.

Ventín Pereira, José Augusto. *Ramón Gómez de la Serna: Primer teórico de la radiodifusión española*. Madrid: Editorial Fragua, 2005.

Vianna, Hermano. *The Mystery of Samba: Popular Music and National Identity in Brazil*. Translated by John Charles Chasteen. Chapel Hill: University of North Carolina Press, 1999.

Villa-Lobos, Heitor. "Villa-Lobos lança um plebiscito para uma nova cultura artística musical." *Diretrizes*, May 15, 1941, 12.

Villavicencio, V. Modesto. "El charleston y nuestro tiempo." *Amauta* 5 (1927): 36.

Vinci de Moraes, José Geraldo. *Metrópole em sinfonia: História, cultura e música popular na São Paulo dos nos 30*. São Paulo: Estação Liberdade, 2000.

Von Eschen, Penny M. *Satchmo Blows Up the World: Jazz Ambassadors Play the Cold War*. Cambridge, MA: Harvard University Press, 2004.

Wade, Peter. *Music, Race, and Nation: Música Tropical in Colombia*. Chicago: University of Chicago Press, 2000.

Washburne, Christopher. "Latin Jazz, Afro-Latin Jazz, Afro-Cuban Jazz, Cubop, Caribbean Jazz, Jazz Latin, or Just . . . Jazz: The Politics of Locating an Intercultural Music." In *Jazz/Not Jazz*, edited by David Ake, Charles Hiroshi Garrett, and Daniel Ira Goldmark, 89–110. Berkeley: University of California Press, 2012.

———. *Sounding Salsa: Performing Latin Music in New York City*. Temple University Press, 2008.

Wasserman, Maria Clara. " 'Abre a cortina do passado': A *Revista da Música Popular* e o pensamento folclorista (Rio de Janeiro: 1954–1956)." Master's thesis, Graduate Program in History, Universidade Federal do Paraná, Curitiba, 2002.

Waxer, Lise. "Situating Salsa: Latin Music at the Crossroads." In *Situating Salsa: Global Markets and Local Meanings in Latin American Popular Music*, edited by Lise Waxer, 3–22. New York: Routledge, 2002.

Williams, Adriana. *Covarrubias*. Austin: University of Texas Press, 1994.

Williams, Daryle. *Culture Wars in Brazil: The First Vargas Regime, 1930–1945*. Durham, NC: Duke University Press, 2001.

Williams, Raymond. *The Politics of Modernism: Against the New Conformists*. London: Verso, 1989.

Wilson, John S. "Brazilian Musicians Present Bossa Nova at Carnegie Hall." *New York Times*, November 22, 1962, 51.

Wisnik, José Miguel. *O coro dos contrários: A música em torno da Semana de 22*. São Paulo: Duas Cidades, 1977.

Wood, Ean. *The Josephine Baker Story*. London: Omnibus, 2010. Kindle edition.

Yanow, Scott. *Afro-Cuban Jazz*. San Francisco: Miller Freeman Books, 2000.

———. *Bebop*. San Francisco: Miller Freeman Books, 2000. Electronic edition.

Yúdice, George. "Postmodernity and Transnational Capitalism in Latin America." In *On Edge: The Crisis of Contemporary Latin American Culture*, edited by George Yúdice, Jean Franco, and Juan Flores, 1–28. Minneapolis: University of Minnesota Press, 1992.

Yurkievich, Saúl. "La pujanza insumisa." In Julio Cortázar, *Rayuela: Edición crítica*, edited by Julio Ortega and Saúl Yurkievich, 2nd ed., 661–74. Madrid: ALLCA XX, 1996.

Žižek, Slavoj. "Multiculturalism, or, the Cultural Logic of Multinational Capitalism." *New Left Review* 225 (September–October 1997): 28–51.

Zwerin, Mike. *Swing under the Nazis: Jazz as a Metaphor of Freedom*. New York: Cooper Square Press, 2000. Orig. pub. 1985.